PERSONALIZED DIGITAL TELEVISION

HUMAN-COMPUTER INTERACTION SERIES

VOLUME 6

The titles published in this series are listed at the end of this volume.

Personalized Digital Television

Targeting Programs to Individual Viewers

Edited by

Liliana Ardissono
Dipartimento di Informatica,
Università di Torino, Italy

Alfred Kobsa
University of California,
Irvine, CA, U.S.A.

and

Mark Maybury
Information Technology Division,
The MITRE Corporation, Bedford, MA, U.S.A.

KLUWER ACADEMIC PUBLISHERS
DORDRECHT / BOSTON / LONDON

A C.I.P. Catalogue record for this book is available from the Library of Congress

ISBN 1-4020-2163-1 (HB)
ISBN 1-4020-2164-X (e-book)

Published by Kluwer Academic Publishers,
P.O. Box 17, 3300 AA Dordrecht, The Netherlands.

Sold and distributed in North, Central and South America
by Kluwer Academic Publishers,
101 Philip Drive, Norwell, MA 02061, U.S.A.

In all other countries, sold and distributed
by Kluwer Academic Publishers,
P.O. Box 322, 3300 AH Dordrecht, The Netherlands.

Printed on acid-free paper

Printed in the Netherlands.

TABLE OF CONTENTS

Preface

This book collects selected research reports on the development of personalized services for Interactive TV. Drawing upon contributions from academia and industry that represent current research in the US, Europe and Asia, these articles represent leading research in personalized television. The individual contributions have been carefully selected by the editors from a pool of about 60 papers presented at four professional meetings in this area, namely:

- TV01 (http://www.di.unito.it/~liliana/UM01/TV.html), which was held within the UM'01 International Conference on User Modeling in Sonthofen, Germany;
- TV02(http://www.di.unito.it/~liliana/TV02/index.html), which was organized in connection with the AH2002 Adaptive Hypermedia Conference in Malaga, Spain;
- TV03 (http://www.di.unito.it/~liliana/TV03/index.html), which was held within the UM 2003 International Conference on User Modeling in Johnstown, PA, USA;
- EuroITV'03 (http://www.brighton.ac.uk/interactive/euroitv/index.htm), the 1st European Conference on Interactive Television, held in Brighton, UK.

The book also includes four papers selected for publication in the special issue on User Modeling and Personalization for Television (http://www.di.unito.it/~liliana/UMUAI-TV/) of the Kluwer Journal "User Modeling and User-Adapted Interaction: The Journal of Personalization Research".

Liliana Ardissono
Torino, Italy

Alfred Kobsa
Irvine, CA

Mark Maybury
Chelmsford, MA USA

Introduction

TV viewers today are exposed to overwhelming amounts of information, and challenged by the plethora of interactive functionality provided by current set-top boxes. While there are hundreds of channels with an abundance of programs available, and large amounts of material that can be retrieved from digital video archives and satellite streams, the available meta-information about this content is poor, so that an informed selection of one's preferred choices is almost impossible. As a result, TV viewers waste a lot of time browsing the available options or end up watching a very limited number of channels.

Future Digital Television (DTV) will have to take usability issues thoroughly into account, to ensure broad adoption of this technology by consumers. Information overload already represents a serious problem for the Internet. It is even less acceptable in DTV because it threatens the entertainment and leisure objectives that most TV viewers have, forcing them to engage in extended information retrieval each time they want to watch a TV show. Serious attention must therefore be paid to facilitate the selection of content on an individual basis, and to provide easy-to-use interfaces that satisfy viewers' interaction requirements.

Given the heterogeneity of TV viewers, who differ e.g. in interests and skills, the provision of personalized services seems to be the only solution to address the information overload problem in an effective manner. The User Modeling and the Intelligent User Interfaces communities have therefore focused on the following main lines of research:

- The provision of Electronic Program Guides recommending TV programs on an individual basis, to prevent users from "being lost in TV program space".
- Information retrieval tools to help users select interesting content in the cases where a prior categorization of the content is not possible (e.g., in news shows).
- The design and development of tools that help users explore large amounts of broadcast television content.
- The provision of adaptive interactive content that can be presented in a personalized way, depending on the viewer's interests.
- The design of suitable user interfaces that enable TV viewers to perform advanced tasks in an intuitive and efficient manner, which is essential for rendering Digital TV usable by any type of viewer, and not merely technical pundits.

Fundamental challenges that must be addressed to enable personalized television include:

- *Viewer Modeling*: The acquisition, representation and utilization of information about viewers, such as their characteristics (e.g., gender and age), preferences, interests, beliefs, and their viewing behavior. This includes models of both individual viewers and groups of viewers.

- *Viewer Identification*: The recognition of the TV viewer(s), which is the basis for the provision of personalized services.
- *Program Processing*: The automated identification, indexing, segmentation (e.g. into components, stories, commercials), summarization, and visualization of television programs, such as interactive documentaries.
- *Program Representation and Reasoning*: representing the general characteristics and specific content of programs and shows, including the possible segmentation of programs into parts. Reasoning about what may make one program similar or dissimilar to others. This can include a range of techniques, including recommendation techniques based on collaborative filtering (e.g., finding unseen programs that others with similar preferences have enjoyed), content analysis, clustering, and data mining.
- *Presentation Generation and Tailoring*: The selection, organization, and customization of television material based on viewer queries, processed programs, and viewer models.
- *Interaction Management*: The design and development of methods of human computer interaction for television, including mechanisms for attention and dialogue management.
- *Evaluation*: The assessment of the benefits for users, including measuring the precision of the techniques to model TV viewers' preferences, the precision and recall associated with the ability of users to find programs they care to watch, the speed and accuracy with which adaptation can be performed, the users satisfaction with the process and result, and the (real or perceived) cognitive load that the system places on the user.

This volume collects leading research addressing some of these challenges. Its chapters have been selected among the highest-quality articles about personalized DTV. The book is organized in three sections:

- The *Electronic Program Guides* (EPG) section includes six papers representing the state of the art in the development of personalized EPGs that customize program recommendations to TV viewers. The described work addresses the identification of the TV viewer's preferences and the personalized recommendation of items to individual users and to groups of users, as is typical of household environments. This section also includes an analysis of TV viewers aimed at defining stereotypical TV viewer classes based on similarities in viewing behavior.
- The *Broadcast News and Personalized Content* section includes three papers presenting the most recent results in the personalization of broadcast (multimedia) content. The papers are concerned with the analysis of the individual TV viewer's information goals, and the subsequent selection of the most relevant news stories. Moreover, the papers propose solutions to the customization of the type and amount of information to be conveyed to viewers, based on an underlying model of the content to be presented. The specification of

meta-level information and the integration of information retrieved from external sources are proposed to extend the presented content and to support the provision of personalized views of such content.

– The *iTV User Interface section* is focused on the design of interactive user interfaces for Digital TV. The two papers included in this section present, respectively, a user-centered approach to the design of the User Interface for a personalized EPG, and a pilot study aimed at evaluating the suitability of 3D interfaces in the exploration of the content in the TV world, including broadcast TV programs and content sharing between TV users.

The papers collected in this book represent the state of the art in personalized recommendation and presentation of TV content. In several cases, the presented proposals have been exploited in commercial applications, which provided positive feedback about the applicability of the approaches in real-world scenarios. The collected experience is also very important for the identification of open research issues that will need to be addressed in the development of future DTV services, a field still in its infancy, but with many opportunities ahead.

Liliana Ardissono
Torino, Italy

Alfred Kobsa
Irvine, CA

Mark Maybury
Chelmsford, MA USA

PART 1: ELECTRONIC PROGRAM GUIDES

Chapter 1

User Modeling and Recommendation Techniques for Personalized Electronic Program Guides

LILIANA ARDISSONO[1], CRISTINA GENA[1], PIETRO TORASSO[1],
FABIO BELLIFEMINE[2], ANGELO DIFINO[2] and BARBARA NEGRO[2]

[1]*Dipartimento di Informatica, Università di Torino, Corso Svizzera 185, 10149 Torino, Italy.*
email: {liliana,cgena,torasso}@di.unito.it
[2]*Telecom Italia Lab, Multimedia Division, Via G. Reiss Romoli 274, 10148 Torino, Italy.*
email: {bellifemine,difino,negro}@tilab.com

Abstract. This chapter presents the recommendation techniques applied in Personal Program Guide (PPG). This is a system generating personalized Electronic Program Guides for Digital TV. The PPG manages a user model that stores the estimates of the individual user's preferences for TV program categories. This model results from the integration of different preference acquisition modules that handle explicit user preferences, stereotypical information about TV viewers, and information about the user's viewing behavior. The observation of the individual viewing behavior is particularly easy because the PPG runs on the set-top box and is deeply integrated with the TV playing and the video recording services offered by that type of device.

1. Introduction

With the expansion of TV content, digital networks and broadband, hundreds of TV programs are broadcast at any time of day. This huge amount of content has the potential to optimally satisfy individual interests, but it makes the selection of the programs to watch a very lengthy task. Therefore, TV viewers end up watching a limited number of channels and ignoring the other ones; see Smyth and Cotter (in this volume) for a discussion about this issue.

In order to face the information overload and facilitate the selection of the most interesting programs to watch, personalized TV guides are needed that take individual interests and preferences into account. As recommender systems have been successfully applied to customize the suggestion of items in various application domains, such as e-commerce, tourism and digital libraries (Resnick and Varian, 1997; Riecken, 2000; Mostafa, 2002), several efforts have been recently made to apply this technology to the Digital TV world. For instance, collaborative filtering has been applied in the MovieLens (2002) and in the PTV Listings Service (Cotter and Smyth, 2000) systems to generate personalized TV listings, and in the TiVo (2002) system to select programs for VCR recording. Collaborative filtering requires that the user positively or negatively rate the programs she has watched; the ranking profiles are collected

L. Ardissono et al. (eds.), Personalized Digital Television, 3–26, 2004.
© *2004 Kluwer Academic Publishers. Printed in the Netherlands.*

in a central server and clustered to identify people having similar tastes. When somebody asks for a recommendation, the system suggests those items that have been
positively rated by the users with the most similar profiles.

Although collaborative filtering suits Web-based applications in an excellent way, we
believe that personalized EPGs should rely on recommendation techniques that can
be applied locally to the user's TV. In fact, an EPG embedded in the set-top box
may continuously track the user's viewing behavior, unobtrusively acquiring precise
information about her preferences. Moreover, the guide can be extended to become
a personal assistant helping the user to browse and manage her own digital archive.

To prove our ideas, we developed the Personal Program Guide (PPG). This is a
personalized EPG that customizes the TV program recommendation and assists
the user in the retrieval of the programs she has recorded. The PPG runs on the user's
set-top box and downloads information about the available TV programs from
the satellite stream. In order to obtain precise estimates of the individual TV viewer's
preferences during the whole lifecycle of the EPG, our system relies on the management of a hybrid user model that integrates three sources of information:

- The user's explicit preferences that may be declared by the user.
- Information about the viewing preferences of stereotypical TV viewer classes.
- The user's viewing behavior.

The system customizes the recommendation of TV programs by taking the user's
preferences for TV program categories and channels into account. The combination
of these two types of information supports accurate suggestions. In fact, the program
categories preferred by the user may be privileged. For instance, movies might be
recommended more frequently than documentaries. Moreover, within each category,
the individual programs selected by the content providers may be prioritized on
the basis of their audience analysis.

While the multi-agent architecture of the PPG has been described in (Ardissono
et al., 2003), this chapter presents the recommendation techniques applied in the
system. The chapter also presents the results of a preliminary evaluation of the
PPG with real users. More specifically, Section 2 outlines the facilities offered by
the PPG and sketches the representation of the information about TV programs. Section 3 presents the management of the user models. Section 4 describes the recommendation techniques applied to personalize the suggestion of TV programs.
Section 5 reports the results of the system evaluation and Section 6 compares our
approach to the related work. Finally, Section 7 concludes the paper and outlines
our future work.

2. Overview of the Personal Program Guide

The PPG offers advanced facilities for browsing TV content. For instance, the user can
search programs by channel, category, viewing time, day, language and cast; see
the buttons located in the left portion of the User Interface shown in Figure 1.1.

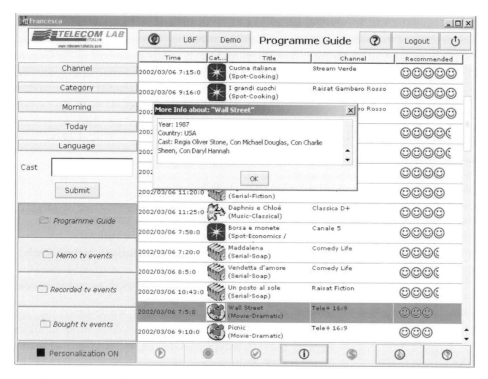

Figure 1.1. User interface of the personal program guide (PC simulator).

Moreover, the user may ask for details about a program (e.g., cast, content description and parental rating), she can record it, ask to be advised when the transmission of the program starts (memo function), and so forth. The user can also retrieve the list of programs she has asked to be alerted about (Memo TV events), she has recorded (Recorded TV Events button), or she has bought (Bought TV Events). Although the system acquires the information about the user's interests in an unobtrusive way, it also accepts explicit feedback about programs that may be rated by clicking on the 'thumb up/down' buttons located in the bottom-right area of the User Interface.

By default, the system works in personalized mode (Personalization ON) and ranks the TV programs by taking the user model into account. The less suitable programs are filtered out and the most promising ones are shown at the top of the list. The recommendation degree of a program is represented by a list of smiling faces close to its description in order to make the ranking information independent of the visualization criterion. The personalization facility can be switched off and in that case the TV programs are sorted on the basis of their starting time.

As described in Ardissono et al. (2001), the information about TV programs is based on an extension of the Digital Video Broadcasting standard (DVB, 2000). A record whose fields specify information such as the starting time, the transmission channel and the stream content, i.e., video, audio or data, describes each TV program. The descriptor includes one or more program categories (*Content* field) representing the program content and format. The program categories are organized in the General Ontology, a taxonomy that includes broad categories, such as Serial, and specializes them in sub-categories, e.g., Soap Opera and Science Fiction Serial.

3. A Hybrid User Model for the Specification of TV Viewing Preferences

In the design of the user model, we considered:

- Explicit *preferences* for TV program categories that the user notifies the system about; e.g., movies and documentaries.
- *Estimates on the viewing preferences* for the program categories. These are related to the number of programs she watches, for each category.
- *Socio-demographic information*, such as her age, occupation, and so forth.
- Information about the user's general *interests, hobbies* and *lifestyles*.
- *Prior information about the preferences of stereotypical classes of TV viewers.*

In order to manage suitably this heterogeneous information, we designed the User Modeling Component (UMC) of the PPG as an agent that exploits three modules, the Explicit Preferences Expert, the Stereotypical UM Expert and the Dynamic UM Expert, each one managing a private user model.

- The *Explicit User Model* stores the information elicited from the user.
- The *Stereotypical User Model* stores the prediction on the user's preferences inferred from prior information about TV viewer categories.
- The *Dynamic User Model* stores the estimates on the user's preferences inferred by observing her viewing behavior.

The predictions generated by the Experts may be affected by uncertainty, e.g., because they have been made in the presence of limited information about the user. In order to take this fact into account, the *confidence* of each prediction is evaluated. The UMC employs this parameter to weight the predictions provided by the Experts into a *Main User Model*, whose contents are exploited to personalize the suggestion of TV programs.

3.1. THE EXPLICIT USER MODEL

This user model stores the user's personal data, (e.g., occupation and age), her declared attitudes towards topics such as cinema, books and politics (henceforth, *general interests*), and her preferences for TV program categories. The system acquires this information by means of a form filled in at registration time.[1] The user may express her interests and preferences by choosing between three values (low, medium, strong) that correspond to numerical values in the user model (0, 0.5, 1).

---

[1]The user may view and modify the form at any time.

In order to limit the overhead on the user, the information about her preferences is elicited on few, broad program categories. As these categories are less detailed than those of the General Ontology, suitable mappings between the concepts are defined to enable the inference of the user's preferences.

A confidence value is associated to each prediction to represent the possible uncertainty of the information. The confidence is a decimal number in [0, 1], where 0 represents the total lack of confidence and is associated to unknown preferences. The 1 value denotes maximum confidence and is associated to the preferences for the categories of the General Ontology that coincide with the declared user preferences.

3.2. THE STEREOTYPICAL USER MODEL

3.2.1. *Representation of the Stereotypical Information*

A knowledge base stores the information about TV viewer classes that are represented as stereotypes (Rich, 1989). We defined the stereotypes by exploiting information about the interests and behavior of TV viewers collected in the Auditel (2003) and Eurisko (2002) studies about the Italian population. These studies enabled us to specify stereotypical preferences for several categories of TV programs that are coarser-grained than those of the General Ontology, but can be easily mapped to such categories (Gena, 2001). Thus, we specified a *Stereotype Ontology* defining the TV program categories to be considered and, similarly to the explicit preferences, we defined mapping rules that relate the corresponding user preferences.

The stereotypical descriptions include the specification of classification data and prediction information. This representation is similar to the one adopted in the SeTA system by Ardissono and Goy (2000). We sketch the representation by considering the stereotype describing the Housewife life style, shown in Figure 1.2.

Each classification datum is represented as a slot with three facets: the *Feature Name*, the *Importance* and the *Values*. The *Importance* describes the relevance of the feature to the description of the stereotype and takes values in [0,1]. The irrelevant

---

Housewife

Classification data

Age *[personal data]*:   *Importance*: 1, *Values*: (less_than_15, 0) (15/24, 0)
                             (25/34, 0) (35/44, 0.5) (45/54, 0.5)
                             (55/64, 0) (more_than_64, 0)

Gender *[personal data]*   *Importance*: 1, *Values*: (male, 0) (female, 1)

Books*[interest]*: *Importance*: 0.6, *Values*: (low, 0.8) (medium, 0.2) (high, 0)

Prediction part

movies-sentimental, *Interest*: 1; serial-soap, *Interest*: 1; TV news, *Interest*: 0,2;

fashion programs, *Interest*: 0,5; cooking programs, *Interest*: 1; ...

Figure 1.2. The 'Housewife' stereotype.

features have importance equal to 0; the essential ones have importance equal to 1. The *Values* facet specifies a distribution of the feature values over the users represented by the stereotype. For each value, the percentage of individuals fitting it within the represented user class is specified. For instance, the interest in *Books* has medium importance in the characterization of the users belonging to the Housewife class (Importance is 0.6). Moreover, 80% of the housewives have low interest in reading books (frequency is 0.8).

The slots in the *prediction part* of a stereotype describe the preferences of the typical user belonging to the represented class. In a prediction slot, the *Program category* specifies the described program category. Moreover, the *Interest* represents the user's preference for the program category and takes decimal values in [0, 1], where 0 denotes lack of interest and 1 is the maximum interest.

3.2.2. Management of the Stereotypical User Model

The user's preferences are estimated in two steps. First, the user is matched against each stereotype S to evaluate how strictly her interests and socio-demographic data correspond to the interests and data of S. The result of this classification is a *degree of matching* with respect to each stereotype. This is a number in [0,1] where 1 denotes perfect match and 0 denotes mismatch.

In the second step, the user's preferences are estimated by combining the predictions of each stereotype, proportionally to the degree of matching with the user. For each program category C of the Stereotype Ontology, the user's interest in C is evaluated as the weighted sum of the interest predicted by the stereotypes; see Ardissono and Goy (2000) and Ardissono et al. (2003) for details. Figure 1.3 shows the stereotypical user model of a user named Francesca.

Interest in TV program categories		Degrees of matching with stereotypes	
Movie-All	0.65	Colleagues	0.34
Movie-Sentimental	0.65	Engaged women	0.24
Movie-Comedy	0.76	Refined women	0.26
Movie-Detective	0.46	Dolphins	0.16
News All	0.73	...	
Serial Fiction	0.54		
...			

Figure 1.3. Portion of Francesca's Stereotypical User Model. The Predictions Have Confidence[2] = 0.43.

---

[2]This value derives from the confidence in the stereotypical classification and is the same for all the program categories because they are specified fully by the stereotypes. Other preferences, not shown in the figure, have lower confidence. Finally, the preferences not specified by the stereotypes have confidence equal to 0.

3.2.3. *Confidence in the Stereotypical Predictions*

Having derived the stereotypes from broad studies such as the Eurisko one, we assume that the classes segment correctly the population of TV viewers. Thus, the confidence in the stereotypical predictions depends on the confidence that the user has been correctly classified by the system. In turn, this depends on the amount of information available at classification time and on 'how stereotypical' is the user.

Confidence in the User Classification with Respect to a Stereotype

The confidence in the classification of the user in a stereotype S represents the confidence that the degree of matching is correct. This measure is evaluated by considering the minimum and maximum degrees of matching that the user might receive, if complete information about her were available.

- The lower bound of the degree of matching (DM_{min}) is evaluated by assuming that, for each classification datum the user has not specified, she matches the less frequent value of the datum, and by classifying her accordingly.
- The upper bound (DM_{max}) is evaluated by assuming that, for each missing classification datum, the user matches the most compatible value.

For instance, the lower bound of the compatibility of Age for 'Housewife' is 0 and suits all the users younger than 35 or older than 55. The upper bound is 0.5 and suits the users between 35 and 54.

DM_{min} and DM_{max} define the interval of admissible values for the degree of matching (DM) : $DM_{min} \leqslant DM \leqslant DM_{max}$. The larger is the interval, the lower the confidence in the classification has to be. In order to model this behavior, we have defined the confidence as:

$$conf_s = 1 - [(DM_{max} - DM_{min})/\Delta]$$

Where Δ is the maximum distance between DM_{max} and DM_{min}. Δ is fixed for each stereotype and it corresponds to the case where no classification datum is set.

The formula defining the confidence in the user classification takes values in [0,1]. When the user is perfectly classified, $DM_{max} - DM_{min} = 0$ and $conf_s = 1$. When no information about the user is available $DM_{max} - DM_{min} = \Delta$ and $conf_s = 0$.

Confidence in the Predictions on the User's Preferences

In order to evaluate the confidence in the predictions, an overall assessment of the quality of the user classification is needed that takes all the classes $\{S_1, \ldots, S_n\}$ of the Stereotype KB into account. The average confidence in the user classification is an approximation of this measure:

$$Conf_{stereotypes} = (\Sigma_{i=1\ldots n} conf_{Si})/n$$

However, this definition does not take the focus of the classification into account. As shown by our experiments (see Section 1.5), the most precise predictions are generated for the 'very stereotypical' users matching a single stereotype or very few stereotypes. Moreover, low-quality predictions are generated for the users that match loosely several stereotypes. Thus, the confidence in the predictions is evaluated by combining the confidence in the classification ($Conf_{stereotypes}$ defined above) with an evaluation of its focus (*Focus*) in a fuzzy and:

$$StereotypicalExpertConfidence = Conf_{stereotypes} * Focus$$

The focalization is derived from the evaluation of Shannon's entropy on the degree of matching of the stereotypes. Suppose that $\{S_1, \ldots, S_n\}$ receive $\{DM_1, \ldots, DM_n\}$ values. Then, the entropy is evaluated as:

$$Entropy = \Sigma_{i=1...n} - \mathbf{DM}_i^* \log_2 \mathbf{DM}_i$$

As the number of stereotypes is fixed, the entropy may be normalized in $[0,1]$, therefore obtaining a normalized entropy *normEntropy*. The focalization is thus:

$$Focus = 1 - normEntropy$$

The focus takes the 0 value when the entropy is the highest, i.e., the classification is very uncertain. In contrast, when a single stereotype matches the user, the focalization is equal to 1. In turn, the confidence is only high when the classification relies on complete information about the user and is very focused.

3.3. THE DYNAMIC USER MODEL

3.3.1. *Acquisition of Information about the User's Viewing Preferences*

The Dynamic User Model specifies the user preferences for the program categories and sub-categories of the General Ontology and for the TV channels. As our system can track the user's actions on the TV, her viewing behavior can be explicitly related to the time of day when the actions occur. Thus, different from the other Experts, the preferences can be acquired for each viewing context and the user's habits during different weekdays and times of day can be identified.

In order to face the uncertainty in the interpretation of the user's viewing behavior, a probabilistic approach is adopted where discrete random variables encode two types of information: preferences and contexts. The sample space of the preference variables corresponds to the domain of objects on which the user holds preferences; the corresponding probability distributions represent a measure of such preferences (interests). The sample space of every context variable is the set of all the possible viewing times.

Figure 1.4 shows the Bayesian Network (Neapolitan, 1990) used to represent the user preferences. In the network, the context variables are associated to the conditions in which the user preferences for the TV programs may occur. A context is characterized by temporal conditions represented by the DAY and VIEWINGTIME

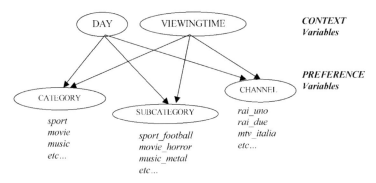

Figure 1.4. Portion of the BN that represents the dynamic user model.

variables. These variables encode, respectively, 7 weekdays and 5 intervals of time in which the day can be subdivided. The context variables are root nodes in the network, since they are not influenced by any other information. The nodes of the Bayesian Network (henceforth, BN) represent the user's contextual preferences, and they provide the probabilities for every program category, sub-category and channel.

For each user, the BN is initialized with a uniform distribution of probabilities on its nodes where all values assumed by the preference variables have equal probability. The BN is updated by feeding it with evidence about the user's selections of TV programs, starting from the first time she watches TV. Each time the user records a program, plays it[3], or asks for more information about it, the system retrieves the category and the sub-category of the program and its transmission channel. Then, it feeds the BN with evidence that a new observation for that category is available.

The BN, implemented using the Norsys' Netica (2001) toolkit, predicts the user preferences by estimating the probabilities of different values for the category, sub-category and channel variables. Exploiting the values of the 'DAY' and 'VIEWINGTIME' variables generates the predictions.

Specifically, Netica provides a simple algorithm for parametric learning that takes the experience of each node of the BN into account. The experience of a node is defined as a function of the number of observed cases. The probability for the state node associated to a new observation is updated as follows:

$$new\_prob = (prev\_prob * prev\_exper + learn\_rate)/new\_exper$$

where

- *learn_rate* is the learning rate of the observed action;
- *prev_prob* and *prev_exper* are the probability and the experience of the node, before the occurrence of the action;
- *new_exper = (prev_exper + learn_rate)* is derived from the previous experience by taking into account the learning rate of the observed action.

---

[3]The system tracks the time spent by the user on a program and compares it to the DVB specification of its duration.

Interest in TV program categories		Interest in transmission	
Movie-All	1	**channels**	
Movie-Sentimental	0.001	RAI 1	0.99
Movie-Comedy	0.49	RAI 2	0.63
Movie-Detective	0.3	Canale 5	1
News All	0.53	Telepiù Bianco	0.56
Serial Fiction	0.001	Telepiù Grigio	0.99
Spot Politics / Society	0.001	...	
...			

Figure 1.5. Portion of Francesca's dynamic user model (evening viewing time). The confidence of the predictions Is 0.5621765.

The probabilities of the state nodes associated to the types of actions that have not been observed are updated, for each viewing time, as follows:

$$new\_prob = (prev\_prob * prev\_exper)/new\_exper$$

Different learning rates are associated to the various action types in order to differentiate their impact on the learning phase. For instance, playing a TV program provides stronger evidence than asking for more information about it.

Figure 1.5 shows the viewing preferences acquired by observing the viewing behavior of user Francesca. The acquired preferences concern the Thursday-Evening context and have been inferred by observing 60 performed actions: 30 Like, 10 Dislike, 3 Memo, 5 Record, 2 Play and 10 request of More Information. [4]

3.3.2. *Confidence in the Predictions of the Dynamic Um Expert*

The confidence in the predictions is based on the quality of the data available to the BN. In turn, the quality depends on the amount of evidence about the user's viewing behavior provided to the BN since the first time the user has interacted with the PPG. In fact, although some noise can be present in her behavior, the BN tolerates it in the presence of a large corpus of data. As the Dynamic User Model is initialized when no viewing data is available, the confidence must be initially equal to 0. The confidence may then increase as long as new user actions are captured by the system.

The Dynamic UM Expert computes the confidence in the predictions by counting how many user actions are observed for a specific context (experience of each node). A sigmoid function defines the confidence, given the number of observed actions. This function is normalized in the [0,1] interval and is defined below:

$$Conf(x) = 1/[1 + e^{(k-x)^* s}]$$

---

[4]The interest values derive from the probability distributions computed by the BN. However, they are normalized in the [0,1] interval to be compatible with the interests predicted by the other UM Experts.

The function returns a confidence close to 0 if no action is observed in a specific context. Moreover, it returns a confidence of 0.5 after k actions are observed and the confidence gets close to 1 after the observation of $2*k$ actions. The s coefficient takes values in [0,1] and defines how steep the function has to be.

3.4. INTEGRATION OF THE PREDICTIONS PROVIDED BY THE UM EXPERTS

The predictions provided by the three Experts are combined by the UMC to estimate the user's preferences employed to personalize the recommendation of TV programs. The possibly conflicting predictions are reconciled by relying on their confidence and the result of this integration is stored in the Main User Model. More specifically, for each category P of the General Ontology, the predictions on P ($Interest_1, \ldots, Interest_n$) provided by the Experts are combined into an overall $Interest$ as follows:

$$Interest = \frac{\sum_{e=1}^{n} Conf_e {}^* Interest_e}{\sum_{e=1}^{n} Conf_e}.$$

This formula merges the predictions in a weighted sum and normalizes the value in [0,1] in order to let the most certain predictions influence the preference estimation in the strongest way. The confidence of the Experts may change along time; at least, the third Expert becomes more and more self-confident. Thus, their predictions are merged in different proportions and, eventually, the Dynamic UM Expert strongly influences the estimation of the user's preferences.

By integrating heterogeneous UM Experts we base the personalization on complementary types of information about the user. In fact, not all the user data are available during the same phases of the life cycle of the EPG. For instance, although the Dynamic UM Expert is expected to learn a precise user model, this module is not able to generate good predictions until a reasonable number of user actions are collected. Moreover, the Explicit Preferences Expert may be unable to provide

Interest in TV program categories		Interest in transmission	
Movie-All	0.91	**channels**	
Movie-Sentimental	0.28	RAI 1	1
Movie-Comedy	0.49	RAI 2	0.63
Movie-Detective	0.37	Canale 5	1
News All	0.79	Telepiù Bianco	0.62
Serial Fiction	0.58	Telepiù Grigio	1
Spot Politics / Society	0.42	...	
...			

Figure 1.6. Portion of the main user model describing francesca's preferences for TV program categories in an evening viewing time.

predictions about several preferences because this specification is not mandatory[5] (although the user may declare her preferences since the first interaction). Finally, the Stereotypical UM Expert may be unable to predict the user's interests if she does not provide her socio-demographic data, or if she clearly differs from stereotypical users. Figure 1.6 shows a portion of Francesca's Main User Model.

4. Recommendation of TV Programs

The recommendation of TV programs is performed in two steps: first, the programs satisfying the user's search query are retrieved and ranked with scores in the range [0,1] representing their suitability to the user. Then, the program list is sorted to reflect the user's preferences and it is possibly pruned, if it includes too many items.

It should be noticed that the programs satisfying the user's search query are retrieved from the system database of TV programs. This database is populated by downloading the program information from the satellite stream. The local storage of the TV content information is essential to support the generation of user-friendly EPGs because it enables the explicit representation of the relations between programs. For instance, the module responsible for populating the database unifies multiple occurrences of the same program, whenever possible. [6] Moreover, the module suitably classifies the serial programs. The availability of this type of information about programs supports the development of flexible presentation strategies. For example, our system simply presents the recommended programs by reporting all the occurrences of each program. However, summary recommendation lists could be generated by removing the redundancies; for example, the timing information of the same programs could be grouped.

4.1. EVALUATING THE SCORE OF A TV PROGRAM

The generation of the scores for the individual TV programs is performed by considering both the user's interests in their program categories and her preferences for the transmission channels (preferences stored in the Main User Model). The former type of information represents the basis for the recommendations, instead we use the latter to refine the suggestions with evidence about the user's viewing habits at the different times of day. It should be noticed that the preference for the channel enables the system to take the user's preferences for individual programs into account without explicitly modeling the characteristics of such

---

[5]The data stored by this module even be unreliable because the users are not always sincere. For instance, in the FACTS project (Bellifemine et al, 99), we noticed that the explicit preferences declared by users are often inconsistent with their real viewing behavior.

[6]The recognition of multiple occurrences is difficult when the information about the programs is delivered by different providers. In fact, although movies and serials are identified by their titles, different descriptions may be broadcast for other programs, such as sport events. The identification is anyway possible when the programs are broadcast by the same provider at different times because, in that case, the DVB information is consistent.

programs. In fact, the system relies on the criteria applied by the broadcasters in the selection of the programs to be shown. The scheduling of TV programs is based on the supposed TV audience in a given time slot that influences the quality and the characteristics of the programs.

The integration of the preferences for program categories and channels is performed according to the algorithm described below. Unfortunately, we cannot rely on complete information about TV programs because the fields of the DVB records broadcast in the satellite stream may be void. Therefore, more or less fine-grained preferences for program categories may be exploited to rank programs. If the program is classified in a sub-category of the General Ontology (e.g., the 'Content' field of the descriptor is sport.basket), the corresponding user preference is employed. Otherwise (sport), the more general user preference is considered.

1. *Prog* = a TV program to be ranked;
2. *Cat* = category of *Prog* (retrieved from the descriptor of *Prog*);
3. *Ch* = transmission channel of *Prog* (retrieved from descriptor);
4. *Ctx* = current context (viewing time);
5. *Score* = user's interest in *Cat*, within *Ctx*;
6. *Interest_Ch* =user's preference for *Ch* in *Ctx*;
7. if *Interest_Ch* is significant
8. then *Score* = update *Score* according to *Interest_Ch;*

Given a TV program *Prog* to be ranked, the system retrieves the category of the program (2) and the transmission channel (3) from the descriptor. Moreover, the current viewing context, *Ctx*, is considered (4). Then, the system retrieves the user's preference (interest related to *Ctx*) for the program category in order to generate the first approximation of the score (5). Finally, the score is possibly refined (6-7-8) to take the user's preference (*Interest_Ch*) for the channel into account.

The approach adopted in the PPG relies on the following assumptions: no inferences can be made if the user's interest in the channel is medium. However, if the user watches the channel very often at the time of day specified by *Ctx*, then this is positive evidence that she appreciates the programs usually broadcast at that time of day. Moreover, if she never watches the channel in a context *Ctx*, this is interpreted as moderate evidence that she does not like the programs broadcast by the channel at that time of day. Two relevance thresholds, set to 0.15 and 0.85, characterize the notions of low, medium and high interest for a channel. We have three cases:

1. *Medium preference for channel.* In this case *Score* coincides with the user's preference for the *Cat* program category; no modification is performed. This happens when *Interest.Ch*, the interest in *Ch* during *Ctx*, is between 0.15 and 0.85.
2. *Very low preference for channel.* If the user's preference for *Ch* is very low (*Interest_Ch* is between 0 and 0.15), the score of the TV event is decreased to represent the fact that the user typically does not watch *Ch* in context *Ctx*.

Thus, the channel reduces evidence that she will like the specific program.[7] In order to decrease the *Score* proportionally with respect to the lack of evidence that the user watches the channel, but to maintain its value in [0,1], *Score* is updated as follows:

$$Score' = Score - \alpha^* Interest\_Ch^* Score$$

Where α, a decimal value in [0,1], tunes the influence of the preference for the channel on the basic preference for the program category.

3. *Very high preference for channel.* If the user's preference for *Ch* is very high (*Interest.Ch* is between 0.85 and 1), *Score* is increased. In fact, *Interest.Ch* provides positive evidence that the user likes watching the programs broadcast in *Ch* in the *Ctx* viewing time. In order to increase the *Score* proportionally to the amount of positive evidence, but to maintain it in [0,1], *Score* is updated as follows:

$$Score' = Score + \alpha^* Interest\_Ch^* (1 - Score)$$

Where α is the same parameter used in case 2. In our experiments, α is set to 0.1 to weakly influence the sorting strategy because we only want to change the order of programs belonging to the same category.

5. Experiments

5.1. THE EVALUATION METHODOLOGY

The recommendations of the PPG are generated by relying on the estimates of the user's preferences stored in the Main User Model (these preferences determine the 'space' devoted to the various TV program categories in the EPG). Thus, an evaluation of the system has to calculate the distance between the recommendations derived from these estimates and the real user's preferences/selections. As the Main User Model results from the combination of the predictions of three UM Experts, we needed three kinds of information for a complete evaluation:

a. The dataset exploited by the Stereotypical UM Expert to classify the users, i.e., socio-demographic data, general interests and lifestyles.
b. The explicit users' preferences for TV programs collected by the Explicit Preferences Expert.
c. The users' observed selections of TV programs, i.e., their viewing behavior.

To obtain this data we involved subjects belonging to the Auditel panel (Auditel, 2003). Auditel is the nonpartisan company that collects daily information about Italian TV audience. This survey classifies the Italian population in several

---

[7]In some contexts, the user may not watch TV at all. Thus, the score of the programs is revised according to the channel preferences only during the viewing times where the user has medium or high preferences for at least one channel.

socio-demographic panels according to the age, gender, education level, type of job and geographic zone. For each panel, the daily audience data is available, grouped by viewing time and TV channels. The Auditel panel includes 5.000 Italian families for a total number of 14.000 subjects. In order to collect datasets *a* and *b* we identified 62 Auditel subjects by following a non-probabilistic blocking sampling strategy. This is a sampling strategy that divides the population in layers related to the variables that have to be estimated, where each layer contains a number of individuals proportional to its distribution in the target population. We identified several layers characterized by different socio-demographic data, interests and TV program preferences. Every layer identifies a possible user of the PPG. We selected a small number of subjects because carrying out the required interviews and collecting the audience data was a complex task. Unfortunately, the complete analysis of the panel is not representative. However, we are currently extending our evaluation to other Auditel subjects to collect information about a representative sample of the Italian TV audience.

In order to acquire the previously mentioned data we operated as follows.

- We interviewed the subjects by means of a questionnaire. To obtain the desired information, we collected: general data (including personal data), information about general interests (books, music, sport, etc.), preferences for TV program categories and sub-categories. The final questionnaire included 35 questions where both the questions and the answers were fixed. The questionnaire was anonymous and introduced by means of a written presentation explaining the general research aims. For the items concerning the general data, the participants were required to check the appropriate answer out of a set of given answers. In the other questions, the subjects had to express their level of agreement with the options associated to the given questions by choosing an item in a 3-point Likert scale. The participants, without the presence of the interviewer, filled in the questionnaires which were collected one week after the distribution. Then, we fed our PPG system with the acquired information to evaluate the validity of the user classification and the accuracy of the recommendations.

- After one year, we fed the PPG with the selections of TV programs made by the test subjects. This information was collected by the Auditel meter[8] and stored in a database. In this way, we could activate the predictions generated by the Dynamic UM Expert. We entered the following information:

  ○ The context variables: day and viewing time.
  ○ The selected TV channel.
  ○ The (play) action suitably related to the TV program categories and sub-categories of our General Ontology.
  ○ The title of the watched program.

---

[8]The meter is an electronic device connected to the TV that constantly monitors the viewing behaviour of the users belonging to the Auditel panel.

5.2. THE RESULTS

To separately test the recommendation capabilities of the three UM Experts we decided to evaluate the system's performance by simulating real scenarios where the Experts take different roles depending on the availability of information about the user. However, we did not evaluate the Explicit Preferences Expert that simply propagates the declared user preferences in the General Ontology.

We started from the Stereotypical UM Expert. We simulated an initial scenario where the user has specified her personal data and general interests, but where she does not declare her TV program preferences. Thus, the recommendations are based only on the stereotypical information. In this first phase, we evaluated the correctness of the stereotypical classification and the accuracy of recommendations by feeding the system with the socio-demographic data and the general interests (dataset *a*) collected by means of the interviews.

Then we simulated a scenario where the system has enough information (datasets *a*, *b* and *c*) to have the three Experts cooperating at the generation of the recommendations. In this second phase we also fed the system with the explicit program preferences and the TV program selections performed by the subjects.

5.2.1. *Evaluation of the Stereotypical Classification*

To evaluate the stereotypical classification, we compared the classification of the subjects computed by the PPG with the classification of two human Eurisko lifestyles experts. The comparison showed that 70% of the users were classified correctly by the system. The remaining 30% were incorrectly classified for two reasons:

- The classification fails for 'non-stereotypical' subjects, whose general interests differ from those evaluated according their socio-demographic data. Indeed, the Stereotypical UM Expert takes both socio-demographic and general interests into account to classify the user. However, the socio-demographic information plays a stronger role in the classification. Thus, if a user *a* has socio-demographic data typical of stereotype *A*, but her interests are typical of stereotype *B*, she is classified as belonging to stereotype *A*.
- The data provided by the Eurisko survey does not cover the whole Italian population. For instance the Retired stereotype only represents low-income users and the other retired users, such as the ex-managers, are not considered. This lack of information has to be overcome to improve the coverage of the stereotypical knowledge base and the consequent classification capabilities of the system.

The first issue deserves further discussion. The misclassification of a 'non-stereotypical' user *a* causes wrong predictions because *a* prefers programs that would be recommended to the users belonging to another stereotype *B*. Indeed, we wanted to preserve the definition of the stereotypes and, at the same time, balance the contribution of the user's socio-demographic data with that of her general interests.

Thus, we employed the declared general interests as another source of information about the user's preferences to be managed by the Explicit Preference Expert.

5.2.2. Evaluation of the System's Recommendation Capabilities

We exploited the *Mean Absolute Error metric* (MAE [9]) to evaluate the distance between the preferences predicted by the system and the users' preferences/selections captured by monitoring their viewing behavior. Good et al. (1999) suggest that, in the evaluation of a recommender system, a satisfactory value of MAE should be about 0.7, in a range of 0–5. We also tested the accuracy of the recommendations by evaluating the *precision* of the collected data, i.e., the ratio between the user-relevant contents and the contents presented to the user; see Salton and McGill (1984).

First of all, we compared the TV program predictions generated by the Stereotypical UM Expert with the preferences expressed by the users and maintained by the Explicit Preferences Expert. Indeed, the users' explicit preferences are expressed as qualitative *low*, *medium* and *high* values. In order to compute the MAE by relying on similar measures, we exploited the numeric preference values generated by the Explicit Preferences Expert starting from the users' declarations. These values are reliable because the Expert derives them in a straightforward way from the qualitative ones.

For each test subject, after having entered the socio-demographic data, the general interests and the explicit preference values in the Explicit User Model, we calculated the differences between the values generated by the Explicit Preferences Expert and those generated by the Stereotypical UM Expert.[10] Specifically, we evaluated the MAE by comparing the TV program category and sub-category predictions with the corresponding explicit preferences, with possible values ranging between 0 and 5. The obtained MAE value was 1,3 with precision 0,40; see Table 1.1.

Although this result cannot be considered satisfactory, we think that the MAE value was strongly influenced by the percentage of misclassified subjects, which was approximately 30%; see Section 5.2.1. Indeed, several subjects matched a high number of stereotypes. In these cases, the focalization of the classification was very low and downgraded the confidence of the predictions generated by the Stereotypical UM Expert, which were generic and corresponded to the users' real preferences

Table 1.1. Evaluation of the system's recommendations

Stereotypical UM Expert	MAE = 1,3 Precision=0.40
Stereotypical UM Expert + Explicit Pref Expert + Dynamic UM Expert	MAE = 0,3 Precision=0.80

---

[9]The MAE metric evaluates the distance between the system predictions and the user's preferences/selections by means of rate vectors. A smaller value means more accurate predictions; see Good et al. (1999).

[10]For the purpose of this evaluation, the recommendations generated by the three UM Experts are recorded in separated log files before being integrated in the Main User Model.

in an approximated way. We think that these values might notably improve if we could extend the stereotypical knowledge base as described in Section 5.2.1.

In the second phase of our evaluation we compared the system's recommendation capabilities with the subjects' viewing behavior. We started from the information about the users already available to the system and we added the explicit preferences, which were omitted in the previous experiment. Next, we entered the TV program selections provided by the Auditel meter. More specifically, we fed the system with the observations collected during the first 10 months to train the Dynamic UM Expert. Then, we exploited those of the last 2 months to evaluate the distance between the system's recommendations and the subjects' observed selections. In this case, the three Experts could generate reasonably confident recommendations and therefore an evaluation of the complete Main User Model was possible.

The resulting MAE was 0.30 and the precision was 0.80; see the second row of Table 1. These values are definitely satisfactory and confirm our hypothesis about the validity of the integration of different sources of information.

We also calculated an ANOVA to investigate the significance of the different MAE results obtained by considering the Stereotypical UM Expert alone and the final merge of the predictions provided by the three Experts. Our analysis showed that the different MAE results are due to a significant correlation between the Experts taken into account (independent variable) and the resulting program recommendations (dependent variable): $F(1.61) = 97.3$ $p < 0.01$.

6. Related Work

Some recommender systems, such as MovieLens (2002), rely on collaborative filtering to personalize the suggestion of items. As discussed in Burke (2002), this technique performs well in domains where the set of items to be recommended is relatively stable, but has problems when new users, or new items, are considered. Other techniques, such as content-based filtering, support the recommendation of new items, but they tend to suggest items very similar to one another. In order to complement the advantages and disadvantages of different recommender systems, hybrid approaches are preferable in several application domains. Similar to the proposal described in Burke (2002), our PPG exploits different preference acquisition techniques, but the main difference is that we excluded collaborative filtering to focus on the techniques that can be efficiently applied locally to the user's set-top box.

The integration of the EPG in the set-top box is an important architectural feature of our system because it enables the continuous tracking of the user's viewing behavior. Thus, the user's preferences can be unobtrusively acquired while she watches TV, without requiring any explicit feedback.[11] In contrast, if a central server manages the EPG, the interaction with the TV is carried out in a distinct thread and can only be monitored while the user browses the program guide, unless special hardware

---

[11]As a matter of fact, the user may rate programs, but the preference acquisition works well even without this type of information.

is employed to connect the TV to the Internet. For instance, Smyth and Cotter's PTV Listings Service is based on a centralized architecture. To overcome the lack of connectivity with the TV, Smyth and Cotter propose the exploitation of GuideRemote, an interactive universal remote control that captures the user's selections while she watches TV.

Another peculiarity of the PPG concerns the integration of alternative preference acquisition techniques to manage the hybrid user model. In other recommender systems, the most promising recommendation methods are selected by applying them in cascade (Burke, 2002), or by relying on a-contextual estimates of the precision of the methods or on the posterior evaluation of the recommendations. For instance, TvScout (Baudisch, 1998; Baudisch and Brueckner, 2002) combines a recommender based on the analysis of size-of-the-audience data in cascade with other two recommendation sources: the user's favorite program categories and the suggestions provided by *opinion leaders*, such as TV critics.As another example, in the TV Show Recommender (Zimmerman et al.) two implicit recommenders and an explicit one are fused by exploiting a neural network that tunes the influence of the competitors on the basis of the accuracy of their recommendations. Finally, the PTV Listings Service integrates a content-based recommender and a collaborative filtering one by merging the items best ranked by each recommender in a single suggestion list. Our approach differs from the previous ones in at least two aspects.

- On the one hand, our PPG combines heterogeneous inference techniques in a finer-grained way and clearly separates the estimation of the user's preferences from the generation of the personalized suggestions. We fuse three preference acquisition modules to acquire precise user models based on different information about the TV viewer. Then we put two recommendation techniques (content-based filtering and adjustment of rates based on the preferences for channels) in cascade to rank the TV programs.
- On the other hand, the system adopts a simpler approach to steer the fusion process. As described in Section 3.4, the PPG tunes the influence of the UM Experts in the estimation of the user's preferences by relying on the confidence in the predictions. Indeed, an accuracy measure should be coupled with the confidence one to evaluate the quality of the predictions in a more precise way. However, in the development of the PPG, we privileged the confidence measure, leaving the accuracy one for our future work, because the confidence can be exploited during the whole lifecycle of the EPG. In fact, it only depends on the amount of information about the user available to the Experts. In contrast, other accuracy measures take some time before being effective for new TV viewers.

The exploitation of stereotype-based techniques has a long tradition in the user modeling field, see Rich (1989); however, the definition of the stereotypical classes has been based on rather different assumptions about the population to be segmented. For instance, Kurapati and Gutta (2002) proposed to define stereotypical classes of TV viewers by clustering the viewing history data of a sample population.

However, they noticed that some of the stereotypes created by the clustering algorithms did not make sense and were very difficult to understand. Instead, Barbieri et al. (2001) proposed to define a set of classical stereotypes, such as Movie Lover and Film Freak, and let the TV viewer explicitly choose the one best matching her mood.

A deeper analysis of TV viewer stereotypes is proposed in a recent survey on the viewing preferences of Japanese TV viewers. Hara et al. group a sample of TV viewers on the basis of the features of the programs they say they have watched thoroughly. The results of the clustering analysis show that the viewers' interests influence their preferences for program categories; moreover, the people having the same socio-demographic attributes, such as age, gender and occupation, frequently differ in their preferences for TV program categories. Thus, Hara et al. propose viewing patterns as the most significant variable for the definition of stereotypical TV viewer classes. In particular, they define 8 viewer groups representing TV viewing 'tastes' and watching styles, such as News/Culture Oriented, Diversion-Seeking Zapper, and so forth.

Although Hara et al.'s findings could discourage the exploitation of socio-demographic information about TV viewers to predict their preferences, we believe that the problem should be put in a different way. Specifically, socio-demographic information is not enough, but it is very useful when coupled with other information aimed at enriching the overall picture of the TV users. Indeed, the stereotypes exploited in our PPG are richer than the previously mentioned ones, as we derived them from complete studies of the TV viewer population under a *socio-demographic* and a *psychographic* point of view. In fact, the lifestyles survey we considered - Sinottica, conducted by Eurisko data analyzers (2002) - clusters the population in groups by taking into account not only socio-demographic data, but also consumer preferences, socio-cultural trends and homogeneous behaviors. Particularly, Sinottica is a psychographic survey on:

- Individuals (characteristics, values, behaviors, styles);
- What they consume (products/goods/services and relative brands);
- Their exposure to the media (a survey in collaboration with Auditel, see 3.2).

By exploiting all these types of information, we could derive a set of stereotypes that partition the population in a precise way and reflect viewing preferences. Notice that these studies are exploited to plan the presentation of commercials within TV programs by the most representative content providers.

7. Conclusions and Future Work

This paper has presented the recommendation techniques applied in the Personal Program Guide (PPG). This is a prototype system generating personalized EPGs for set-top box environments. The PPG is based on a multi-agent architecture that facilitates the integration of different user modeling techniques for the recognition of the TV viewer's preferences and the suggestion of the programs to watch.

As shown by our preliminary experimental results, the management of a hybrid user model, relying on different sources of information about the user's preferences, supports high-quality recommendations. This is not surprising: in fact, the recommendations based on explicit user information are subject to failures, because users are often unable to declare their real preferences. Moreover, the recommendations based on the observation of the user's viewing behavior take some time before being effective and, mirroring the user's usual selections, they fail to support the variety in the system's recommendations. In order to enable the system to generate high-quality suggestions since the first interaction with the user, we enriched the user models with community preferences by exploiting two main sources of information: on the one hand, the stereotypical preferences for program categories derived from lifestyle and audience data provide information about the preferences of similar TV viewers. On the other hand, the user's preferences for TV channels, at different times of day, support the refinement of the recommendations based on the audience analysis performed by the content providers.

In our future work, we want to extend the PPG in two main aspects. First, we want to enhance the TV program recommendations by taking household preferences into account and by refining the management of the hybrid user model. Second, we will redesign the User Interface to take usability issues into account.

Modeling household preferences is important because people rarely watch TV alone. As discussed in this volume by Masthoff, several recommendation strategies may be applied to satisfy the individual group members and avoid frustration. Although our system does not address household preferences, its recommendation capabilities can be extended in a rather straightforward way. In fact, the system architecture facilitates the integration of new User Modeling Experts and a Household Preference Expert could be added to handle group models. This UM Expert could employ the same preference acquisition techniques applied in our Dynamic Preference Expert to learn household profiles. Indeed, we believe that the most relevant issue to be solved is the automatic recognition of the user(s) in front of the TV. This issue is still unsolved, but some researchers, such as Goren-Bar and Glinansky (2002), are working to address it. The extension of the hybrid user model mainly involves the refinement of the fusion technique adopted to merge the predictions of the User Modeling Experts. As described in the previous part of this chapter, the predictions generated by the Experts are combined in a weighted sum, depending on their confidence. Although this approach has produced satisfactory results, we want to tune the fusion process by taking an accuracy measure into account, as well. In the multi-agent systems area, an established approach for the integration of possibly heterogeneous agents is based on the joint evaluation of the agents' *self-confidence* and *reputation*. The self-confidence is a subjective evaluation of the agents' decision capabilities. The agent's reputation is an objective parameter evaluated by a third party. In the PPG, we already model the Experts' self-confidence that corresponds to the confidence in the preference predictions. Moreover, we will introduce the reputation that will be computed by the UMC by comparing the predictions provided by the Experts with the user's viewing behavior. The UMC will exploit the Experts' confidence and reputation to merge their preference predictions. Notice however that the UMC has to rely on the sole confidence for the fusion process until it has collected a significant amount of information about the user's viewing behavior.

As far as the User Interface is concerned, a lot of work has to be done to redesign it according to usability standards. However, as a first step in this direction, we want to focus on the presentation of the system's recommendations. At the current stage, the PPG suggests TV programs by coupling each item with a number of faces representing the recommendation degree. Moreover, the system limits the length of the recommendation list by omitting the presentation of the programs receiving very bad scores. As noticed in Zimmerman et al., the TV viewer's trust in the EPG would increase if she could be informed about all the available options, not only about the most interesting ones. The question is therefore how such possibly long list of alternatives could be presented in a clear and acceptable way, from the user's point of view. Other projects have encountered serious difficulties in making TV viewers accept prototype User Interfaces for Interactive TV; e.g., see Tinker et al. (2003). Therefore, some researchers are applying user-centered design to the definition of new User Interfaces for Electronic Program Guides; see van Barneveld and van Setten, in this volume.

Acknowledgments

The Personal Program Guide has been developed in a joint project between Telecom Italia Lab and the University of Torino. This work has been partially supported by the Italian M.I.U.R. (Ministero dell'Istruzione dell'Università e della Ricerca) through the Te.S.C.He.T. Project (Technology System for Cultural Heritage in Tourism).

We are grateful to Flavio Portis, who helped us in the development of the Stereotypical UM Expert of the PPG.

References

Ardissono, L., Gena, C., Torasso, P., Bellifemine, F., Chiarotto, A., Difino, A. and Negro, B.: 2003, Personalized Recommendation of TV Programs. In: *LNAI n. 2829. AI*IA 2003: Advances in Artificial Intelligence*, Springer-Verlag, pp. 474–486.
Ardissono, L. and Goy, A.: 2000, Tailoring the Interaction with Users in Web Stores. *User Modeling and User-Adapted Interaction* **10**(4), 251–303.
Ardissono, L., Portis, F., Torasso, P., Bellifemine, F., Chiarotto, A. and Difino, A.: 2001, Architecture of a system for the generation of personalized Electronic Program Guides. *Proceedings UM'01 Workshop on Personalization in Future TV*, Sonthofen, Germany.
Auditel : 2003, Auditel. http://www.auditel.it.
Barbieri, M., Ceccarelli, M., Mekenkamp, G. and Nesvadba, J.: 2001, A personal TV receiver with storage and retrieval capabilities. In: *Proceedings UM'01 Workshop on Personalization in Future TV*, Sonthofen, Germany.

Baudisch, P.: 1998, Recommending TV programs on the Web: How far can we get at zero user effort? *In Recommender systems: papers from the 1998 workshop. Technical Report WS-98–08*, AAAI Press, Menlo Park, pp. 16–18.

Baudisch, P. and Brueckner, L.: 2002, TV Scout. Lowering the entry barrier to personalized TV program recommendation. In: *Proceedings 2nd Int. Conf. On Adaptive Hypermedia and Adaptive Web-based Systems (AH2002)*, Malaga, Spain, pp. 58–68.

Bellifemine, F. et al.: 1999, Deliverable A12D1 'Agent-system software for the AVEB Phase 1 Demonstrator'. FACTS (FIPA Agent Communication Technologies and Services) is the ACTS project number AC317 of the European Commission.

Burke, R.: 2002, Hybrid Recommender Systems: Survey and Experiments. *User Modeling and User-Adapted Interaction* **12**(4), 331–370.

Cotter, P. and Smyth, B.: 2000, A Personalized Television Listing Service. *Communications of the ACM*, **43**(8), 107–111.

DVB (2000). Digital video broadcasting. http://www.dvb.org.

Eurisko (2002). Sinottica. http://www.eurisko.it.

Gena, C.: 2001, Designing TV Viewer Stereotypes for an Electronic Program Guide. In: *Proceedings of the 8th Int. Conf. on User Modeling*, Sonthofen, Germany, pp. 274–276.

Good, N., Schafer, J. B., Konstan, J. A., Botchers, A., Sarwar, B. M., Herlocker, J. L. and Riedl, J.: 1999, Combining collaborative filtering with personal agents br better recommendations. In: *Proceedings of the 16th National Conference on Artificial Intelligence*, Orlando, Florida, pp. 439–446.

Goren-Bar, D. and Glinansky, O.: 2002, Family Stereotyping - A Model to Filter TV Programs for Multiple Viewers. In: *Proceedings AH'02 Workshop on Personalization in Future TV*, Malaga, Spain, pp. 101–108.

Hara, Y., Tomomune, Y. and Shigemori, M.: 2004, Categorization of Japanese TV viewers based on program genres they watch. In this volume.

Kurapati, K. and Gutta, S.: 2002, TV Personalization through Stereotypes. In: *Proceedings AH'02 Workshop on Personalization in Future TV*, Malaga, Spain, pp. 109–118.

Masthoff, J.: Group modeling: selecting a sequence of television items to suit a group of users. In this volume.

Mostafa, J.: 2002, *IEEE Intelligent Systems: Information Customization*, **17**(6).

MovieLens : 2002, MovieLens: Helping you find the right movies. http://www.movielens.umn.edu/.

Neapolitan, R. E.: 1990, *Probabilistic Reasoning in Expert Systems: Theory and Algorithms*. John Wiley & Sons, New York.

Netica (2001). Application for Belief Networks and Influence Diagrams, User's Guide. http://www.norsys.com.

Resnick, P. and Varian, H. R.: 1997, *Communications of the ACM: Special Issue on Recommender Systems* **40**(3).

Rich E.: 1989, Stereotypes and User Modeling. In: A., Kobsa, W., Wahlster, (eds.): *User Models in Dialog Systems*. Springer-Verlag, Berlin, pp. 31–51.

Riecken, D.: 2000, *Communications of the ACM: Special Issue on Personalization* **43**(8).

Salton, G. and McGill, M.: 1984, *Introduction to Modern Information Retrieval*, McGraw-Hill Book Company.

Smyth, B. and Cotter, P.: The Evolution of the Personalized Electronic Programme Guide. In this volume.

Tinker, P., Fox, J. and Daily, M.: 2003, A zooming, electronic programming interface. 3rd Workshop on Personalization in Future TV (TV'03), Johnstown, PA, pp. 7–11.

TiVo, Inc. (2002). TiVo: TV your way. http://www.tivo.com

Van Barneveld, J. and van Setten, M.: Designing Usable Interfaces for TV Recommender Systems. In this volume.

Zimmerman, J., Kurapati, K., Buczak, A. L., Schaffer, D., Martino, J. and Gutta, S.: TV Personalization System. In this volume.

Chapter 2

TV Personalization System
Design of a TV Show Recommender Engine and Interface

JOHN ZIMMERMAN[1]*, KAUSHAL KURAPATI[2]*, ANNA L. BUCZAK[3]*,
DAVE SCHAFFER[4], SRINIVAS GUTTA[4] and JACQUELYN MARTINO[5]*
[1]*Carnegie Mellon University*
[2]*IBM Corporation*
[3]*Lockheed Martin Corporation*
[4]*Philips Research*
[5]*MIT*

Abstract. The arrival of PVRs (Personal Video Recorders)—tapeless devices that allow for easy navigation and storage of TV content—and the availability of hundreds of TV channels in US homes have made the task of finding something good to watch increasingly difficult. In order to ease this content selection overload problem, we pursued three related research themes. First, we developed a recommender engine that tracks users' TV-preferences and delivers accurate content recommendations. Second, we designed a user interface that allows easy navigation of selections and easily affords inputs required by the recommender engine. Third, we explored the importance of gaining users' trust in the recommender by automatically generating explanations for content recommendations. In evaluation with users, our smart interface came out on top beating TiVo's interface and TV Guide Magazine, in terms of usability, fun, and quick access to TV shows of interest. Further, our approach of combining multiple recommender ratings—resulting from various machine-learning methods—using neural networks has produced very accurate content recommendations.

Key words. electronic program guide (EPG), interactive TV, personalization, trust, TV interface, TV recommender, user interface

1. Introduction

The increase in TV viewing options from digital cable and digital satellite has created a world where many US homes have access to hundreds of channels. In addition, the arrival of Personal Video Recorders (PVRs) such as TiVo™ and ReplayTV™ has begun to change how people watch TV. PVRs allow easy navigation of TV-show schedules through electronic program guides (EPG) for selection and storage on hard disks. In observing PVR users, we noticed that within two to three days they shifted from watching live to stored TV programs almost exclusively. So now, instead of having to select a single program to watch from hundreds of channels, PVR users instead select a small set of TV shows to store from the tens of thousands broadcast each week.

---

*Work done while at Philips Research

L. Ardissono et al. (eds.), Personalized Digital Television, 27–51, 2004.
© 2004 *Kluwer Academic Publishers. Printed in the Netherlands.*

In order to address this looming content selection overload issue and improve the TV show selection and viewing experience, we created a TV show recommender to help users find something 'good' to watch. During its creation we pursued three related research themes. First, we developed a recommender engine that could track users' TV-preferences and deliver accurate content recommendations. An accurate recommender can extract shows users want to see from an ocean of less interesting fare. Second, we designed a user interface that allows easy navigation of selections and supports inputs required of the recommender engine. A recommender without an easy to use interface can potentially make finding something *good* to watch more difficult than not using a recommender. Finally, we explored the importance of gaining users' trust in the recommender, because if users don't trust a recommender, they will not use it or pay for it as a feature or service.

Our recommender engine combines two user information streams: explicit and implicit. The explicit stream allows users to take control by specifying their preferences and enables the system to begin working right away. The implicit stream unobtrusively observes users to learn their preferences. Implicit methods reduce the amount of work required of users to get recommendations and allow for changes in taste to be captured over time. We obtain accurate recommendations by fusing both recommenders' outputs using neural networks. Our interface runs on a touch-screen remote control. The use of a finger as a floating cursor greatly improves efficiency over traditional remote control interfaces that employ jumping highlights. In addition, our interface allows users to select how much or how little interaction they want with the recommender, making them feel *in control*. Finally, we build user trust by providing (i) accurate recommendations, (ii) flexible access to the recommender, and (iii) appropriate feedback on why users might want to try a *new* TV show.

Our research on both the engine and interface follows a user-centered iterative design process: analyze, design, and evaluate (repeat). At this point our work is still in the preliminary stages. We have focused on a longer-term evaluation with a small set of test subjects instead of a larger, statistically significant study.

2. Related Work

2.1. RELATED WORK ON TV RECOMMENDER SYSTEMS

With respect to recommendation engines, the TV Advisor of Das & Horst (1998), PTV system of Cotter & Smyth (2000), EPG work of Ardissono et al. (in this volume), and our prior work Gutta et al. (2000), and Kurapati et al. (2001) stand out as some of the earliest TV recommender systems. In addition, TiVo and Predictive Networks offer commercially available systems that provide TV recommendations. For a history of the evolution of personalized electronic program guides, refer to Smyth & Cotter (in this volume).

The TV Advisor of Das & Horst (1998) employs explicit techniques to generate recommendations for a TV viewer. Such techniques require individual users to take the initiative and explicitly specify their interests in order to get high quality recommendations. Although this method is a good first step and one that is easy to implement in a set-top box, it burdens users who want minimal interaction with the recommender. Moreover the system is static and does not allow evolution of user profiles over time.

Cotter & Smyth's PTV (2000) uses a mixture of case-based reasoning and collaborative filtering as a means of learning users' preferences in order to generate recommendations. Initially users state their preferences about channel, genre, and viewing time while registering with the system, similar to the explicit recommender of Das & Horst. However, the heart of the PTV recommender infers users' preferences as they enter their feedback on TV shows they have watched. Also, PTV is Internet based, requiring the users to log on to a web site in order to see their recommendations. This approach removes users from the TV viewing environment thereby questioning the system's ability to be useful in the real setting.

Case-based recommendation relies on input of programs that users liked in the past (Balabanovic & Shoham 1997, Hammond et al. 1996, Smyth & Cotter 1999). Collaborative filtering (Balabanovic & Shoham 1997, Billsus & Pazzani 1998) recommends TV shows that other users, having characteristics similar to a given user's profile, liked. The advantage of collaborative filtering is that it does not need content descriptions (titles are sufficient). However, collaborative filtering does not completely protect users' privacy since information about a user's likes and dislikes is used to make recommendations to other users. Additionally, collaborative filtering cannot work for programs that are completely new, not known to at least one of the viewers. This often happens with TV when new programs and made-for-TV movies are broadcast.

Ardissono et al. (in this volume) created the Personalized EPG that employs an agent-based system designed for set-top box operation. Three user modeling modules collaborate in preparing the final recommendations: Explicit Preferences Expert, Stereotypical Expert, and Dynamic Expert. The Explicit Preferences Expert deals with preferences declared by the users during initial setup. The Stereotypical Expert exploits users' personal data known to the system and the explicit preferences stated in order to classify individual users into one of the lifestyle (stereotypical) groups. The Dynamic Expert analyzes users' watching behaviors, and based on it builds and adapts its model of the user. The Personalized EPG recommender is a very interesting mixture of explicit, stereotypical and implicit user preferences allowing the final recommendation to take advantage of the three complementary methodologies involved. This work further validates hybrid approaches to generating content recommendations.

One of the earliest commercially available TV recommenders comes from TiVo, Inc. TiVos generate personalized recommendations that are displayed to users. Their recommender learns by tracking which programs users choose to record and user feedback of 'thumbs-up' or 'thumbs-down' to indicate how they feel about TV shows (on a 1 to 7 scale).

Predictive Media, Inc. provides another commercially available recommender system. They use a mixed model approach that combines statistical analysis, expert systems, and neural networks to generate content recommendations. Their system is primarily implicit in nature. Predictive Media's recommender results can be plugged into any UI for presentation. This decoupling lessens the usefulness of a TV recommender in our opinion.

All of the techniques described above share one common characteristic: users only see a very limited number of recommendations. A unique feature of our system is that it creates a prioritized list of *all* TV shows. This allows users to browse both highly rated and lowly rated programs, and to actively tune the recommender and improve its performance.

2.2. RELATED WORK ON INTERFACE DESIGN

With respect to TV recommender interfaces, Double Agents by Meuleman et al. (1998), Personalized Contents Guide by Lee et al. (2001), TV Scout by Baudisch & Brueckner (2001), Time-pillars by Pittarello (in this volume), the interface explorations of Barneveld and Setten (in this volume), and the commercial PVR by TiVo all stand out.

Double Agents, designed by Meuleman et al. (1998) employs animated characters to help users find programs of interest. Each character represents a different genre. When a highly recommended program is being broadcast, the character representing the genre of this program changes its posture using human-like behavioral characteristics to let users know something *good* is on. This model can work well when working with the relatively small number of shows being broadcast live, however, unlike our interface it would have a problem with the one to two weeks worth of shows that PVRs present.

The Advanced Contents Guide of Lee et al. (2001) offers an interface where users can select from recommended TV shows. This interface uses user inputs such as selection, fast-forward, and rewind to learn user preferences, but unlike our system it offers users no direct input to the recommender. The interface presents a list of recommended programs by genre. However, the interface at present has only been used with data from four channels based on two weeks of data. It would be interesting to see if it can support hundreds of channels.

The TV Scout interface by Baudisch & Bruekner (2001) offers a fully featured TV show recommender interface that progressively reveals its filtering features to users over time. Users produce queries to find shows of interest, and the system learns what they like by tracking their queries. Unlike our interface, TV Scout only allows users to organize programs by time. However, this limitation may be only an artifact of a limited implementation as opposed to a limitation of the actual interface design. A more difficult problem is that the interface runs on a PC and has a very strong PC look and feel.

Time-pillars by Pittarello (in this volume) provides users with a 3D world populated by pillars that appear similar to architectural wonder, *Traian's column*, found in Rome. Each pillar represents a TV channel, with individual shows ordered by broadcast time spiraling up from the bottom to the top of the pillar. The Time-pillars interface seems most concerned with generating a pleasurable user experience where as our interface focus more on balancing a pleasurable user experience that also reduces the amount of time spent searching for something interesting to watch.

The interface explorations by Barneveld and Setten (in this volume) offer great insights into users' expectations. The conducted user research through participatory design and surveys to help clarify both which features users want and what those features might look like. They specifically looked at Predictions (how recommendations appear on the screen), Feedback (how users explicitly enter preferences to the recommender), and Explanations (how recommendations are justified to users). Their designs for feedback do not support the flexible interaction with the recommender our participants demanded (Section 5.2); however, their evaluation of explanations completely supports our design of the reflective history interface element (Section 7.1).

TiVo currently offers a TV show recommender interface as a commercial product in the United States and in England. Users can enter up to three thumbs up or thumbs down to indicate how much they like or dislike a TV program. To see what programs have been recommended, users have two options. First, they can check the hard disk contents and view programs TiVo has recorded for them that they did not explicitly request. Second, users can navigate to a list of highly recommended programs coming up in the next two weeks. This list never exceeds 100 program titles.

TiVo's recommender interface has two limitations. First, the interface does not allow users to access the recommender when filtering programs by genre such as Action-Movies, or by time such as *show me the recommended programs that are on now*. Second, the interface does not offer users any indication of why a program has been recommended. While there is much to complain about the limitations of TiVo's recommender interface, it must be noted that the interface is quite easy to use, and it is available on store shelves today.

2.3. RELATED WORK ON TRUST

Related work with respect to trust literature includes Herlocker et al.'s (2000) visualization of collaborative filtering recommendation; Lerch & Prietula's (1989) work on trust of machine advice; Fogg & Tseng's (1999) elaboration on the elements of computer credibility; Cassel & Bickmore's (2001) exploration of trust of virtual characters that participate in small talk; and Wheeless & Grotz's (1977) research on the use of self disclosure in developing trust.

Herlocker et al. (2000) built on the theory that providing explanations to collaborative filtering recommenders increases users acceptance. They prototyped and user tested several visualizations explaining how collaborative filtering works. They found that bar charts showing nearest neighbors were very effective in communicating how a recommender system works and in offering confidence in the recommendation.

Looking more abstractly at the relationship between computers and people, Lerch & Prietula (1989) conducted a study to measure the difference between people's trust of machines and their trust of people. They found that people trusted advice from expert computer systems about as much as advice from novice humans. Expert humans were the most trusted. They also noted that bad advice given early in the use of a system had a strong, adverse effect on trust.

Fogg & Tseng (1999) synthesized the research done on computer credibility. They noticed that in the past people thought of computers as 'virtually infallible' but that people's trust in machines had greatly eroded. They proposed new conceptual frameworks for and offered methods for evaluating computer credibility.

Bickmore & Cassel (2001) explored the use of conversational agents to help people trust computers. They created a virtual reality realtor who would engage people in small talk before trying to sell a house. They discovered that small talk was effective in increasing the trust of extroverted people but that it had almost no effect on introverts.

Wheeless & Grotz (1977) researched the relationship between trust and self-disclosure. They created a method for measuring individualized trust and compared it to many different kinds of self-disclosure. Their results indicate that both intentional disclosure and increased amounts of disclosure create a higher level of trust.

3. Recommender Engine

Our recommender engine contains several components (Figure 2.1). We currently use both Bayesian and Decision Tree (DT) methods to produce implicit recommendations. Test subjects keep paper diaries detailing their viewing histories and based on these implicit recommendations are calculated. The explicit recommender allows users to directly input their preferences using two different interfaces (see Section 5.2). When we feed meta-data describing upcoming shows into the system, each of the different recommenders generates a rating for each show. An artificial neural network fuses the outputs of the different recommenders into a single set of improved recommendations.

3.1. METADATA

Our recommender engine relies on metadata from Tribune Media Services. Everyday we downloaded an updated TV-schedule for the next 12 days with channels (85+) and times associated with the Briarcliff Manor, New York area. Currently we have approximately four years of data, enabling us to re-run our recommenders on historic data as needed.

The metadata describes each TV-show using 205 fields, many of which are often not populated or relevant. We selected 21 fields for the implicit recommender, including:

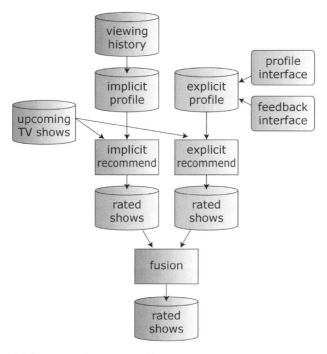

Figure 2.1. Recommender system architecture.

title, broadcaster, air time, air date, unique show key (indicating format such as series, movie, etc.), genres (comedy, action, adventure, news, etc.), actors, producers, directors, writers, hosts, synopsis, year, language, and content rating (mature, children, etc.). A subset of 14 fields from the 21 inputs to the implicit recommender is shown in Table 2.1.

Table 2.1. Metadata sample

Field	Value
⟨Program Code⟩	EP1151270151
⟨Title⟩	Friends
⟨Short Title⟩	Friends
⟨Episode Title⟩	The One With the Wedding
⟨Synopsis⟩	Rachel serves as a bridesmaid in her ex-fiancé Barry's wedding.
⟨Genres⟩	Situation, Comedy
⟨Channel⟩	WPIX (NBC Affiliate)
⟨Air Time⟩	2000
⟨Air Date⟩	20020912 (Sep. 12, 2002)
⟨Actors⟩	Jennifer Aniston, Courteney Cox, Lisa Kudrow, Matt LeBlanc, Matthew Perry, David Schwimmer
⟨Producers⟩	Marta Kauffman
⟨Directors⟩	
⟨Writers⟩	
⟨Language⟩	English

3.2. IMPLICIT RECOMMENDERS

The implicit recommenders generate profiles based on users' viewing histories. The implicit nature stems from the fact that users need only watch TV. We selected our two implicit methods, one based on Bayesian statistics (Kurapati et al. 2001) and one on Decision Trees (Gutta et al. 2000), for three main reasons. First, both methods work with relatively noisy data. We knew that users would occasionally watch shows they do not like and would sometimes not watch show they do like. Second, both methods do not require sharing histories with a central server. In conducting evaluations of the implicit recommenders and of sample user interfaces, all users liked the fact that our system protected their privacy. Third, both methods can run in a processor and memory-constrained environment such as a set-top box or TV.

3.2.1. *The Viewing History*

We assume that in a final product, such as a set-top box or TV, viewing histories can automatically be collected. For our study, however, we chose to use paper diaries for reasons of both cost and accuracy. First, it is very expensive to build custom set-top boxes for a small set of users. In addition, requiring users to use a device different from their current TV viewing setup seemed disruptive to their normal TV viewing behavior. We also considered a small device to collect all RF commands (Radio Frequency waves are a means of wireless communication—in this case between a remote control and a TV set) but the problem with this is that a single missed command would be impossible to find and would render any collected data meaningless. Therefore, we asked participants in our study to record which programs they watched each day into a paper journal, and we collected these journals each month. The two classes of TV shows of interest include: *C1* (shows that interest the viewer) and *C2* (shows that do not interest the viewer). However, practically we obtain information only on the classes: C+ (shows the viewer watched) and C− (shows the viewer did not watch), which are approximations of classes C1 and C2.

A major element of uncertainty lies in determining what is 'not-watched' by users. For each watched show—which can be ascertained clearly—there are numerous ones 'not-watched'. The key question is how to sample the universe of shows to appropriately populate the 'not-watched' class, C−. We recognize that users could be asked to provide information on shows they do not like, thus gathering information directly on shows belonging to class, C2 (shows disliked by the user). However, when we consider the pure implicit method, we have to rely on a sampling technique to populate class C−. To approximate class C−, one option is to select a not-watched show broadcast in the same time-slot as the watched show. An inference that the watched show is preferable to the not-watched shows seems reasonable in this case. Unfortunately, this scheme prevents learning preferred viewing times.

We chose instead to sample one not-watched show for each watched show from the previous week of shows, randomly selecting the day, time, and channel. This helped preferred viewing times to become statistically discernable; however, the issue of how many not-watched shows to sample is one that could profit from more research. We chose a one-to-one sampling ratio because it makes the Bayesian a priori probability of each class equal. Since we sample uniformly in time, the not-watched class represents a sample of the general run of shows being broadcast and therefore the implicit recommenders should find patterns of features that distinguish what is liked from this general run of material.

For three years we collected viewing histories on eight participants. However, because participants relocated during the study we do not have a full three years for each individual. Participants were recruited from the community around Briarcliff Manor, New York. They ranged in age from late teens to early sixties and were of mixed gender. None of the participants worked for Philips Research. Because of the small number of subjects, the results presented in this paper are preliminary in nature.

3.2.2. Bayesian Recommender

Our Bayesian implicit recommender uses the Bayesian classifier (Billus & Pazzani 1998, Duda & Hart 1973) approach to compute the likelihood that the user will like or dislike a particular TV program. We approached the problem with a 2-class Bayesian decision model, where a show either belongs to the class 'watched', or the class 'not watched'. Ideally, we would like to have ground truth information on whether a TV-show was *liked* or *not liked* by the user, but the implicit profiling technique allows us to have information only on the classes watched and not watched. The user profile, in the Bayesian context, is a collection of features together with a count of how many times each occurs in the positive and negative examples (i.e. classes $C+$ and $C-$). An excerpt from a user profile is shown in Table 2.2. Note that a feature is an attribute-value pair and that only a small sample has been shown.

Our Bayesian model computes the prior probabilities directly from the counts in the viewer profile. Then we compute the conditional probabilities that a given feature, f_i, will be present if a show is in class $C+$ or $C-$: $P(f_i|C+) = k(f_i|C+)/k(C+)$, where $k(f_i|C+)$ represents the number of shows in which feature f_i is present given that the show belongs to class watched ($C+$) and $k(C+)$ represents the count of all shows

Table 2.2. User profile excerpt

Feature	Watched (C+)	Not-watched (C−)
Total_programs	66	66
Station: ABC	10	56
Station: BBC	20	10
Title: BBC News	10	2
Actor: Jim Carrie	2	0
Genre: comedy	1	7
Keyword: murder	5	1

belonging to class watched (C+). The recommendation scores for upcoming shows are computed by estimating the aposteriori probabilities, i.e. the probability that a show is in class $C+$ and $C-$ given its features: $P(C+|\mathbf{x})$, where $\mathbf{x}$ is the feature vector. For details on the computation, we refer to Kurapati et al. (2001).

3.2.3. *Decision Tree Recommender*

Like the Bayesian recommender, our Decision Tree (DT) recommender uses the 'watched' and 'not watched' shows. The decision tree employs Quinlan's C4.5 (Quinlan 1983, 1991) and uses an information-theoretical approach based on entropy. C4.5 builds the decision tree using a top-down, divide-and-conquer approach: select an attribute, divide the training set into subsets characterized by the possible values of the attribute, and follow the same procedure recursively with each subset until no subset contains objects from more than one class. The single-class subsets correspond to leaves of the decision tree.

The DT has nodes and leaves where nodes correspond to some test to be performed and leaves correspond to the two classes: 'watched' and 'not watched'. Testing an unknown show involves parsing the tree to determine which class the unknown show belongs to. When computing a recommendation for each TV show, a probability is computed that the show will be in the class 'watched' and the class 'not watched' based on the shows it correctly classified during training. However, if at a particular decision node we encounter an unknown attribute value, so that the outcome of the test cannot be determined, the system then explores all possible outcomes and combines the resulting classifications: the class with the highest probability is assigned as the predicted class.

As decision trees become large, with increasing viewing histories, they become difficult to understand because each node in the tree has a specific context established by the outcomes of tests at antecedent nodes. We then rewrite the tree as a collection of rules, which is usually more accurate than a decision tree (Gutta et al. 2000).

3.3. EXPLICIT RECOMMENDER

Based on participants' request for interaction with the recommender and our need for a recommender that could work quickly 'out of the box', we developed an explicit recommender (Kurapati et al. 2001) that relies on user inputs. By default our system assigns a neutral 4 for all channels, genres, days, and times of day. Individual users can then indicate their preference on a 1 to 7 scale (1 for 'hate the feature', 7 for 'love the feature') for as many or as few features as they prefer. We compute an explicit recommender score as follows:

$$E = wDayT * rDayT + wCh * rCh + (1/K) * \Sigma wGenre_i * rGenre_i \tag{1}$$

where $rDayT$ is the profile rating for the feature daytime, rCh – profile rating for channel, $rGenre_i$–profile rating for ith genre describing a given show (from K genres describing it; in Tribune Media Services metadata up to six genres describe a show) and the corresponding heuristically determined weights are: $wDayT = 0.1$, $wCh = 0.2$ and $wGenre_i = 0.7$ (for each genre). Users have two methods of inputting their preferences as described in Section 5.2.

4. Increasing Accuracy through Fusion

Results of testing the explicit and two implicit recommenders with real users (Kurapati et al. 2001) suggested reasonable recommender accuracy. However different recommenders seemed to perform well for different users with no easy way to pre-match individual recommenders to individual users. Further analysis revealed that different recommenders performed well for very different sets of shows. As a follow-up we attempted to improve accuracy by *fusing* (combining) recommender outputs using a neural network. We chose to use a neural network because it might detect correlations that simple heuristics cannot. We believe that such an approach improves the robustness of our system.

The fusion system combines the following individual recommenders:

1. Implicit Bayesian based on individual view history
2. Implicit Bayesian based on household view history
3. Implicit Decision Tree based on individual view history
4. Implicit Decision Tree based on household view history
5. Explicit

The individual and household view histories were used separately in order to determine whether a TV recommender could just do with one profile per box in a household or if we needed to make fine grain distinctions between individual household members.

We developed two approaches to fusion. The first method uses a single Radial Basis Function (RBF) neural network for all the users. We trained this network on partial data from a subset of our eight viewing history participants. This approach has the advantage that it can be developed using ground truth data from a small set of participants to improve accuracy for a large set of users in a deployed product. The second approach uses a custom network for each user. This neural network was trained on each of our viewing history participants. This approach ensures that the network is responsive to a particular user's characteristics. For example, certain participants obtained better recommendations using an individual profile while others did better using a household profile. Also the importance of explicit recommenders varied from participant to participant. A challenge this second approach faces is that it requires ground truth data from all users. This is not likely in a final product as we do not expect users to be willing to inform the system if they actually liked each show they watched and did not want to see each show the system selects as 'not-watched'.

4.1. RADIAL BASIS FUNCTION NEURAL NETWORKS

We chose Artificial Neural Networks because of their ability to recognize patterns in the presence of noise and from sparse and/or incomplete data. They perform matching in high-dimensional spaces, effectively interpolating and extrapolating from learned data. We chose Radial Basis Function (RBF) networks (Moody & Darken 1989) because they are universal approximators and train rapidly; usually orders of magnitude faster than back propagation. Their rapid training makes them suitable for applications where on-line, incremental learning is desired such as a set-top box observing TV viewing. The ways we used RBF networks are explained in Sections 4.3 and 4.4.

4.2. EVALUATION

In order to generate a set of ground truth data, we asked our eight viewing history participants to rate a set of approximately 300 TV shows. At the time of this evaluation one of our participants had recently relocated, so we have data on seven people, referred to as A, C, D, F, G, H and I. Using Likert scales—an attitude measurement method that allows users to rate on a discreet scale of 'strongly agree' to 'strongly disagree'—participants rated each show as 'would watch' (1), 'may watch' (0.5) and 'wouldn't watch' (0). In addition, participants could rate a show as 'do not know' (DNK) when they were not familiar with its title. Only the shows known to the user were utilized (there were 1348 such shows).

We compared fusion results using three metrics: Hit Rate (HR), False Positive Rate (FPR), and Mean Squared Error (MSE). Hit Rate and False Positive Rate were computed for only those shows that were crisply classified by the user either as 0 (wouldn't watch) or 1 (would watch). For the shows classified as 0.5 (may watch) it is disputable whether they should be recommended or not. For computing Hit Rate and False Positive Rate, a threshold value needs to be chosen. A higher threshold value will lead to both lower Hit Rate and False Positive Rate, and a lower threshold will result in higher Hit Rate and False Positive Rate.

The main advantage of using the Mean Squared Error is that it can be computed for shows with any ground truth rating (yes-1, no-0, and may be-0.5). Its additional advantage is that it does not require a determination of a threshold value, which can be quite cumbersome. This metric suits our goal of producing a 'degree of match' for each show with a profile, rather than a hard yes or a no vote on a particular show. In the end, based on user evaluation, our recommender interface displays all shows, ordering them from most to least recommended.

4.3. FUSION METHOD 1: SINGLE RBF NET FOR ALL USERS

RBF networks with five inputs, one output and a varying number of hidden nodes were trained. We used scores from the five individual recommenders—listed at the beginning of Section 4—as inputs to the RBF network, which produces fused recommendations as the output. The higher the output value, the higher the recommender rating assigned to a show. We used 15% to 40% of data from subjects A, C, and D as a training set. This represents 26% of the whole data set. For the networks' cross-validation, we used 14% to 45% of data from subjects D, F, and G. This represents 13% of the whole data set. The remaining data was employed for the end tests (testing recall). Data from users H and I were neither used in training nor in cross-validation as these users had no household values. The best performance of RBF networks in terms of Hit Rate (HR) and False Positive Rate (FPR) was obtained by cross-validation for a network with 15 hidden nodes. A threshold of 0.5 was used to compute HR and FPR.

Figure 2.2 depicts the hit rate for all the subjects. Hit rate obtained by fusion is on average 29% higher then the average of the hit rates from nine separate recommenders.

Figure 2.3 shows the FPR for each of the users. The lower the FPR, the better the final recommendation. FPRs are mixed, since for certain users a lower FPR is obtained by fusion, for others the average of nine recommenders gives an improved FPR. On average the fused FPR is higher by 5% than that obtained by the average of recommenders. False positive rates cannot however be compared by themselves without comparing hit rates since both are interrelated, and linked by the threshold value. By using a higher threshold value, FPR can be easily lowered; this of course causes hit rate to get lower as well. Therefore if for fusion the hit rate is better on average by 29%, and FPR is worse on average by 5%, still the combined fusion results are more advantageous than the average of recommenders.

The top curve on Figure 2.4 shows the average MSE for nine recommender combinations (all five recommenders plus each implicit method combined with the explicit recommender); the middle curve shows the single-network MSE. The single-net MSE varies for different users from 0.1 to 0.17 per user while the average MSE for nine recommender combinations are much higher (it varies from 0.17 to 0.32

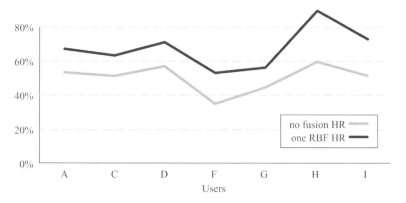

Figure 2.2. Comparison of no fusion Hit Rate and one RBF net Hit Rate.

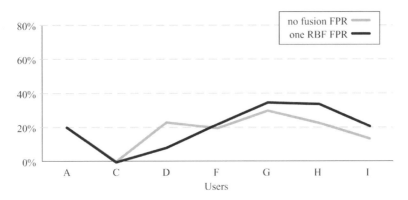

Figure 2.3. Comparison of no fusion FPR and one RBF net FPR.

per pattern). For all users, with the exception of user *F*, fused MSE performs better than the average of non-fused results. For user F, the average MSE of non-fused results is as good as the fused MSE. This user is however an outlier whose behavior is completely different from the other users. This is the only user for whom recommenders based on individual viewing history were superior to recommenders based on household history (Kurapati et al. 2001) and the only one for whom the Explicit Recommender is the least reliable. It is remarkable that for such an outlier the single network still works so well.

4.4. FUSION METHOD 2: SEPARATE RBF NETWORK PER USER

We also trained a separate RDF network for each individual participant. Approximately 40% of the data were used for training, 15% for cross-validation, and the rest for testing. The number of hidden units for each user's fusion network was determined by checking the performance of a set of trained RBF networks on the cross-validation set. The network that gave the best performance in terms of HR and FPR on the cross-validation set was the one chosen.

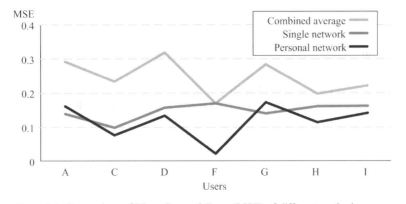

Figure 2.4. Comparison of Mean Squared Error (MSE) of different methods.

The overall performance of fusion can be characterized by MSE that is shown as the bottom curve in Figure 2.2. The separate networks give excellent results, consistently better than the average of recommendations: MSE of the fused results varies for different users from 0.02 to 0.17 (compared with 0.17 to 0.32 for the average of individual recommenders).

It is worth noting the superior performance of fusion for user F. Since training took place on the data from this outlier, RBF network weights have stabilized to better describe this user, resulting in the smallest MSE of all. This shows that separate networks work especially well for outliers who cannot be well described by a common (stereotype) network.

5. Interface Design

We began our design by reviewing participant feedback from evaluations of two previous interfaces. Three issues emerged. First, users complained that both our earlier designs and current commercial products required too many button clicks and navigation of too many screens to complete a single task. Second, users wanted more flexible interaction with the recommender. Some users wanted to have almost no interaction; some users wanted to take complete control; and some users wanted to have more limited interaction with the recommender. Third, users displayed a lack of trust with the recommender. When we recommended shows they regularly watched, they felt the recommender worked well. However, when we recommended a show they had never heard of, instead of thinking the recommender had found something new to watch, they assumed it was broken. The design of the Touch and Drag interface focused on addressing these three user interface issues.

5.1. EASE OF USE

Traditional TV interfaces, including our two previous designs, force users to maneuver a jumping highlight across a series of screens making the completion of a single task quite time consuming. For example, if users want the fifth item on a list, they must press the cursor-down button four times and then press OK. We chose to address this problem by (i) placing our interface on a *touch-screen remote control* where users could employ their finger as a floating cursor, and (ii) designing a series of *expanding and collapsing interface elements* so individual tasks could be solved on a single screen.

We designed the screens to read from left to right (Figure 2.5). The far left contains a *Themes Ring* and below this the *Profile Ring*. By accessing these elements, users can indicate who they are and what kind of content they are searching/browsing for. Moving right, users encounter the *Results List* with a default sort by recommender rating. To the right of the *Results List* are *Details* for the highlighted TV show and tools (called *Markers*) for taking action such as storing or access to the feedback interface.

Figures 2.5 and 2.6 with the expanded *Themes Ring* offer an example of the collapsing and expanding elements. When users touch the collapsed *Themes Ring*

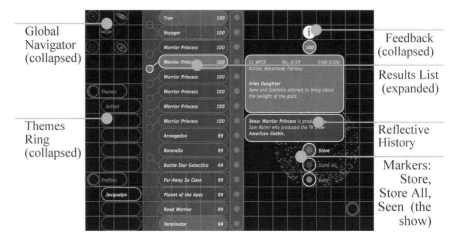

Figure 2.5. Interface screen with expanded *Results List*.

(Figure 2.5) it automatically expands to provide users access to this tool. At the same time the *Results List* collapses (Figure 2.4) to create more room on the screen. In addition, the details and other tools disappear as they only operate on the highlighted show, which is no longer visible.

5.1.1. *Touch, Drag and Stroke*

The design offers three interaction methods: 'Touch', 'Drag', and 'Stroke'. Touch allows users to select different elements on the screen. For example, if users want

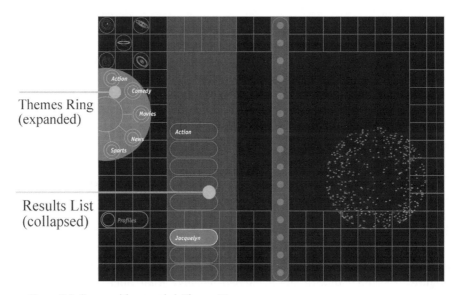

Figure 2.6. Screen with expanded *Themes Ring*.

to record a TV show, they can touch the *Marker* element labeled 'Store' (Figure 2.5). To record multiple episodes of the same show, users can touch the *Marker* labeled 'Store All.'

Figure 2.6 offers an example of the Drag interaction. In order to see all of the items on the *Themes Ring*, users drag their finger clockwise or counter clockwise, causing the ring to rotate. When they find a desired theme, they drag it onto the collapsed *Results List*. The Drag action not only reduces the number of steps needed to complete a task, it also creates a more naturalistic interaction. If users wish to see Action shows on the *Results List*, they drag the Action element there.

Many other recommenders address the problem of long lists of shows by hiding shows that fall below a threshold or by displaying only the top N number of shows. However, our view history participants were uncomfortable with this approach. They did not trust any recommender enough for it to eliminate possible selections. Therefore our interface presents all of the next weeks shows matching the *Themes Ring* selection, sorted from highest to lowest rated. This means users often must deal with very long lists. To address this problem we developed the Stroke interaction. When users want to rapidly scroll the list, they stroke their finger up or down on the list. When the finger is lifted, the system sets a velocity and then slowly decelerates. If users see an item they are interested in scroll by, they touch the list to stop it from moving. This idea works somewhat like the wheel of a bicycle that has been turned upside down. People can Stroke the wheel to make it spin. They can then either watch it decelerate or touch the wheel to stop it.

Use of expanding and collapsing elements combined with the use of a finger as a pointing device greatly reduces the number of screens users need to navigate and the number of steps (button clicks) needed to complete a single task. For example, consider the task of browsing for movies. Using the Touch and Drag interface, users navigate two screens (Global Navigator and Find TV) and perform three Touches and three Drags in order to produce a personalized list of movies. Using TiVo, users need to visit five screens and perform a minimum of fourteen button clicks in order to see a alphabetical listing of movies.

5.2. FLEXIBLE RECOMMENDER INTERACTION

During evaluation of the earlier designs and of the implicit recommenders, some users expressed a desire to interact more directly with the system. This led in turn to our definition of three different user groups and two interfaces to communicate with the explicit recommender.

5.2.1. *Do it for Me Users*

The implicit recommender works well for the *Do it for me* users. This recommender monitors viewing history and then makes recommendations. All a user needs to do is watch TV. In addition, the Touch and Drag interface automatically displays upcoming programs sorted by recommender rating. Placing highly recommended programs at the top of the list reduces the number of shows users need to browse.

5.2.2. *Let's Do it together Users*

The *Feedback* interface (Figure 2.7) supports the *Let's do it together* users and the *Let me drive* users. This interface allows users to access the part of their explicit profile that corresponds to the currently highlighted show. When users see a recommendation they disagree with or when they just want to better understand why a show has a certain rating, they can expand the *Feedback* interface and view or modify the ratings.

5.2.3. *Let Me Drive Users*

Let me drive users can take more control by selecting Profiles on the *Global Navigator*. This transitions them to the Profiles interface (Figure 2.8). Here they can rate all program attributes on a 0 to 100 scale. The system initially gives all items a neutral rating of 50. Users can quickly look through the listed items and change as few or as many as they want.

The interface supports flexible access to the recommender without the need for users to select a novice or expert mode. Users that want little or no interaction are free to simply watch TV. Users that want some interaction can choose how much or how little control they want to take by using the *Feedback* interface and the Profiles screen.

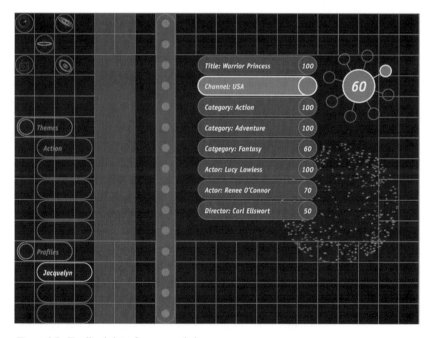

Figure 2.7. Feedback interface expanded.

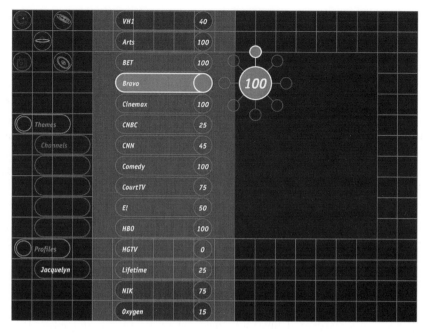

Figure 2.8. Profiles interface.

6. Testing Ease-of-Use

After completing the Touch and Drag interface design, we performed a *proof of concept* test. Our questions included:

1. Does the use of collapsing and expanding elements improve ease of use over nested menu systems?
2. Does the use of a finger as a floating cursor improve ease-of-use over a jumping highlight and traditional four-cursor remote control?
3. How do users feel about a large touch-screen remote control?

For this evaluation we recruited six subjects (not the participants in our viewing history study), three men and three women, ranging in age from 21 to 60. They were all moderate to heavy TV viewers. Each participant rated items for the explicit recommender in order to generate individual recommendations.

We chose a task-based approach to the test, asking subjects to complete two common TV tasks using TV Guide Magazine™, Touch and Drag, and TiVo™. Task 1 asked users to find three upcoming movies they *wanted* to watch. Task 2 asked participants to find the next broadcast of the TV show *Roseanne*. Participants tested only one system at a time, starting first with TV Guide, then Touch and Drag, and finally TiVo. They were each allowed to play with one of the systems and then asked to complete both tasks. When all tasks had been completed on all systems, we asked subjects to answer qualitative questions about the three systems. One of the challenges of testing came from the recommender. TV guide magazine clearly has no recommender, and in addition, since TiVo does not employ an explicit recommender, we had no way of tuning this device to personalize the content for users.

Subjects found the Touch and Drag interface much easier than either TV Guide magazine or TiVo at finding a list of movies they wanted to watch. The reduced number of screens and clicks along with the personalized listing of movies significantly reduced the amount of time users spent with our system compared to TiVo. TiVo was also handicapped by the fact that the list of movies and individual descriptions of movies appear on separate screens, forcing users to constantly move back and forth between screens. TV guide was most significantly handicapped by a lack of a single listing for all movies and offered no method of filtering for the channels an individual participant received.

Finding the next broadcast of *Roseanne* proved easiest on TiVo; however, Touch and Drag took only slightly longer. TiVo's on screen keyboard made title input quite easy. Our system suffered from lack of labeling on our Sort tool that allows users to resort the *Results List* by title instead of the default sort by rating. Once participants discovered this tool, they had no problems completing the task. TV Guide proved nearly impossible for this task. Only one of the six participants completed this, and he ended up looking at every page until he found *Roseanne*.

Participants rated twelve qualitative questions using 1 to 5 Lickert scales Responses show that users preferred Touch and Drag and particularly found it attractive and fun to use (Table 2.3). One participant, when playing with the *Stroke* interaction on the *Results List*, told the evaluator, 'Don't show this to Vegas.' He found the stroke action similar to slot machines and immediately associated it with fun.

Table 2.3. Participant responses to qualitative questions

	Question	TV Guide	Touch & Drag	TiVo
Q1	Frequency of use	3.33	4.33	3.67
Q2	Usefulness for finding shows of interest	2.83	4.33	4.00
Q3	Confidence in using system at home	4.17	3.42	3.42
Q4	Ease of finding shows of interest	3.33	4.58	3.67
Q5	Ease of use of system	3.33	4.17	3.83
Q6	Feeling in control of system	3.33	4.17	3.83
Q7	Adequate information structure	2.83	2.92	3.33
Q8	Intuitiveness of UI	3.08	3.67	3.25
Q9	Attractiveness of info layout	3.00	4.5	3.67
Q10	Fun to use	1.33	4.67	4.00
Q11	Information quantity	4.17	3.83	4.00
Q12	Ease of learning	3.50	4.00	4.25
	Average Score	3.19	4.05	3.74

Participants offered differing views on the touch-screen versus remote control. Some liked the touch-screen and felt it would be the best system to use at home. However, others stated that they would rather see the information on the TV screen. They suggested that the Touch and Drag interface be adapted to work with a standard remote or even a remote control with a track pad similar to laptop computers.

The results of this evaluation offered insights into how we might reshape the design. However, it is important to note that this test only offered users a few minutes to use each system. For a more thorough evaluation, we would need a much more robust system we could place in users' homes.

7. Improving Trust

During evaluation of our earlier recommenders and interfaces we encountered a difficult problem. When our system recommended programs participants regularly watched, they thought it worked great. However, when the system recommended programs they did not know, participants felt the recommender was 'broken'. This created a serious problem. A recommender that only finds programs users know they like will have limited value. In order to create a recommender that provides real value it must help users find new shows to watch and present these new shows in a way that they might try them.

Experimental evidence has shown that providing explanations of how a recommender works can help to improve user acceptance of a recommender system (Herlocker et al. 2000). The Touch and Drag interface allows users to glimpse how the recommender is working through the feedback interface (Figure 2.5) and the Profiles screen (Figure 2.6). However, these interfaces do not specifically address new shows.

Looking deeper into the value of new shows we were quite surprised to discover that people generally *do not want to be challenged* when selecting programs to watch. The majority of television viewing takes place in the evening (Kubey & Csikszentmihalyi 1990), at a time when people want to relax after a hard day. People often choose to watch television at this time because it makes them *feel* relaxed (Kubey & Csikszentmihalyi 1990). In addition, much of television watching is nonselective (Lull 1990). Viewers *coast* from one show to another, watching whatever program comes on.

We found a good analogy in food. People do not want to try new food at each meal. Often they want *comfort food*, particularly when they are stressed such as at the end of a workday. Menus offer people a chance to try something new by listing the main ingredients. When people try a new food, they have some expectation of what it will be like based on foods they have eaten in the past.

7.1. REFLECTIVE HISTORY

Based on the food analogy we developed the *Reflective History* (Figure 2.3), an interface element designed to motivate people to try a new TV show when they were

Table 2.4. Text strings used in reflective history

Task	NewTask	OldTask
Director	is directed by	directed the TV show
Producer	is produced by	Produced the TV show
Writer	is written by	wrote
Actor	stars	plays ⟨Character⟩ in

Example: *Boston Public* stars Jeri Ryan who plays Seven of Nine in *Star Trek: Voyager.*

in the mood. The element needed to be subtle, since the mood to try new things is rare. We wanted it to tempt the user as opposed to cramming new programs down their throats. This element appears when 'new' and 'highly rated shows' are highlighted in the results list.

We generate these conversational sentences by comparing users' viewing histories used by the implicit recommender with the metadata about upcoming TV shows. Our system looks for highly rated new programs (programs not already in a user's viewing history). Next, it searches for a common person between the new TV show and TV shows the user has already seen. When it finds an appropriate match, the system generates a conversational sentence using the following structure: ⟨NewProgram⟩ ⟨NewTask⟩ ⟨Person⟩ who ⟨OldTask⟩ ⟨OldProgram⟩. Table 2.4 offers examples of the text strings for ⟨Task⟩, ⟨NewTask⟩, and ⟨OldTask⟩.

The reflective history sentence uses a conversational structure; making it sound like something one friend might say to another. This builds on Reeves and Nash's theory that people interact with computers as if they were people (Reeves & Nass 1999). The sentence reveals some of what the system knows about the user. This is a type of self-disclosure, which can help to build trust (Wheeless & Grotz 1977). The short, conversational sentence also works well with our interface design. Its size and location make it easy for users to ignore. However, its appearance and disappearance as new shows move into the highlight position on the results list make it easy to find for users who are in the mood to try something new.

8. Conclusions

The Touch and Drag personalization system integrates an accurate TV show recommender engine and an easy to use interface that supports the way people want to watch and store TV shows. In addition, our interface design offers appropriate insights into how the recommender engine works, helping people both refine and trust the recommendations they receive. Preliminary testing of the previous and current recommender engines and interfaces indicate that we are moving in the right direction.

Our recommender engine employs a robust design, combining both an explicit and implicit recommender. Our explicit recommender allows users to enter and modify their preferences to allow for both a system that can run out of the box, and to allow users to *feel in control*. The interface offers two methods for entering and modifying preferences and in addition, preloads all ratable items with a neutral value of fifty. The combination of the two interfaces and the pre-rated items allows the interface to seamlessly support users that want very little interaction with the recommender as well as users that want to really take control. This easy access encourages users to slowly tweak the explicit recommender until they get the results they want.

Our implicit recommender monitors all TV shows users watch, adjusting recommendations based on current and changing tastes. This recommender supports users that want *no* interaction with the recommender. By simply watching TV the system can learn their likes and dislikes. The viewing history also provides an opportunity for increasing user trust. By mining the viewing history, the user interface can subtly recommend *new* programs based on people that the programs have in common. Our conversational approach builds on the person-to-person model of self-disclosure to improve users trust.

Our touch-screen based interaction makes both browsing and profile management easy, efficient, and fun. The collapsing and expanding interface elements along with the use of a finger as a floating cursor help users to complete tasks on a single screen. The improvement in efficiency allows users to get back to doing what they like most: watching TV. The naturalistic style through the *Touch*, *Drag*, and *Stroke* interactions helps to clarify the relationships between the different interface elements and to make the interface as entertaining to use as watching an actual TV show.

Finally, we generate accurate recommendations by fusing the results of both the implicit and explicit recommenders using a radial basis neural network. We developed two RBF network-based approaches to fusing recommendations. The first method trains the network to be responsive to all users while the second one employs a separate RBF net for each user. Both methods achieve a beneficial combination of the strengths of individual recommenders.

The results of both approaches are very encouraging and superior to the average of recommendations. For most users separate networks perform the best because they are well adapted to a given user's characteristics. The most remarkable separate network performance is obtained for an outlier whose individual recommender characteristics were almost the opposite from the mainstream user. For this user a separate net gives much superior results to the single (stereotype) network. For the mainstream users the difference between separate and single nets is much less pronounced.

The power of the single-network method is that such a fusion network can be developed based solely on the data from subjects in our study, whose behavior conforms to the mainstream, and then deployed in the field where it can perform well for users it has not encountered earlier. Later it could be tuned to a specific user behavior by using feedback data collected by the system. We should however stress that the method developed is a proof-of-concept demonstration and testing on a larger user population is needed to obtain statistically significant results.

This increased accuracy works with the whole interface design to help improve user trust of the recommender. In addition, the improved accuracy helps bring the *best*

TV shows for users to the top of long lists of shows, making it much faster and more interesting for users to find something they *want* to watch.

Acknowledgements

We would like to thank Jeanne de Bont, Henk Lamers, Guy Roberts, Lira Nikolovska, Lesh Parameswaran, John Milanski, and Jenny Weston of Philips Design for their assistance in design and evaluation of the interface. We would also like to thank Henk van der Weij of Big Camp in Eindhoven, the Netherlands, for his assistance with the implementation of the Touch and Drag interface.

References

Ardissono, L., Gena, C., Torasso, P., Bellifemine, F., Chiarotto, A., Difino, A. and Negro, B.: User Modeling and Recommendation Techniques for Personalized Electronic Program Guides. This Volume.

Smyth, B. and Cotter, P.: The Evolution of the Personalized Electronic Program Guide. This Volume.

Balabanovic, M. and Shoham, Y.: 1997, FAB: Content-Based Collaborative Recommender. *Communications of the ACM* **40**(3), 66–72.

Barneveld, J. V. and Setten, M. V.: Designing Usable Interfaces for TV Recommender. This Volume.

Baudisch, P. and Bruekner, L.: 2001, TV Scout: Guiding Users from Printed TV Program Guides to Personalized TV Recommendation. *Second International Conference on Adaptive Hypermedia and Adaptive Web Based Systems: Workshop on Personalization in Future TV*, Malaga, Spain, pp. 151–160.

Bickmore, T. and Cassell, J.: 2001, Relational Agents: A Model and Implementation of Building User Trust. *Conference on Human Factors in Computing*, Seattle, WA, USA, pp. 80–87.

Billsus, D. and Pazzani, M. J.: 1998, Learning Collaborative Information Filters. *Fifteenth International Conference on Machine Learning*, Wisconsin, USA, pp. 46–54.

Cotter, P. and Smyth, B.: 2000, PTV: Intelligent Personalized TV Guides. *Seventeenth National Conference on Artificial Intelligence*, Austin, TX, USA, pp. 957–964.

Das, D. and ter Horst, H.: 1998, Recommender Systems for TV. Technical Report WS-98-08 *Recommender System, Papers from the 1998 Workshop*, Madison, WI. Menlo Park, CA: AAAI Press, pp. 35–36.

Duda, R. and Hart, P.: 1973, *Pattern Recognition and Scene Analysis*. John Wiley & Sons, New York.

Fogg, B. J. and Tseng, H.: 1999, The Elements of Computer Credibility. *Conference on Human Factors in Computing Systems*, Pittsburgh, PA, USA, pp. 80–86.

Gutta, S., Kurapati, K., Lee, K. P., Martino, J., Milanski, J., Schaffer, D. and Zimmerman, J.: 2000, TV Content Recommender System. *Seventeenth National Conference on Artificial Intelligence*, Austin, TX, USA, pp. 1121–1122.

Hammond, K. J., Burke, R. and Schmitt, K.: 1996, A Case-Based Approach to Knowledge Navigation. In D. Leake (ed.), *Case-Based Reasoning Experiences, Lessons and Future Directions*, Cambridge, MA: MIT Press, pp. 125–136.

Herlocker, J., Konstan, J. and Riedl, J.: 2000, Explaining Collaborative Filtering Recommendations. *Conference on Computer Supported Cooperative Work*, Philadelphia, PA, USA, pp. 241–250.

Kubey, R. and Csikszentmihalyi, M.: 1990, *Television and the Quality of Life: How Viewing Shapes Everyday Experiences.* Hillsdale, NJ: Lawrence Erlbaum Associates.

Kurapati, K., Gutta, S., Schaffer, D., Martino, J. and Zimmerman, J.: 2001, A Multi-Agent TV Recommender. *Eighth International Conference on User Modeling: Workshop on Personalization in Future TV*, Sonthofen, Germany, http://www.di.unito.it/~liliana/UM01/kurapati.pdf.

Lee, H., Nam, J., Bae, B., Kim, M., Kang, K. and Kim, J.: 2001, Personalized Contents Guide and Browsing based on User Preference. *Second International Conference on Adaptive Hypermedia and Adaptive Web Based Systems: Workshop on Personalization in Future TV*, Malaga, Spain, pp. 131–150.

Lerch, F. J. and Prietula, M. J.: 1989, How do we Trust Machine Advice? In: G. Salvendy and M. J. Smith (eds.), *Designing and Using Human-Computer Interfaces and Knowledge Based Systems*, Amsterdam, the Netherlands: Elsevier Science Publishers B. V., pp. 410–419.

Lull, J.: 1990, *Inside Family Viewing: Ethnographic Research on Television's Audiences.* New York: Routledge.

Moody, J. and Darken, C. J.: 1989, Fast Learning in Networks of Locally Tuned Processing Units. *Neural Computation* 1(2), pp. 281–294.

Mueleman, P., Heister, A., Kohar, H. and Tedd, D.: 1998, Double Agents - Presentation and Filtering Agents for a Digital Television Recording System. *Conference on Human Factors in Computing Systems*, Los Angeles, CA, USA, pp. 3–4.

Pittarello, F.: Time-pillars World: A 3D Paradigm for the New Enlarged TV Information Domain. This Volume.

Predictive Media, Inc. - http://www.predictivemedia.com/

Quinlan, J. R.: 1983, Learning Efficient Classification Procedures and their Application to Chess End Games. In: R. S. Michalski, J. G. Carbonell and T. M. Mitchell (eds.), *Machine Learning: An Artificial Approach*, Vol. 1. Morgan Kaufmann Publishers Inc, Palo Alto, California.

Quinlan, J. R.: 1991, *C4.5: Machine Learning Programs*, Morgan Kaufmann Publishers, Palo Alto, California.

Smyth, B. and Cotter, P.: 1999, Surfing the Digital Wave: Generating Personalised TV Listings using Collaborative Case-Based Recommendations. *International Conference on Case-Based Reasoning*, Springer-Verlag, Germany, pp. 561–571.

Smyth, B. and Cotter, P.: The Evolution of the Personalized Electronic Program Guide. This Volume.

TiVo, Inc. - http://www.TiVo.com

Tribune Media Services - http://www.tms.tribune.com/

Wheeless, L. and Grotz, J.: 1977, The Measurement of Trust and Its Relationship to Self-disclosure. *Communication Research* 3(3), pp. 250–257.

Zimmerman, J. and Kurapati, K.: 2002, Exposing Profiles to Build Trust in a Recommender. *Conference on Human Factors in Computing Systems*, Minneapolis, MN, pp. 608–609.

Chapter 3

Case-Studies on the Evolution of the Personalized Electronic Program Guide

BARRY SMYTH[1] and PAUL COTTER[2]

[1]*Smart Media Institute, Department of Computer Science, University College Dublin, Belfield, Dublin 4, Ireland. e-mail: barry.smyth@ucd.ie*
[2]*Changing Worlds Ltd. South County Business Park, Leopardstown, Dublin 18. Ireland. e-mail: paul.cotter@changingworlds.com*

Abstract. The Digital TV revolution promises unprecedented access to programming content across hundreds of channels. Early indications are that this leads to a new information overload problem for DTV viewers and although the current generation of electronic program guides provides viewers with on-screen access to schedule information, their usefulness is compromised by the sheer volume of information that exists. Personalized guides that learn about the viewing habits of individual users have been proposed as a solution to this problem and in this paper we examine recent developments in this area of research and chart the progress of the PTV family of personalized online TV guides. Three different case-studies are examined as we look at how personalized guides can be deployed across a variety of devices and the implications this may have on their functionality and interface design.

Key words. electronic program guide, personalization, PTV.

1. Introduction

Digital TV (DTV) has been made possible by a number of important technology and infrastructure developments, the definition of new broadcasting standards, and the emergence of range of new Digital TV operators and services. For the end-consumer Digital TV means sharper pictures (including true widescreen format) and clearer audio, as well as a range of new interactive features, from online shopping to games, email and messaging. In addition to all of this, Digital TV offers the consumer a hugely expanded channel choice with many services offering more than 100 channels as standard. For example, at the time of writing, Sky Digital, the UK's leading digital operator, offers nearly 200 hundred channels as part of its premium subscription package. Moreover, many of these new channels offer niche programming (news, music, movies, documentaries, comedy etc.) as theme-based channels become commonplace.

On the face of it Digital TV appears to offer subscribers an entirely new type of TV experience – certainly the expanded channel line-up provides unprecedented access to programming content. However, upon closer inspection there is a serious problem facing subscribers. Put bluntly: subscribers are finding it increasingly difficult to access

L. Ardissono et al. (eds.), Personalized Digital Television, 53–71, 2004.
© *2004 Kluwer Academic Publishers. Printed in the Netherlands.*

the right content at the right time. The Digital TV operators are not unaware of this problem, however, and provide subscribers with access to so-called Electronic Program Guides (EPG) as part of their service; see for example [24]. The now common EPG is essentially an on-screen version of the traditional TV guide, providing users with channel by channel access to schedule information and program details. Unfortunately, while the EPG is a step in the right direction, its usefulness is limited as users must still browse through screen after screen of schedule information to locate relevant schedules [6, 14]. The unfortunate result is that today many subscribers have a tendency to limit their DTV habits to a restricted set of 'favorites' and this is likely to impact the success of DTV going forward.

Our primary research objective has been the development of technologies to assist the DTV subscriber when it comes to locating show and scheduling information. Our approach has been to concentrate on the development of personalized EPGs (pEPGs), EPGs that pro-actively recommend relevant shows to individual users based on their learned viewing preferences; e.g. [26–28]. These pEPGs exploit recent advances in user modeling and recommender systems research to automatically learn about the viewing habits of individual users in order to compile personalized program guides that reflect these preferences; see also a range of related articles in this volume by Ardissono et al., Zimmerman et al. and O'Sullivan et al. We have developed a sequence of pEPG systems and in this article we provide an overview of this research, focusing on three separate case-studies that describe different aspects of this research. A particular emphasis is placed on the different devices that we have explored as the vehicles for these personalized guides (Web, mobile phone, PDA and digital remote controls).

2. Motivations

Let us first look in detail at many of the reasons why personalized EPGs are an important research topic in the context of future DTV services. With most DTV services offering subscribers 100–200 separate channels, it is clear that DTV ushers in a new era of program choice. And looking to the future it is not unreasonable to expect hundreds of channels to be available to the average consumer. Many of these channels are likely to be focused on a particular theme (e.g. news, comedy, movies) which further complicates the choice for subscribers. In the introduction we highlighted that this range of choice is not without its problems and, for the consumer at least, navigating through this sea of alternatives to find a relevant show is not an appealing prospect; for sure, the traditional paper-based TV guide is rendered virtually useless as means of rapid access to schedule information.

This doesn't just introduce problems for Digital TV subscribers. The television channels themselves are faced with the significant problem of how to ensure that viewers will notice their programming content within a sea of alternatives. This is particularly problematic for the smaller channels and could ultimately have a negative impact on their ability to attract advertising revenue. Indeed this probably limits the range of channels that will eventually come to be offered unless a solution can be found.

Of course, dissatisfied subscribers and content providers are a recipe for disaster for DTV operators in the long-term and a model in which subscribers pay for access to hundreds of channels, but actually view only a small handful of favorites, is unlikely to be sustainable going forward. The response of the DTV industry has been to offer subscribers access to an Electronic Program Guide as their primary interface with the DTV service. EPGs allow users to browse through scheduling information, set reminders for relevant shows, request additional show information, purchase pay-per-view content etc. However, while they offer a certain level of convenience they do not yet properly address the core information overload problem. Of course, EPGs come with their own usability issues many of which are a direct consequence of the information overload problem itself. For example, [6] report results from an EPG usability study which concluded that more than two thirds of users experienced problems using the EPG as a source of schedule information; see also [14].

To get a more precise sense of the scale of the information overload problem it is worth considering the sample EPG screen-shot present in Figure 3.1 This EPG is capable of displaying 90 minutes worth of viewing time across 7 channels. This means that a 24-hour schedule across a relatively modest 70-channel lineup will require 160 screens of schedule information alone. In the US ReplayTV^{TM} users are typically faced with guide information for two weeks in advance and for 200 channels. This requires a staggering 6400 screens of content.

How can subscribers gain efficient access to programming content as DTV services scale-up to many hundreds or perhaps even thousands of channels? We believe that personalization technology (e.g. [2, 4, 19]), which provides for the compilation of

Ally McBeal			KTVU Cable 2
9:00pm-10:00; Starts in 12 minutes			8:48pm
Clips and interviews with cast members highlight the show's most memorable moments; host Bill Maher. Calista Flockhart, Gil Bellows, Greg Gorman, Courtney Thorne-Smith, Tracy			
Mon 3/22	8:30pm	9:00pm	9:30pm
2 KTVU	The Road to Fa...	Ally McBeal	
3 NIKP	CatDog	Brady Bunch	The Wonder Ye...
4 KRON	Caroline in the...	Law & Order	
5 KPIX	The King of Qu...	Everybody Lov...	Becker
7 KGO	20/20	John Sanford 's Mind Prey	
8 FXP	The X-files	NYPD Blue	
9 KQED	Antiques Road...	The American Experience	

Figure 3.1. An example EPG listing programs for a sample of 7 channels over a one-hour time slot (Courtesy of ReplayTV,www.replaytv.com).

schedule information that suits the viewing preferences of an individual subscriber, offers a sustainable solution in this regard.

As programming content grows so too does the requirement for enhanced levels of personalization. Figure 3 2 captures this viewpoint by charting the level of personalization required to support different levels of programming content. For example, in the 'good ol' days' of terrestrial television, with tens of channels, the volume of programming content was limited and therefore the need for personalization was also limited. Viewers were quite happy to refer to paper-based TV guides as their primary source of schedule information; the so-called 'zone of usefulness' is wide in this region of the chart. Indeed during this period teletext-based TV guides, the forerunners of today's EPGs, proved to be a useful source of online schedule information. As channel numbers increased this zone of usefulness narrowed and more flexible EPG-like services began to emerge. For example, a range of Internet-based online TV guides (e.g. www.tvguide.com, www.entertainmentireland.com) offered users limited levels of personalization in order to cope with the increase in programming content. For example, users were able to set their channel favorites, search for specific shows, organise their guide by genre etc., and similar services found their way into the first generation of DTV EPGs.

Looking to the future, we argue the need for fully personalized EPGs that are capable of automatically learning about the viewing needs and preferences of individual users and of alerting these users to the right programs at the right times; see [1, 3, 5, 7, 9–13, 17, 18, 20, 22, 29] and also articles by Ardissono et al., Zimmerman et al., O'Sullivan et al. and Judith Mastoff in this volume. This type of EPG effectively removes traditional channel boundaries to offer viewers their own personalized television channel, drawing together relevant programming content

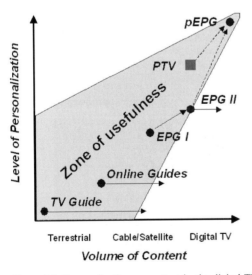

Figure 3.2. Personalization vs content in the digital TV domain.

from across the full range of available channels, large and small. In this way viewers are guaranteed to receive the right information at the right time and even the smallest channels will benefit from viewership as long as their program content is relevant to these viewers. A good commercial example of the personalized EPG is offered by the Tivo system (www.tivo.com), which is by far the most popular pEPG on the market today (in terms of units sold). Tivo combines digital recording technology with collaborative filtering style personalization (e.g. [4, 23] allowing subscribers to benefit from automatic recording of their favorite shows.

It is this goal, the development of a fully personalized EPG that is capable of learning about, and responding to, the changing viewing preferences of individual viewers, that we are primarily interested in. And in the following sections we outline a sequence of pEPG applications (called PTV) that we have developed in order to evaluate a variety of a different personalization strategies, presentation formats and delivery platforms [7, 8, 26–28]. In particular, for the purpose of this article, we will focus on less conventional delivery platforms, describing our experiences using PC, mobile phone, PDA and remote control devices as a means of delivering listings information to subscribers.

Before continuing with an overview of recent research that has been carried out in pursuit of the personalized EPG, it is worth further elaborating the reason for our focus on different delivery devices. The main reason is quite simple: the availability and functionality of these devices strongly suggests that they will have at least a part to play in the future of Digital TV. For example, advanced high-end remote controls have been around for a number of years and continue to evolve in terms of the functionality offered to end-users. For instance, the latest generation of these remote controls share many technical features in common with PDAs (high-resolution color screens, significant processing power and as much as 8MB of on-board RAM). As we shall see in future sections, recent developments highlight how these control devices can be used to deliver EPG information directly to the user, by-passing the more traditional on-screen set-top-box based EPG. In turn, many applications exist for current PDAs so that they can offer similar control functionality and Internet-enabled mobile phones are likely to follow suit. Thus it is vitally important to understand how such devices influence EPG services, particularly in terms of the input and output capabilities. These devices, especially mobile phones and PDAs, are becoming more commonplace and so are likely to represented a cost-effective alternative to set-top-box solutions given that many users will already own a PDA and mobile phone.

3. The Evolution of the Personalized EPG

The personalized electronic program guide has come about as a result of a number of factors: the arrival of Digital TV and increased programming content; the availability of sophisticated *recommender systems* [2, 4, 19]; and the popularity of the Internet and a whole new range of information access devices. The result is that since the mid 1990's researchers have been using recommender systems technologies to develop the next generation of EPG applications on a range of devices.

In general, personalized EPGs can be usefully catagorized along three distinct dimensions: recommendation strategy; feedback method; delivery device. In the following sections we will discuss these dimensions in more detail and survey recent work in pEPG development as it relates to this catagorization.

3.1. RECOMMENDATIONS, FEEDBACK & DEVICES

The recommendation strategy used by a pEPG refers to the type of recommendation technique that is employed, be it content-based, collaborative of some hybrid technique. Content-based techniques rely on the availability of program descriptions that can be compared against user profiles in order to determine a degree of similarity. This is used to rank order programs for recommendation; in short, new programs are recommended because they are similar to those the target user has liked in the past (see [1, 2, 13, 26, 27]).

In the case where program descriptions are not available, collaborative filtering techniques may be used (see [2, 4, 19]). These rely on the availability of user profiles in which individual program items are graded according to their relevance to a particular user and new recommendations are generated for a target user by leveraging the profiles of a set of similar users, users whose graded profiles are highly correlated with the target user; in short, programs that are graded highly by similar users are likely to be recommended to the target user; see also the work of O'Sullivan et al. in this volume.

The feedback method used by a particular pEPG refers to the way in which preference data is gathered from the user when constructing or updating the user profile. In general there are two options. *Explicit feedback* techniques ask the user to provide profile information directly, for example, by filling out online forms or by grading recommendations (e.g. [18, 26, 27]). In contrast, *implicit feedback* techniques attempt to detect preference information without the need to ask users directly. Approaches include transforming normal user behaviors (program selection, bookmarking etc) into profile data. For example, a user who repeatedly requests more information for episodes of 'Buffy the Vampire Slayer' is likely to be interested in this show; see for example [13, 22]. Feedback is a critical issue in pEPGs because without up-to-date profile information, guide quality will be compromised; see also the work of Hara et al. in this volume which compares demographic preferences with viewing preferences as a source of profiling data.

Finally, because of recent developments in the device industry it is now possible to deliver information services across a rich variety of device-types. As such, the concept of delivering an EPG service through the TV set is no longer the only option. Increasingly we find EPG applications being developed as Internet services available to desktop and handheld devices and this introduces a whole new set of issues related to interface design, feedback strategies etc. [8, 28].

3.2. RECENT DEVELOPMENTS

Perhaps one of the earliest descriptions of a personalized EPG is provided by [13]. In terms of recommender technologies, they describe a *content-based* approach to program recommendation in which each program is associated with a set of descriptive features and a number of similarity metrics are used to compare programs and user profiles in order to identify a set of recommendable programs for a particular user. For example, program descriptions are made up of predefined genre categories in line with the Digital Video Broadcast (DVB) standard (see www.dvb.org), with each genre of show associated with a set of attributes (e.g., title, year, participants, producers etc.). It is worth noting that the authors have added additional genre categories as part of their application. Fuzzy-matching techniques are used to generate program recommendations and explicit and implicit feedback techniques are also considered as part of this work. Users are required to fill out an initial profile description (or select from a pre-defined set of standard profile *stereotypes*) and selection actions made by users are logged and analyzed during profile update. It is worth noting that the availability of stereotypical profiles goes some way to addressing the critical *cold-start* problem in recommender systems—how to generate high quality recommendations for new users in the absence of a rich individual user profile. This is a recurring theme in pEPG research as well, as we shall see below.

The work of [1] introduces the use of multi-agent architectures for the generation of personalized EPGs; see also [10, 21]. Once again the core recommender uses a content-based strategy based on the DVB meta-data standard and the use of a combination of explicit feedback and profile stereotypes is proposed, with new users automatically classified in relation to a given stereotype based on their initial profile data. In addition, the pEPG is delivered through the user's set-top-box and, as such, profiles can be dynamically updated by tracking and classifying a user's actual viewing behavior.

The availability of rich program descriptions is a major stumbling block for content-based approaches to recommendation. At best it can be expensive to source reliable and informative content descriptions for TV programs and very often only minimal descriptions are available that are not compatible with the use of content-based techniques. This problem is a familiar one in most other recommender system application domains where collaborative filtering techniques have formed at least part of a solution in order to compensate for description shortcomings. Collaborative filtering techniques rely on ratings-based user profiles rather than program descriptions to make their recommendations and recent pEPG research has investigated the use of collaborative filtering, often in conjunction with content-based methods. For example, [9] describe a hybrid recommender, combining content-based and collaborative techniques, that takes advantage of both explicit and implicit profiling and feedback methods. Similarly, as we will discuss in the next section, and as described in detail in [26, 27], the PTV systems also combined content-based and collaborative techniques. [29] describe a multi-agent approach to integrating different recommendation strategies, but propose a combination of probabilistic and collaborative recommendation strategies in a Web-based pEPG that relies on explicit feedback.

In general, hybrid recommender systems must solve the additional problem of how to choose a final set of recommendations from those sets of recommendations generated by each of the individual recommendation strategies or recommender agents. For example, [9] outline a reinforcement-learning strategy for assessing the likely accuracy of an individual recommender agent. Related work by [30] describes a generic framework for combining different prediction strategies which is claimed to facilitate the rapid creation and evaluation of hybrid recommendation techniques.

We mentioned above that one of the critical issues in the development of successful pEPGs is related to the cold-start problem in recommender systems research. In short, pEPGs must be capable of responding intelligently to new users even in the absence of high-quality profile information. As a result a number of complementary research initiatives are evident from the literature. Of course one approach is to look at the use of implicit profiling techniques so that user profiles are maintained constantly without the need for explicit updates from the user; for example, see [13, 22]. Reference [18] suggests that in the case where explicit feedback is required then natural language dialogs should be used as a means of enhancing the user experience. An adaptive recommendation strategy is outlined that allows users to provide explicit requirements information in the form of natural language question and answer dialogs.

One common way to minimise (or even eliminate) the need to collect initial profile information from users is to take advantage of profile stereotypes. The basic idea is to associate a new user with one of a set of pre-defined stereotypes based on minimal information about this user. Each stereotype contains a rich set of profile information that is unlikely to be very accurate in relation to the new user, but that will nevertheless serve as a knowledge-source for early recommendations. For instance, [20] propose the use of stereotypical profiles derived from the usage patterns of real users, although the results reported are limited in nature due to the small numbers of users available as the source of the stereotypes. An alternative approach is described by [15, 16] in which stereotypes are constructed from an analysis of pre-existing user lifestyle surveys. Once again preliminary studies are promising, indicating that the resulting sterotypes are useful sources of recommendation knowledge if the target user is well suited to the stereotype in question.

To a large extent work on pEPGs has focused primarily on the generation of *accurate* program guides for users, the ultimate goal being to select a set of programs that a user is likely to enjoy. Recently researchers have begun to investigate other factors that are likely to be important to end-users. For example, the work of [5] argues that *trust* is also an important factor to consider. The basic idea is that in order for end-users to appreciate novel recommendations they must trust the recommender; see also [32]. Reference [5] address this by attempting to explain novel recommendations to users in order to rationalise the recommendation; for instance, the example provided by [5] in relation to the first-time recommendation of 'Boston

Public' to a user is that 'Boston Public stars Jeri Ryan who plays Seven of Nine in Star Trek: Voyager'. They argue that these *conversational explanations* are well-suited to TV recommenders and that they appear to help in the building of trust between user and recommender. In a similar vein the work of [25] argues for the importance of diversity in recommender systems—the idea that recommended items be diverse (different from one another) while being similar to the user profile in order to maximise recommendation coverage—a point which is investigated within the TV domain by [31].

4. PTV Case-Studies

The PTV family of applications are well-known examples of personalized electronic program guides; see [7, 8, 26, 27]. The original PTV was launched as a Web-based pEPG, combining content-based and collaborative filtering techniques with explicit, ratings-based feedback, in 1999. And since that time PTV has proven to be extremely successful and popular. It has attracted in excess of 20,000 users in the Irish market and the core technology has been licensed to a number of portal sites and telecommunication companies, including the Irish Times newspaper group and Vodafone. Indeed the current version of PTV, now called PTVPlus (www.ptvplus.com), has been adapted for a range of delivery platforms including the mobile Internet and next-generation remote control units. In this section we will summarise each of these different versions of PTV highlighting the pros and cons of each against a set of application objectives and novelties.

4.1. CORE TECHNOLOGY

The core PTV architecture is presented in Figure 3.3. In brief, it consists of a number of core functional units (*profiler, recommender, compiler*) and databases (*profile database, program database, schedule database*).

The profile database contains an individual profile for each registered user. Each profile encodes the TV preferences of a given user, listing channel information, preferred viewing times, program and genre preferences, guide preferences etc.

This program database contains the program content descriptions (program cases). Each entry describes a particular program using features such as the program title, genre information, the creator and director, cast or presenters, the country of origin, and the language. This information repository is crucial for the content-based (case-based) recommendation component of PTV.

This schedule database contains TV listings for all supported channels. Each listing entry includes details such as the program name, the viewing channel, the start and end time, and typically some text describing the program in question. The schedule database is constructed automatically from electronic schedule resources.

The profiler is responsible for maintaining and updating all profile information. Preliminary profile information is collected from the user at registration time in order

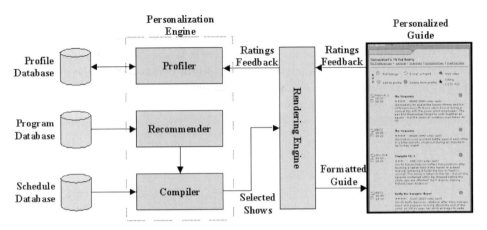

Figure 3.3. The PTV core architecture combines a sophisticated hybrid personalization engine and rendering engine to deliver personalized EPG content in a variety of formats.

to bootstrap the personalization process. However, the majority of information is learned from grading feedback provided by the user; each recommended program is accompanied with grading icons or links that allow the user to explicitly evaluate the proposed recommendation.

The recommender component is the intelligent core of PTV. Its job is to take user profile information and to select new programs for recommendation to a user. As mentioned already, PTV uses a hybrid recommendation approach that combines content-based and collaborative recommendation strategies. Each recommendation strategy produces a set of ranked recommendations which are then interleaved to produce a final guide by the compiler.

The compiler component produces a generic guide format in XML, which is automatically converted into an appropriate presentation format by the rendering engine through the use of XSLT stylesheets. While individual guides are converted into single HTML pages for the Web, they are converted into multiple WML pages (or cards) for mobile phone usage; this is necessary to solve the problems of limited presentation space (and memory space) that exist on current WAP phones. This separation of presentation logic from the underlying recommendation logic allows PTV to be readily adapted for use on a wide range of devices.

4.2. CASE STUDY 1 – PTV ON THE WEB

The main objective of the Web version of PTV was to serve as a test-bed for our recommendation techniques within the TV domain [7, 26, 27]. It produces personalized daily TV guides for each registered user based on its hybrid recommendation engine. A sample guide is presented in Figure 3.4 showing part of a Web guide that consists of 4 program recommendations. Each program recommendation is accompanied by critical program information such as the channel and time of broadcast, a brief episode summary, and some information about what other users have thought of this show; for example, 2628 users have rated 'Buffy the Vampire Slayer' with a 4-star average rating. Importantly, 'The Simpsons' recommendations have been made because this user is already known to enjoy this show; the show is already among the positive programs in the user's profile and the icon to the right of the program title allows the user to remove this show from their profile. In contrast, the other two recommendations have not been commented on previously by the user and so they are suggested along with a set of rating icons, which allow the user to positively or negatively rate each program, and, in so doing, update their profile. To measure the personalization quality of the personalized guides produced by PTV we carried

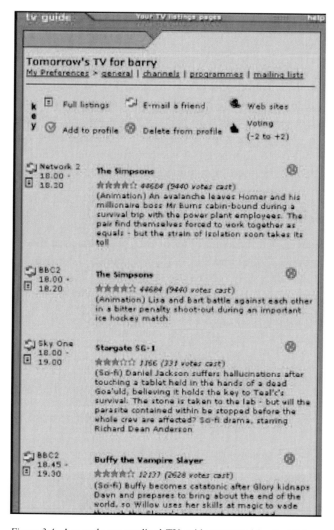

Figure 3.4. A sample personalized TV guide generated by the Web version of PTVPlus.

out a user study in which users were asked to evaluate the system in terms of guide precision, ease of use, and speed of service. Very briefly, in total 310 PTV users were included in the evaluation. They were selected from a population of regular and new PTV users at random. The selected users varied in age, gender and Internet usage patterns and represented a broad cross-section of PTV's users at the time. In terms of guide quality they were asked to rate the appropriateness of their personalized guides.

The results are presented in Figure 3.5 and are clearly very positive. The average personalized guide contained between 10 and 15 programs and, critically, 97% of users rated the quality of these guides as satisfactory or good, with only 3% of users rating the guides as poor in quality. What is more, the vast majority of users indicated that they were at least satisfied with PTV's ease of use and speed of recommendation.

While it is clear that, as a Web-based application, PTV has enjoyed some success in relation to its ability to produce high-quality personalized TV guides, its ultimate usefulness as an EPG is limited because of the fact that it operates largely in what might be termed a *disconnected* mode. In other words, PTV users have on-screen access to personalized guide via their PC but not from their TV. As a result many PTV users report that they use the system to print out personalized guides, which they then use as a form of paper-based, personalized TV guide. In the next two case-studies we describe efforts to address this issue by attempting to 'get PTV into the livingroom' so that it may be used in conjunction with TV viewing.

4.3. CASE STUDY 2 – PTV MOBILE

Our next edition of PTV leveraged the availability of Internet-enabled mobile devices such as WAP-enabled mobile phones and PDAs [8]. Of course, the advantage that

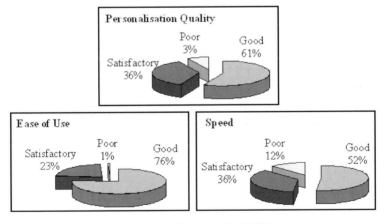

Figure 3.5. Summary results from a live-user trial of PTV.

these devices have over a traditional PC is their portability. As a result, by developing a mobile version of PTV it is possible to provide users with the ability to bring their electronic guide into the livingroom and interact with it more directly as an EPG.

Since the PTV architecture separates the recommendation logic from the presentation logic, the adaptation of PTV for use on new devices, such as mobile phones, is not technically difficult. Briefly, it involves a careful redesign of the core PTV page format stylesheets in order to take account of the presentation restrictions that exist on hand-held devices.

Example screen-shots from the latest version of the mobile edition of PTV are shown in Figure 3.6 showing a sample of the homepage, a personalized guide, and an individual program page. It should be clear that a number of significant changes have been made in relation to the Web-based PTV format from an interface perspective. For example, due to page size restrictions only limited program information can be presented as part of each personalized guide; see Figure 3.6(b). The additional episode detail and ranking information is now provided as part of a new program information page (see Figure 3.6(c)), which provides detailed information about one specific show. Indeed this adjustment, combined with some recent developments within the mobile sector, have made it possible to offer the end-user a whole host of additional show-related services. For instance, the program information page provides the user with access to MMS (Multi-Media Messaging) services—allowing the user to send a picture or animation from the show in question to their friends—and ringtone services to name but two.

In addition to these presentation changes, we have made a more explicit separation between recommendations that have been made because the user has previously expressed an interest (these are now called *reminders*) and recommendations that are new suggestions that have not been commented on in the past by the target user (now called *recommendations*). As a result, each user's personal homepage now provides direct access to top ranking reminders and new recommendations (see Figure 3.6(a)) as well as direct access to individual channel and themed guides.

With this latest mobile edition of PTV we have demonstrated that it is possible to deliver a compelling EPG presentation to the end user via their mobile handset; although it is worth highlighting that the screen-shots shown in Figure 3.6 are not compatible with the original WAP phones, which support a monochrome text-based interface only. In addition, by making personalized TV guides available through a mobile phone the average user at least has access to their personalized guide while watching TV, making it easier for them to request up-to-the-minute guide information and simpler for them to rate programs.

4.4. CASE STUDY 3 – PTV REMOTE

The mobile edition of PTV goes some way to addressing the issue of the *connection*, or lack thereof, between the personalized guide and the TV viewing experience. Nevertheless important shortcomings are still evident because the connection remains weak.

(a)

(b)

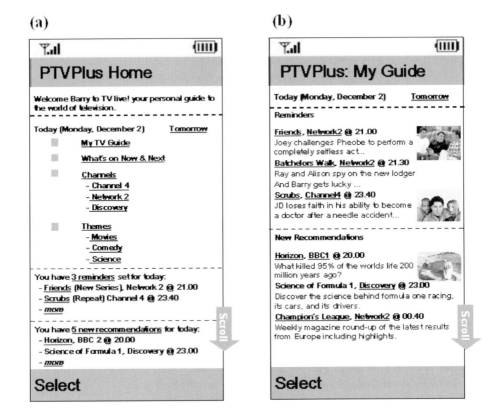

(c)

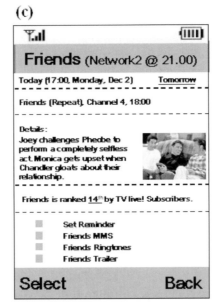

Figure 3.6. A sample of screen-shots for a version of PTVPlus designed for delivery over the new generation of enhanced WAP-enabled, color mobile phones.

The user can still not switch between programs and channels from PTV, a basic feature of all set-top-box based EPGs. Moreover, user feedback remains explicit, with the user providing ratings for individual shows.

Both of these issues are addressed in our final case-study, which sees PTV being used to drive a personalzied EPG that is made available through a next-generation remote control unit called the GuideRemote™ (by Evolve Communications Inc.). GuideRemote is an interactive universal remote control that integrates Internet and LCD technology to offer consumers a combined handheld EPG and universal remote control facility.

Figure 3.7 shows an example of the GuideRemote displaying a 30-minute viewing slot over 4 channels. The user can scroll through the EPG using the device's main navigation keys to switch directly to a program that is currently showing or to set up a reminder for a show that is soon to air. The EPG offers a 7-day listings service and a range of added-value services including advertising messages, retail coupons for t-commerce services, interactive games, voting services for shows, plus the ability to request more information for a given show from the Internet. The consumer 'synchs' their GuideRemote with a base Web site, through their PC, on a weekly basis, to download new listings and information (including coupons and advertisements) and to upload their recent actions; thus an always-on Internet connection is unnecessary.

Of course the familiar EPG information-overload problem takes on an even more acute form in the context of the GuideRemote. With its single screen able to present a 30-minute listings window across only 4 channels, a week's worth of viewing over 100 channels will require more than 8000 screens of information, and even a single

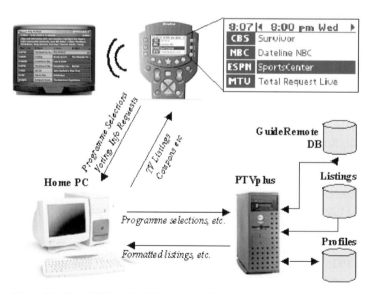

Figure 3.7. The PTVPlus-GuideRemote architecture.

day's viewing may require up to 1200 screens, and this covers only the program titles. By using PTV as the GuideRemote base Web site, and provider of TV listings, this overload problem can be significantly reduced since PTV can download personalized guides to each device at synchronization time, in addition to the static listings information; see also [28]. In this way PTV acts as a proxy, mediating the interaction between the device and the back-end listings content, and prioritizing relevant content for the particular target device (see Figure 3.7).

Moreover, the GuideRemote integration also solves the *connection* problem. Now users can use their EPG to actually control the TV set (after all GuideRemote provides fully-fledged remote control features) but it also allows users to *vote* for specific programs using the device's 'vote' button. This information can then be interpreted by PTV as grading information. Indeed, this can be taken one step further. Guide-Remote can capture the selections that users make as they use the EPG, including switching to a specific program for viewing, or requesting more information, for example. This information can be used by PTV as a source of grading data, obviating the need for the program voting that is currently supported as the dominant form of feedback. In other words, instead of expecting users to grade a program positively (or negatively) it is possible to capture the same information by determining whether they have switched channels to tune into (or tune out of) that program when it airs. From a usability perspective this will allow users to benefit fully from PTV's personalization facilities without the need to elicit extra user information.

It is worth highlighting that the GuideRemote device comes with the problem of how to cater for multiple users of the same device, users who are likely to have different interest profiles. Currently this is solved by asking users to log-on to the device but we are looking at alternative strategies including ways of predicting which user is likely to be using the device based on their usage patterns and the time of day.

5. Conclusions

The DTV industry needs to properly address the information overload problem that is facing DTV subscribers. Even today subscribers are finding it difficult to locate programming content quickly and easily leading many researchers to question the usability of the current generation of EPGs [6, 14]. The recent success of personalization technologies in general [2, 4, 19], and the specific success of personalized EPGs (e.g. [1, 3, 9, 27]) suggests that the personalized EPG is a real and viable solution to this information overload problem. Indeed the recent progress that has been made by many researchers in this space looks to be a clear indication that a new generation of personalized EPGs may be just around the corner.

In this article we have taken the opportunity to checkpoint a number of developments in the pEPG arena. In particular, we have focused on the PTV family of applications and how they have provided users with access to a variety of personalized TV guides across a number of devices, from their PC to the mobile phone to the TV remote control.

References

1. Ardissono, L., Portis, F. and Torasso, P.: 2002, Architecture of a System for the Generation of Personalized Electronic Program Guides. In: *Proceedings of the 1st Workshop on Personalization in Future TV at the 8th International Conference on User Modeling.* Sonthofen, Germany.
2. Balabanovic, M. and Shoham, Y.: 1997, FAB: Content-Based, Collaborative Recommendation. *Communications of the ACM* **40**(3), 66–72.
3. Baudisch, P. and Brueckner, L.: 2002, TV Scout: Lowering the Entry Barrier to Personalized TV Program Recommendation. In: *Proceedings of the Second International Conference on Adaptive Hypermedia and Adaptive Web-Based Systems.* Malaga, Spain: Springer-Verlag, pp. 58–68.
4. Billsus, D. and Pazzani, M. J.: 1998, Learning Collaborative Information Filters. In: *Proceedings of the 15th International Conference on Machine Learning.* Wisconsin, USA, pp. 46–54.
5. Buczak, A. L., Zimmerman, J. and Kurapati, K.: 2002, Personalization: Improving Ease-of-Use, Trust and Accuracy of a TV Show Recommender. In: *Proceedings of the 2nd Workshop on Personalization in Future TV at the 2nd International Conference on Adaptive Hypermedia and Adaptive Web-Based Systems.* Malaga, Spain, pp. 3–12.
6. Concejero P., Gil, S., Ramos, R., Collado, J. A. and Angel, M.: 1999, Usability Testing of an Electronic Program Guide and Interactive TV Applications. In: *Proceedings of the 17th International Symposium on Human Factors in Telecommunication.* Copenhagen, Denmark.
7. Cotter, P. and Smyth, B. PTV: 2000, Intelligent Personalised TV Guides. In: *Proceedings of the Seventeenth National Conference on Artificial Intelligence and Twelfth Conference on Innovative Applications of Artificial Intelligence.* Austin, Texas: AAAI Press/The MIT Press, pp. 957–964.
8. Cotter, P. and Smyth, B.: 2000, Waping the Web: Content Personalisation for WAP–Enabled Devices. In: *Proceedings of the International Conference on Adaptive Hypermedia and Adaptive Web-Based Systems.* Trento, Italy: Springer–Verlag, pp. 98–108.
9. Dai, W. and Cohen, R.: 2003, Dynamic Personalized TV Recommendation System. In: *Proceedings of the 3rd Workshop on Personalization in Future TV at the 9th International Conference on User Modeling.* Pittsburgh, USA, pp. 12–21.
10. Difino, A., Negro, B. and Chiarotto, A.: 2002, A Multi-agent System for a Personalized Electronic Program Guide. In: *Proceedings of the 2nd Workshop on Personalization in Future TV at the 2nd International Conference on Adaptive Hypermedia and Adaptive Web-Based Systems.* Malaga, Spain, pp. 13–22.
11. Dimitrova, N., Agnihotri, L., Jasinschi, R., Zimmerman, J., Marmaropoulos, G., McGee, T. and Dagtas, S.: 2000, Video Scouting Demonstration: Smart Content Selection and Recording. In: *Proceedings of the Eighth ACM International Conference on Multimedia.* Calfornia, USA: ACM Press, pp. 499–500.
12. Dimitrova, N., Jasinschi, R., Agnihotri, L., Zimmerman, J., McGee, T. and Li, D.: 2001, Personalizing Video Recorders Using Multimedia Processing and Integration. In: *Proceedings of the 9th ACM International Conference on Multimedia.* Orrawa, Canada: ACM Press, pp. 564–567.
13. Ehrmantraut, M., Hrder, T., Wittig, H. and Steinmetz, R. 1996, The Personal Electronic Program Guide–Towards the Pre–selection of Individual TV Programs. In: *Proceedings of the 5th International Conference on Information and Knowledge Management.* Maryland USA: ACM Press, pp. 243–250.

14. Eronen, L. and Vuorimaa, P.: 2000, User Interfaces for Digital Television: A Navigator
    Case Study. In: *Proceedings of the Working Conference on Advanced Visual Interfaces*.
    Palermo, Italy: ACM Press, pp. 276–279.
15. Gena, C.: 2001, Designing TV Viewer Stereotypes for an Electronic Program Guide.
    In: *Proceedings of the 8th International Conference on User Modeling*. Sonthofen,
    Germany: Springer–Verlag, pp. 274–276.
16. Gena, C. and Ardissono, L.: 2002, On the Construction of TV Viewer Stereotypes Starting
    from Lifestyles Surveys. In: *Proceedings of the 1st Workshop on Personalization in Future
    TV at the 8th International Conference on User Modeling*. Sonthofen, Germany.
17. Goren–Bar, D. and Glinansky, O.: 2002, Family Stereotyping – A Model to Filter TV
    Programs for Multiple Viewers. In: *Proceedings of the 2nd Workshop on Personalization
    in Future TV at the 2nd International Conference on Adaptive Hypermedia and Adaptive
    Web-Based Systems*. Malaga, Spain, pp. 95–102.
18. Johansson, P.: 2003, Natural Language Interaction in Personalized Epgs. In: *Proceedings
    of the 3rd Workshop on Personalization in Future TV at the 9th International Conference
    on User Modeling*. Pittsburgh, USA, pp. 27– 31.
19. Konstan, J. A., Miller, B. N., Maltz, D., Herlocker, J. L., Gordon, L. R. and Riedl, J.: 1997,
    Grouplens: Applying Collaborative Filtering to Usenet News. *Communications of the
    ACM* **40**(3), 77–87.
20. Kurapati, K. and Gutta, S.: 2002, TV Personalization through Stereotypes. In: *Proceedings
    of the 2nd Workshop on Personalization in Future TV at the 2nd International Conference
    on Adaptive Hypermedia and Adaptive Web-Based Systems*. Malaga, Spain, pp. 103–112.
21. Kurapati, K., Gutta, S., Schaffer, D., Martino, J. and Zimmerman, J.: 2001, A Multi–Agent
    TV Recommender. In: *Proceedings of the 1st Workshop on Personalization in Future
    TV at the 8th International Conference on User Modeling*. Sonthofen, Germany.
22. Lee, H.-K., Lee, H.-K., Nam, J., Bae, B., Kim, M., Kang, K. and Kim, J.: 2002, Perso-
    nalized Contents Guide and Browsing Based on User Preference. In: *Proceedings of
    the 2nd Workshop on Personalization in Future TV at the 2nd International Conference
    on Adaptive Hypermedia and Adaptive Web-Based Systems*. Malaga, Spain, pp. 131–140.
23. O'Sullivan, D., Wilson, D. and Smyth, B.: 2002, Using Collaborative Filtering Data in
    Case-Based Recommendation. In: *Proceedings of the 15th International FLAIRS
    Conference*. Florida, USA, pp. 121–128.
24. Peng, C. and Vuorimaa, P.: 2000, A Digital Television Navigator. In: *Proceedings of the
    eighth ACM International Conference on Multimedia*. California, USA: ACM Press,
    pp. 429–431.
25. Smyth, B. and McClave, P.: 2001, Similarity v's Diversity. In: D. Aha and I. Watson (eds.):
    Proceedings of the International Conference on Case-Based Reasoning. Vancouver,
    Canada: Springer, pp. 347–361.
26. Smyth, B. and Cotter, P.: 2000, A Personalized Television Listings Service. *Communica-
    tions of the ACM* **43**(8), 107–111.
27. Smyth, B. and Cotter, P.: 2001, Personalized Electronic Program Guides. *Artificial
    Intelligence Magazine* **21**(2), 89–98.
28. Smyth, B., Cotter, P. and Ryan, J.: 2002, Evolving the Personalized EPG an Alternative
    Architecture for the Delivery of DTV Services. In: *Proceedings of the 2nd Workshop
    on Personalization in Future TV at the 2nd International Conference on Adaptive
    Hypermedia and Adaptive Web-Based Systems*. Malaga, Spain, pp. 161–170.
29. Uchyigit, G. and Clark, K.: 2002, An Agent Based Electronic Program Guide. In:
    *Proceedings of the 2nd Workshop on Personalization in Future TV at the 2nd International
    Conference on Adaptive Hypermedia and Adaptive Web-Based Systems*. Malaga, Spain,
    pp. 46–58.

30. van Setten, M., Veenstra, M. and Nijholt, A.: 2002, Prediction Strategies: Combining Prediction Techniques to Optimize Personalization. In: *Proceedings of the 2nd Workshop on Personalization in Future TV at the 2nd International Conference on Adaptive Hypermedia and Adaptive Web-Based Systems*. Malaga, Spain, pp. 23–32.
31. Wilson, D., Smyth, B. and O'Sullivan, D.: 2003, Sparsity Reduction in Collaborative Recommendation: A Case-Based Approach. *International Journal of Pattern Recognition and Artificial Intelligence* **17**(5), 863–884.
32. Zimmerman, J. and Kurapati, K.: 2002, Exposing Profiles to Build Trust in a Recommender. In: *CHI '02 Extended Abstracts on Human factors in Computer Systems*. Minnesota, USA: ACM Press, pp. 608–609.

Chapter 4

Interactive Television Personalization
From Guides to Programs

DERRY O' SULLIVAN[1], BARRY SMYTH[1], DAVID WILSON[2],
KIERAN Mc DONALD[3] and ALAN F. SMEATON[3]
[1]*Department of Computer Science, University College Dublin, Dublin 4, Ireland.*
e-mail:{dermot.osullivan,barry.smyth}@ucd.ie
[2]*Department of Software & Information Systems, University of North Carolina at Charlotte,*
USA. e-mail:davils@uncc.edu
[3]*Centre for Digital Video Processing, Dublin City University, Dublin 9, Ireland.*
e-mail:{kmcdon,asmeaton}@computing.dcu.ie

Abstract. The personalized Electronic Program Guide (pEPG) has been touted as a possible solution to the information overload problem faced by Digital TV (DTV) users. It leverages artificial intelligence and user profiling techniques to learn about the viewing preferences of individual users in order to compile viewing guides that fit their individual preferences. In this chapter, we focus on the recommendation technology used by existing pEPG's and argue that certain important shortcomings (related to profile sparsity and recommendation diversity) exist that impact the future success of pEPG's. We describe how data mining approaches can be used to alleviate many of these problems and present results of a comprehensive evaluation of such approaches.

Key words. data mining, electronic program guides, personalization, personalized broadcasts

4.1. Introduction

Recent years have seen dramatic changes in the TV sector on a number of fronts. The advent of Digital TV (DTV) services has offered consumers a greater range of channels and programming content in addition to a host of new interactive services. In parallel, new breeds of TV-based consumer devices have emerged, such as personal video recorder (PVR) technologies, for example, TiVo (http://www.tivo.com/) and WinTV (http://www.hauppauge.com/). As a result, consumers are faced with a new challenge, namely how to search and browse for relevant video content—collected by this new range of consumer devices and made available through a variety of online services—in an intuitive and efficient way. The personalized Electronic Program Guide (pEPG) [11–14, 16, 30–32] and digital video library [7] comprise part of an overall answer to this challenge, and together they can provide users with a direct interface to program content that is tailored to their needs. Such systems employ user profiling and information filtering techniques to

L. Ardissono et al. (eds.), *Personalized Digital Television*, 73–91, 2004.
© 2004 *Kluwer Academic Publishers. Printed in the Netherlands.*

learn about the viewing preferences of individual users in order to pro-actively promote relevant programs.

As part of our ongoing research program into personalized TV services [12, 13], we have been developing a range of personalization and recommendation techniques that are well suited to the TV domain [4–6, 3]. In this chapter we describe recent work on the application of data mining methods to extract new program metadata from user profiles, which can significantly augment knowledge about program similarity and relevance in order to address the *sparsity problem* normally associated with collaborative filtering (CF) recommendation techniques. Deriving item meta-data in order to empower recommendation is similar in spirit to work on deriving user meta-data for enhancing recommendation [24, 33]. We should emphasize that data mining is one of many possible approaches to generating additional similarity knowledge; we have simply chosen data mining as a reasonable initial technique to demonstrate the feasibility of our new recommendation strategy. Evaluations of this approach have show that it delivers superior personalization accuracy across a range of experimental conditions [1]. Our earlier work in this area has already shown great promise for explicit ratings-based user profiles as the central source of preference information [2], and recently new results from the collection of implicit behavioral profile data [7] have shown that implicit profiles are as accurate, if not more, than their explicit counterparts [3]. This chapter provides a synopsis of our research to date in the area of personalization and recommendation in the DTV arena and goes on to discuss future avenues of research including the progression from personalized guides to personalized programs in recommendation.

4.2. Background

In order to ground our discussion on recommendation, we briefly overview the key techniques that have been used to drive recommender systems, emphasising opportunities that exist for improving these techniques. We go on to provide detailed information on the state-of-the-art PTVPlus [16] (pEPG) and Fìschlàr [7] (PVR) systems that serve as testbeds for our research.

4.2.1. RECOMMENDER TECHNIQUES

Recommender systems combine techniques from user modelling and information filtering in order to build systems that are better able to respond to the preferences of individual users during their search for a particular item or product. Collaborative filtering (CF) techniques generate recommendations for a target user by leveraging the preferences of like-minded individuals—individuals whose profiles display a significant degree of similarity to the target user's profile [15–17]. The success of collaborative filtering depends on the ability to successfully identify a set of similar users to the target. Typically, collaborative filtering techniques employ simple notions of profile similarity that exploit direct overlaps or correlations between matching profile elements and their ratings. This lack of flexibility in measuring similarity gives rise to the so-called *sparsity problem* in collaborative filtering; that is, individual users typically rate only a small portion of the available items and so the expected item overlap between two random users tends to be low. In other words, the user-item ratings matrix is sparsely populated. As a consequence relevant users may be missed, and this may result in the failure to select suitable profiles as recommendation partners for a given target user.

Case-based reasoning (CBR) and, more generally, content-based approaches to recommendation can be viewed as complimentary to collaborative techniques [18, 22, 27]. In the case-based approach, a feature-based representation of the current user's interests is used as a retrieval probe or query into a library of item descriptions and the best matching descriptions (according to some similarity metric) are retrieved. In some ways, case-based approaches to recommendation are strongly related to collaborative filtering techniques—one can usefully treat collaborative profiles as cases, and the identification of like-minded individuals can be thought of as a form of case retrieval [22]. Interestingly, case-based systems usually adopt more sophisticated models of similarity that go beyond the computation of direct overlaps between case features. Case-based systems allow for the fact that two cases may be similar even though they contain none of the same features [22].

A key insight in our research is that by extending collaborative filtering systems to exploit more sophisticated models of case-based similarity [22, 27], the sparsity problem may be significantly ameliorated by supporting the detection of a wider range of profile similarities (Section 4.3). Previous work demonstrated the validity of using data mining techniques with CF and CBR for recommendation and its effect in combating the sparsity problem [1]. Using datasets from the DTV domain, we seek to corroborate these results here (Section 4.4).

4.2.2. PTVPLUS—PERSONALIZED ELECTRONIC PROGRAM GUIDE

PTVPlus (www.ptvplus.com) is an established online recommender system deployed in the television listings domain with over 20,000 users [16]. It uses its recommendation engine to generate a set of TV program recommendations for a target user, based on their profiled interests, and it presents these recommendations in the form of a personalized program guide (see Figure 4.1) [12, 14]. The uniqueness of PTVPlus stems from its combination of complementary recommendation results from separate collaborative and case-based recommendation strategies. The key to PTVPlus's personalization facility is an accurate database of interactively acquired user preference profiles that contain collaborative filtering style ratings lists. These are employed directly in the collaborative filtering component and by transformation to a content summary *profile schema* for matching in the case-based component [16]. While this means that each set of recommendations can help to make up for the shortfalls of the other set's personalization strategy, each set still

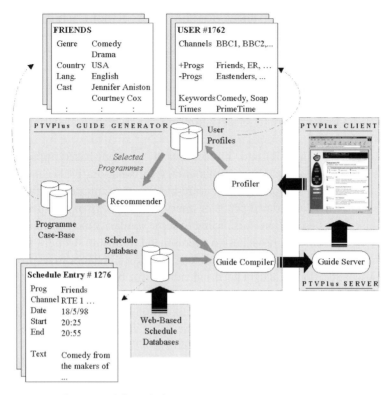

Figure 4.1. Structure of the PTVPlus system.

faces the limitations of its own strategy and the information that it has at its disposal.

4.2.3. THE FÌSCHLÀR DIGITAL VIDEO LIBRARY SYSTEM

Fìschlàr [7] is a video library system which allows users to record, browse, search and watch television programs online using their web browser. The system is in use by over 2000 students and lecturers within the campus of Dublin City University and on campus student residences for over 2 years. Users browse personalized television schedules, provided by the PTVPlus-ClixSmart personalization engine [16], to select programs to be recorded by the system; currently 8 terrestrial channels are available for recording. These programs are captured digitally and then analyzed to support browsing and interactive searching of their content; up to 300 hours of programs are available at any given time. While browsing a program, a user can decide to play all or part of that program. The system maintains a distinct user-base from PTVPlus (and thereby datasets in our evaluation); as well as this, user profiling of both explicit and implicit data may be captured, thus providing us with a valuable method of comparing these datasets (see Figure 4.2).

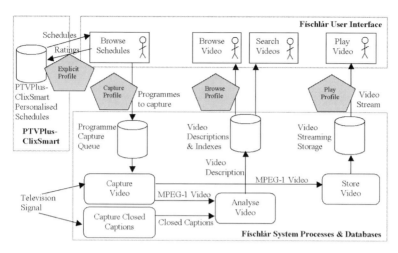

Figure 4.2. Structure of the Fìschlàr system.

4.3. Similarity-Based Recommendation

Our new approach to recommendation borrows ideas from CF and CBR style techniques. Specifically we advocate the use of association rule mining techniques to learn program similarity knowledge from ratings-based profiles and then use this similarity knowledge to drive a content-based recommendation technique.

4.3.1. ASSOCIATION RULE MINING FOR RECOMMENDATION

Association rule mining [19] and specifically in our case, the Apriori algorithm [20], generates rules of the form $A \Rightarrow B$, where A and B are sets of programs. In data mining terms, whenever a transaction (profile) contains a certain set of programs A, then the transaction probably contains another set of programs B. The probability that a given rule holds, rule confidence, is the percentage of transactions containing B given that A occurs. These confidence values are taken as probabilities and used to fill in an program-program similarity matrix, which provides the additional similarity knowledge necessary to compare non-identical profile items [1]. We term this association-rule harvested knowledge as *Direct*; an example of a direct rule is *Friends* $\Rightarrow$ *Frasier* with rule confidence of 70%. An extension to this knowledge (termed *Indirect*) is made by rule chaining; we combine rules and their confidences to find new rules, thus providing further similarity knowledge; e.g. given rules *Friends* $\Rightarrow$ *Frasier* with 70% confidence and *Frasier* $\Rightarrow$ *ER* with 50% confidence, we can chain these to give *Friends* $\Rightarrow$ *ER* with a confidence of 35% (using a multiplicative model for combination).

The availability of this item similarity knowledge facilitates a new type of similarity-based recommendation strategy that combines elements from case-based and collaborative recommendation techniques. It facilitates the use of more sophisticated CBR-like similarity metrics on ratings-based profile data, which in turn make it possible to generate improved recommendation lists by leveraging indirect similarities between profile cases. The recommendation strategy consists of two basic steps:

1. The target profile, t is compared to each profile case, $c \in C$, to select the k most similar cases.
2. The items contained within these selected cases (but absent in the target profile) are ranked according to the relevance to the target, and the r most relevant items are returned as recommendations.

4.3.2. PROFILE MATCHING

The profile similarity metric is computed as the weighted-sum of the similarities between items in the target and source profile cases Equation (1.1). In the situation where there is a direct correspondence between an item in the source, c_i, and the target, t_j, then maximal similarity is assumed Equation (1.2). However, the nature of ratings-based profile cases is such that these direct correspondences are rare and in such situations the similarity value of the source profile item is computed as the mean similarity between this item and the n most similar items in the target profile case $(t_1, \ldots, t_n)$, based on the learned similarity knowledge Equation (1.3).

$$P\,\text{Sim}(t, c, n) = \sum_{c_i \in c} w_i \cdot I\,\text{Sim}(t, c_i, n) \tag{1.1}$$

$$I\,\text{Sim}(t, c_i, n) = 1 \quad \text{if } \exists t_j = c_i \tag{1.2}$$

$$= \frac{\sum_{j=1..n} \text{Sim}(t_j, c_i)}{n} \tag{1.3}$$

4.3.3. RECOMMENDATION RANKING

Once the k most similar profile cases ($\hat{C}$) to the target have been identified, their items are combined and ranked for recommendation using three factors to prioritize: (1) items that have a high similarity to the target profile case, (2) items that occur in many of the retrieved profile cases, and (3) items that are recommended by profiles most similar to the target. Accordingly we compute the *relevance* of an item, c_i, from a retrieved profile case, c, with respect to the target profile, t, as shown in Equation (1.4); where $C^i \subseteq \hat{C}$ is the set of retrieved profile cases that contain c_i.

$$\text{Rel}(c_i, t, \hat{C}) = I\,\text{Sim}(c_i, t, k) \cdot \frac{|C^i|}{|\hat{C}|} \cdot \sum_{c \in C^i} P\,\text{Sim}(c, t, k) \tag{1.4}$$

Finally, the top-N ranked items are returned for recommendation.

4.4. Experimental Results

Here, we describe our most recent set of evaluations which use a range of different profile datasets from the DTV domain to test the recommendation accuracy of a number of different recommendation algorithms including standard collaborative filtering and a number of variations of our association-rule mining strategy.

4.4.1. TEST DATA

The PTVPlus and Fìschlàr systems are used to provide a range of different profile datasets collected from real user interactions with both systems over the past two years. The user profiles available from both systems are made up of explicit program ratings, although it is worth noting that for the purpose of this evaluation only positive ratings are used in the PTVPlus and Fìschlàr profiles. Fìschlàr has the added advantage of providing implicit profiles because the recording, playback and browsing actions of Fìschlàr users are tracked and can be translated directly into simple implicit ratings. As a result the following individual profile datasets are used:

- Explicit Datasets

    1. **PTVPlus**: 622 profiles from PTVPlus users.
    2. **Fìschlàr**: 650 profiles from Fìschlàr users.

- Fìschlàr Implicit Datasets

    1. **Record**: 650 profiles containing recorded programs.
    2. **Browse**: 650 profiles containing browsed programs.
    3. **Play**: 650 profiles containing played programs.
    4. **Combined**: A combination of the previous 3 datasets.

The above profile datasets are composed of profiles selected randomly from the PTVPlus and Fìschlàr user populations. Each profile consists of a list of rating-program pairs and the number of profiles represent the standard dataset sizes available from each system. Only positive ratings have been used for the purposes of this experiment; our system is also capable of dealing with negative ratings and current work involves amalgamating recommendations from both positive and negative ratings to see what effects may accrue.

4.4.2. TEST ALGORITHMS

A traditional collaborative filtering algorithm is used as a benchmark against which to evaluate the success of our family of similarity-based recommendation methods. We test a number of variations on our approach: one relies on *direct* association rules only as the basis for similarity knowledge, while a set of variations seek to exploit *indirect* similarity knowledge based on rule chaining, each differing in the way that the individual rule confidences are combined. In summary, the following test algorithms are evaluated:

- **CF**: Standard collaborative filtering similarity found by calculating the percentage of overlapping programs between profiles.
- **DR**: The so-called direct approach to similarity-based recommendation in which only those association rules discovered by Apriori are used for similarity knowledge (see Section 4.3).
- **Indirect**: A range of so-called indirect approaches to similarity recommendation that utilize additional similarity knowledge by chaining the mined association rules; results are shown for the average performance of these approaches.

4.4.3. EXPERIMENTAL SETUP

In order to evaluate recommendation accuracy we need some way to judge whether the recommendations made by a particular algorithm are relevant to a target user. An initial stage of our experiments is calculating rule threshold parameters for the Apriori algorithm [20]; this has been discussed in detail previously [3]. We then adopt a standard evaluation methodology in which each profile set is divided into a *training set*, containing 40% of the profiles, and a *test set*, containing the remaining 60% of the profiles. The training profiles are used as the basis for collaborative and similarity-based recommendation by the various test algorithms. In other words, only the ratings in the training profiles are used as the basis for profile comparisons prior to recommendation and only the training profiles are mined to discover similarity knowledge for similarity-based recommendation.

Once a set of recommendations is generated for a specific user with a given recommendation algorithm, their accuracy is evaluated with reference to the ratings contained in the test profile for that user; that is, those recommendations that we know to be relevant. We use two metrics in calculating accuracy:

Recall: The proportion of items in the user's test profile that are recommended, averaged over all users.

Hit Rate: The proportion of users for which at least one item from the user's test profile is recommended.

Recall is a stringent accuracy criterion, and a result of 100% here means the system is able to recommend all of the blocked out items. Hit Rate serves as a looser measure of accuracy where we focus on the ability of a system to generate at least one useful recommendation. A precision metric is not used as it would refer to the proportion of correct-to-all recommendations thus not being as revealing an accuracy measure as the two currently employed.

4.4.4. RECOMMENDATION ACCURACY

In the following experiments we measure the recall and hit rate statistics across all profile datasets and test algorithms. In addition, we distinguish between two types of accuracy experiment depending on whether the training profiles and the test profiles are taken from the same original profile set. For example, in the intra-dataset experiment the training profiles and the test profiles come from the same dataset; that is, if the recommender contains training profiles from the Play dataset then its recommendations are evaluated with respect to the corresponding test profiles in the Play dataset. In contrast, in the inter-dataset experiment a recommender that contains training profiles from the Play dataset might be evaluated with respect to test profiles from another dataset. By comparing respective results, it is possible to evaluate the degree to which explicit ratings are useful predictors of real user behaviors such as recording and playback.

4.4.4.1. *Intra-Dataset Accuracy*

Figures 4.3 & 4.4 present the recall and hit rate scores for the various recommendation algorithms across the six datasets. For example, the recall results for the PTV-Plus dataset indicates that the DR algorithm, which exploits similarity knowledge derived directly from the Apriori association rules, achieves a recall of 20%. In other words, on average, 20% of test profile items are present in the recommendations made by DR. In fact DR outperforms all of the algorithm variations that exploit indirect rules generated by rule-chaining. These indirect algorithms achieve a maximum recall of 18%. In turn the basic collaborative filtering algorithm, CF, which does not avail of the mined similarity knowledge, achieves a significantly lower recall 8%. A similar ordering of algorithms is found in the hit rate values for the PTVPlus dataset. The difference between indirect and CF algorithms as well as direct and CF algorithms was found to be significant at the 99% level. These results

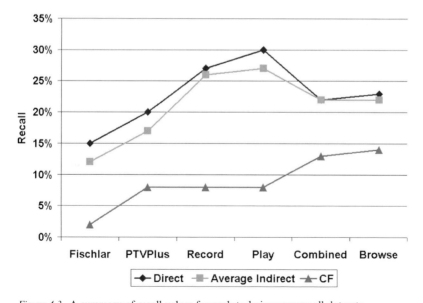

Figure 4.3. A summary of recall values for each technique across all datasets.

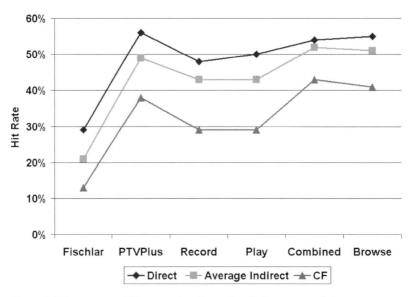

Figure 4.4. A summary of hit rate values for each technique across all datasets.

highlight the usefulness of the mined similarity knowledge during recommendation; in the PTVPlus dataset the DR recall value, with its direct similarity knowledge, is 2.5 times greater than CF recall results. However, the indirect recall and hit rate values are less than those for DR. This suggests that the additional similarity knowledge available to the indirect algorithms is of lower quality that the knowledge available to DR.

The remaining datasets follow a similar trend to that found for PTVPlus, with direct methods outperforming indirect, and indirect outperforming standard collaborative filtering. Again, we found that the difference between algorithms using our association rule approach and standard CF algorithms was significant at the 99% level.

Looking at Figures 4.3 & 4.4 from an overlying algorithm viewpoint, the dominance of DR over indirect over CF techniques should be clear—there is a clear and consistent separation between the DR and indirect recall (or hit rate) values and the CF recall (or hit rate) values.

Overall these summary results indicate that there is considerable added-value to be derived from the newly generated similarity knowledge when it comes to recommendation accuracy. On average, across all datasets, the DR recall value is 3.4 times that of the CF recall value, and the DR hit rate value is 1.6 times the CF hit rate value. The fact that the direct similarity knowledge outperforms the indirect knowledge perhaps should not be so surprising. It indicates that the chaining procedure has a tendency to produce lower-quality similarity knowledge—this may be expected given the nature of the chaining and confidence combination process.

4.4.4.2. *Inter-Dataset Accuracy*

In the previous section we tested and evaluated recommendation accuracy by drawing training and test profiles from the same dataset. Because of the relationship that exists between the five Fischlàr datasets (Fischlàr, Play, Record, Browse, Combined) it is also possible, and informative, to examine the impact of using various combinations of explicit and implicit (behavioral) profiles during the training and testing parts of the evaluation. In Figure 4.5, the recall results are displayed for recommender systems that are trained using explicit Fischlàr profiles, but tested using implicit profiles.

The results show that even though the recommender is generating recommendations from explicit, ratings-based profiles, recall is greater when the test profiles are from an implicit dataset. For example, we see that the recall of DR, using Fischlàr training profiles, but tested with respect to Fischlàr Play profiles, is about 26%. Compare this to a 15% recall value when the test profiles are explicit ratings-based profiles. The same result is found across all of the behavioral profiles, indicating that, in general, explicit ratings-based profiles are just as capable of predicting real behaviors (recording, playback and browsing) as they are at predicting future ratings. Of course it is this prediction of real behaviors that is ultimately the most important consideration in a system like Fischlàr; after all, it is more important for Fischlàr to recommend programs that a user will ultimately record, play, or browse than programs they will simply rate positively.

When we compare the recall results in Figure 4.5 to corresponding recall results in Figure 4.3, we find only marginal differences. For example, as mentioned above

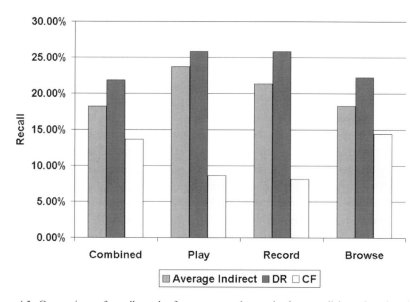

Figure 4.5. Comparison of recall results for recommenders trained on explicit, ratings-based Fischlàr profiles, but tested on implicit, behavioral profiles.

the recall of DR, using explicit training profiles, but tested with Play profiles, is 26%. In Figure 4.3 we see that the same DR technique achieves a recall value of 30% when it uses Play profiles for training and testing. In other words, the explicit ratings-based profiles are almost as good predictors of real behavior as the behavioral profiles themselves.

4.5. Implications

The techniques developed in this chapter and their application in the Digital TV space have highlighted a number of important issues, not just for personalized EPGs but for recommender systems in general. In this section, we discuss these broader implications as they relate to profiling, sparsity and recommendation diversity.

4.5.1. EXPLICIT vs IMPLICIT PROFILING

Results from Section 4.4 indicate that playback, recording, browsing and combined behaviors in Fìschlàr serve as competent interest indicators when it comes to profiling user preferences. In each case we find an increase in the quality of recommendations made from profiles containing implicit information. Moreover, the scale of this increase is largest in the case of our new technique, due to the fact that this recommender directly mines the profiles in order to generate program similarity knowledge as the basis for recommendations. The availability of the higher quality implicit profiles helps to improve the similarity rules used by our technique when compared to the similarity rules mined from explicit profiles. We believe this more than justifies the validity of using implicit profiling in future applications requiring DTV user input.

4.5.2. DENSITY vs ACCURACY

At the beginning of this chapter we explained that one of our primary motivations in this work is to look for ways to overcome the sparsity problems associated with typical profile spaces. Any set of ratings-based profiles can be translated into a ratings matrix, with each row corresponding to an individual profile and each column corresponding to an individual item, so that user ratings are represented as values with the appropriate cells in the matrix. The sparsity problem occurs because most of the cells in a typical ratings matrix are empty—most users have rated very few items; conversely most items are rated by very few users.

Sarwar et al. [21] suggest measuring the density of such a matrix for a particular dataset as shown in Equation (1.5). We can now rank-order different datasets according to the degree to which they suffer from the sparsity problem—this results in the sequence Fìschlàr (0.00358), PTV-Plus (0.00575), Record (0.00809), Play (0.00843), Combined (0.01182) and Browse (0.01191) in increasing density.

$$\text{Density (Dataset)} = \frac{\text{Number of nonzero entries}}{\text{Total number of entries}} \qquad (1.5)$$

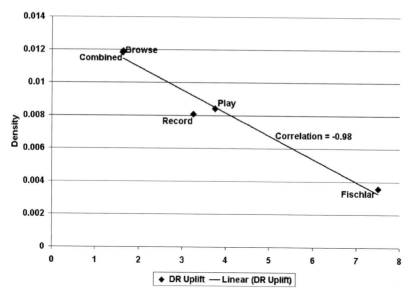

Figure 4.6. Dataset density vs recall uplift.

Interestingly there appears to be a strong correlation between the success of our new similarity-based techniques (relative to the standard collaborative technique) and the density of the ratings matrix in a given dataset. This can be seen more clearly in Figure 4.6, which graphs dataset density against the increase in DR recall relative to CF recall for the Fischlàr explicit and implicit datasets. For example, DR recall is more than 7 times that of CF recall in the explicit Fischlàr dataset, with its density of 0.00358. A similar graph can be obtained for the indirect recommendation techniques, as well as for the hit rate metric. Moreover, all of these graphs indicate a strong correlation between dataset density and the increase in recommendation accuracy (recall or hit rate) for our new similarity-based techniques relative to the standard CF method. For example, the correlation between the DR increase for the dataset density is -0.98.

This suggests that datasets with high degrees of sparsity (low density) are likely to offer the greatest opportunity for improvements on collaborative recommendation by exploiting our similarity-based techniques. Clearly, this particular result is of key importance for recommender systems in general if the relationship holds outside of the TV domain. Of course there is nothing special about the TV related profile datasets used here that would lead us to suspect that this density relationship would not hold in other domains. In fact, in recent work we have demonstrated a similar relationship for movie recommenders [2].

4.5.3.   RECOMMENDATION DIVERSITY

A more recent evaluation concern has arisen when assessing the quality of various recommendation algorithms; this concern relates to the issue of *recommendation diversity*. Recommendation diversity refers to the degree of dissimilarity that exists between the items in a given recommendation set. Higher dissimilarity means higher diversity, and higher diversity means that the recommendations made provide greater coverage of the item space. Diversity can be important in many recommendation scenarios where the number of recommended items is necessarily limited. For example, recommender systems designed for use on the mobile Internet will be restricted by the limited screen space available to current and future mobile handsets. If only a few recommendations can be made, then there is limited value if they are all very similar to each other. Increasing recommendation diversity may have an impact on recommendation accuracy, however, and as such the critical objective is to develop recommendation techniques that maximize recommendation accuracy and diversity.

The traditional collaborative filtering recommendation strategy benefits from some natural diversity advantages relative to content-based or case-based techniques [18, 22], and recent research on content-based recommenders has shown that it is possible to increase recommendation diversity while maintaining recommendation accuracy [28, 29]. Recent experiments in the movie domain have shown that our new technique has comparable diversity in recommendations with traditional collaborative filtering methods; we will shortly be conducting similar experiments in the DTV domain to corroborate the claim that both diversity and accuracy can be preserved in recommendations.

4.6. Towards Personalized Broadcasting: Fìschlàr News

The research presented in this chapter deals with the personalized retrieval of programs in which the complete program is the personalized and retrieved unit. In contrast, our current research concentrates on personalization and retrieval of finer-grained units of audio-visual programs such as scenes from general TV content or stories from TV news. The aim is to construct personalized news magazine broadcasts for users [25]. This new direction requires advances in automatic scene and story segmentation of audio-visual content and advances in collaborative- and content-based recommendation techniques for semantic sub-units of audio-visual programs. It also requires work on the development of user interfaces to desktop, PDA and other mobile devices in order to really take advantage of this new level of access and personalization, which we believe will better satisfy users' needs [34–36]. These interfaces are necessary as they provide usage information to guide the development and evaluation of recommendation algorithms and they also provide feedback into personalization from active users.

In this work we are building upon the existing *Fìschlàr News* Retrieval System [8] by developing, evaluating and integrating story-based access to TV news. Our *Fìschlàr-News-Stories* system automatically captures local Irish TV news each day and analyzes the captured video so that it can be browsed and played online using a PC or a mobile PDA. We currently have a manual story segmentation system running with a desktop interface, which allows us to capture usage profiles and rating from users, and which we are using to evaluate recommendation techniques for this type of content. We also have developed and are improving upon fully automatic news story segmentation outlined below.

4.6.1. AUTOMATIC NEWS STORY SEGMENTATION

Automatic news story segmentation is performed in *Fìschlàr-News-Stories* using a Support Vector Machine (SVM) classifier that takes as its input shot boundaries, detected advertisement breaks, detected faces and anchorperson shot clustering, and provides as output a set of story boundaries [8]. These story boundaries are integrated with the content's MPEG-7 description, which like Fìschlàr-TV [9] can be visualized in a device-independent manner using XSL transformations. We are evaluating this technique as part of TRECVID 2003, the TREC video track [10] with a collection of over 60 hours of ABC and CNN broadcast news. The instance of this classifier used in *Fìschlàr-News-Stories* has been trained solely on local evening news and therefore should be able to achieve high performance on this specific content. We are also working on further improvements on the accuracy of this detector, such as the inclusion of more features to be used as input into the SVM.

4.6.2. USER INTERFACES FOR NEWS STORY RETRIEVAL

News stories provide a logical high-level unit for browsing and searching of a collection of television news. At its simplest level when a user accesses *Fìschlàr-News-Stories* she is provided with a list of stories for today and can also view stories for any other date (see Figure 4.7). As part of future work we intend that this presentation of stories

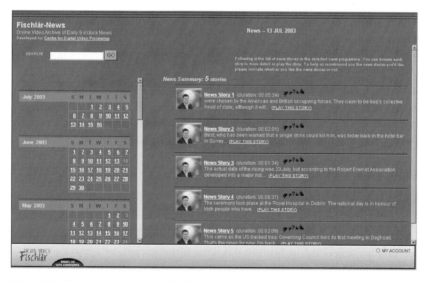

Figure 4.7. News stories on a specific day.

Figure 4.8. Browsing a specific news story.

will take into account recommended stories ranked by the personalization engine using techniques described elsewhere in this chapter. Similar to the Fìschlàr-TV system where programs are rated and personalized, news stories in *Fìschlàr-News-Stories* can be rated, played and browsed. Browsing the story displays its closed-captions and keyframes (see Figure 4.8) and also provides a list of related stories which the user can browse. Currently, the calculation of 'related stories' is implemented using text similarity among closed captions but we are exploring the idea of taking account of user-story recommendations in combination with content-based matching.

We currently provide story searching in *Fìschlàr-News-Stories* using a simple text query with results displayed as a list of ranked stories that match the query. This provides an alternative entry point into story exploration and browsing than selection of a date. The grouping of results based on their similarity might also be beneficial.

Currently, as an additional service and incentive to use *Fìschlàr-News-Stories*, we alert our users to the first three stories of the news each day with an email. The purpose of this email is to entice them to use the Fìschlàr news story retrieval system and as a result to produce user ratings, browse logs, and play logs, which will form the basis of our development and evaluation of our news story personalization engine. In future, this email itself will be personalized to recommend stories each day to users.

4.6.3. RECOMMENDATION ENGINE FOR AUDIO-VISUAL STORIES

The techniques described in Section 4.3 have already been adapted to operate using the new data available through this story based system. Due to the presence of both implicit and explicit profiling within this system, we hope to conduct tests similar to those described in Section 4.4. Once the system is fully integrated, we aim to conduct user feedback surveys to analyze the usefulness and usability of the system.

We hope that this work will provide a good insight into personalization for video news stories and will lead to synergy between news story retrieval and recommendation systems.

4.7. Conclusions

The Digital TV domain is a fertile ground for recommender systems research [11–13]. Digital TV subscribers are faced with an important information overload problem: selecting relevant programming content from a sea of possibilities. This represents a genuine business need and serves as a strong motivator for the development of personalization solutions that attempt to respond better to the personal preferences of individual users and recommender systems are an important part of these solutions.

In this chapter we have made a number of important contributions. We have shown the usefulness of a novel recommendation technique which leverages the use of association-rule mining and case-based methods in recommender systems. Using this technique, recommendation accuracy is higher than with traditional CF approaches, with greater benefit seen among sparser datasets. We believe that this approach provides a solid foundation for the single-user model of recommendation but that the techniques are general enough to apply for other models of personalization, such as for groups of people [26]. By comparing the use of implicit and explicit profiling through the Fìschlàr system, we have seen that implicit interest indicators are comparable to explicit interest indicators in terms of recommendation accuracy, thus creating a chance to alleviate the burden of explicit ratings from DTV users.

Finally we have reported our recent work which is exploring the use of our recommendation techniques for the compilation of personalized news programs instead of personalized guides.

Acknowledgments

The authors would like to thank Informatics Research Initiative of Enterprise Ireland for their support.

References

1. O' Sullivan, D., Wilson, D. C. and Smyth, B.: 2002b, Using Collaborative Filtering Data in Case–Based Recommendation. In: S. M. Haller and G. Simmons (eds.): *Proceedings of the Fifteenth International Florida Artificial Intelligence Research Society Conference.* May 14–16, 2002, Pensacola Beach, Florida, USA, pp. 121–128.
2. O' Sullivan, D., Wilson, D. C. and Smyth, B.: 2002a, Improving Case-Based Recommendation: A Collaborative Filtering Approach. In: S. Craw and A. D. Preece (eds.): *Advances in Case-Based Reasoning, 6th European Conference, ECCBR 2002 Aberdeen*, Scotland, UK, September 4–7, 2002, Proceedings, Vol. 2416 of Lecture Notes in Computer Science, pp. 278–291.

3. O' Sullivan, D., Smyth, B., Wilson, D. C. McDonald, K. and Smeaton, A.: 2003, Improving the Quality of the Personalised Electronic Program Guide, In: L. Ardisonno, M. Maybury and Alfred Kobsa (eds.): *UMUAI Special Issue on User Modeling and Personalization for Television*. In Press.
4. Wilson, D. C., Smyth, B. and O'Sullivan, D.: 2003, Sparsity Reduction in Collaborative Recommendation: A Case-Based Approach, In: I. Russell and S. Haller (eds.): *International Journal of Pattern Recognition and Artificial Intelligence (IJPRAI)*, **17** (5), pp. 863–884, World Scientific, 2003.
5. O'Sullivan, D., Smyth, B. and Wilson, D.: 2003b, Explicit vs Implicit Profiling - A Case-Study in Electronic Programme Guides, In: G. Gottlob and T. Walsh (eds.): *Proceedings of the Eighteenth International Joint Conference on Artificial Intelligence*, (IJCAI–03), Acapulco, Mexico, pp. 1351–1356, Morgan Kaufmann, 2003.
6. O' Sullivan, D., Smyth, B. and Wilson, D.: 2003a, Preserving Recommender Accuracy and Diversity in Sparse Datasets, In: S. Haller and I. Russell (eds.): *International Journal of Artificial Intelligence Techniques (IJAIT)*. In Press.
7. Smeaton, A. F., Murphy, N., O' Connor, N. E., Marlow, S., Lee, H., McDonald, K., Browne, P. and Ye, J.: 2001, The Físchlàr Digital Video System: A Digital Library of Broadcast TV Programmes, In: *Proceedings of the 1st ACM/IEEE-CS Joint Conference on Digital Libraries*, pp. 312–313.
8. Smeaton, A. F., Lee, H., O'Connor, N., Marlow, S. and Murphy, N.: 2003, TV News Story Segmentation, Personalisation and Recommendation, In: *Intelligent Multimedia Knowledge Management 2003 AAAI Spring Symposium*, Technical Report SS-03-04, AAAI Press, 2003.
9. Smeaton, A. F., Murphy, N., O'Connor, N., Marlow, S., Lee, H., McDonald, K., Browne, P. and Ye, J.: 2001, The Físchlàr Digital Video System: A Digital Library of Broadcast TV Programmes, In: *Proceedings of JCDL 2001 – ACM+IEEE Joint Conference on Digital Libraries*, Roanoke, VA , 24–28 June 2001.
10. Smeaton, A. F. and Over, P.: 2003, TRECVID: Benchmarking the Effectiveness of Information Retrieval Tasks on Digital Video, In: *Proceeding of the International Conference on Image and Video Retrieval*, Urbana, IL, USA, July 2003, Springer, LNCS 2728, pp. 19–27.
11. Ardissono, L. and Faihe, Y. (eds.): 2001, In: *Proceedings of the 1st Workshop on Personalisation in Future TV, UM, 2001*, Sonthofen, Germany.
12. Ardissono, L. and Buczak, A. (eds.): 2002, In: *Proceedings of the 2nd Workshop on Personalisation in Future TV, AH 2002*, Malaga, Spain.
13. Ardissono, L. and Maybury, M. (eds.): 2003, In: *Proceedings of the 3rd Workshop on Personalisation in Future TV, UM 2003*, Johnstown, PA, USA.
14. Buczak, A. L., Zimmerman, J. and Kurapati, K.: 2002, Personalization: Improving Ease-of-Use, Trust and Accuracy of a TV show Recommender, In: L. Ardissono and A. Buczak (eds.): *Proceedings of the 2nd Workshop on Personalisation in Future TV*, Malaga, Spain, pp. 9–18.
15. Konstan, J. A., Miller, B. N., Maltz, D., Herlocker, J. L., Gordon, L. R. and Riedl, J.: 1997, GroupLens: Applying Collaborative Filtering to Usenet News, In: D. Crawford (ed.): *Communications of the ACM*, **40** (3), pp. 77–87.
16. Smyth, B. and Cotter. P.: 2001, Personalised Electronic Programme Guides, *Artificial Intelligence Magazine*, **21** (2), pp. 210–217.
17. Balabanovi, M. and Shoham, Y.: 1997, Fab: Content-based, Collaborative Recommendation, In: D. Crawford (ed.): *Communications of the ACM*, **40** (3), pp. 66–72.
18. Wilson, D. C. and Leake, D. B.: 1998, Maintaining Case-Based Reasoners: Dimensions And Directions, *Computational Intelligence*, **17** (2).

19. Hipp, J. Güntzer, U. and Nakhaeizadeh, G.: 2000, Mining Association Rules: Deriving a Superior Algorithm by Analyzing Today's Approaches, In: D. A. Zighed, H. J. Komorowski and J. M. Zytkow (eds.): *Proceedings of the 4th European Symposium on Principles of Data Mining and Knowledge Discovery*, pp. 159–168.

20. Agrawal, R., Mannila, H., Srikant, R., Toivonen, H. and Verkamo, A. I.: 1996, Fast Discovery of Association Rules. In: U. M. Fayyad, G. Piatetsky-Shapiro, P. Smyth and R. Uthurusamy (eds.): *Advances in Knowledge Discovery and Data Mining*. AAAI Press, Chapter 12, pp. 307–328.

21. Sarwar, B., Karypis, G., Konstan, J. and Riedl, J.: 2001, Item-based Collaborative Filtering Recommendation Algorithms. In: V. Y. Shen and N. Saito and M. R. Lyu and M. E. Zurko (eds.): *Proceedings of the Tenth International Conference on World Wide Web*. pp. 285–295.

22. Hayes, C., Cunningham, P. and Smyth, B.: 2001, A Case-Based View of Automated Collaborative Filtering. In: D. W. Aha and I. Watson (eds.): *Case-Based Reasoning Research and Development, 4th International Conference on Case-Based Reasoning, ICCBR 2001*, Vancouver, BC, Canada, July 30 – August 2, 2001, Vol. 2080 of Lecture Notes in Computer Science. pp. 234–248.

23. Billsus, D. and Pazzani, M. J.: 1998, Learning Collaborative Information Filters. In: J. W. Shavlik (ed.): *Proceedings of the Fifteenth International Conference on Machine Learning (ICML 1998)*, Madison, Wisconson, USA, July 24–27, 1998. pp. 46–54.

24. Hara, Y., Tomomune, Y. and Shigemori, M.: 2003, Categorization of Japanese TV Viewers Based on Program Genres They Watch, In this volume.

25. Maybury, M., Greiff, W., Boykin, S., Ponte, J., McHenry, C. and Ferro, L.: 2003, Personalcasting: Tailored Broadcast News, In this volume.

26. Masthoff, J.: 2003, Group modeling: Selecting a Sequence of Television Items to Suit a Group of Viewers, In this volume.

27. Burke, R.: 2000, A Case-Based Reasoning Approach to Collaborative Filtering, In E. Blanzieri and L. Portinale (eds.): *Proceedings of EWCBR-00*, Trento, Italy, 1898, Springer, pp. 370–379.

28. Bradley, K. and Smyth, B.: 2001, Improving Recommendation Diversity, *Proceedings of (AICS 2001)*, Limerick, Ireland, pp. 85–94.

29. McSherry, D.: 2001, Increasing Recommendation Diversity Without Loss of Similarity, *Proceedings of the 6th UK CBR Workshop*, December 2001, Cambridge, UK, pp. 23–31.

30. Ardissono, L., Gena, C. and Torasso, P.: 2003, User Modeling and Recommendation Techniques for Personalised Electronic Program Guides, In: L. Ardisonno, M. Maybury and A. Kobsa (eds.): In this volume.

31. Zimmerman, J., Kurapati, K., Buczak, A. L., Schaffer, D., Martino, J. and Gutti, S.: 2003, TV Personalisation System: Design of a TV Show Recommender Engine and Interface, In this volume.

32. Smyth, B. and Cotter, P.: 2003, The Evolution of the Personalized Electronic Programme Guide, In this volume.

33. Dimitrova, N., Zimmerman, J. and Janevski, A.: 2003, Content Augmentation of Personalized Entertainment Experience, In this volume.

34. Pittarello, F.: 2003, The Time–Pillars World: A 3D Paradigm for the New Enlarged TV Information Domain, In this volume.

35. Rambhia, A., Wen, G. and Cheung, S.: 2003, Content Morphing: A Novel System for Broadcast Delivery of Personalizable Content, In this volume.

36. van Barneveld, J. and van Setten, M.: 2003, Designing Usable Interfaces for TV Recommender Systems, In this volume.

Chapter 5

Group Modeling: Selecting a Sequence of Television Items to Suit a Group of Viewers

JUDITH MASTHOFF
University of Brighton, UK. e-mail: judith.masthoff@brighton.ac.uk

Abstract. Watching television tends to be a social activity. So, adaptive television needs to adapt to *groups* of users rather than to *individual* users. In this paper, we discuss different strategies for combining individual user models to adapt to groups, some of which are inspired by Social Choice Theory. In a first experiment, we explore how *humans* select a sequence of items for a group to watch, based on data about the individuals' preferences. The results show that humans use some of the strategies such as the Average Strategy (a.k.a. Additive Utilitarian), the Average Without Misery Strategy and the Least Misery Strategy, and care about fairness and avoiding individual misery. In a second experiment, we investigate how satisfied people believe they would be with sequences chosen by different strategies, and how their satisfaction corresponds with that predicted by a number of satisfaction functions. The results show that subjects use normalization, deduct misery, and use the ratings in a non-linear way. One of the satisfaction functions produced reasonable, though not completely correct predictions. According to our subjects, the sequences produced by five strategies give satisfaction to all individuals in the group. The results also show that subjects put more emphasis than expected on showing the best rated item to each individual (at a cost of misery for another individual), and that the ratings of the first and last items in the sequence are especially important. In a final experiment, we explore the influence viewing an item can have on the ratings of other items. This is important for deciding the order in which to present items. The results show an effect of both mood and topical relatedness.

Key words. adaptation, group modeling, interactive television, recommender, social choice

1. Introduction

Interactive television offers the possibility of personalized viewing experiences. Different domains have been identified in which this personalization would have a great impact, such as education (Masthoff and Luckin, 2002), news (Maybury et al., 2004), advertising (Lekakos et al., 2001), and electronic program guides (Cotter and Smyth, 2000). Adapting television to *individual* viewers is a topic in itself, and a lot of research has already been done, particularly in the area of electronic program guides (e.g., O'Sullivan et al., 2004). This research tends to build on decades of work on content-based and social filtering. In this paper, we will explore an even more difficult issue: adaptation to a *group* of viewers. We believe this to be essential for interactive television as, in contrast to the use of PCs, television viewing is largely a family or social activity (Barwise and Ehrenberg,

L. Ardissono et al. (eds.), Personalized Digital Television, 93–141, 2004.
© *2004 Kluwer Academic Publishers. Printed in the Netherlands.*

1988; Kasari and Nurmi, 1992). Unfortunately, television-viewing statistics do not include data on the average number of people watching television together and who watches television with whom (as also noted by Gillard, 1999). It is very likely to be culturally dependent, as the number of televisions per household varies widely. According to a large research study in the UK (Livingstone and Bovill, 1999), television is the medium most often shared with family. Watching television together is top of the list of activities shared between parents and children, and more than two thirds of children watch their favorite programme with somebody else, nearly always family. Children most often watch with their siblings (Van Evra, 1998). Young people would like to watch television with friends, though (due to a lack of resource) many do not manage to do so (Livingstone and Bovill, 1999). Given the rising number of televisions in bedrooms it is likely that watching television with friends will be an increasingly popular activity. Already, television is the most popular conversation topic of young people with friends (Livingstone and Bovill, 1999). For these reasons, we believe that adaptive television should be able to *adapt to groups of people* watching together. These groups can be quite heterogeneous, and age, gender, intelligence, and personality influence what types of TV programmes people enjoy (Kotler et al., 2001; Gillard, 1999; Livingstone and Bovill, 1999). The question then arises how one can adapt to a group of viewers, in such a way that each individual enjoys (and in educational programs, benefits from) the broadcast.

2. Strategies for Combining User Models

User modeling has been widely studied, particularly the modeling of user preferences (directly or indirectly via observation and inference) (see UMUAI journal, User Modeling conferences). In contrast, *group modeling*—combining individual user models to model a group—has hardly been investigated in our field. There are only three main adaptive systems that use it: MUSICFX (McCarty and Anagnost, 1998), POLYLENS (O'Conner et al., 2001), and INTRIGUE (Ardissono et al., 2002). MUSICFX is used in a company's fitness center to select background music to suit a group of people working out at any given time. POLYLENS is a group recommender extension of MOVIELENS, which recommends movies based on an individual's taste as inferred from ratings and social filtering. It allows users to create groups and ask for a recommendation for that group. INTRIGUE recommends places to visit for tourist groups taking into account characteristics of subgroups within that group (such as children and disabled). Though some exploratory evaluation of MUSICFX and POLYLENS has taken place, for none of these systems it has been investigated how effective their group modeling strategies really are, and what the effect would be of using a different strategy. Besides, the application domains of both POLYLENS and MUSICFX differ from television viewing in the sense that these systems do not need to select a group of items: people normally only see one movie per evening, and music stations can play forever.[*] For INTRIGUE, on

---

[*]This would have been different if MUSICFX selected individual songs rather than radio stations.

the other hand, it is quite likely that a tourist group would visit multiple attractions during their trip, but the selection of a balanced sequence has not been addressed yet. Our view on adaptive interactive television is that reasonably *small* video segments would be concatenated (this is in line with Maybury et al., 2004, who mention that their newsitems on average are only 51 s long). The smaller the segments the more adaptation and real interactivity can take place.

Though group modeling has hardly been studied in our field, the related issue of *social choice* (also called group decision making)—deciding what is best for a group given the opinions of individuals—has been studied extensively in economics, politics, sociology, and mathematics (see, e.g. Condorcet, 1785; Pattanaik, 1971; Taylor, 1995). Their construction of a *social welfare function* is very similar to our group modeling problem. Other areas in which the problem has been studied are Meta-Search, Database Middleware, Collaborative Filtering, and Multi-Agent systems. In Meta-Search, the ranking lists produced by multiple search engines need to be combined into one list (they call this the problem of rank aggregation). See, for instance, Dwork et al. (2001), and Cohen et al. (1999). Dwork et al. base their work on social choice theory, and use a variant of the method of Kemeny, which uses an extended Condorcet principle (see Section 2.2. for an explanation of the ordinary Condorcet principle, and why we object to it). In Database Middleware, objects have to be ordered where each object has numerical values for multiple fields (see for instance, Fagin et al., 2003). In Collaborative Filtering, preferences of a group of individuals have to be aggregated to produce a predicted preference for somebody outside the group. See Pennock et al. (2000) for an explanation of how social choice theory applies to collaborative filtering. In multi-agent systems, agents need to take decisions that are not only rational from an individual's point of view, but also from a social point of view. See Hogg and Jennings (1999) for a discussion of social rationality for agents and its links to Social Choice Theory. See Ephrati and Rosenschein (1996) for how a social decision mechanism (namely the Clarke Tax mechanism) can be used to reach consensus between multiple non-cooperative (possibly cheating) agents.

In this section, we will discuss some of the issues, and present a number of example strategies.

2.1. FOCUSING OUR PROBLEM AND INTRODUCING AN EXAMPLE

Assume the television has a set of items to choose from. These can be news items, quiz questions, MTV music clips, television programs, etc. For our discussion we will just call them items (and video clips in the experiments). Assume the television needs to adapt to a group of viewers. Assume the television knows who the viewers are, and the system has preference ratings for each of them (say from 10, really like, to 1, really hate). The problem now is which items should the television show, given that it has time for a certain number but not all of them?

An example of this situation is given in Table I. There are three viewers, John, Adam and Mary, and the television has ten items to select from (A to J). For each

Table I. Example ratings for a group of three viewers

	A	B	C	D	E	F	G	H	I	J
John	10	4	3	6	10	9	6	8	10	8
Adam	1	9	8	9	7	9	6	9	3	8
Mary	10	5	2	7	9	8	5	6	7	6

item, it knows the preference ratings, for instance, John really likes A, but Adam really hates it. The problem is what should the TV show if it has time for only one item? What if it has time for two items? Etc.

The example in Table I will be used to illustrate the strategies described below, and will also be used in the experiments presented in Sections 3 and 4.

Note that we have made a number of simplifications: we have assumed that a number of problems have been solved while actually they are still a focus of much research. For example:

- *How will the television know who is watching it?* Solutions have been proposed in the form of an individual infrared card which registers viewers automatically (Lieberman et al., 1999), an individual token which you have to put on the television, a login procedure (which can take a conversational form, with the television asking who is watching it tonight), and a probabilistic mechanism using the time of day combined with a known probability of a viewer watching at that time (Goren-Bar and Glinansky, 2002).

- *How will the preferences of the individual users be determined?* Social, and content-based filtering can be used, combined with stereotypes (see many papers in Ardissono and Buczak, 2002). Obviously, there is a complication in that it is difficult to make inferences from actions when a group watches the television, but actions at times the user watches alone could be used combined with a probabilistic model when watching in company. Plua and Jameson (2002) describe a mechanism by which groups of people who know each other well can help each other to specify their preferences. An additional complication is that an individual's ratings might depend on the group they are in. For instance, a teenager might be very happy to watch a programme with his younger siblings, but might not want to see it when with his friends.

- *Dealing with differences in rating tendencies.* Not all people have the same rating behavior. Some people only use the ends of the scale, they either 'really hate' or 'really love' an item. Others only use the middle, never being very positive, and never being really negative. A '7' by Pete, who is always very negative, may be a far more positive review than a '9' by Tim, who likes everything. Note that similar differences may occur when ratings are inferred from viewing behavior. These differences in behavior should be taken into account when using ratings as input for a group model. One way to do this is to normalize them. Though we have not assumed the ratings of John, Adam and Mary to be completely comparable (and indeed some differences in rating tendencies can be seen in the example, e.g. between John and Adam), we have simplified our problem by giving all individuals 'reasonable' rating behaviors. For instance, none of them only uses the ends of the scale.

- *Dealing with uncertainty.* The preferences as determined by filtering mechanisms do not have to be correct (though accuracy is growing). For the research in this paper, we will assume the ratings to be accurate. We will revisit this issue in the Areas for Further Work section in the conclusions.

- *Changing groups.* We assume that the group remains the same during the whole sequence. If one member of the group needs to leave early (a child, for instance, who has to go to bed) then it is likely that the preferences of that person should have greater weight when they are present.

- *Dealing with multidimensionality.* Often, you have ratings in multiple dimensions, rather than just one dimension. For instance, in adaptive instruction, there are many reasons for selecting an item, such as the student's existing knowledge (does it fulfill the prerequisites), learning goal and learning style, the educational flow (does it built on what has been explained before), etc. One way to match this onto the modeling as discussed above would be to construct a single rating for each item based on how it scores on these criteria. Masthoff (2003) describes a way in which the aggregation methods discussed in this paper can be used to aggregate ratings of different criteria.

- *How will the recommendations be presented to the group?* We assume that the television decides which items to show, so, does not give the viewers a choice. One kind of application we are considering is a personalized news program. So, instead of watching a news broadcast that is the same for all viewers (like the BBC news), you would watch a news program with items in it that are automatically selected for the group of people you are watching with. Most recommender systems, in contrast, would present their list of recommendations to the user, and different ways have been devised on how to do this. For instance, Zimmerman et al. (2002) discuss using celebrities (a photo combined with text) to present generated content recommendations (for instance, for an Electronic Program Guide).

All of these problems merit more research, but are beyond the scope of this paper.

2.2. DESIRABLE PROPERTIES

In Social Choice Theory, some consensus exists about desirable properties of voting systems, but it has been proven that no system can have all these properties (Arrow, 1950), and, arguably, this is why different voting systems exist in different countries, institutions, and societies (see Cranor, 1996, for about 20 of these, and Section 2.3 for a selection). One analysis of 27 democracies over a period of 45 years found a staggering 70 different voting systems being used for national elections (Lijphart, 1994).

Some examples of desirable properties that have been proposed:

- *Pareto rule* (Pareto, 1897).
  If at least one person prefers x to y and nobody prefers y to x, then x should
  be above y in the ranking. If nobody prefers x to y and nobody prefers y
  to x, then x and y should share a place in the ranking.
  In our example, everybody prefers F to G. Hence, F should precede G in the
  group list. Similarly, F should precede H, as John and Mary prefer it and Adam
  does not mind.
  In this manner, we find:

B should precede C	D should precede B,C,G
E should precede G,I	F should precede B,C,D,G,H,J
H should precede B,C,G,J	J should precede C,G

- *Anonymity* (May, 1952).
  If the ratings of two individuals are swapped for all alternatives, then the resulting sequence should remain the same. Note that dictatorship violates this rule,
  and that it can be well defended that in real life television viewing not everybody
  has to have equal rights all the time. For instance, if it is John's birthday than
  maybe it is fair to give John more satisfaction on that day than the others.
- *Positive Association.* (Arrow, 1951).
  If alternative x preceded alternative y in the sequence, then an increase in an
  individual's rating of x should maintain x's position before y in the sequence.
  If alternative x appeared equal to alternative y in the sequence, then an increase
  in an individual's rating of x should lead to x being before or equal to y in
  the sequence. Note that it is tempting to say that x should precede y in the
  latter case, but this is too strong a condition. For instance, if the sequence
  was determined on the basis of Plurality Voting (see below), then x and y could
  be equal because as many people preferred x to y as preferred y to x. Increasing
  the rating of x for one individual does not necessarily change this.
- *Condorcet winner criterion* (Condorcet, 1785).
  An alternative x is a Condorcet winner if for each other alternative y:
  x is preferred to y by the majority of individuals.
  The criterion states that if a Condorcet winner exists then it should *top the group
  list on its own.*
  A weaker version allows it to *share* the top of the group list.
  The criterion becomes stronger when modifying the Condorcet winner
  definition to
  'x is preferred *or equal* to y by the majority of individuals.'
  In our example, both E and A are Condorcet winners using this definition.
  We do not agree with this criterion (not even in its weakest form). Assume an item
  x is rated 10, 1, 10 (as A is in our example). Assume all other items are rated
  9, 9, 9. Item x is then a Condorcet winner, but it can be argued that it should
  not top the group list, given the misery it produces for the second individual.

Our resistance to the Condorcet winner criterion highlights another property we might want our voting systems to have:

- *Each individual's satisfaction with the results should be above a certain threshold.*

  When a sequence of items is selected for a group to watch, the individual's satisfaction could be measured at the end of the sequence, or, in a stronger version of this rule, at any moment in the sequence. Note that the latter does not necessarily mean that the individual's satisfaction with each item should be above a certain threshold, as satisfaction is considered in the *context* of the items shown so far. For instance, consider a sequence '8 9 3 10'. If we want to measure satisfaction at any moment in the sequence, then we would have to measure the satisfaction after having seen '8', after having seen '8 9', '8 9 3', and '8 9 3 10'. The satisfaction of the individual after having seen '8 9 3' could well be higher than the satisfaction with '3' on its own, so this sequence might pass this criterion, while a sequence '3 8 9 10' might fail.

We will need to determine empirically whether typical TV viewers share our negative feelings about the Condorcet winner criterion, and whether they agree with our individual satisfaction rule.

2.3. EXAMPLE STRATEGIES

Many strategies, also called 'social choice rules', 'group decision rules', and 'rank aggregation functions', have been devised for reaching group decisions given individual opinions. We will discuss some simple ones (the first five originate from social choice theory and the latter five from our specific use), and illustrate them with the example introduced above. The example will show the 'group list' resulting from the strategy, a sequence indicating in which order the items would be chosen. Sometimes, two items score the same, like E and F in the Additive Utilitarian strategy. That is indicated in the group list by placing them between brackets. This means that either E is followed by F, or F followed by E. The main purpose of this section is to show that many different, all seemingly logical, strategies can be devised, all of which have quite distinct results when applying them to the example.

1. *Plurality Voting* (also called 'first past the post'). Each voter votes for his or her most preferred alternative. The alternative with the most votes wins. This method is, for instance, used in UK elections. When a sequence of alternatives needs to be selected, this method can be used repetitively: first, an election is held for the first place in the sequence, next for the second place, etc. In the example, John would like to vote for A, E, or I (all ratings of 10). Adam for B, D, F, or H, and Mary for A. Traditionally in Plurality voting, each individual has only one vote, so, John would have to decide whether to vote for

A, E, or I. If John were aware of the preferences of the others, then it is likely that he would vote for A, as with Mary's vote this would secure a majority. In our scenario, with only three individuals and ten items, it is quite likely that a vote would end in a tie (in contrast to politics, where the number of individuals tends to be a lot larger than the number of alternatives). If John were to vote for E or I, then all three individuals would vote for a different item, and there would be no winner. It would clearly be in John's interest to vote A. In our case, the television would decide on a choice for the group, and as the television would be aware of all individuals' preferences, it could easily accommodate strategic voting, to prevent ties. Our interpretation of Plurality Voting in this context will therefore be that rather than giving individuals one vote, we allow them to vote for all items that have the highest rating. In our example, this gives A two votes, and it becomes the start of the sequence. Next, John likes to vote for E or I, Adam for B, D, F, or H and Mary for E. With two votes E has most votes, and becomes second in the sequence.

	1	2	3	4	6	7	8	10
John	A,E,I	E,I	I	I	H,J	J	G	C
Adam	B,D,F,H	B,D,F,H	B,D,F,H	B,D,H	B,H	B	B	C
Mary	A	E	F	D,I	H,J	J	B,G	C
Group	A	E	F	D,I	H	J	B,G	C

Group List: AEF(I,D)HJ(B,G)C

Instead of using the method repetitively, each voter could vote for x alternatives (with x being the length of the sequence).

	1	2	3	4	5	6	7	8
John	AEI			AEIF	AEIFHJ		AEIFHJDG	
Adam	BDFH				BDFHJC		BDFHJCE	BDFHJCEG
Mary	A	AE	AEF	AEFDI		AEFDIHJ		AEFDIHJBG
Group	A	AE	AEF	F(AEDI)	F(AEDIHJ)	FHJ(AEDI)	FHJED(AI)	FHJEDG(AIB)

2. *Utilitarian Strategy.* Utility values for each alternative (expressing the expected happiness) are used, instead of just using ranking information (as in plurality voting). This can be done in multiple ways:
   Additive. Ratings are added, and the larger the sum the earlier the alternative appears in the sequence. Note that the resulting group list will be exactly the same as when taking the average of individual ratings. For this reason this strategy was called the 'Average strategy' in (Masthoff, 2002). This strategy (often in a weighted form, where weights are attached to individual ratings) is used in multi-agent systems (Hogg and Jennings, 1999) and Collaborative filtering.

This is also the strategy used in the INTRIGUE system (Ardissono et al., 2002), with a weighting depending on the number of people in the subgroup and the subgroup's relevance (children and disabled had a higher relevance).

	A	B	C	D	E	F	G	H	I	J
John	10	4	3	6	10	9	6	8	10	8
Adam	1	9	8	9	7	9	6	9	3	8
Mary	10	5	2	7	9	8	5	6	7	6
Group	21	18	13	22	26	26	17	23	20	22

Group List: (E, F) H (D, J) A I B G C

Multiplicative. Instead of *adding* the utilities, they are multiplied, and the larger the product the earlier the alternative appears in the sequence.

	A	B	C	D	E	F	G	H	I	J
John	10	4	3	6	10	9	6	8	10	8
Adam	1	9	8	9	7	9	6	9	3	8
Mary	10	5	2	7	9	8	5	6	7	6
Group	100	180	48	378	630	648	180	432	210	384

Group List: F E H J D I (B, G) A C

A disadvantage of the utilitarian strategy is that an individual viewer might always lose out, because their opinion happens to be a minority view. This is more likely to cause problems the larger the group. After all, in a small group the opinion of each individual will have a large impact on the average/product.

3. *Borda Count* (Borda, 1781). Points are awarded to each alternative according to its position in the individual's preference list: the alternative at the bottom of the list gets zero points, the next one up one point, etc. For instance, in our example John has the lowest rating for C, and hence, C is awarded 0 points. A problem arises when an individual has multiple alternatives with the same rating. We have decided to distribute the points. So, for example, in Mary's list B and G share the place one up from the bottom and get $(1+2)/2 = 1.5$ points each. To obtain the group preference ordering, the points awarded for the individuals are added up.

	A	B	C	D	E	F	G	H	I	J
John	8	1	0	2.5	8	6	2.5	4.5	8	4.5
Adam	0	7.5	4.5	7.5	3	7.5	2	7.5	1	4.5
Mary	9	1.5	0	5.5	8	7	1.5	3.5	5.5	3.5
Group	17	10	4.5	15.5	19	20.5	6	15.5	14.5	12.5

Group List: F E A(H, D) I J B G C

4. *Copeland Rule* (Copeland, 1951). This is a form of majority voting. It orders
the alternatives according to the Copeland index: the number of times an alternative beats other alternatives minus the number of times it loses to other
alternatives. For instance, in the example A beats B as both John and Mary
prefer it.

	A	B	C	D	E	F	G	H	I	J
A	0	–	–	–	0	–	–	–	0	–
B	+	0	–	+	+	+	0	+	+	+
C	+	+	0	+	+	+	+	+	+	+
D	+	–	–	0	+	+	–	0	0	–
E	0	–	–	–	0	–	–	–	–	–
F	+	–	–	–	+	0	–	–	–	–
G	+	0	–	+	+	+	0	+	+	+
H	+	–	–	0	+	+	–	0	+	–
I	0	–	–	0	+	+	–	–	0	–
J	+	–	–	+	+	+	–	+	+	0
Index	+7	–6	–9	+1	+8	+5	–6	0	+3	–3

Group List: E A F I D H J (B, G) C

Note that in the example the resulting group list is almost identical to the one
resulting from repetitive plurality voting.

5. *Approval Voting*. Voters are allowed to vote for as many alternatives as
they wish. This is intended to promote the election of moderate alternatives: alternatives that are not strongly disliked. This type of voting is used
by several professional societies, like the IEEE. In our example, we could
assume that John, Mary, and Adam vote for all alternatives with a rating
above a certain threshold. They could vote for all alternatives with a rating
higher than 5, as this means voting for all alternatives they like at least
a little bit.

Threshold 5.

	A	B	C	D	E	F	G	H	I	J
John	1			1	1	1	1	1	1	1
Adam		1	1	1	1	1	1	1		1
Mary	1			1	1	1		1	1	1
Group	2	1	1	3	3	3	2	3	2	3

Group List: (D, E, F, H, J) (G, A, I) (B, C)

Threshold 6.

	A	B	C	D	E	F	G	H	I	J
John	1				1	1		1	1	1
Adam		1	1	1	1	1		1		1
Mary	1			1	1	1			1	
Group	2	1	1	2	3	3	0	2	2	2

Group List: (E, F) (A, D, H, I, J) (B, C) G

6. *Least Misery Strategy*. Make a new list of ratings with the minimum of the individual ratings. Items get selected based on their rating on that list, the higher the sooner. The idea behind this strategy is that a group is as happy as its least happy member. POLYLENS (O' Conner et al., 2001) uses this strategy, assuming groups of people going to watch a movie together tend to be small and a small group to be as happy as its least happy member. A disadvantage is that a minority opinion can dictate the group: if everybody really wants to see something, but one person does not like it, then it will never be seen.

	A	B	C	D	E	F	G	H	I	J
John	10	4	3	6	10	9	6	8	10	8
Adam	1	9	8	9	7	9	6	9	3	8
Mary	10	5	2	7	9	8	5	6	7	6
Group	1	4	2	6	7	8	5	6	3	6

Group List: F, E, (H, J, D), G, B, I, C, A

7. *Most Pleasure Strategy*. Make a new list of ratings with the maximum of the individual ratings. Items get selected based on their rating on that list, the higher the sooner.

	A	B	C	D	E	F	G	H	I	J
John	10	4	3	6	10	9	6	8	10	8
Adam	1	9	8	9	7	9	6	9	3	8
Mary	10	5	2	7	9	8	5	6	7	6
Group	10	9	8	9	10	9	6	9	10	8

Group List: (A, E, I), (B, D, F, H), (C, J), G

8. *Average Without Misery Strategy*. Make a new list of ratings with the average of the individual ratings, but without items that score below a certain threshold (say 4) for individuals.

	A	B	C	D	E	F	G	H	I	J
John	10	4	3	6	10	9	6	8	10	8
Adam	1	9	8	9	7	9	6	9	3	8
Mary	10	5	2	7	9	8	5	6	7	6
Group	–	18	–	22	26	26	17	23	–	22

Group List: (E, F), H, (D, J), B, G (threshold 4); (E, F), H, (D, J), I, B (threshold 3)

MUSICFX (McCarty and Anagnost, 1998) uses a more complex version of this strategy. Their users rate all music stations, from $+2$ (really love this music) to -2 (really hate this music). These ratings are converted to positive numbers (by adding 2) and then squared to widen the gap between popular and less popular stations. An Average Without Misery strategy is used to generate a group list. To avoid starvation and always picking the same station, a weighted random selection is made from the top m stations of the list (m being a system parameter).

9. *Fairness Strategy*. Top items from all individuals are selected. When items are rated equally, the others' opinions are taken into account. The idea behind this strategy is that it is not so bad to watch something you hate, as long as you get to watch the things you really love as well. This strategy is often applied when people try to fairly divide a set of items: one person chooses first, then another, till everybody has made one choice. Next, everybody chooses a second item, often starting with the person who had to choose last on the previous round. It continues till all items have been used. In our example, if we assume John chooses first, then John would like A, E, or I. He could choose E because it causes the least misery to others and has the highest average. Next it is Adam's turn. Adam would like B, D, F, or H. He could choose F because it has the best ratings for the others. Mary would choose A (her highest rating). Next, Mary would like E, which has already been shown, and then F, which also has already been shown. Therefore, it makes sense to let Adam choose. He likes B, D, or H. He chooses H, as that has the best ratings for the others. Following this strategy, we could end up with a group list like: E, F, A, H, I, D, B, etc. The list would, of course, be different if we let Mary or Adam choose first. However, we would expect A to be within the first three items, as it is the item Mary prefers most.

10. *Most Respected Person Strategy (Also called 'Dictatorship')*. The ratings of the most respected person are used – in our example assume that is Adam–, only taking the ratings of the others into account to choose between similarly rated items. The idea behind this strategy is that groups may be dominated by one person. For instance, some research shows that the television remote control is most often operated by the oldest male present. Similarly, adults may have more influence than children (could depend on the time of day, adults having more influence later in the day). Visitors may have more influence than

inhabitants of the house. Special circumstances, like birthdays, illness, etc. can influence who is 'the most respected' person on a particular moment. This strategy is used often in collaborative filtering under the name of 'the nearest neighbor strategy': only the preferences of the individual closest in taste to the outsider are used.

A more sophisticated use of differences in social status would be to assign weights to the individuals' ratings. As mentioned above, this has also been used in collaborative filtering and in the INTRIGUE system (Ardissono et al. 2002), both of which use a weighted additive utilitarian strategy.

	A	B	C	D	E	F	G	H	I	J
John	10	4	3	6	10	9	6	8	10	8
Adam	1	9	8	9	7	9	6	9	3	8
Mary	10	5	2	7	9	8	5	6	7	6
Group	1	9	8	9	7	9	6	9	3	8

Group List: F H D B J C E G I A

2.4. SUMMARY OF STRATEGIES AND THE ISSUE OF SATISFACTION

Table II summarizes the results of the previous section. As can be seen, the different strategies described led to quite different results when applied to our example. One major difference between strategies is the emphasis placed on *individual* satisfaction, particularly *avoidance of misery*, compared to the satisfaction of the *majority* of the group. A clear example is the location of A in the group lists, an item that is very much hated by Adam (rating 1), but loved by both John and Mary (ratings 10). Plurality Voting puts A at the top of its list, and it ranks also highly

Table II. Summary of group lists produced by the strategies discussed above when applied to our example

	1	2	3	4	5	6	7	8	9	10
Fairness Strategy	Depends on order of choice, but A within first three items.									
Most Pleasure	A or E or I			B or D or F or H				C or J		G
Plurality Voting	A	E	F	I or D		H	J	B or G		C
Copeland Rule	E	A	F	I	D	H	J	B	G	C
Borda Count	F	E	A	H or D		I	J	B	G	C
Utilitarian Multiplicative	F	E	H	J	D	I	B or G		A	C
Least Misery	F	E	H or J or D			G	B	I	C	A
Average Without Misery Threshold 4	F or E		H	J or D		I	B			
Threshold 3						B	G			
Utilitarian Additive	F or E		H	J or D		A	I	B	G	C
Approval Threshold 6	F or E		H or J or D or A or I					B or C		G
Voting Threshold 5	F or E or H or J or D					A or I or G			B or C	
Most Preferred Person Adam	F	H	D	B	J	C	E	G	I	A

in the lists of the Copeland, Borda, Most Pleasure and Fairness strategies. In contrast, the Average Without Misery strategy completely ignores A, and A also ranks at the bottom of the lists of the Least Misery and Utilitarian Multiplicative strategies.

A second major difference between the strategies is whether they use only the relative position of items in each individual's preference list, or also the strengths of these preferences. The Plurality, Copeland, Borda, and Most Respected Person strategies only use relative positions, unlike the Utilitarian, Least Misery, Average Without Misery, and Most Pleasure strategies.

As discussed in Section 2.2, we believe strategies should have a property like '*Each individual's satisfaction with the results should be above a certain threshold*'. So, to determine how good the strategies are we need a way of *measuring* each individual's satisfaction with the sequences they produce. Note that this is something the choice strategies do not tell us. One way of doing this would be to have a *Satisfaction Function* that takes as input a sequence and an individual's and their friends' ratings and produces as output a number that quantifies the individual's satisfaction with that sequence. Ideally, such a Satisfaction Function would be empirically validated, for example by predicting individuals' satisfaction with sequences and then measuring in an experiment how satisfied they really are (see Experiment 2, Section 4). A good Satisfaction Function would be a fast way to test how strategies perform under many different circumstances (like group size, ratings, sequence length, etc.). Additionally, the construction of a good Satisfaction Function would provide valuable insights into what makes a good strategy.

2.4.1. *A Basic Satisfaction Function*

In its simplest form, a Satisfaction Function would take as input a *set* of ratings for any sequence of clips and produce as output a real number. One such function that has been used a lot is *Addition*: the summation of the individual's ratings of the clips concerned. So, for instance, John's satisfaction with FEAHD would be 43 $(9 + 10 + 10 + 8 + 6)$, while Mary's would be 40 $(8 + 9 + 10 + 6 + 7)$. Though without thresholds we cannot say whether these numbers amount to high or low satisfaction, the function would predict that John would be more satisfied than Mary.

2.4.2. *The Issue of Normalization*

A basic Satisfaction Function as sketched above only considers the ratings of the selected clips. It does not take into account how these ratings compare to those of the *unselected* clips. So, for instance, ratings of '6 5 6 7' would produce the same satisfaction whether the other clips had ratings of '9 10 10 10 10 9' or '1 2 1 3 1 4'. To counteract this, *normalization* can be used, by dividing the sum of ratings of the selected clips by the maximal 'possible' sum for that individual. For instance, the maximum sum for John for a sequence of five items is 47 (namely $10 + 10 + 10 + 9 + 8$), while the maximum for Mary is 41. So, John's satisfaction with FEAHD would be 0.91 (43/47), while Mary's would be 0.98 (40/41). We could then conclude that Mary would be more satisfied than John (in contradiction with the results without normalization). Normalization is one way to counteract differences in rating tendencies.[*]

2.4.3. *The Issue of Linearity*

An issue that has not been taken into account by any of the described strategies is that ratings are not necessarily linear. The question arises whether the difference between a '9' and a '10' should really be as big as between a '6' and a '7'. We have the hypothesis that the further away from the middle point of the scale (in our example 5.5 can be seen as Neutral), the larger the difference between subsequent ratings. So, both the differences between a 9 and a 10 and between a 1 and a 2 are larger than the difference between a 6 and a 7. To achieve this, we could convert the ratings '1 2 3 4 5 6 7 8 9 10' for our satisfaction function into '$-25 -16 -9 -4 -1 +1 +4 + 9 + 16 + 25$'. This has for instance as a result that FE would give Mary a higher satisfaction ($16 + 4 = 20$) than JC ($9 + 9 = 18$), while the satisfaction would be equal if ratings were considered linear ($FE = 9 + 7 = 16$, $JC = 8 + 8 = 16$).

2.4.4. *The Issue of Misery*

Another question is whether satisfaction depends on pleasure only (the sum of the positive numbers as a proportion of the maximum achievable pleasure) or whether it is also affected negatively by disagreeable experiences (more than because of losing out on possible pleasure).

2.4.5. *The Issue of Order*

Until now, we have considered the Satisfaction Function to take as input a *set* of ratings (whether only of selected or also of unselected items). This assumes that the *order* of the sequence does not impact the Satisfaction. However, the impact of viewing an item on the user's happiness is likely not only to depend on the viewer's liking for the item in isolation, but also on the *context* in which the item is shown. It is well known in the advertising world that the context of an advertisement has an impact on its effectiveness and resulting brand evaluation. In particular, studies have shown that the viewer's *mood* (as induced by watching the preceding program) has a signifi-cant effect on brand evaluations (Meloy, 2000; Gardner, 1985), with the viewer respond-ing more positively if they were in a more positive mood. The *liking* of a television program has a similar significant effect (Murray et al., 1992; Schumann and Thorson, 1990). So, we hypothesize that an item that is rated as, say, a 3 could be perceived more highly after having watched a 10, and less highly after having watched a 1. There is

---

[*]Note that normalization only works when we assume each individual to have some items they like. For instance, we would not want to conclude that a selection of '2 2 2 2' with other items of '1 1 1 1 1', would make this individual 100% satisfied.

also an interaction between the emotional tone of commercials and programs (Kamins et al., 1991): viewers preferred a sad commercial in the middle of a sad program, and a humorous commercial in a humorous program. This forms the basis for consistency theory, which suggests that viewers try to maintain a mood throughout a program. For example, after watching a 'September 11th' news item, viewers might prefer watching another sad item, rather than a funny one, even when normally they would rate the funny one higher. Other content aspects are also likely to play a role. An item about 'the position of the Kurds in Iraq' may be appreciated more than its individual rating suggests, after having just seen an item about 'the US position on Iraq'.

2.4.6. *The Issue of Solidarity*

Is it possible to determine an individual's satisfaction without considering the satisfaction of the others in the group? Would a person be as satisfied with a certain sequence when his friend got a sequence of '1 2 1 3' as he would be when his friend got a sequence of '7 8 6 8'? Hogg and Jennings (1999) deal with this issue in multi-agent systems by adding a weighted measure of the satisfaction of the society. They consider weights between 0 (a very selfish agent) and 1 (a very sociable agent). In fact, the situation could be even more complicated: somebody could be jealous of the pleasure of their friend, so their satisfaction would decrease if their friend's ratings increased. Note that this is quite likely when siblings are watching television together.

So, how do we decide which is the best Satisfaction Function? A way to find such function is to determine some plausible functions *before* measuring (reported) human satisfaction in an experiment, and to use these functions to *predict* the experimental outcomes. A comparison between the predictions and the real outcomes would then produce insights into the relative merits of the Satisfaction functions and their weaknesses. Additionally, the experiment could produce the needed threshold value. We will report on such an experiment in Section 4. First, however, we have explored how people act when confronted with the task our strategies perform.

3. Experiment 1: How Real People Do It

One can easily create hundreds of strategies (the strategies above are only the tip of the iceberg). The important question is which strategy is most effective and will be most liked by viewers. As a starting point, we want to determine what strategy real people use. We have performed a first experiment to explore this.

3.1. EXPERIMENTAL DESIGN

3.1.1. *Method*

Subjects were divided into two groups, experiencing different experimental conditions. In both conditions, subjects were given the same individual ratings of three people,

John, Adam, and Mary, for a set of video clips. In seven questions, they were asked which clips the three should view as a group, given that they only had time to see respectively 1, 2, 3, 4, 5, 6, or 7 clips, and why they made that selection. The task presented to both groups differed only in that in condition 2, 'John, Mary and Adam' had been replaced by 'John (29), Mary (32), and their grandfather Adam (81)' (see Appendix A for exact task wordings). A between-subject design was used, as a pilot test revealed large order effects: subjects felt compelled to change their group ratings in favor of Adam, if they received condition 2 *after* condition 1. The individual ratings had been chosen primarily to enable differentiating between the strategies we expected subjects to use (same ratings were used as in Section 2). In addition, we ensured that John and Mary had quite similar ratings, while Adam's ratings were frequently the opposite of the ratings of the other two. We also ensured that for one clip, namely clip A, John and Mary had maximal positive ratings (10), while Adam had a maximal negative rating (1). The latter would give a good idea of the importance subjects assigned to avoiding misery. The ratings can also be seen as representing different rating behavior: Adam has not used the maximum of the scale (10), while John has used it three times.

3.1.2. *Research Questions*

We wanted answers to the following research questions:

- Do subjects follow a clear strategy? Is it possible to describe subjects' individual behavior in terms of a logical strategy? Are the strategies discussed above being used?
- Is there a dominant strategy? Is one strategy used by a majority of subjects, and, if so, which strategy is it?
- Do subjects take pleasure, misery, and fairness into account? Which do they find most important?
- Do subjects follow the rules (exhibit the desirable properties as discussed in Section 2.2)?
- Is social standing taken into account? Does subjects' behavior change if one person in the group can be regarded as more important?

We expected the results of both experimental conditions to provide some answers to the first four questions, and the difference between the conditions to provide some insight in the last question. Our hypothesis was that in Condition 2, Adam would be regarded as more important (because of his age), and the selections would be more geared toward his taste. Note that we have deliberately chosen to make this experiment an *indirect* one: rather than having an actual group sit down to decide what to watch, subjects were asked what they *thought* people should watch. There are two reasons for this. Firstly, we really wanted our subjects to think about what would be best for the group as a whole. Giving them a role to play (i.e. to represent John, Adam or Mary) could lead to them trying to defend their own interests (even with clear instructions to consider the group as a whole). Secondly, as discussed in our literature review in Section 2, individuals behave differently depending on who else is in the group. Some people tend to be more accommodating of others, some are more timid and others more outspoken, some are better at arguing their case, or are just more respected. We did not want the eloquence with which John, Mary and Adam argued their case to influence the outcomes.

3.1.3. *Subjects*

Thirty nine subjects participated in the experiment. All were final-year undergraduate students of the IT faculty attending a lecture of the Adaptive Interactive Systems module. The students were studying various courses (B.A. Computer and Information Systems, B.Sc. Computer Studies, B.Sc. Computer Science, and B.Sc. Software Engineering). The experiment took place in a lecture room. Subjects were assigned to experimental condition depending on where they sat: the left of the room was assigned to condition 1 (18 subjects, 16 male, 2 female, average age 28, standard deviation 9.7), the right to condition 2 (21 subjects, 15 male, 6 female, average age 24, standard deviation 3). Students participated in the experiment voluntarily (in addition to the numbers mentioned above, 9 students chose not to participate). The spread over courses was similar for both conditions.

3.2. RESULTS AND DISCUSSION

Subjects do not seem to answer the questions independently: they responded which new clip should be added to the sequence they had already chosen for the previous question. This made it possible to present the results in the way we have done in Tables III and IV (for respectively, Condition 1 and 2), only showing the new clip selected for each question. However, from an experimental point of view, this is not ideal: it might have influenced their strategy, making it perhaps less likely that they use the 'fair strategy' (which only makes sense when selecting a larger group of clips). We need to explore whether the results would be different if we asked the subjects immediately to select, say, six clips. A between-subject design could be used to distinguish between different set sizes.

Table III shows the results for Condition 1, and Table IV for Condition 2. As can be seen in the tables, subjects did not always make a unique selection for a clip, sometimes they answered 'D or J'. We have tried to keep the tables as simple (and uncrowded) as possible: if a cell does not have a clip name in it, then the first name above it applies. For instance, sub11 replied F to the first question. Subjects have been ordered to make the tables as easy to view as possible. The tables include information about how well the subjects' replies fit some of the strategies discussed in Section 2:

- Bold borderlines indicate replies that are in correspondence with the Average Strategy. So, for instance, all replies of sub 14 were the same as those by

Table III. Results for Condition 1 (see above for meaning of shading and borderlines)

	1	2	3	4	5	6	7	Summary ⋆
sub14	E	F	H	J	D	A	I	Average Strategy throughout
sub2	F	E				I	B	Average without Misery Strategy throughout
sub11						G	B	Least Misery Strategy throughout
sub10								
sub4							I	Least Misery Strategy, except for last choice
sub7							A	
sub9				D or J	D or J	A	I	Average Strategy throughout
sub17				D	J	B	G	Average without Misery Strategy throughout
sub3		J	H	D		G	I	Least Misery Strategy, except for last choice
sub18					G	D	B	First four choices correspond to Least Misery
sub16			G	H			A	First three choices correspond to Least Misery
sub6			A	H	J		I	Only first two choices correspond to strategy
sub13								
sub5			D			G	B	Least Misery Strategy throughout
sub1							A	Least Misery Strategy, except for last two choices
sub12		H	J	D	E	G		Only first choice corresponds to a strategy
sub15		G		E	D	H		
sub8			E	A	B	D	H	

⋆When we say something like 'Average Strategy throughout', we mean that the subjects' choices are identical to those of this strategy. This does not necessarily mean that the subject was consciously applying this strategy.

the Average Strategy. The first two replies by sub16 were the same as those by the Average Strategy, but sub16's later replies differed.

- Gray cell shading indicates replies that are in correspondence with the Least Misery Strategy. So, for instance, all replies of sub11 were the same as those by the Least Misery Strategy. The first three replies by sub16 were the same as those by the Least Misery Strategy, but sub16's later replies differed.
- Bold dotted borderlines indicate replies that are in correspondence with the Average Without Misery Strategy. So, for instance, all replies of sub2 were the same as those by the Average Without Misery Strategy.

Note that strategies can have overlapping starts of their group lists. For instance, both the Average Strategy and the Least Misery Strategy allow a start of FEHDJ. This means that cells can have both a gray cell shading and a bold borderline. So, for instance, sub7's replies followed the Average Strategy for the first five clips, and in correspondence with the Least Misery Strategy for the first six clips. Also, note, we have only used the Bold dotted borderlines, when the Average Without Misery Strategy starts deviating from the Average Strategy.

3.2.1. *Do Subjects Follow a Clear Strategy?*

There is evidence that human subjects use the strategies mentioned above, particularly the Average Strategy, the Average Without Misery Strategy and the Least Misery Strategy.

Table IV. Results for Condition 2 (see above for meaning of shading and borderlines)

	1	2	3	4	5	6	7	Summary ★
SUB1	F	E	H	J	G	D	B	First four choices correspond to Least Misery and Average strategies
SUB2				D		B	G	Average without Misery Strategy throughout
SUB14								
SUB8						A	I	Average Strategy throughout
SUB16								
SUB11								
SUB20						G	A	Least Misery Strategy, except for last choice
SUB12							B	Least Misery Strategy throughout
SUB5						I		Average without Misery Strategy throughout
SUB9					A	D	I	First four choices correspond to Least Misery and Average strategies
SUB15				A	D	J		Only first three choices correspond to a strategy
SUB19				D	J	A		Average Strategy throughout
SUB10						G	B	Least Misery Strategy throughout
SUB3							A	Least Misery Strategy, except for last choice
SUB4			D	H			I	
SUB18			G	J	H	D	B	Only first two choices correspond to a strategy
SUB21		G	D			B	E	Only first choice corresponds to a strategy
SUB17		J	H	E	D	G	B	
SUB13		H	D		J			
SUB6	E or F	E or F	H	J or D	D or J	A	I	Average Strategy throughout
SUB7	E	F	J	A	H	G	D	Only first two choices correspond to a strategy

★When we say something like 'Average Strategy throughout', we mean that the subjects' choices are identical to those of this strategy. This does not necessarily mean that the subject was consciously applying this strategy.

- *Average Strategy.* Two subjects in Condition 1 (sub14 and 9) and five subjects in Condition 2 (SUB8, 16, 11, 19, and 6) exactly followed the Average Strategy. Their papers tended to show additions on them.
- *Least Misery Strategy.* Three subjects in Condition 1 (sub11, 10, and 5) and two subjects in Condition 2 (SUB12, and 10) exactly followed the Least Misery Strategy. Three subjects in Condition 1 (sub4, 7, 3) and three in Condition 2 (SUB20, 3, 4) followed the Least Misery strategy almost completely. For clip 7, three selected A ('while Adam hates it, the others really like it so he will just have to put up with it', 'Mary seems to lose out in most clips, so A is for her', 'Might as well please two out of three'), three selected I ('Closest', 'At least the majority will be satisfied').
- *Average Without Misery Strategy.* Two subjects in Condition 1 (sub17, 2) and three subjects in Condition 2 (SUB2, 14, 5) exactly followed the Average Without Misery Strategy. Three subjects used a threshold of 4 or 5 and two subjects (sub2, SUB5) used a threshold of 2 or 3. As expressed by one subject 'I try to please all of them making sure that no is lower than five'. Note that the resulting sequence for the Average Without Misery Strategy for a

threshold of 2 or 3 coincides with Multiplicative Utilitarianism (but no signs of multiplications where found on the papers).

- *Fairness Strategy.* Two subjects (sub6, 13) used some kind of a Fairness Strategy. Both selected A relatively early. They made comments like 'Although Adam gave 1 mark for A, he gets to see F', 'Although some gave some clips low marks, they all get to see some they rated highly'. Other subjects applied fairness towards the end: 'Mary's average ratings have been low, so give her something she will enjoy' (sub1, explaining selecting A), 'Mary seems to lose out in most clips, so A is for her' (SUB3), 'As Adam did not like A, pick D next as he scored it a 9' (SUB15).

- *Approval voting.* The subjects' explanations did not show any sign of using Approval voting. Nevertheless, thirteen subjects' sequences fall within those permitted by Approval voting with threshold 5, and eleven within those permitted by Approval voting with threshold 6 (seven of which are in common with threshold 5). These seem high numbers, but it has to be taken into account that Approval voting (particularly with threshold 5) did not put many restrictions on the sequences it allowed.

- Nobody used plurality voting (in either form) and nobody used the Copeland rule. Nobody completely followed the Borda count (though two subjects' behavior on the first four items coincides with it: sub6 and sub13).

3.2.2. *Is There a Dominant Strategy?*

There does not seem to be a clearly dominant strategy, but Average, Average Without Misery, and Least Misery are all plausible candidates for implementation. Fairness plays a role, but our human subjects did not have a clear strategy for applying it.

3.2.3. *Do Subjects Take Misery into Account?*

Many subjects take misery into account, as evidenced by the high proportion of subjects using the Least Misery and Average Without Misery strategies. Even subjects that do completely deviate from the Least Misery or Average With Least Misery strategies, like sub12, sub15, SUB21, SUB18, SUB17, and SUB13 avoid misery: all left out A and I from their selection. Therefore, preference should be given to a strategy that takes misery into account.

3.2.4. *Is Social Standing Taken into Account?*

We did not find any statistically significant differences between the conditions. Only one subject explicitly mentioned age as a reason for a selection: 'A is not chosen because only the young ones like the topic' (SUB5). Our intention of making Adam the most respected person did not completely succeed: one subject (SUB7) actually

Table V. Ways in which subjects broke the Pareto rule

	B (4,9,5) before D (6,9,7)	B (4,9,5) before H (8,9,6)	G (6,6,5) before D (6,9,7)	G (6,6,5) before H (8,9,6)	G (6,6,5) before J (8,8,6)	G (6,6,5) before E (10,7,9)	J (8,8,6) before H (8,9,6)
sub8	X	X	X	X	X	X	
sub18			X				X
sub16			X	X			X
sub15			X	X	X	X	X
sub3			X				X
SUB1			X				
SUB18			X	X	X		X
SUB21			X	X	X	X	X
SUB7			X				X
SUB17							X

mentioned 'Adam's scores have been ignored to some extend because of age', another (SUB21) said 'overall pick the average highest, if there is any difference attempt to match the two people with the same age'. Overall, it seems that this part of the experiment was not successful: in future we will have to make it more obvious that one person is socially more important (perhaps by making it their birthday).

3.2.5. *Do Subjects Follow the Rules?*

No, subjects sometimes exhibit completely unexpected behavior. Four subjects in Condition 1 and four in Condition 2 selected G (ratings 6,6,5) before D (ratings 6,9,7). This seems rather illogical, and breaks the Pareto rule. Two of these subjects explained using disparities in ratings as a basis for selection. This would mean that a group is happy if everybody were equally happy or miserable. Overall, ten subjects broke the Pareto rule, in ways as shown in Table V.

The only plausible explanation seems to be that subjects thought fairness to be more important than pleasure. Subjects also do not follow the Condorcet winner criterion. In its stronger form, A and E were both Condorcet winners, but almost all subjects started their sequence with F. This backs up our resistance against the Condorcet winner criterion.

4. Experiment 2: How People Judge the Sequences Produced

In the previous experiment, we have investigated what strategies people follow and what they find important when making a decision on behalf of a group (for instance, misery, fairness, etc). However, the fact that, for instance, many people used a Least Misery strategy does not necessarily mean that our television should use this strategy (though it seems a reasonable option, given the results of Experiment 1). Similarly, the fact that nobody used the Copeland rule does not necessarily mean that the television should definitely not use that strategy. Perhaps that strategy was just to complex for a human to apply. In this experiment, we have turned the game around: instead of asking subjects to produce a satisfying sequence, we have presented subjects with sequences produced by the strategies, and asked them how satisfied they would be with such a sequence. We wanted to determine which strategy produces the most *satisfaction* for all members of the group. To gain a better understanding of what determines an individual's satisfaction, we have also compared a number of satisfaction functions (see Section 2.4) to see which provides the best predictions.

4.1. EXPERIMENTAL DESIGN

4.1.2. *Method*

Subjects were told that they were going to watch video clips with their two friends. They were given the same individual ratings of three people, themselves, Friend1, and Friend2, for a set of video clips. The ratings used were the same as those in Experiment 1, with John's ratings corresponding to their own, Adam's ratings to Friend1's, and Mary's ratings to Friend2's.[*] They were told the TV had selected a sequence of clips for them, and were asked how satisfied they and their friends would be given that sequence, and why. This was repeated three times: all subjects were given three different sequences on three pieces of paper, stapled together. (See Appendix B for the exact wording.) Table VI shows the sequences used, and the reason for using them.

Sequences have been kept as short as possible, not to overburden the experimental subjects. Some of the sequences are longer (6 items) than others (5 items),

Table VI. Sequences used and reasons for using them

Sequence	Reason
FEAHD	Social choice according to Borda Count
EAFID	Social choice according to Copeland rule
AEFID	Social choice according to Plurality voting (one for one)
FEHJDI	Social choice according to Utilitarian multiplicative
EFHDJB	Social choice according to Average without misery
FEHJDG	Social choice according to Least misery
AEIBDF	Social choice according to Most pleasure
EFHDJA	Social choice according to Utilitarian additive
AIEFD	Social choice set according to Plurality voting and Copeland rule, but in another sequence with the most negative items for Adam at the start. Together with EAFID and AEFID used to see if the order of the sequence influences the results.

[*]We decided to use 'Friend 1' and 'Friend 2' rather 'Adam' and ' Mary' to avoid any influence on the subjects' behavior. After all, names imply gender. It would have been better to use three male names in Experiment 1. Though we did not detect any influence, we decided to avoid the risk in this experiment.

because they would not distinguish between voting strategies otherwise. Though we used 'I', 'Friend1' and 'Friend2' in the text of the experiment, we will use 'John', 'Adam' and 'Mary' in our discussion (this makes it easier to compare between experiments). Note: as before we have chosen for an *indirect* experiment: rather than having an actual group sit down and *measure* how satisfied each individual would be with a certain sequence, subjects were asked how satisfied they *thought* all members of the group would be. Measuring satisfaction would require subjects to really experience the clips, and this would have required a set of clips with ratings accurately reflecting our subjects' tastes. To compare multiple sequences, we either would need different groups of people with the same tastes (difficult to find and control) or use a within subject design. However, order effects could have been large, as showing a clip multiple times would influence its rating.

4.1.3. *Satisfaction Functions We Will Use to Make Predictions*

We have used six simple satisfaction functions to predict the outcomes of this experiment:

1. Linear Addition without Normalization: The most basic satisfaction function discussed in Section 2.4, where the individual's ratings of the selected items are summed.
2. Linear Addition with Normalization: As the previous one, but now with normalization (as described in Section 2.4.2)
3. Quadratic Addition, Pleasure only, without Normalization: Ratings are transformed as described in Section 2.4.3 (10 becomes 25, 1 becomes -25 etc). The individual's *positive* ratings of the selected items are summed. Negative ratings are ignored.
4. Quadratic Addition, Pleasure only, with Normalization.
5. Quadratic Addition, Pleasure minus Misery, without Normalization: As Quadratic Addition, Pleasure only, but now the negative ratings are also incorporated in the sum.
6. Quadratic Addition, Pleasure minus Misery, with Normalization.

The differences in predictions between 1,3,5 on the one hand and 2,4,6 on the other hand will provide insight into whether subjects use Normalization. The differences in predictions between 3,4 on the one hand, and 5,6 on the other hand will provide insight into whether the subjects deduct misery. The differences in predictions between 1,2 on the one hand, and 3,4,5,6 will provide insight into whether subjects use the ratings as linear.

We have not used the order of the sequence as input for our satisfaction functions. We did consider adding a satisfaction function that uses the sequence of the ratings: increasing the added satisfaction of an item if the previous rating was high. However, we decided to leave this to future research, as we want to resolve some of the other issues first, and did not know enough yet about the influence ordering could have.

4.1.4. *Predictions of the Satisfaction Functions*

Figure 5.1 shows the predictions of the satisfaction functions. Some of the more prominent differences are:

- *Effect of Normalization.* (Comparing the left hand graphs with the right hand graphs). FEAHD, AIEFD, AEIBDF: John beats Mary without normalization, Mary beats John with normalization. EFHDJB: John beats Mary without normalization, Mary and John almost equal with normalization. FEHJDG: Adam beats John with normalization, and they are quite equal without.

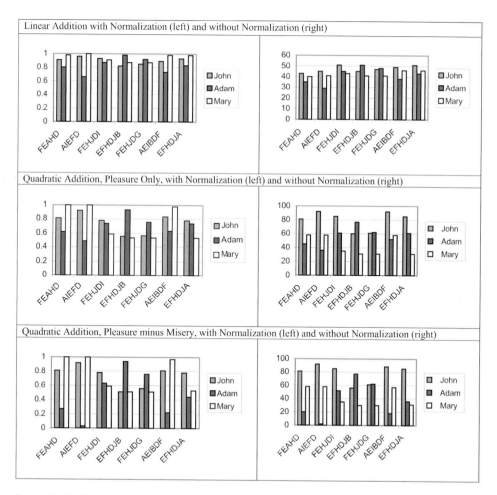

Figure 5.1. Predictions of the satisfaction functions.

John beats Mary without normalization, and they are quite equal with normalization.

- *Effect of deducting Misery*. (Comparing the middle two graphs with the bottom two graphs). EFHDJA: Adam beats Mary without deduction of misery. With deduction, Mary beats Adam (or is almost equal to Adam, without normalization).
- *Effect of Quadratic versus Linear*. (Comparing the top two graphs with the bottom four graphs). FEHJDI: In Linear Addition, John and Mary are quite equal. In the others, John clearly beats Mary. FEHJDG: In Quadratic, Adam clearly beats Mary. In Linear, Adam and Mary are quite equal. EFHDJA: In Linear, Mary beats John (or is equal to John without normalization). In Quadratic, John beats Mary.

4.1.5. *Research Questions*

1. Is one of our satisfaction functions a good predictor of subject behavior? The satisfaction functions above predict how each individual's satisfaction compares to that of the other two individuals for a particular sequence, as well as how it compares to their own satisfaction for other sequences. For instance, according to the Quadratic-Addition-Pleasure-Only satisfaction functions, John and Mary would be more satisfied with AIEFD than Adam, and both would prefer AIEFD to FEHJDI. The predictions of the various satisfaction functions differ, and in the experiment we can compare these predictions with the satisfactions as indicated by our experimental subjects. A main question was whether the predictions of one our satisfaction functions would closely match those of our subjects. We also wanted answers to the following related questions, to better understand what makes a good satisfaction function:

- Do subjects use *normalization*?
- Do subjects deduct *misery*?
- Do subjects use *linear rating scales*?

We can use the differences in predictions as discussed above to answer these three questions.

If one of the satisfaction functions is a very good predictor, then it might be possible to also determine thresholds. Let s be the predicted satisfaction of an individual with a sequence. We would like to determine thresholds t1, t2, t3, t4 and t5, such that:

- $s < t1$: individual is very dissatisfied with the sequence (score of 1 on the scale of the experiment)
- $t1 \leqslant s < t2$: individual is dissatisfied with the sequence (score of 2 or 3 on the scale)
- $t3 \leqslant s < t4$: individual is satisfied with the sequence (score of 5 or 6 on the scale)
- $t4 \leqslant s$: individual is very satisfied with the sequence (score of 7 on the scale)

If one of the Normalized satisfaction functions were a good predictor, then all thresholds would have to be between 0 and 1.

2. Does the *order of the sequence* influence subjects' satisfaction ratings? What aspects of order do subjects mention? We have given the subjects *sequences* of selected items, rather than sets. This allows the subjects to use this information if they want to. We hope that the subjects' explanations will provide us with more insight into how order influences satisfaction. To study this further, we have included three experimental conditions (EAFID, AEFID, AIEFD) that are exactly the same, with the same set of items being selected, except that they are presented in a different order. Note that in our experiments we have deliberately abstracted items (A to J) instead of telling the subjects about the item content. This ensures that subjects use the ratings provided rather than their own personal opinions. This has as side effect that the subjects cannot use content information (the emotional tone or how the content is related to the content of other items). So, our experiment will be restricted to the impact of the *ratings profile* of a sequence on satisfaction (for instance, exploring the difference between '7 1 9 3 9' and '1 3 7 9 9'), and not the emotional or content profile. It might be possible to change this in a future experiment, but it is a tricky issue to handle: for instance, telling subjects an item is 'sad' might influence their opinion of that item in isolation, not just as part of a sequence.

3. Do subjects use *social aspects* to determine individual satisfaction? We have not used social aspects (solidarity or jealousy) in our satisfaction functions. Without having resolved the other issues first, it would have led to an explosion in possible satisfaction functions. Even more so, as the selfishness/sociality of our individual subjects would have an impact, and different 'average sociality' weightings would have been needed for the predictions. However, we hoped that subjects' explanations would indicate whether they had taken social aspects into account.

4. Is there one strategy (or multiple ones) that is clearly better than the others, in terms of keeping all members of the group happy? As subjects would indicate the satisfaction of all members of the group, we could investigate whether there is a sequence (i.e. the result of a particular selection strategy) with positive satisfaction (i.e. score 5 or above) on average – or better even for all subjects – for all members of the group.

4.1.6. *Subjects*

Twenty-two subjects participated in the experiment. All were academic staff of the University of Brighton. Subjects were assigned to experimental condition at random. To control for order effects, each sequence appeared similarly often as first, second and third paper. Permutated sequences AIEFD, AEFID, and EAFID were not given to the same subjects, so, there was a complete between-subjects design for those. Each sequence was studied by at least seven subjects (some by eight).

4.2. RESULTS AND DISCUSSION

Figure 5.2 shows the average satisfaction scores per condition.

4.2.1. *Do Subjects Use Normalization?*

Comparing the results with the prominent differences between the predictions of the satisfaction functions (see Section 4.1.4), we find:

- FEAHD: There is a trend that Mary beats John, as predicted by normalization. This is not statistically significant, but 'without normalization' predicted John to beat Mary.
- AIEFD, AEIBDF: John and Mary are quite equal, which is more in tune with normalization.
- EFHDJB: Mary and John almost equal, as predicted by normalization.
- FEHJDG: There is a trend that Adam beats John, as predicted by normalization, but this is not statistically significant. However, John clearly beats Mary, as predicted by 'without normalization' (this is statistically significant, $p < 0.01$).

So, overall, there is some evidence that normalization has taken place, but with a contradictory result for FEHJDG (which is a strange case, as will be discussed below).

4.2.2. *Do Subjects Deduct Misery?*

Comparing the results with the predictions of the satisfaction functions (see Section 4.1.4), we find:

- EFHDJA: There is a trend that Mary beats Adam as predicted by deducting misery. This is not statistically significant, but without deducting misery it was predicted that Adam beats Mary.

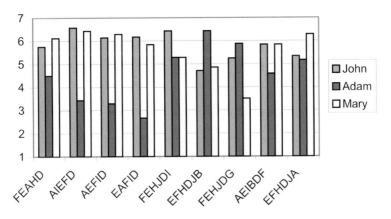

Figure 5.2. Average satisfaction scores per condition.

So, there is some evidence that misery is taken into account (deducted). This is in line with the results of Experiment 1.

4.2.3. Do Subjects Use Linear Rating Scales?

Comparing the results with the predictions of the satisfaction functions (see Section 4.1), we find:

- FEHJDI: John beats Mary, as predicted by Quadratic. This is statistically significant ($p < 0.01$).
- FEHJDG: Adam clearly beats Mary, as predicted by Quadratic. This is statistically significant ($p < 0.001$)

So, there is clear evidence that Quadratic is a better measure than Linear.

4.2.4. Does the Order of the Sequence Influence Satisfaction?

Order is mentioned by six subjects:

- One subject (S22) mentioned that the first clip mainly influenced his ratings. Another subject (S3) explained a low rating for Adam in AIEFD: 'had to endure his two least favorite clips. Then he gave up and went away.'
- One subject (S20) considered how the individuals' experience changed over time. For FEHJDH he mentions the problem of John feeling a decline of 'quality' from the second clip onwards. He also mentioned that John would be quite satisfied with EFHDJA 'ending in a high' (in addition to seeing good clips). In support of this, another subject explained a low satisfaction of Adam with EFHDJA by 'never finish on a bad one' (S7). A third subject (S18) shared this interest in the end of the sequence: she mentioned that Adam and Mary would be more satisfied than John with FEAHD (contrary to general belief) because they get more favorite clips towards the end. She also gave John a low rating (3) for EFHDJA because she assumed it to be boring to see too many favorites in a row!
- One subject (S13) explicitly indicated not having taken order into account.

No statistically significant differences were found between the results of EAFID, AEFID, and AIEFD. This is not surprising given the small number of subjects who mentioned order. Most subjects treated the sequences as sets. The ordering issue will need to be studied further in future experiments, particularly investigating the impact of the start of the sequence, the end, and the increase or decrease of pleasure over time.

4.2.5. Do Subjects Use Social Aspects to Determine Individual Satisfaction?

Most subjects did not explicitly do so.

- Only three subjects (S15, S12, and S11) mentioned taking the mood of the others into account when determining the satisfaction of an individual. Another subject (S16) mentioned 'If satisfaction depends on others being satisfied I could not assess this, because there was too much to hold in short-term memory. I had no overall model of the situation, and merely did the three evaluations independently.'

- One of these subjects (S11) mentioned that it would be important to know more about the context: 'if watching at your own house, your visitors' satisfaction becomes more important'.

4.2.6. *Is One of the Satisfaction Functions a Good Predictor?*

Comparing the average profile above with the profile of the normalized 'Quadratic Addition, Pleasure minus Misery' satisfaction function, it can be concluded that they are quite similar. There are, however, still a number of noticeable differences:

- Adam's satisfaction for AIEFD (and its permutations) is low, but not as low as predicted. Similarly, Adam's satisfaction for AEIBDF is higher than expected. Perhaps the numbers associated with low ratings (like -25 for a rating of 1) should be less negative than we have them. So, deducting misery, but less severely.
- The difference between John's and Mary's satisfaction for FEHJDG is larger than expected. Comparing Mary's satisfaction for FEHJDG with that for EFHDJB shows a significant difference ($p < 0.05$). This is strange as the only difference between both sequences (except order) is the G in one sequence and the B in the other, both of which have the same rating for Mary. Perhaps subjects did take a social aspect into account: preferring B (which at least gives pleasure to Adam) to G (which gives pleasure to nobody), and feeling more upset about missing favorite A because G pleases nobody. Many subjects mention missing A as the reason for giving a low mark.
- John's satisfaction for EFHDJA is lower than expected (compared to Adam's and Mary's satisfaction). This might be partly caused by the somewhat odd behavior of subject S18 (See order section above). Another subject mentioned giving John a low rating (3) because of missing out on one of his favorites (I).
- The last two points (and the frequency with which subjects used the argument of missing the favorite for giving a lower mark) indicates that a higher weight has to be given to favorites, such that satisfaction goes down when all favorites are missed.

These differences have made it impossible to determine thresholds.

4.2.7. *Is There a Strategy that Keeps Everyone Happy?*

On average, John, Adam and Mary were all reported to be *not dissatisfied* with FEAHD (Borda Count), FEHJDI (Multiplicative Utilitarian), EFHDJB (Average without Misery), AEIBDF (Most pleasure) and EFHDJA (Additive Utilitarian). Looking at individual subjects' responses, FEHJDI (Multiplicative Utilitarian) is the only sequence that has ratings of at least 4 for all subjects for all individuals. The average ratings for this sequence are even above 5 for John, Adam, and Mary, showing a certain degree of satisfaction for all of them. So, Multiplicative Utilitarian seems the most promising strategy, but the others are not bad either. Of course, we need to investigate this issue further, using different individual ratings and different lengths of the sequence. However, on the basis of this experiment, we can reduce the number of strategies to be investigated (discarding Copeland rule, Plurality voting, Least misery).

4.2.8. *Other Issues*

- One subject mentioned that the length of the clips would be important. (S19) This is a valid point, as viewing something you hate for five minutes or an hour would indeed make a big difference.
- One subject mentioned that other factors would influence satisfaction, like the discussion on the basis of the clips (S18).
- Almost all subjects talked about including (or not having included) the favorite clip(s). This seemed to be a more important issue than expected.

5. Algorithms for Presenting a Sequence: The Issues of Order and Ratings

Until now we have focused on how a *set* of items suitable for a group can be selected based on the individuals' ratings. The television will also need to decide in which *order* to show the items. In this section, we will sketch three algorithms that take ordering issues into account, and we will empirically explore the assumptions underlying these algorithms.

5.1. ALGORITHMS

5.1.1. *Algorithm 1: Using the Group List Ranking*

As the selection strategies described produce a ranked group list, the simplest algorithm is to show the items in the same order as they appear in the list. We have applied this method when producing the sequences for Experiment 2. The algorithm is depicted in Figure 5.3. Note that this algorithm might need to be slightly modified if the time durations of items vary. Television programmes (such as the news) tend to have a fixed length. Items, on the other hand, could have varying lengths, with one item being longer than another. It is possible that at the end of the sequence

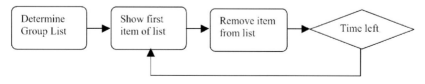

Figure 5.3. Algorithm for deciding sequence using group list ranking.

an item lower in the group list ranking needs to be selected to fill the available time, as the item which turn it was might be too long.

5.1.2. Algorithm 2: Changing Order

Using the group list ranking to determine the order will produce a sequence with items liked by the group at the start and a decline in quality afterwards. However, this might not be the best order for keeping everybody optimally satisfied. As indicated in Section 2.2 we believe that a good sequence should keep each individual's satisfaction above a threshold at each moment during the broadcast. Our example in that section already showed that the order of the items impacts whether or not a sequence meets this criterion. Comments made by some subjects in the previous experiment show that there might be additional aspects that decide how good a sequence is, like having a strong ending. As discussed in Section 2.4.5, it is also likely that the *mood* induced by watching an item and the *topic* of an item influences what is the best item to show next. So, instead of showing items in the order of the group list, a more advanced algorithm could merely use the group list to decide which set of items to show and then order this set taking certain constraints into account (see Figure 5.4). For instance, it could order the set such that the sequence

- *Keeps individuals sufficiently satisfied throughout the broadcast*: The predicted satisfaction of each individual at each point in the sequence is above a certain threshold
- *Has a strong ending:* The predicted satisfaction of each individual with the last M items is above a certain threshold
- *Exhibits consistency in mood:* The predicted mood induced by each two adjacent items in not 'too wide apart' on a mood scale. For instance, it might be fine to succeed a 'Very Happy' item with a 'Happy' item, but not with a 'Very Sad' item.
- *Has a good narrative flow:* Topically related items are as close as possible in the sequence.

Note that these constraints are both speculative and vague. Though they might seem reasonable, we have not proven yet that they are, and we have not specified them in detail (for instance, how far apart are two adjacent items allowed to be on the mood scale, what is the value of M, etc.). Also, the constraints could conflict: two items can be highly topically related but induce widely different moods. Additionally, the television will need information about the mood and topicality of the items to be able to use them for ordering. This requires either explicit

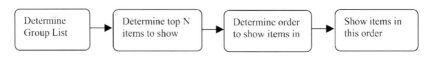

Figure 5.4. Algorithm for deciding sequence using ordering constraints.

annotation (rather unlikely to happen for small television items), or an inference mechanism based on what is known about the item. The main source of information about items will be their subtitles, complemented by the audio and video signal. We expect that it might be possible to automatically estimate the mood of an item based on an analysis of its subtitles (e.g. looking for words like murder, disaster, dead, etc) and the tone of voice of the people in the video. Topical relatedness could perhaps be estimated by comparing the frequencies of (non-common) words in the subtitles. In the experiment below we will explore our assumptions that mood and topical relatedness should have an impact on the order. The practical issue of how to automatically determine the mood or topicality is beyond the topic of this paper.

5.1.3. *Algorithm 3: Changing Ratings*

There seems to be one major flaw in the reasoning above: until now we have tacitly assumed that we can first select a set of items and then order them, ignoring that ratings might change as an effect of viewing an item. Having shown an item to the group, issues like mood consistency and topical relatedness might well lead to an item outside the selected set being more suitable to show next than the items in our selected set. We believe that the individuals' ratings should be recalculated taking into account the items they have seen so far. This leads to the algorithm depicted in Figure 5.5. Different rules could be used for the recalculation of ratings, and the following are some speculative examples:

- If an item is topically related to the item shown, then increase its rating (by an amount proportionate to the relatedness).
- If an item has the same mood as the item shown, then increase it's rating, and decrease the rating if the moods conflict (by an amount proportionate with the intensity of the mood). A question is whether changes in ratings need to apply only for the duration of the next selection or for longer. For instance, suppose the TV shows a 'very sad' item. This might lead to a reduction in ratings for 'happy' items. If the TV were to show a 'neutral' item next, should the ratings for the 'happy' items be restored to their previous value, or remain reduced?
- If the (predicted) viewer's satisfaction is high after watching the items so far, then increase ratings, and if the (predicted) satisfaction is low then decrease ratings. To give an example of how this might work: Assume Adam is shown a number of items he likes. This gives him high satisfaction. Because of this,

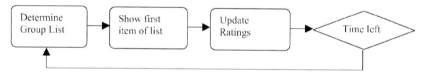

Figure 5.5. Algorithm for deciding sequence using rating modification.

his ratings for other items (like the ones he normally hates) will increase. This makes it more likely these items will be selected (for instance, by passing the threshold in an Average Without Misery strategy). Assume as a consequence an item he normally hates is shown, like item A. This reduces his satisfaction and therefore his ratings for other items, making it more likely he will see something he enjoys soon.

Note that this algorithm allows items to be shown multiple times. This can be counteracted by sharply decreasing the rating of items that have been shown, or by adding a constraint to the 'Show first item of the list' that it has to be the first item not already shown. Whilst showing a news item multiple times needs to be avoided, this might not be equally true for all types of programmes and viewers. Toddlers, for instance, very happily watch something they like multiple times. Similarly, a music clip might warrant watching multiple times for a fan. It seems therefore best to leave this issue to be dealt with by the sub-algorithm that determines each individual's ratings.

To investigate whether this algorithm is indeed better than the other two algorithms discussed, our next step is to explore if people do indeed adjust their ratings. More particularly, we would also like to gain insight into the effects of mood, satisfaction, and topical relatedness on the ratings of items after having viewed another item.

5.2. EXPERIMENTAL DESIGN

5.2.1. *Method*

Subjects were told that they were going to watch the evening news, and that the television would select a sequence of news items for them. They were asked to rate seven news items on how much they would want to watch them and how they might expect the news item to make them feel. After they had rated all seven items, subjects were told what the first item on the news was, an item that they had not yet seen. They were asked to rate this first item on how much they would want to watch it and how they might expect the item to make them feel. Next, they were asked to rate the other seven news items again, given that they had just watched that first item. There were two experimental conditions. In Condition A, the first news item was 'Brighton University Watts Building on Fire: hundreds feared dead'. In Condition B, it was 'England football team has to play Bulgaria in the next round'. (See Appendix C for the exact wording.) Table VII shows the news items used, and the reason for using them.

5.2.2. *Research Questions*

We wanted answers to the following research questions:

- *Do people adjust ratings?* Does having watched the first news item influence the ratings for the other news items? If this is the case, then a new group list will

Table VII. News items used and reasons for using them

News item	Reason
'[Insert name of your favorite sport's club] wins important game'	Expect that most subjects would want to see this item and that it would make them feel very happy.
'Fleet of limos for Jennifer Lopez 100-metre trip'*	This item and the next two were real news items that were chosen to be *not* topically related to the 'England football team has to play Bulgaria in the next round' and 'Brighton University Watts Building on Fire: hundreds feared dead' items.
'Heart disease could be halved'*	Expect that it would make most subjects happy.
'Is there room for God in Europe?'*	Expect that subjects would differ in opinion.
'Earthquake hits Bulgaria'	Expect that most subjects would want to see this item and that it would make them feel sad. Also picked 'Bulgaria' to make this item weakly topically related to the 'England football team has to play Bulgaria in next match' item.
'UK fire strike continues'	Expect that most subjects would not want to see this item at the start. The UK fire strike had already been in the news for months. Item is weakly topically related to 'Brighton University Watts Building on Fire: hundreds feared dead' item.
'Main three Bulgarian players injured after Bulgaria–Spain football match'	Expect that most subjects would not want to see this item at the start. Item is strongly topically related to the 'England football team has to play Bulgaria in next match' item.
'Brighton University Watts Building on Fire: hundreds feared dead' (only in Condition A)	Most of the subjects' lectures take place in Watts Building. We therefore expected them to be both very interested in and very sad about this item. Constructed to investigate the effect of mood.
'England football team has to play Bulgaria in the next round' (only in Condition B)	Topically related to two other items, with a different degree of relatedness. Constructed to investigate the effect of topical relatedness.

*These news headlines were taken from the Yahoo news site http://uk.news.yahoo.com/ on 28-2-2003.

have to be determined after each presented item, as in Algorithm 3 of the previous section. If the ratings stay the same, then we could apply an ordering algorithm to the group list, as in Algorithm 2 of the previous section. Our hypothesis was that in both conditions the ratings would change.

- *Does mood influence the way ratings are adjusted?* Condition A was constructed to test this. We expected all subjects to feel very sad after viewing the 'Brighton University Watts Building on Fire: hundreds feared dead' item. Our hypothesis was that this would influence their ratings, particularly of items of a conflicting ('happy') mood, such as the '[Insert name of your favorite sport's club] wins important game' item.

- *Does topical relatedness influence the way ratings are adjusted?* Does having watched the first news item influence the ratings of topically related items to a higher extent than the ratings of topically unrelated items? Condition

B was constructed to test this. Our hypothesis was that after watching the 'England football team has to play Bulgaria in the next round' item, subjects would change their ratings for the 'Main three Bulgarian players injured after Bulgaria–Spain football match' item, and, to a lesser extent, for the 'Earthquake hits Bulgaria' item.

- *Does the subject's satisfaction influence the way ratings are adjusted?* Does a subject with a high rating for the first item increase the ratings of the other items? Does a subject with a low rating for the first item decrease the ratings of the other items? We can only test this on items that are topically unrelated and in the same mood (or these aspects might cause a change). Our hypothesis was that the rating for the 'Earthquake hits Bulgaria' item would increase after having seen the 'Brighton University Watts Building on Fire: hundreds feared dead' item, as both are sad items, topically unrelated, and the 'on fire' item is expected to have a high interest rating.
- *Is there an interaction between these factors?* Is there an interaction between the subject's satisfaction of an item and the effect of topical relatedness on ratings for other items? Our hypothesis is that subjects who express an interest in the 'England football team has to play Bulgaria in the next round' item are more likely to increase the rating of the topically related 'Main three Bulgarian players injured after Bulgaria–Spain football match' item than subjects who were not interested.

5.2.3. *Subjects*

Thirty-four subjects participated in the experiment. All were final-year undergraduate students of the IT faculty attending a lecture of the Adaptive Interactive Systems module.* The students were studying various courses (B.A. Computer and Information Systems, B.Sc. Computer Studies, B.Sc. Computer Science, and B.Sc. Software Engineering). The experiment took place in a lecture room. Subjects were randomly assigned to an experimental condition. Students participated in the experiment voluntarily (in addition to the numbers mentioned above, two students chose not to participate). The spread over courses was similar for both conditions.

5.3. EXPERIMENTAL RESULTS AND DISCUSSION

5.3.1. *Influence of Viewing an Item on Ratings for Other Items*

The results for Condition A ('Brighton University Watts Building on Fire: hundreds feared dead') clearly confirm our hypothesis that there can be a large influence of viewing an item on the ratings of other items. Figure 5.6 shows a dramatic

---

*Note: this experiment took place almost a year after Experiment 1, so none of these subjects had participated before.

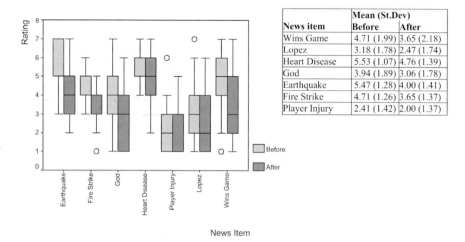

News item	Mean (St.Dev)	
	Before	After
Wins Game	4.71 (1.99)	3.65 (2.18)
Lopez	3.18 (1.78)	2.47 (1.74)
Heart Disease	5.53 (1.07)	4.76 (1.39)
God	3.94 (1.89)	3.06 (1.78)
Earthquake	5.47 (1.28)	4.00 (1.41)
Fire Strike	4.71 (1.26)	3.65 (1.37)
Player Injury	2.41 (1.42)	2.00 (1.37)

Figure 5.6. Box plot and summary table for Condition A showing the mean, standard deviation, median, and quartiles, and outliers (circles) of the subjects' ratings for the various news items before and after seeing the 'Brighton University Watts Building on Fire: hundreds feared dead' item.

decrease in ratings after seeing this item. All subjects modified at least one rating, and the difference in ratings was statistically significant. We can therefore conclude that Algorithm 3 is the best candidate.

5.3.2. *Influence of Mood*

The results for Condition A ('Brighton University Watts Building on Fire: hundreds feared dead') were hoped to shed some light on the influence of mood. We clearly succeeded in producing an item that made all subjects expect to feel sad. All subjects chose 'very sad', with the exception of two who chose the category just above that. However, we probably succeeded too well: subjects were expecting to be sad to the extent that most decreased their ratings across the board. Some subjects expressed this by making comments like 'I would not be interested to see anything anymore, when worried about friends dying'. This does confirm our hypothesis that mood can influence ratings, but not our more particular hypothesis about the way it would affect them. We did not find that the ratings of happy items decreased more than those of sad items. On the contrary, the Heart Disease item (judged by subjects as making them happy) showed a smaller decrease than the sad Earthquake item. So, contrary to our hypothesis and the literature described in Section 2.4.5, it might be that subjects actually prefer a happy item to distract them from the sad news. Subjects' comments also indicate that there is more to items than mood and topic: namely, an importance dimension. Subjects commented that after seeing the Brighton University On Fire item, they were no longer in the mood for irrelevant items, such as the Wins Game and Lopez items.

We also did a small pilot test using an – as we thought – positive mood inducing item 'War avoided by negotiation'. This proved problematic: our pilot subjects varied in opinion on how happy this item would make them feel. Their comments show that this was due to the subjects' opinion on the desirability of avoiding a war in Iraq. Note that we never specified which war was supposedly avoided. This shows the difficulty in constructing items with a certain fixed mood or interest.

5.3.3. *Influence of Satisfaction*

We could not draw any conclusions about the influence of satisfaction from the 'Earthquake in Bulgaria' item in Condition A, because the 'University on Fire' item had had the unexpected effect of changing all ratings. Also, no effect was found in Condition B. Therefore, we have not found any proof to support the recalculation of ratings dependent on the rating of the previous item. However, we need still to investigate whether satisfaction would have an influence if there were no other influencing factors (like mood and topical relatedness). It might also be that the influence of satisfaction is not a *conscious* influence, one that people are aware of, and that a more realistic experiment in which subjects were really viewing video clips is needed.

5.3.4. *Influence of Topical Relatedness*

The results for Condition B ('England football team has to play Bulgaria in the next round') confirm our hypothesis that viewing an item can influence the ratings of topically related items. Figure 5.7 shows that subjects increased the ratings of

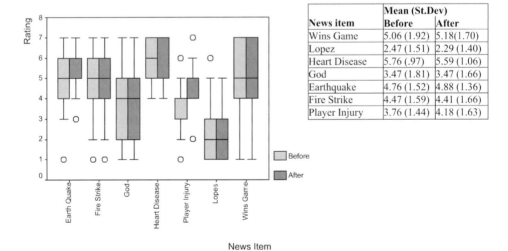

News item	Mean (St.Dev)	
	Before	After
Wins Game	5.06 (1.92)	5.18(1.70)
Lopez	2.47 (1.51)	2.29 (1.40)
Heart Disease	5.76 (.97)	5.59 (1.06)
God	3.47 (1.81)	3.47 (1.66)
Earthquake	4.76 (1.52)	4.88 (1.36)
Fire Strike	4.47 (1.59)	4.41 (1.66)
Player Injury	3.76 (1.44)	4.18 (1.63)

Figure 5.7. Box plot and summary table for Condition B showing the mean, standard deviation, median, quartiles, and outliers (circles) of the subjects' ratings for the various news items before and after seeing the 'England football team has to play Bulgaria in the next round' item.

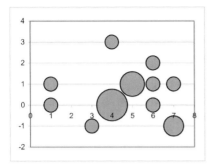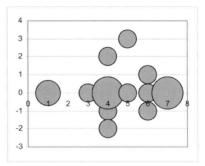

Figure 5.8. Rating differences for 'Main three Bulgarian players injured after Bulgaria–Spain football match' (left) and 'Earthquake hits Bulgaria' (right) after seeing the 'England football team has to play Bulgaria in the next round' news item (y-axis), plotted against the rating of the subject for the latter (x-axis). Size of the bubbles indicates number of subjects.

the topically related items, while the ratings of the topically unrelated items remained similar (actually, the means even show a small decline in ratings for these items). The strongly topically related 'Main three Bulgarian players injured after Bulgaria–Spain football match' also showed a larger change in ratings than the weakly related 'Earthquake hits Bulgaria'.

5.3.5. *Interaction Between Satisfaction and the Effect of Topical Relatedness*

We expected the effect of topical relatedness to depend on the interest the subject had for the item they viewed. For instance, if a subject were completely uninterested in the English football team, then we would not expect an effect on their ratings for the related 'Main three Bulgarian players injured after Bulgaria–Spain football match'. On the contrary, if a subject were very interested in the English football team, then we would expect their ratings for the related item to go up. Figure 5.8 shows the effect of watching the first (England–Bulgaria) item on the topically related items (Bulgarian Player Injury, and Earth Quake in Bulgaria) as a function of the subjects' ratings for the first item. The figure to a certain extent supports our hypothesis, with the increases in ratings mainly for subjects who expressed some interest (rating 5 and above), and the decreases in ratings mainly for subjects who were not that interested (ratings 4 and below).

6. Conclusions

Group modeling is an interesting research area with a wide possibility of applications, both in interactive television and beyond. In this paper, we have defined the problems associated with adaptation to groups, described our initial research in this area, discovered some answers and many more questions that need answering.

6.1. CONCLUSIONS FROM THE STUDY

The main results from this study are:

- People use some of the choice strategies described in Section 2, such as the Average Strategy (a.k.a. Additive Utilitarian), the Average Without Misery Strategy and the Least Misery Strategy, and care about fairness and avoiding individual misery. (Experiment 1)
- People use normalization: their satisfaction does not only depend on the selected items, but also on the not selected ones. (Experiment 2)
- People deduct misery: their satisfaction is negatively affected by disagreeable experiences, more than because of losing out on possible pleasure. (Experiment 2)
- People use the ratings in a non-linear way: i.e. the difference in ratings between say 9 and 10 is regarded as larger than that between 7 and 8. (Experiment 2)
- The 'Normalized Quadratic Addition, Pleasure minus Misery' satisfaction function produced reasonable, though not completely correct predictions. (Experiment 2)
- The sequences produced by five choice strategies (Borda Count, Multiplicative Utilitarian, Average without Misery, Most pleasure, and Additive Utilitarian) gave, in our example, on average satisfaction to all individuals in the group. (Experiment 2)
- Multiplicative Utilitarian seems the best strategies as it's sequence produced satisfaction for all individuals in the group according to all subjects. (Experiment 2)
- People's opinion about items can change dramatically as a result of watching another item. Hence, ratings need to be recalculated after showing each item, and a new Group list needs to be determined before selecting the next item. (Experiment 3)
- People's opinion about items can change as a result of the mood induced by watching an item. Watching a very sad item can decrease the ratings for other items. Contrary to expectation, it does not seem to decrease the ratings of conflicting mood items more than those of similar mood. (Experiment 3)
- People's opinion about items can change as a result of their topical relatedness to a shown item. There is a trend towards an interaction with Satisfaction: if the person is interested in the shown item, then the ratings of topically related items are more likely to increase. (Experiment 3)

6.2. LIMITATIONS OF THE STUDY

6.2.1. *Indirectness of the Experiments*

As discussed in Sections 3 and 4, we have deliberately chosen to make the experiments *indirect*. In Experiment 1, rather than having an actual group sit down to decide what to watch, subjects were asked what they *thought* people should watch. In Experiment 2, rather than having an actual group sit down and *measure* how satisfied each individual would be with a certain sequence, subjects were asked how satisfied they *thought* all members of the group would be. In Experiment 3, real news headings were used for items, rather than the abstract items used in the earlier experiments. But again, we did not really show the items to the subjects, but asked them how much they wanted to see them and how they *expected* viewing them would make them feel. We explained the reasons for this indirect approach in Sections 3 and 4, and they mainly had to do with controlling the experiment. However, as always, the more an experiment is controlled, the less it resembles the real world.

6.2.2. Subjects Used in the Experiments

The sets of subjects were quite homogeneous, particularly the level of education: either having or studying for a degree, mostly in computing. Subjects were also from a relatively narrow age range (though not as narrow as the word 'student' suggests, as we have a large proportion of mature students), and the majority of subjects in Experiments 1 and 3 were male. This raises some doubts about the generalisability of the results, as the demographic of a television audience is a lot more heterogeneous. However, as the indirectness of our experiments did require a certain level of education, it would have been impossible to use a cross section of the population. This would also have required a rather large group of subjects. Nevertheless, the generalisability of the results remains to be proven.

6.2.3. Example Used in the Experiments

In both Experiments 1 and 2, we have used the example of a group of three people, with particular ratings for these three people. It still needs to be proven that our result about the suitability of the strategies is generalisable to larger groups, and different rating distributions.

6.2.4. Assumptions Made

As discussed in Section 2, we have made a number of assumptions. In a sense, all of them are limitations of this study. The most important limitation seems our assumption that ratings are accurate: recommender systems need to be able to deal with uncertainty. This might mean that rather than having an accurate rating for an individual for an item, we might have a probability distribution that indicates the likelihood of certain ratings for that item. Or it might mean that we have an estimated rating with an indication of how certain the system is about its estimation. Taking uncertainty into account would have made our experiments far more complicated. We had, therefore, decided to separate concerns, and start with the assumption that ratings were accurate. We believe that most results – in the sense of what is important to people, like avoiding misery – would still hold when dealing with uncertainty, but that an additional set of rules would apply in that case.

6.3. AREAS FOR FURTHER WORK

Our research has only just started, and raises many questions that warrant further research. For example:

- The Multiplicative Utilitarian strategy seems a good strategy to use, but more experiments are needed to confirm this. These experiments would need to deal with the limitations mentioned above.
- One way to reduce the effort involved in empirical evaluations would be to have a good Satisfaction Function to predict experimental results. The 'Normalized Quadratic Addition, Pleasure minus Misery' satisfaction function is a promising start, but needs further improvement to become more accurate.
- Finding a highly accurate Satisfaction Function would also allow us to mathematically determine the optimal strategy.
- The ordering of the sequence requires more investigation. This is not only a group adaptation issue, but applies also when dealing with only one viewer. We need to determine what exactly the effect of mood is, how to correctly predict the size of the effect of topical relatedness on ratings, and how to deal with the importance dimension. On a more practical level, we need to investigate how mood, topicality, and importance can be automatically detected based on subtitles, audio, and video.
- Invisible members can be added to a group (to represent teachers, or parents) to ensure that a viewer's (student or child) overall viewing experience is more appropriate. It should be investigated how this can be done and can be made both acceptable and beneficial for the viewer. Similarly, television critics could be added as members of a group. Their ratings would accurately reflect their opinions.
- An individual's satisfaction might be influenced by adequate user interface design. For instance, when showing an item, it could be indicated to the viewers what the next item(s) will be (for instance, using a subtitle). This tells viewers who do not like the current item that the next one will be to their taste. This might avoid dissatisfaction, boredom, and walking away from the television.

Acknowledgements

The author would like to thank the anonymous reviewers for constructive suggestions and comments which aided in improving the article, and the Nuffield Foundation for support via grant NAL/00258/G.

References

Ardissono, L. and Buczak, A. (eds.) (2002). *Proceedings of the 2nd Workshop on Personalization in Future TV*, Malaga, Spain.
Ardissono, L., Goy, A., Petrone, G., Segnan, M. and Torasso, P. (2002). Tailoring the recommendation of tourist information to heterogeneous user groups. In: S. Reich, M. Tzagarakis, and P. De Bra (eds.), *Hypermedia: Openness, structural awareness, and*

adaptivity, International Workshops OHS-7, SC-3, and AH-3, 2001. Lecture Notes in Computer Science 2266, Berlin: Springer Verlag, pp. 280–295.

Arrow, K. (1950). A difficulty in the concept of social welfare. *Journal of Political Economics*, **58**, 328–346.

Arrow, K. (1951). *Social Choice and Individual Values.* New York: John Wiley and Sons.

Barwise, P. and Ehrenberg, A. (1988). *Television and Its Audience.* London: Sage.

Borda, J.C. (1781). *Mémoire sur les elections au scrutine.* Histoire de l'Académie Royale des Sciences.

Cohen, W., Schapire, R. and Singer, Y. (1999). Learning to order things. *Journal of Artificial Intelligence Research*, **10**, 243–270.

Condorcet, Marquis de (1785). Essai sur l'application de l'analyse à la probalité des décisions rendues à la pluralité des voix. Paris.

Copeland, A.H. (1951). *A Reasonable Social Welfare Function.* Mimeo, University of Michigan.

Cotter, P. and Smyth, B. (2000). PTV: Intelligent personal TV guides. *12th Innovative Applications of Artificial Intelligence Conference*, Austin, Texas, pp. 957–964.

Cranor, L.F. (1996). Declared-strategy voting: An instrument for group decision-making. Ph.D. Thesis, Washington University. http://ccrc.wustl.edu/~lorracks/dsv/diss/node4.html

Dwork, C., Kumar, R., Naor, M. and Sivakumar, D. (2001). Rank aggregation methods for the web. *Tenth International World Wide Web Conference*, Hong Kong, pp. 613–622.

Ephrati, E. and Rosenschein, J.S. (1996). Deriving consensus in multi agent systems. *Artificial Intelligence*, **87**, 21–74.

Fagin, R., Lotem, A. and Naor, M. (2003). Optimal aggregation algorithms for middleware. *Journal of Computing System Sciences,* **66**, 614–656.

Gardner, M. (1985). Mood states and consumer behavior: A critical review. *Journal of Consumer Research*, **12**, 281–300.

Gillard, P. (1999). The child audience: Who are they and how are they using TV and new media? Paper presented at the Children's Television Policy Forum and Reception, Sydney, 22 July. As accessed on http://www.aba.gov.au/abanews/conf/1999/pdfrtf/20years_gillard.rtf.

Goren-Bar, D. and Glinansky, O. (2002). Family stereotyping: A model to filter TV programs for multiple viewers. In: L. Ardissono and A. Buczak (eds.) *Proceedings of the 2nd Workshop on Personalization in Future TV*, Malaga, Spain, pp. 95–102.

Hogg, L. and Jennings, N.R. (1999). Variable sociability in agent-based decision making. *Sixth International Workshop on Agent Theories Architectures and Languages,* Orlando, FL, USA, pp. 276–289.

Kamins, M.A., Marks, L.J. and Skinner, D. (1991). Television commercial evaluation in the context of program induced mood: Congruency versus consistency effects. *Journal of Advertising*, **20**(2), 1–14.

Kasari, H., Nurmi, S. (1992). TV audience segments based on viewing behaviour. In: *Advertising Research Foundation (ARF) and European Society for Opinion and Marketing Research (ESOMAR)*, Worldwide Broadcast Audience Research symposium. Toronto.

Kotler, J., Wright, J. and Huston, A. (2001). Television use in families with children. In: J. Bryant and J.A. Bryant (eds.), *Television and the American family.* Mahwah, N.J.: Lawrence Erlbaum Associates, 33–48.

Lekakos, G., Papakiriakopoulos, D. and Chorianopoulos, K. (2001). An integrated approach to interactive and personalized TV advertising. In: L. Ardissono and Y. Faihe (eds.) *Proceedings of the 2001 Workshop on Personalization in Future TV*, Sonthofen, Germany.

Lieberman, H., van Dyke, N. and Vivacqua, A. (1999) Let's browse: A collaborative web browsing agent. *1999 International Conference on Intelligent User Interfaces,* Los Angeles, CA, pp. 65–68.

Lijphart, A. (1994). *Electoral Systems and Party Systems: A Study of Twenty-seven Democracies 1945, 1990.* Oxford: Oxford University Press.

Livingstone, S. and Bovill, M. (1999). Young people, new media. Summary report of the research project: Children, young people and the changing media environment. As accessed on http://www.lse.ac.uk/Depts/Media/people/slivingstone/young people report.pdf.

Masthoff, J. (2002). Modeling a group of television viewers. *Future TV: Adaptive Instruction in Your Living Room Workshop,* San Sebastian, Spain, pp. 34–42.

Masthoff, J. (2003). Modeling the multiple people that are me. In: P. Brusilovsky, A. Corbett, and F. de Rosis (eds.) *Proceedings of the 2003 User Modeling Conference,* Johnstown, PA, Berlin: Springer Verlag, pp. 258–262.

Masthoff J. and Luckin, R. (eds.) (2002). *Proceedings of the workshop Future TV: Adaptive Instruction in Your Living Room, associated with the Intelligent Tutoring Systems Conference,* San Sebastian, Spain.

May, K.O. (1952). A set of independent, necessary and sufficient conditions for simple majority decision. *Econometrica,* **20,** 680–684.

Maybury, M.T., Greiff, W. Boykin, S., Ponte, J., McHenry, C. and Ferro, L. (2004). Personal Casting: Tailored broadcast news. **14,** 119–144 (this issue).

McCarthy, J. and Anagnost, T. (1998). MusicFX: An arbiter of group preferences for computer supported collaborative workouts. *ACM 1998 Conference on CSCW,* Seattle, WA, pp. 363–372.

Meloy, M. (2000). Mood-driven distortion of product information. *Journal of Consumer Research,* **27,** 345–359.

Murray, J., Lastovicka, J. and Singh, S. (1992). Feeling and liking responses to television programs: An examination of two explanations for media-context effects. *Journal of Consumer Research,* **18,** 441–451.

O' Conner, M., Cosley, D., Konstan, J.A. and Riedl, J. (2001). PolyLens: A recommender system for groups of users. In: *Proceedings of ECSCW 2001,* Bonn, Germany, pp. 199–218. As accessed on http://www.cs.umn.edu/Research/GroupLens/poly-camera-final.pdf.

O' Sullivan, D., Smyth, B., Wilson, D.C., McDonald, K. and Smeaton, A. (2004). Improving the quality of the personalized electronic program guide. **14,** 5–35 (this issue).

Pareto, V. (1897). *Cours d'economie politique.* Lausanne: Rouge.

Pattanaik, P.K. (1971). *Voting and Collective Choice.* Cambridge: Cambridge University Press.

Pennock, D., Horvitz, E. and Giles, C. L. (2000). Social choice theory and recommender Systems: Analysis of the axiomatic foundations of collaborative filtering. *17th National Conference on Artificial Intelligence,* Austin, TX, pp. 729–734.

Plua, C. and Jameson, A. (2002). Collaborative preference elicitation in a group travel recommender system. In F. Ricci and B. Smyth (eds.) *Proceedings of the AH'2002 Workshop Recommendation and Personalization in eCommerce,* Malaga, Spain, 148–154.

Schumann, D. and Thorson, E. (1990). The influence of viewing context on commercial effectiveness: A selection-processing model. *Current Issues and Research in Advertising,* **12,** 1–24.

Taylor, A. (1995) *Mathematics and politics: Strategy, voting, power and proof.* New York: Springer Verlag.

Van Evra, J. (1998). *Television and Child Development.* Mahwah, N.J.: Lawrence Erlbaum Associates.

Zimmerman, J., Parameswaran, L. and Kurapati, K. (2002). Celebrity recommender. In: L. Ardissono and A. Buczak (eds.) *Proceedings of the 2nd Workshop on Personalization in Future TV,* Malaga, Spain, pp. 33–41.

Appendix A

SCENARIO 1

John, Mary, and Adam are going to watch video clips together. We know how interested they are in the topics of the clips. Each clip is rated from 1 – really hate this topic, to 10 – really like this topic.

Clip	John	Adam	Mary
A	10	1	10
B	4	9	5
C	3	8	2
D	6	9	7
E	10	7	9
F	9	9	8
G	6	6	5
H	8	9	6
I	10	3	7
J	8	8	6

1. They only have time to watch one clip. Which clip should they watch? Why?
2. They only have time to watch two clips. Which clips should they watch? Why?
3. They only have time to watch three clips. Which clips should they watch? Why?
4. They only have time to watch four clips. Which clips should they watch? Why?
5. They only have time to watch five clips. Which clips should they watch? Why?
6. They only have time to watch six clips. Which clips should they watch? Why?
7. They only have time to watch seven clips. Which clips should they watch? Why?

SCENARIO 2

John (29), Mary (32), and their grandfather Adam (81) are going to watch video clips together. We know how interested they are in the topics of the clips. Each clip is rated from 1 – really hate this topic, to 10 – really like this topic.

Clip	John	Adam	Mary
A	10	1	10
B	4	9	5
C	3	8	2
D	6	9	7
E	10	7	9
F	9	9	8
G	6	6	5
H	8	9	6
I	10	3	7
J	8	8	6

1. They only have time to watch one clip. Which clip should they watch? Why?
2. They only have time to watch two clips. Which clips should they watch? Why?
3. They only have time to watch three clips. Which clips should they watch? Why?
4. They only have time to watch four clips. Which clips should they watch? Why?
5. They only have time to watch five clips. Which clips should they watch? Why?
6. They only have time to watch six clips. Which clips should they watch? Why?
7. They only have time to watch seven clips. Which clips should they watch? Why?

Appendix B

Age: Gender: M/F

You and two friends (Friend1 and Friend2) are going to watch video clips together. The Television knows how interested you are in the topics of the clips. Each clip is rated from 1 – really hate this topic, to 10 – really like this topic.

Clip	You	Friend1	Friend2
A	10	1	10
B	4	9	5
C	3	8	2
D	6	9	7
E	10	7	9
F	9	9	8
G	6	6	5
H	8	9	6
I	10	3	7
J	8	8	6

It decides to show you the following sequence of clips: E A F I D

	Very dissatisfied		Neutral				Very satisfied
How satisfied would you be?	1	2	3	4	5	6	7

Why?

How satisfied do you believe Friend1 would be? 1   2   3   4   5   6   7
Why?

How satisfied do you believe Friend2 would be? 1   2   3   4   5   6   7
Why?

Appendix C

Age: Gender: M/F

You are going to watch the evening news. A number of things have happened today, and the news programme has to make a selection about what to show you. Decide for the following news items how *interested* you would be to see them, and how you think they would make you *feel*. Each news item is described by its headline, more detail would be given in the news. Assume all news items to be true.

'[Insert name of your favorite sport's club] wins important game'

	Really Hate to		Neutral		Really Want to	
How much would you want to watch this news item?	1	2	3	4	5	6	7

	Very Sad		Neutral		Very Happy	
How might you expect this news item to make you *feel*?	1	2	3	4	5	6	7

'Fleet of limos for Jennifer Lopez 100-metre trip'

	Really Hate to		Neutral		Really Want to	
How much would you want to watch this news item?	1	2	3	4	5	6	7

	Very Sad		Neutral		Very Happy	
How might you expect this news item to make you *feel*?	1	2	3	4	5	6	7

'Heart disease could be halved'

	Really Hate to		Neutral		Really Want to	
How much would you want to watch this news item?	1	2	3	4	5	6	7

	Very Sad		Neutral		Very Happy	
How might you expect this news item to make you *feel*?	1	2	3	4	5	6	7

'Is there room for God in Europe?'

	Really Hate to		Neutral		Really Want to	
How much would you want to watch this news item?	1	2	3	4	5	6	7

	Very Sad		Neutral		Very Happy	
How might you expect this news item to make you *feel*?	1	2	3	4	5	6	7

'Earthquake hits Bulgaria'

	Really Hate to		Neutral		Really Want to	
How much would you want to watch this news item?	1	2	3	4	5	6	7

	Very Sad		Neutral		Very Happy	
How might you expect this news item to make you *feel*?	1	2	3	4	5	6	7

'UK fire fighter strike continues'

	Really Hate to		Neutral		Really Want to	
How much would you want to watch this news item?	1	2	3	4	5	6	7

	Very Sad		Neutral		Very Happy	
How might you expect this news item to make you *feel*?	1	2	3	4	5	6	7

'Main three Bulgarian players injured after Bulgaria-Spain football match'

	Really Hate to		Neutral		Really Want to	
How much would you want to watch this news item?	1	2	3	4	5	6	7

	Very Sad		Neutral		Very Happy	
How might you expect this news item to make you *feel*?	1	2	3	4	5	6	7

The first item on the news is 'Brighton University Watts Building on Fire: hundreds feared dead'

	Really Hate to		Neutral		Really Want to	
How much would you want to watch this news item?	1	2	3	4	5	6	7

	Very Sad		Neutral		Very Happy	
How might you expect this news item to make you *feel*?	1	2	3	4	5	6	7

Given that you have just seen this item, how much would you now want to watch these items?

	Really Hate to			Neutral			Really Want to
'[Insert name of your favorite sport's club] wins important game'	1	2	3	4	5	6	7
'Fleet of limos for Jennifer Lopez 100-metre trip'	1	2	3	4	5	6	7
'Heart disease could be halved'	1	2	3	4	5	6	7
'Is there room for God in Europe?'	1	2	3	4	5	6	7
'Earthquake hits Bulgaria'	1	2	3	4	5	6	7
'UK fire fighter strike continues'	1	2	3	4	5	6	7
'Main three Bulgarian players injured after Bulgaria-Spain football match'	1	2	3	4	5	6	7

Has watching the 'Brighton University Watts Building on Fire: hundreds feared dead' news item changed your opinion? How and why?

Condition B: Same as condition A, only now
'Brighton University Watts Building on Fire: hundreds feared dead' is replaced by 'England football team has to play Bulgaria in the next round'.

Chapter 6

Categorization of Japanese TV Viewers Based on Program Genres They Watch

YUMIKO HARA, YUMIKO TOMOMUNE[1] and MAKI SHIGEMORI[2]
NHK Broadcasting Culture Research Institute
e-mail: {hara.y-ig, tomomune.y-iy, shigemori.m-ek}@nhk.or.jp

Abstract. Although program preferences can be characterized on the basis of demographic attributes like sex, age or occupation or by taking the cultural studies approach focused on ethnic or social traits, preferences for programs often differ among people of the same sex, age, occupation and social class. We think that nothing can describe subjects' viewing preferences more accurately than what programs they had watched in the past. To verify our hypothesis, we surveyed the viewing behavior of more than 1,600 randomly chosen individuals, and utilized this data to analyze people's program choices. We categorized the respondents by the similarity of the programs they had watched and examined the groupings that emerged and the features of these groups.

From our analysis, it became clear that a 'more/less serious' and 'more/less fictional' axes are involved in program selection.

Our results show that eight groups (stereotypes) explain viewers' contact with television, their motivation for choosing programs to watch, and their interest in matters other than television. Applying these stereotypes to the process of program selection or recommendation will be useful for the future design of personalized adaptive systems.

Key words. audience segmentation, Japan, personalized TV, program genre, stereotype, TV, user study, viewer, viewing preference

1. Aims

Although program preferences can be characterized on the basis of demographic attributes like sex, age or occupation or by taking the cultural studies approach focused on ethnic or social traits (Webster et al. 1983; Morley, 1992; Ang, 1996), preferences for programs often differ among people of the same sex, age, occupation and social class. We think nothing can describe subjects' viewing preferences more accurately than what programs they watched in the past. The aim of this paper is to propose an effective method for determining viewer groups based on an analysis of individuals' viewing behavior, to contribute to the future design of personalized adaptive TV systems.

---

[1]Yumiko Tomomune now works at the Japan Prize Secretariat in NHK.
[2]Maki Shigemori now works at the Corporate Planning Bureau in NHK.

L. Ardissono et al. (eds.), Personalized Digital Television, 143–173, 2004.

Previous studies in Japan have already attempted to define TV viewer types. Major studies were: (a) Sugiyama (1968); (b) Izumi (1973); (c) Fujiwara (1983); (d) Miwa (1986); (e) Nagashima (2000), and (f) Video Research Ltd., (2000). Studies (a)–(d) were carried out by the NHK Broadcasting Culture Research Institute, while (e) and (f) were done by Video Research Ltd., a viewer ratings research company. In all cases, these studies attempted to group viewers according to factors other than demographic characteristics and to elucidate the features of viewer groups.

Studies (b), (e) and (f) were based on existing viewer ratings data, and although researchers could determine which programs individual samples had watched, there was no data available on attitudes toward television. Studies (a), (c) and (d), meanwhile, were carried out using new survey designs intended to group viewers into stereotypes. They also included data on exposure to and attitudes toward television, which made the data used similar to ours. Study (d) examined television viewing characteristics of senior citizens and used attitudes toward television as the basis for developing viewer stereotypes. Studies (a) and (c) analyzed data using methods similar to those adopted by the authors of this paper, grouping viewers on the basis of specific programs watched. However, both studies were done over twenty years ago, when trends among viewers and the character of the TV programs themselves were quite different from today.

Building on past research conducted in Japan, we believed there was ample space for a new analysis, as presented in this study.

2. Method

2.1. TYPE OF DATA USED AND ANALYSIS FLOW

Our study is based on data from the Station Image Survey conducted by the NHK Broadcasting Culture Research Institute in March 2000 (Tomomune et al. 2000a; Hara et al. 2000). This study was done to determine the public images of NHK and commercial broadcasters.

The survey was conducted between Saturday February 26 and Sunday March 12, 2000 and involved 2,200 people aged 16–65 in Tokyo and six other Kanto region prefectures. The number of respondents was 1,683 and the response rate was 76.5%. One of the important characteristics of this survey is that the same respondents were surveyed both with regard to their attitudes and their actual viewing of programs.

Figure 6.1 describes the analytical process that was used to define viewer stereotypes using data from the Station Image Survey. The shaded areas in Figure 6.1 correspond to the Station Image Survey. Based on program viewing data in the study, respondents were grouped by quantification method III (see Section 2.3 and footnote 4) and the K-means cluster method. The viewer groups obtained in this way were then matched against the data from the attitude survey in order to elucidate the characteristics of each group.

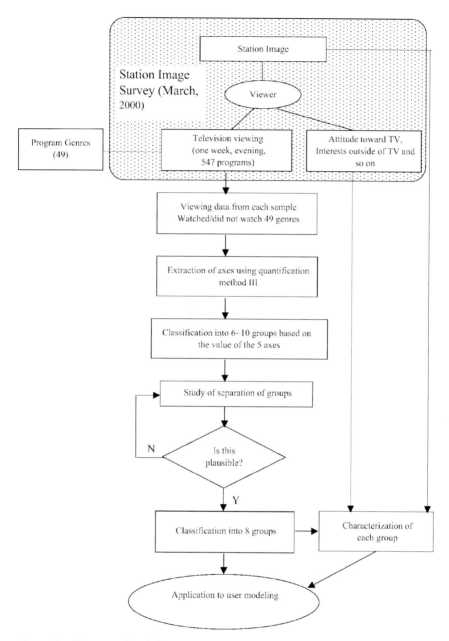

Figure 6.1. Sequence of analysis.

2.2. CLASSIFICATION OF PROGRAM GENRES

The sample in the Station Image Survey is limited from age 16–65 because we considered that people over 65 would find this complicated survey difficult to endure. The random sample of respondents consisted of 1,683 persons as described in

Table I. Sample composition

Male	No. of respondents	Female	No. of respondents
Total	864	Total	819
Age 16–19	58	Age 16–19	54
20–29	203	20–29	185
30–39	176	30–39	162
40–49	171	40–49	160
50–59	177	50–59	176
60–65	79	60–65	82

Table I. The actual program viewing survey consisted of 547 programs aired in the evening from Monday, 6 to Sunday, 12 March, 2000, on all terrestrial channels and the BS-1 and BS-2 satellite channels operated by NHK. Figure 6.2 shows the questionnaire employed in this study. The program listings for the one-week period were distributed to respondents' homes beforehand and retrieved later. Respondents were asked to circle the programs that they had 'watched thoroughly' and to indicate their reasons for viewing those particular programs.

Analyzing this data, we tabulated respondents' answers as to whether they had watched the programs 'thoroughly' or not. Working with 547 programs yielded too many possible combinations of viewing options, so we decided to group the 547 programs based on program categories already in use by television stations. We decided that the program categories generally used by NHK since 1971 were not appropriate for use in this analysis. The categories are outdated and have not kept up with current television viewing. For example, the variety program genre, which is also part of the 'entertainment/other entertainer' genre, is very popular today, and there are numerous types of variety programs.[3] What is known as reality-based programming in the United States comes under the 'variety' genre in Japan, as are programs that include singing interspersed with amusing talk. The 'variety' genre is therefore very broad and needs to be further subdivided.

We decided to develop our own classification of program types for this study. We taped and watched the 547 programs and classified them into genres and sub-genres, and developed definitions for each (Table II). For variety programs, using the programs' viewer functions and performance manner as variables, we developed 16 sub-genres to ensure balanced numbers. For example, among the viewer functions are 'makes viewers laugh and is enjoyable to watch' or 'good for watching late at night,' and among performance manner are 'features television personalities doing skits' or 'features adroit conversation.' Through this method we arrived at our final classification of 49 program genres and sub-genres (Tomomune et al. 2000b; hereafter referred to as 49 program genres). Using the definitions

---

[3]Variety programs in Japan began to proliferate from the second half of the 1980s, especially in the evening line-ups of commercial broadcasters. Variety program types became even more diversified in the 1990s. For the characteristics of variety programs, see Tomomune et al. (2001).

in Table II, anyone can classify programs the same way and obtain the same results. However, this classification system would need to be reviewed if new program types with very different content and formats should appear in a few years. Also, since this classification only considers the evening programs during a specific one-week period, some genres are not included (such as professional baseball and morning news summaries).

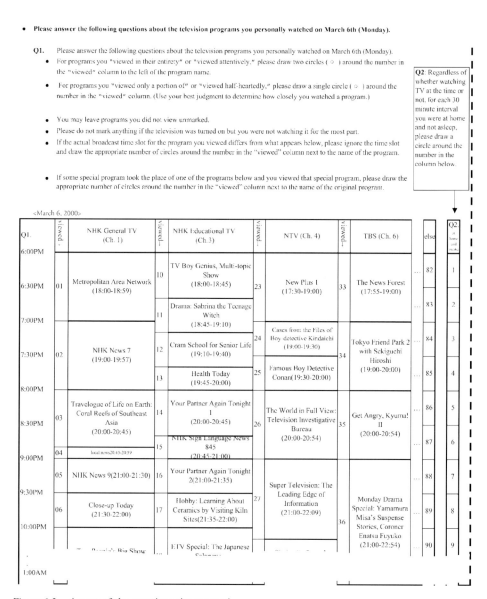

Figure 6.2. A part of the questionnaire we used.

Asking about the programs you watched thoroughly
Q3. Please give us the numbers of the   Q4. Please select the motives among below which suited best why you
programs you watched.   watched each program.

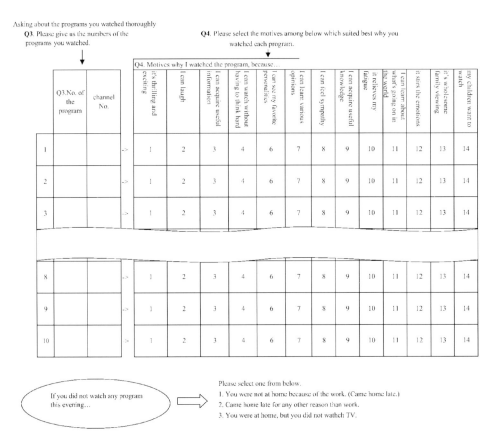

Figure 6.2. Continued.

Next, we mapped the 547 programs on the 49 genres. When we were uncertain about the classification of a particular program, we watched the program again before assigning it. We also asked the 1,683 respondents whether or not they had watched the respective programs 'thoroughly'. Table III shows the genres, the number of programs pertaining to each genre, and the ratio of viewers who 'had watched them thoroughly.'

2.3. DETERMINATION OF AXES RELATED TO PROGRAM SELECTION

Our analysis is based on the data of Table III. There are various methods for analyzing this type of data, and we used quantification method III, which was also employed by (a) Sugiyama (1968) and (c) Fujiwara (1983) (see Section 1). This is a pattern classification method developed by Chikio Hayashi, which accommodates simultaneous analysis of variables and samples. This method is used when there are no external criteria for analyzing qualitative data. In other parts of the world it is called 'analyse des correspondences' (Benzecri, 1973), 'optimal scaling'

Table II. Names and definitions of genres and sub-genres

Variety

Programs enjoyable to watch for their comedy, ability to move the emotions, stimulate identification or fear, or bring intellectual fulfillment

Basically studio programs hosted by personalities or celebrities and which also include several other personalities

In many cases, they include a variety of entertainment types, as the name of this genre implies

Skits/comedy	Calculated professional performances, such as skits, imitations or gags by personalities
Talk and gossip	Shows featuring interesting talk or skillful repartee
Debate	Debate on various subjects, either by personalities or members of the general public
Game-playing	Mainly personalities engaging in various games or contests
Talk and singing	At first glance, looks like a singing show, but is a program with a twist, with talk as the main element
Cooking/food	Features cooking, recipes, information about ingredients, gourmet restaurants/shops, etc.
General knowledge	Presents knowledge or information that viewers can then talk about
Information on daily life	Tips and information on clothing, food, housing, health and other topics related to daily living
Local community	Focuses on information concerning a specific area or community
Major events/incidents	Presents shocking or unusual events occurring in Japan or other countries
Adventure and challenge	Personalities or members of the general public attempt to perform difficult tricks or sports, acquire professional qualifications, etc.
True story/personal problem	Shows people making the most of their situation, or looking for solutions to personal problems
People-watching	'Candid Camera'-type situations orchestrated by a television station, where people's behavior is observed
Trend	Provides the latest information on fashions, music, films, etc.
Child-oriented	Presents video games, pastimes, animation and songs popular among children
Late-night	Programs appealing to certain tastes, or with adult content, for relaxed or unfocused late-night viewing

News

Programs communicating information acquired through news gathering

In most cases, the program is led by an anchorman in the studio and includes video clips

General news/early evening	General news broadcast in the 6 p.m. slot, reporting not only the day's news and weather but also presenting topics relating to family life, etc.
General news/mid-evening	General news broadcast in the 7 p.m., 8 p.m. or 9 p.m. slot, reporting the day's news and weather and also regional information, etc.
General news/late evening	General news broadcast at 10 p.m. or later, including detailed information on the day's news, special reports, sports results, weather, and currency/stock market reports.
Special topic	In-depth presentation reporting on one or several topics
Weekend	Omnibus program on the week's news events, broadcast on Saturdays or Sundays

---

(Continued)

Table II. (Continued)

Sports news	Results of sports matches in Japan and abroad, sports-related information
English-language Japanese news	News about Japan in English
Foreign-produced	Foreign-produced news or documentary programs aired for Japanese viewers

Documentary/report

Programs composed mainly of truth-based film shot on a specific theme

People	Features the life or philosophy of a certain personage
Society	Communicates social phenomena or situations, or probes social issues
Nature/science	Presents information about nature or science (animals, the environment, earth science, medical care, etc.)
Around town/living/food	Presents travel information, everyday food, dress and housing or unusual landscapes, local delicacies and local points of interest
Special	A television station orchestrates a situation and records exactly what happens
Hobby	Highlights a specific recreational activity_fishing, automobiles, etc.
Travelogue	Describes the people, customs and culture of various regions in Japan and other countries
Art/trend	Presents art works and artists

Drama

Fictional stories presented by actors

Crime/suspense	Stories about crime or suspense
Romance	Stories about love and romance
Foreign-produced	Imported from abroad
Life/youth	Themes that give viewers food for thought about life, or that are about youth
Historical drama	Set in old Japan
Others	Not included in the above

Live event

Special events, sports matches, concerts, etc. broadcast live or taped

Soccer	Soccer matches
Other sports	Basketball or other sports matches, excluding soccer
Performing arts/others	Broadcasts of concerts, presentation ceremonies, etc.

Instructional

Teaches or describes specific content or a specific activity
Features a presenter in the role of teacher

Daily life-related	How to cook, maintain fitness, etc.
Cultural/educational	Art, sociology, history, etc.
Hobby/game	Ceramics, drawing, handicrafts, dancing, etc.

We omit describing definitions of the genres without sub-genres, like Animation, Singing, Personality talk show, Movie and Others.

Table III. Program genres and viewers' rating

Genre	Sub-genre	No. of programs on the 7 terrestrial channels	'Watched thoroughly' ratio (%; $n = 1,683$)
Variety	Skits/comedy	12	31
	Talk and gossip	9	19
	Debate	3	12
	Game-playing	11	24
	Talk and singing	9	22
	Cooking/food	7	12
	General knowledge	14	35
	Information on daily life	3	23
	Local community	4	17
	Major events/incidents	3	13
	Adventure and challenge	6	18
	True story/personal problem	11	15
	People-watching	12	37
	Trend	11	3
	Child-oriented*	5	2
	Late-night	18	8
News	General news/early evening	29	19
	General news/mid-evening	26	19
	General news/late evening	34	31
	Special topic	9	12
	Weekend	3	8
	Sports news	13	11
	English-language Japanese news*	0	0
	Foreign-produced*	0	0
Documentary/ report	People	13	15
	Society	8	6
	Nature/science	6	10
	Around town/living/food	4	10
	Specials	6	8
	Hobby	2	3
	Travelogue	6	5
	Art/trend*	3	1
Drama	Crime/suspense	8	22
	Romance	10	33
	Foreign-produced	7	5
	Life/youth	5	25
	Historical drama	8	19
	Others	2	7
Animation		28	24
Singing		8	18
Personality talk show		6	7
Live event	Soccer	1	5
	Other sports	1	4
	Performing arts/others	3	6

(*Continued*)

Table III. (*Continued*)

Genre	Sub-genre	No. of programs on the 7 terrestrial channels	'Watched thoroughly' ratio (%; $n = 1,683$)
Movie		4	22
Instructional	Daily life-related	22	3
	Cultural/educational*	16	1
	Hobby/game*	4	1
Others*		3	1

*watched thoroughly by the least number of respondents.

Table IV. Types of multivariate analysis

External criteria	Explanatory variables (Characteristics of the data)	Methods
With quantitative	Quantitative	Multiple regression analysis Multiple correlation analysis
	Quantitative and/or qualitative	Quantification method I
With qualitative	Quantitative	Discreminant function Canonical correlation analysis
	Quantitative and/or qualitative	Quantification method II
Without	Quantitative	Component analysis Factor analysis
Without	Quantitative and/or qualitative	Quantification method III Quantification method IVEij Quantification method VKL Quantification method VI

or 'homogeneity analysis' (Gifi, 1981). Table IV shows the matrix of different methods available, categorized by whether or not external criteria are included as well as characteristics of the data.[4]

From the 49 genres, we excluded seven which were watched thoroughly by the least number of respondents (these are marked by * in Table III). The 42 remaining program genres were subject to quantification method III which uses the variable of whether or not the programs were 'watched thoroughly.' Our analysis yielded five axes, whose meanings were based on the scores for the 42 program genres.

The first axis (Figure 6.3) serves to group program genres into the two categories 'watched thoroughly' and 'not watched thoroughly.' The second axis obtained (Figure 6.4) has genres like Documentary/report at one end, and Personality talk

---

[4]Quantification method III is a method of structural analysis for multi-variable categorical data. Unlike methods I and II, it has no external criteria. Quantification method III has a long history, originating from Richardson and Kuder's (1933) method of reciprocal averages. Others (Guttman 1941; Maung 1941; Hayashi 1952) later obtained the same method from different criteria, and it was further refined by Benzecri (1973), Nishizato (1980) and others. Source: Takeuchi et al. (1989).

Variety: People-watching	0	
Variety: Skits/comedy	0	0 = not watched
Variety: Game-playing	0	1 = watched
Variety: General knowledge	0	
Variety: Talk and gossip	0	
Variety: Information on daily life	0	
Variety: Talk and singing	0	
Variety: Local community	0	
News: General news/late evening	0	
News: General news/early evening	0	
Variety: Adventure and challenge	0	
Variety: True story/personal problem	0	
Drama: Romance	0	
Animation	0	
Drama: Crime/suspense	0	
Drama: Life/youth	0	
Singing	0	
Variety: Cooking/food	0	
Variety: Major events/incidents	0	
Documentary/report: People	0	
Variety: Debate	0	
Movie	0	
Documentary/report: Around town/living/food	0	
⋮	⋮	

Singing	1
News: Sports news	1
Variety: Skits/comedy	1
Documentary/report: People	1
Variety: People-watching	1
Documentary/report: Hobby	1
Variety: Information on daily life	1
Variety: Debate	1
Drama: Foreign-produced	1
Variety: Talk and singing	1
Live event: Performing arts/others	1
Variety: Major events/incidents	1
News: General news/early evening	1
News: Weekend	1
Drama: Other	1
Variety: Adventure and challenge	1
Variety: Game-playing	1
Documentary/report: Around town/living/food	1
Variety: Cooking/food	1
Documentary/report: Specials	1
Variety: Talk and gossip	1
Personality talk show	1
Variety: True stories/personal problems	1
Variety: Late-night	1
Variety: Local community	1
Variety: Trend	1

Figure 6.3.   Program genres on Axis 1 (sorted by scores).

show, Singing and Drama at the other end. This axis was used to distinguish the seriousness of the genres watched. The third axis (Figure 6.5) consists of Live events, News, and Documentary/report at the one end, and at the other end genres such as Drama and Singing. This axis is thought to separate programs with more fictional content from those with less fictional content.

Documentary/report: Travelogue   1
Documentary/report: Society   1
News: Special topic   1
News: General news/mid-evening   1
Documentary/report: Nature/science   1   0 = not watched
Drama: Historical drama   1   1 = watched
News: Weekend   1
Instructional: Daily life-related   1
Documentary/report: Around town/living/food   1
Documentary/report: Hobby   1
News: General news/early evening   1
Singing   1
Variety: General knowledge   1
Variety: Information on daily life   1
News: Sports news   1
Documentary/report: People   1
News: General news/late evening   1
Drama: Crime/suspense   1
Variety: Skits/comedy   0
Live event: Soccer   1
⋮   ⋮

Drama: Foreign-produced   1
Live event: Other sports   1
Drama: Historical drama   0
Drama: Life/youth   1
News: General news/mid-evening   0
Variety: General knowledge   0
Variety: Major event/incidents   1
Animation   1
Variety: Game-playing   1
Variety: People-watching   1
Drama: Romance   1
Variety: Talk and gossip   1
Personality talk show   1
Variety: Adventure and challenge   1
Variety: Skits/comedy   1
Variety: Talk and singing   1
Variety: Late-night   1
Drama: Others   1
Variety: Trend   1

Figure 6.4. Program genres on Axis 2 (sorted by scores).

The fourth axis obtained appears to distinguish programs relating to daily life and practical information from art-related programs and programs with high production quality. The principle of its classifying effect was however not as clear as that of Axes 2 and 3. The significance of the fifth axis obtained was even more difficult to discern.

Live event: Other sports	1
Live event: Soccer	1
Variety: Trend	1
News:Sports news	1
Variety: Late-night	1
Documentary/report: Society	1
News:Weekend	1
Documentary/report :People	1
Documentary/report :Nature/science	1
News:General news/late evening	1
News:Special topic	1
Documentary/report: Hobby	1
Personality talk show	1
Documentary/report: Specials	1
Variety: Talk and gossip	1
Drama: Crime/suspense	0
Drama: Life/youth	0
Variety: Skits/comedy	1
Animation	0
Variety: Game-playing	1
⋮ ⋮	

0 = not watched
1 = watched

Variety: Adventure and challenge	1
News: Sports news	0
Drama: Romance	1
Movie	1
Documentary/report: Travelogue	1
News: General news/late evening	0
Variety: Major event/incident	1
News: General news/early evening	1
Instructional: Daily life-related	1
Variety: Information on daily life	1
Live event: Performing arts/others	1
Documentary/report: Around town/living/food	1
Animation	1
Drama: Historical drama	1
Singing	1
Drama: Others	1
Drama: Foreign-produced	1
Drama: Life/youth	1
Variety: True story/personal problem	1
Drama: Crime/suspense	1

Figure 6.5.   Program genres on Axis 3 (sorted by scores).

Based on the above, we regarded Axes 2 and 3 as the most effective in distinguishing the characteristics of the different program genres. The attributes of the program genres and respondents were therefore examined using these two axes.

2.3.1. *Close Distribution of Genres Viewed by the Same Viewer*

As shown in Figure 6.6, the positions of each program genre were plotted on a graph with Axis 2 as the horizontal axis and Axis 3 as the vertical axis. Genres in News and Documentary/report appear on the left side of the graph, while most of the Variety genres appear on the right. Genres in Drama are in the upper half, and genres consisting of Sports, Information and Talk are scattered across the lower half.

Quantification method III gives similar values to similar responses and respondents, and brings them together. Accordingly, for program genres located close to each other in this graph, the rate at which each genre was viewed by the same viewers is high, while for those located far apart from each other the rate at which they were viewed by different viewers is high.

The genres Variety: People-watching, Variety: Talk and singing, Variety: Game-playing, Variety: Skits/comedy, Variety: Talk and gossip, and Drama: Romance are located within a short distance of each other. Also close to one another are News: General news/early evening, Variety: Information on daily life, Instructional: Daily life-related, Documentary/report: Around town / living / food, Live event: Performing arts/others, Singing, and Animation. For each of these genres, the rate at which the same viewers watched the adjacent genres is high.

2.3.2. *Position of Average Values for Sex, Age Bracket and Occupational Group*

Figure 6.7 shows the average values according to respondents' sex, age bracket, and occupational group, also plotted along Axes 2 and 3. The average value for female viewers is on the 'less serious' side of Axis 2 (the horizontal axis) and on the 'more fictional' side of Axis 3 (the vertical axis), in other words, in the upper right quadrant. The average for males is directly opposite, in the third (lower left) quadrant (comparatively serious and less or non-fictional genres). The average values by age bracket show a wide distribution along Axis 2. The lower age brackets fall towards the 'less serious' side, the higher age brackets fall towards the 'more serious' side. For occupational groups, the averages for specialists/freelancers and housewives were in the 'more fictional' direction; agriculture/forestry/fisheries, unemployed/retired, self-employed, and managerial people were in the 'more serious,' 'less fictional' quadrant; students fell into the 'less serious,' 'less fictional' quadrant; and engineers, technicians, office workers and part-time/casual workers clustered near the center of the graph. Axis 2 has a strong correlation to age bracket, yielding a score of 0.619 when calculated according to Pearson's correlation factor (significant at the 1% level). Axis 3 showed some correlation to sex, with a correlation factor of 0.219 (significant at the 1% level). No axes showed a correlation with occupational group.

2.4. CLASSIFICATION INTO EIGHT VIEWER GROUPS

As was the case for Sugiyama (1968) and Fujiwara (1983), we used quantification method III to identify axes by analyzing whether or not individual programs

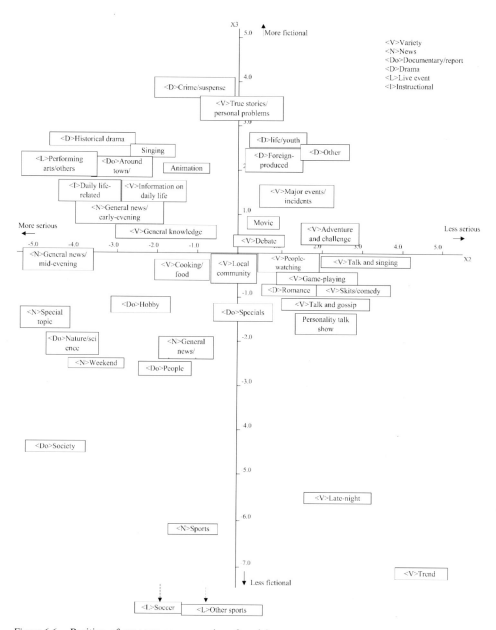

Figure 6.6. Position of program genres on Axes 2 and 3.

had been thoroughly watched. However, subsequent sample cluster grouping in those two studies was based on a combination of plus and minus scores added to just two axes. We used not only the two axes, whose meaning was clear, but also the others whose meaning had not been clearly interpreted, to group the samples. Each sample has a score vis-à-vis Axes 1 to 5, which we used to conduct a

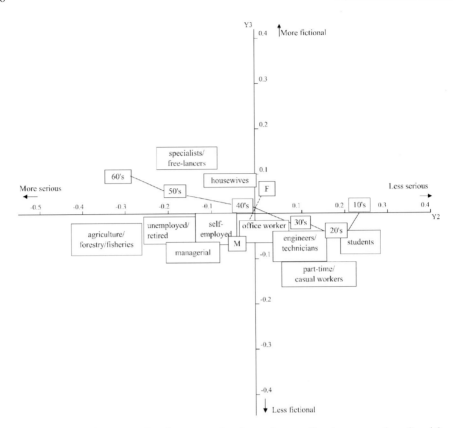

Figure 6.7.   Position of average values for sex, age bracket and occupational group on Axes 2 and 3.

K-means cluster analysis. Since samples with similar scores for each axis can be placed in the same group using this method, we believed that we found the optimum grouping after experimenting with several viewer clusters. Other methods, such as hierarchical clustering, are not appropriate for analyzing samples of over sixteen hundred cases. If we had grouped on the basis of predetermined factors, we would have excluded the possibility of identifying new factors for selecting programs. This includes the atmosphere of programs, the type of actors, and so on.

We examined the results obtained when six to ten viewer group clusters were used. We looked at the distribution and compared the characteristics of each group. Based on this, we determined that using eight groups yielded the clearest trends for program genres viewed. Accordingly, we adopted eight viewer groups.

3. Results

3.1. NAMING, DISTRIBUTION, CHARACTERISTICS

To better characterize the traits of each of the eight viewer groups, we gave them distinctive names. We analyzed them based on the Station Image Survey and identified the characteristics of each group, specifically with respect to their interests and attitude towards TV.

We gave these viewer groups the following names: 'laughter-/stimulation-seeker,' 'diversion-seeking zapper,' 'romance-/fiction-oriented,' 'trend-conscious TV devotee,' 'easygoing interest-seeker,' 'barely interested,' 'wholesome and practical type,' and 'news-/culture-oriented.'

The 'diversion-seeking zapper,' as the name suggests, hopped frequently between channels. The 'trend-conscious TV devotee' was keenly interested in trends and fads in general, not only in relation to television. The 'barely interested' type watched only a small number of programs thoroughly. Each group will be described in more detail below.

3.1.1. *Relative Position of the Eight Viewer Groups*

Figure 6.8 plots the eight viewer groups on axes 2 and 3. Each group is represented by an ellipse, whose center point represents the group's average score and whose size indicates the number of people in the group. When the viewer groups are superimposed on the program genres of Figure 6.6, some viewer groups overlap with program genres. This indicates that viewers in that group watched those genres thoroughly. As for the correlation among the viewer groups in terms of the program genres they watched, groups located close to one another had much in common while those far apart had almost nothing in common.

3.1.2. *Distribution and Characteristics of the Eight Viewer Groups*

Table V shows the ratio of males to females among the eight viewer groups. The 'diversion-seeking zapper,' 'barely interested' and 'news-/culture-oriented' groups had a significantly higher proportion of males, while the 'romance-/fiction-oriented,' 'trend-conscious TV devotee' and 'wholesome and practical type' groups included a significantly higher proportion of females.

Figure 6.9 shows the distribution of the eight viewer groups in the various age brackets, in five-year increments.[5] The overall average on the graph shows that the 'barely interested' group accounted for one-third of all respondents, while the 'trend-conscious TV devotee' group made up the smallest portion. This figure also shows which viewer groups are more common among the younger and older age brackets and which are spread evenly in all age brackets. In other words, different viewer groups can be found within the same age bracket.

---

[5]The elderly account for a high proportion of Japan's population, but the maximum age of Station Image Survey respondents was set at 65. We assumed that it would be difficult for older people to respond when asked about images in abstract terms, and therefore only surveyed individuals between 16 and 65 in this study.

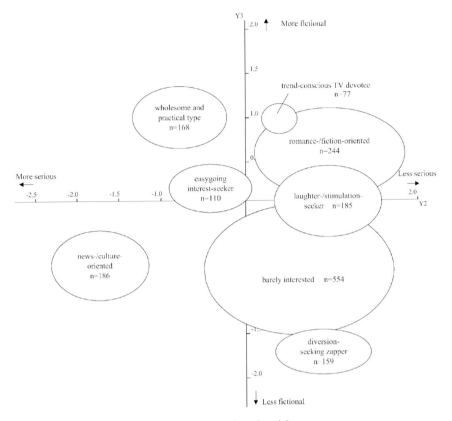

Figure 6.8. Position of eight viewer groups on Axes 2 and 3.

3.2. TV VIEWING TASTES

The genres of programs watched thoroughly by each viewer group are listed in Table VI (100% equaling the number of the people in the each group). Table VII lists the motivations of individuals, based on the number of programs they watched (100% equaling the total number of programs watched thoroughly by viewer group). Ranking in order of decreasing numbers is used for Tables VI and VII. Table VIII, showing data from the questions on television viewing attitude, records the proportion of respondents who answered 'yes' to each of six questions. These three tables will be used to describe the characteristics of the eight viewer groups.

3.2.1. *Characteristics of Each Group*

The laughter-/stimulation-seeker frequently watches Animation, Movie, Variety: Major events/incidents, and Variety: Skits/comedy, indicating that he/she likes laughter and stimulation. Many people in this group cite 'because I can laugh' or 'because I can watch without having to think hard' as the reasons why they watched the programs.

Table V. Ratio of male vs. female among the each viewer groups

	No. of respondents	% male	% female
Viewer group	1,683	51%	49%
Laughter-/stimulation-seeker	185	51%	49%
Diversion-seeking zapper	159	74%	26%
Romance-/fiction-oriented	244	31%	69%
Trend-conscious TV devotee	77	21%	79%
Easy going interest-seeker	110	55%	46%
Barely interested	554	59%	41%
Wholesome and practical type	168	37%	63%
News-/culture-oriented	186	59%	41%

The diversion-seeking zapper likes several Variety genres, including People-watching, Skits/comedy and Game-playing, and News genres such as General news/late evening. Motivations for watching television ranked in first and second place are the same as for the laughter-/stimulation-seeker, along with 'because I can see my favorite personalities.' The proportion of people in this group who hop between channels is significantly higher compared to the other groups.

The romance-/fiction-oriented viewer loves Drama: Romance, as well as Drama: Life/youth and Variety: People-watching. In other words, she/he likes to watch people on television. The top-ranking motivations for watching are similar to those in other groups, but 'because it stirs the emotions' is also an important motivation.

In the trend-conscious TV devotee group, when programs are extracted which more than 20% of respondents have watched thoroughly, we find a wide variety of genres are watched including the less to the more serious programs. Table VIII

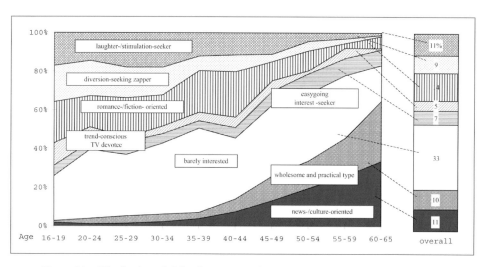

Figure 6.9. Distribution of eight viewer groups by age bracket.

Table VI. Genres watched thoroughly by the eight viewer groups, in descending order of relative frequency

Laughter-/stimulation-seeker		Diversion-seeking zapper	
No. of respondents 185		No. of respondents 159	
Animation	68%	Variety: People-watching	73%
Movie	63%	Variety: Skits/comedy	65%
Variety: Major events, incidents	59%	Variety: Game-playing	62%
Variety: Skits/comedy	54%	News: General news/late evening	59%
Variety: People-watching	49%	Variety: Talk and singing	54%
Variety: General knowledge	41%	Variety: Talk and gossip	52%
Variety: Debate	32%	Drama: Romance	50%
Variety: Adventure and challenge	31%	Variety: Late-night	42%
Drama: Life/youth	31%	News: Sports news	40%
Variety: Game-playing	28%	Variety: Local community	37%
Drama: Romance	25%	Variety: Adventure and challenge	35%
Variety: Talk and gossip	21%	Variety: General knowledge	33%
News: General news/late evening	21%	Documentary/report: People	26%
		Personality talk show	23%
		Variety: Information on daily life	21%
		Live event: Soccer	21%
		Animation	20%
		Variety: Cooking/food	20%
Romance-/fiction-oriented		Trend-conscious TV devotee	
No. of respondents 244		No. of respondents 77	
Drama: Romance	79%	Drama: Life, youth	81%
Drama: Life/youth	63%	Drama: Romance	79%
Variety: People-watching	48%	Variety: Talk and singing	64%
Variety: Skits/comedy	42%	Variety: Skits/comedy	60%
Variety: Talk and singing	40%	Animation	60%
Drama: Crime/suspense	31%	Variety: People-watching	57%
Animation	28%	Drama: Other	57%
News: General news/late evening	26%	Variety: General knowledge	55%
Variety: Game-playing	24%	Movie	52%
Singing	24%	Singing	49%
		News: General news/late evening	48%
		Variety: Game-playing	46%
		Variety: Information on daily life	40%
		Variety: Talk and gossip	39%
		Variety: Adventure and challenge	36%
		Live event: Performing arts/others	36%
		Documentary/report: People	33%
		News: General news/early evening	31%
		News: General news/mid-evening	29%
		Drama: Crime/suspense	27%
		Drama: Historical drama	25%
		Drama: Foreign-produced	25%
		Variety: Local community	22%
		Variety: Major events/incidents	22%
		Variety: True story/personal problem	21%
		Documentary/report: Special	21%

(Continued)

Table VI. (Continued)

Easygoing interest-seeker	
No. of respondents 110	
Variety: Local community	65%
Variety: General knowledge	61%
Variety: People-watching	60%
Variety: Skits/comedy	54%
Variety: Information on daily life	54%
Variety: True story/personal problem	49%
Variety: Game-playing	48%
News: General news/early evening	45%
Variety: Talk and gossip	43%
Variety: Major events/incidents	42%
Variety: Adventure and challenge	41%
News: General news/late evening	39%
Variety: Cooking/food	39%
Variety: Debate	33%
Drama: Crime/suspense	33%
Drama: Historical drama	33%
Animation	29%
Documentary/report: Around town/living/food	28%
Movie	27%
Variety: Talk and signing	25%
Documentary/report: People	22%
Documentary/report: Special	22%
News: General news/mid-evening	21%

Barely interested	
No. of respondents 554	
News: General news/early evening	17%
Drama: Romance	16%
Variety: People-watching	16%
Variety: General knowledge	16%
Variety: Skits/comedy	15%

Wholesome and practical type	
No. of respondents 168	
Drama: Crime/suspense	68%
Drama: Historical drama	61%
Variety: Information on daily life	58%
Variety: General knowledge	57%
News: General news/late evening	54%
Singing	47%
Variety: True stories/personal problems	46%
Variety: People-watching	41%
Documentary/report: Around town/living/food	39%
Variety: Local community	38%
News: General news/mid-evening	36%
Variety: Game-playing	31%
Drama: Romance	29%
Drama: Life/youth	29%
News: General news/late evening	26%
Variety: Cooking/food	23%
Variety: Talk and singing	22%
Animation	22%

News-/culture-oriented	
No. of respondents 186	
News: General news/mid-evening	74%
Variety: General knowledge	68%
News: General news/late evening	62%
News: Special topic	58%
Documentary/report: Nature/science	43%
Singing	40%
Variety: Information on daily life	37%
Drama: Historical drama	36%
Documentary/report: People	35%
News: General news/early evening	32%
Documentary/report: Society	30%
News: Weekend	26%
News: Sports news	24%
Documentary/report: Travelogue	23%
Drama: Crime/suspense	21%
Movie	20%

100% = No. of people per viewer group.
Extracted when watched thoroughly by 20% or more per viewer group.
However, in the 'barely interested' viewer group, none of the programs were watched thoroughly by over 20%, so in this case programs watched thoroughly by 15% or more were extracted.

Table VII. Motivation for watching 'thoroughly-watched programs' among the eight viewer groups, in descending order

Laughter-/stimulation-seeker	No. of thoroughly-watched proglams 2,209	
	Because I can laugh	34%
	Because I can watch without having to think hard	31%
	Because it's wholesome family viewing	18%
	Because it's thrilling and exciting	16%
	Because my children want to watch	16%
	Because it stirs the emotions	15%
Diversion-seeking zapper	No. of thoroughly-watched proglams 2,298	
	Because I can laugh	43%
	Because I can see watch without having to think hard	33%
	Because I can see my favorite personalities	21%
	Because I can acquire useful information	17%
	Because I can learn about what's going on in the world	17%
Romance-/fiction-oriented	No. of thoroughly-watched proglams 2,251	
	Because I can laugh	31%
	Because I can watch without having to think hard	29%
	Because I can see my favorite personalities	24%
	Because it stirs the emotions	18%
	Because it's wholesome family viewing	17%
	Because it's thrilling and exciting	16%
	Because it relieves my fatigue	15%
Trend-conscious TV devotee	No. of thoroughly-watched proglams 1,606	
	Because I can laugh	29%
	Because I can watch without having to think hard	27%
	Because it's wholesome family viewing	23%
	Because I can see my favorite personalities	20%
	Because it relieves my fatigue	16%
	Because it's thrilling and exciting	16%
	Because it stirs the emotions	16%
	Because I can acquire useful information	15%
Easygoing interest-seeker	No. of thoroughly-watched proglams 1,925	
	Because I can watch without having to think hard	30%
	Because I can laugh	30%
	Because I can acquire useful information	27%
	Because I can acquire useful knowledge	24%
	Because I can learn about what's going on in the world	21%
	Because it's wholesome family viewing	21%
	Because it relieves my fatigue	16%
	Because it stirs the emotions	16%
Barely interested	No. of thoroughly-watched proglams 1,816	
	Because I can watch without having to think hard	25%
	Because I can laugh	23%
	Because I can learn about what's going on in the world	21%
	Because I can acquire useful information	20%
	Because I can acquire useful knowledge	15%
	Because it stirs the emotions	15%

(Continued)

Table VII. (*Continued*)

Wholesome and practical type	No. of thoroughly-watched proglams 2,477	
	Because I can watch without having to think hard	25%
	Because it's wholesome family viewing	20%
	Because I can learn about what's going on in the world	19%
	Because I can acquire useful information	18%
	Because I can acquire useful knowledge	17%
	Because I can laugh	15%
News-/culture oriented	No. of thoroughly-watched proglams 2,563	
	Because I can learn about what's going on in the world	41%
	Because I can acquire useful information	32%
	Because I can acquire useful knowledge	28%
	Because I can watch without having to think hard	21%
	Because it's wholesome family viewing	15%

100%: total number of programs 'watched thoroughly' by each viewer group.
Motivation extracted for programs watch thoroughly by 15% or more of each viewer group.

shows that this viewer group ranks first among the eight groups in four out of the six questions, answering 'yes,' for example, to 'there are programs I look forward to every week' and 'I set time aside so that I can watch television.' This viewer group has a keen interest in watching television.

The easygoing interest-seeker ranks Variety programs, including those on Local community and General knowledge, from first to seventh place among program genres watched. This indicates that this viewer type wants to watch programs with rewarding content, in an easygoing manner. Third-ranked motivation for watching is 'because I can acquire useful information.'

The barely interested viewer group was given this name because there was no program that over 20% of them had watched thoroughly (Table VI). Table VIII also indicates that these individuals are not particularly interested television viewers.

The wholesome and practical viewer group watches Drama: Crime/suspense, Drama: Historical drama, Variety: Information on daily life and Variety: General knowledge. Compared to the other viewer groups, fewer people are motivated to watch television 'because I can laugh.' Their second-ranked motivation is 'because it's wholesome family viewing'.

The news-/culture-oriented viewer group often watches News: General news/mid-evening, News: General news/late evening, News: Special topic, Variety: General knowledge and Documentary/report: Nature/science. In this group, motivation for watching is very different than in the other groups, with 'because I can learn about what's going on in the world,' 'because I can acquire useful information' and 'because I can acquire useful knowledge' as the top-ranking reasons. This was the only viewer group for which the programs watched 'because I can laugh' make up less than 15% of the programs they watched thoroughly.

Table VIII. Television viewing attitude by the eight viewer groups

	Total	Laughter-/ stimulation- seeker	Diversion- seeking zapper	Romance-/ fiction- oriented	Trend- conscious TV devotee	Easygoing interest- seeker	Barely interested	Wholesome and practical type	News-/ culture- oriented
No. of respondents who answered yes to …	1,683	185	159	244	77	110	554	168	186
'There are programs I look forward to every week'	76%	82%*	83%*	83%*	97%*	85%*	60%*	87%*	75%
'I sometimes watch programs so that I can hold my own in conversations with family and friends'	23	28	22	24	42*	21	20*	26	16*
'I set time aside so that I can watch television'	29	35	31	35*	57*	40*	18*	29	27
'I'll even record programs that I want to watch'	48	51	56*	62*	65*	48	43*	36*	38*
'I generally have the TV program schedule memorized'	30	31	30	34	33	42*	21*	42*	33
'I sometimes channel-hop'	57	60	72*	57	57	64	57	47*	46*

*With a significant difference.

3.3. TOPICS OF INTEREST OTHER THAN TELEVISION

Topics of interest other than television among the eight viewer groups are listed in Table IX which shows the proportion of people in each viewer group who indicated that they were 'interested' in the topics named as choices in the Station Image Survey.

According to this, many diversion-seeking zapper and barely interested viewers are interested in work. Many barely interested individuals are probably busy with work and have little time for television. Many news-/culture-oriented viewers are interested in politics/economy, while many belonging to the easygoing interest-seeker and wholesome and practical type show an interest in health/diet. In the trend-conscious TV devotee group, many people are interested in trends/fashion and fitness/dieting, the source of this viewer group's name. While multiple answers were allowed in the case of topics of interest, the trend-conscious TV devotees include more items to which many respondents answered 'interested.' They not only watched many television programs thoroughly but were also very involved in other daily activities.

Although viewers were assigned to the eight groups solely on the basis of programs watched thoroughly, it seems there are also relationships between respondents' viewing tastes and topics of interest other than television, depending on the topic. This signifies that people's choices of TV programs are closely related to their lifestyles and senses of value.

4. Application of Results

4.1. APPLICATION TO A TV PROGRAM RECOMMENDATION SYSTEM

The method that we employed in this study measures similarities among users based on the sole criterion of their TV program selection behavior. We believe that this is the most useful approach for personalizing television viewing.

Murasaki et al. (2001) developed a prototype of a program selection system that is based on a multi-agent architecture. It employs stereotypes of television viewing behaviors to create a user model for each individual viewer. The system has a two-layered structure for managing individual user data that are used in program selection. One layer consists of a 'user profile' that manages data specific to a user, such as name, age, occupation, interests, and program history. The other layer consists of a 'user model' that employs statistical data on viewing patterns obtained from our research. Specifically, this user model manages the eight viewer stereotypes, and attempts to determine from calculations the extent to which an individual fits each of these stereotypes. At the time of program selection, the user model can identify new programs that potentially suit the tastes and needs of the individual in question by using the user profile as supplementary data, and can respond flexibly to changes in viewer tastes through the use of agents. Although this system is currently only a prototype, the underlying technique could be developed further into a personalized TV program selection system.

Table IX. Interests of the eight viewer groups beyond television

	Total	Laughter-/ stimulation- seeker	Diversion- seeking zapper	Romance-/ fiction- oriented	Trend- conscious TV devotee	Easygoing interest-seeker	Barely interested	Wholesome and practical type	News-/ culture- oriented
No. of respondents	1,683	185	159	244	77	110	554	168	186
Work	37%	33%	46%	30%	27%	35%	45%	29%	32%
Politics/economy	31	20	34	20	23	30	33	31	50
Volunteerism/social contribution	13	15	8	11	27	18	11	13	17
Savings/pension	21	18	16	20	20	29	18	25	29
Family issues	37	40	33	39	44	36	34	40	37
Local issues	16	18	12	11	21	18	13	20	23
Relations with people close to me	26	29	23	27	34	26	25	24	22
Education/ learning	23	27	21	29	38	16	24	15	16
Hobbies/recreation	58	63	65	59	51	59	59	48	58
Health/diet	51	42	47	55	48	62	44	66	56
Trends/fashion	20	18	37	29	36	19	18	10	7
Fitness/dieting	19	22	15	23	30	23	16	24	13

4.2. OTHER POSSIBLE APPLICATIONS

An analysis conducted using our stereotypes of different viewers reveals that programs categorized under the same genre do in fact appeal to very different viewer stereotypes.

To give an example, Figure 6.10 shows the results of a comparison, based on data from viewer surveys used in this analysis, of two news magazines: 'News 9,' public broadcaster NHK's 9 p.m. news broadcast, and 'News Station,' aired at 10 p.m. by a commercial broadcaster. A comparison of the viewer types of individuals who actually watched these two programs revealed interesting differences in the two audiences: whereas half of those who watched 'NHK News 9' were news-/ culture-oriented types, a large proportion of 'News Station' viewers were diversion-seeking zapper types who like to watch variety and sports programs, and laughter-/stimulation-seeker and romance-/fiction- oriented types who do not watch news programs very often. Using the stereotypes identified in this study, therefore, TV producers/broadcasters can reveal program characteristics that viewer demographics cannot.

The distribution of the eight viewer types in the five-year age brackets also reveals that different viewer types are present even within the same age bracket (Figure 6.9). A final application of our results would be the targeted development of

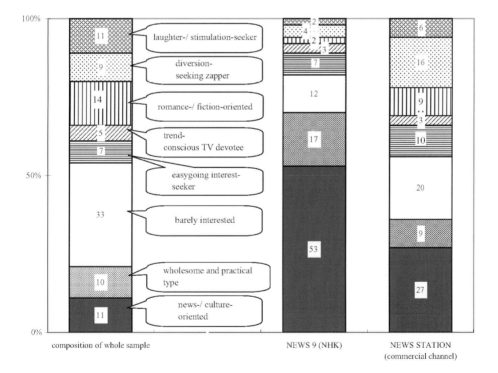

Figure 6.10. Composition of eight viewer groups for two news programs.

programs for viewer types that were identified in our study, taking their preferred program genres into account.

5. Conclusion

A variety of factors determine what television programs people choose to watch. Their actual selection also depends on diverse situational factors, such as the viewer's environment and mood, and the availability of competing programs. It is impossible to account for all these factors when grouping viewers based on similarities, but we believe that they can be appropriately grouped by considering the types of programs they 'watch thoroughly'. Using this approach, we studied data on programs actually viewed by respondents, and grouped them into eight viewer groups according to similarities in the types of programs they watched.

The question remaining is whether the central characteristics of programs that determine similarity in program selection been correctly identified. We watched television programs and established 49 genres that we believe express best the characteristics of the programs that we considered in our study.

We used quantification method III to analyze similarities in program selection, based entirely on similarities of the programs rather than predetermined elements such as program type or demographic characteristics. From our analysis it was clear that the 'more/less serious' and 'more/less fictional' axes are involved in program selection, but we do not yet clearly know the meaning of the other discriminatory axes.

The viewer stereotypes based on similarity in TV program selection that were obtained in this way can be applied to developing programs targeted to specific viewers or diagnosing the characteristics of certain channels. We believe that they can make a major contribution to the development of personalized adaptive systems, such as the recommendation of programs to suit viewer tastes and the sale of packages in multi-channel broadcasting.

6. Discussion

Our method of analysis (which is based on data about whether or not a particular program was watched thoroughly) can also be applied on a long-term basis.

The categories of program genres used, however, cannot be applied indefinitely. Our genre categories are based on viewer perceptions of different programs. These perceptions are related to the content and format of programs. As broadcast content evolves, changes must accordingly be made to the categorization of genres. This does not necessitate constant, extensive alteration, but it will be necessary to review the genre classifications periodically.

The history of television programming in Japan shows that major changes in trends take place approximately every ten years (Iyoda, Y. 1998). Evening variety programs only began to show great diversity in the mid-1990s, and so far this trend has not changed. We believe that the program genre categories we have developed will remain applicable at least until programs appear with a very new format or content that also attract a substantial number of viewers.

Other program characteristics that were not sufficiently reflected in this analysis but would be worthwhile including in our view are elements such as personalities appearing on programs, and program orientation and tempo. These elements may make it possible to interpret the meaning of other axes that influence program selection. That topic will require further research.

Additionally, in the present study, people who did not watch very many TV programs during the survey period accounted for roughly one-third of the total sample. Although this is a rather large number, we did not analyze those viewers further and placed them into a single 'barely interested' group. It would be necessary to grasp their TV preferences through more extensive research and subcategorization.

References

Ang, I.: 1996, *Living Room Wars*. London: Routledge.

Benzecri, J. P.: 1973, L'Analyse des Donnés, vol. 1, vol. 2. Dunod: Paris.

Gifi, A.: 1981, *Nonlinear multivariate analysis*. Leiden: DSWO Press.

Fujiwara, N.: 1982, 1983, Prime-time Television Program Viewer Types (in Japanese) *NHK Monthly Report on Broadcast Research*, October 1982, 26–38, December 1982, pp. 29–40, February 1983, pp. 34–46, Tokyo: Nihon Hoso Shuppan Kyokai.

Hara et al.: 2000. Eight Types of TV Viewers and Their Perception of TV Station. (in Japanese) *NHK Annual Bulletin of Broadcasting Culture Research* No. 45, Tokyo, NHK Broadcasting Culture Research Institute, Tokyo, Japan, 165–223.

Hayashi, C.: 1993, *Quantification: Theory and Method* (in Japanese). Tokyo: Asakura Shoten.

Iyoda, Y.: 1998, *A Television History Handbook* (in Japanese). Tokyo: Jiyu Kokuminsha.

Izumi, Y.: 1973, Viewer Types Based on Program Genres (in Japanese), *NHK Monthly Report on Broadcast Research*. July 1973, Tokyo: Nihon Hoso Shuppan Kyokai, 39–45.

Miwa, T.: 1986, Classification of Viewer Types According to Their Attitudes toward Television (in Japanese). *NHK Monthly Report on Broadcast Research*. Tokyo: Nihon Hoso Shuppan Kyokai, 46–61.

Moores, S.: 1993, *Interpreting Audiences: The Ethnography of Media Consumption*. London, Sage.

Morley, D.: 1992, *Television, Audience and Cultural Studies*. London: Routledge.

Murasaki, Y. et al.: 2001, TV Program Selection System based on a User Model Agent *the IEICE Technical Report, AI2001-50*, 25–31 (http: //db. ieice. org/gakkai/show. php?id=135200)

Nagasawa, H.: 2000, Trying to Describe TV 'Viewers Personalities' (in Japanese) *Video Research Digest*, August 2000, Tokyo, Video Research Inc. 1–8.

Nishizato, S.: 1980, *Analysis of Categorical Data: Dual Scaling and Its Applications*. Toronto: University of Toronto Press.

O'Sullivan et al.: 2003, Improving the Quality of the Personalized Electronic Program Guide, Special issue on User Modeling and Personalization for Television, User Modeling and User-Adapted Interaction: The Journal of Personalization Research.

Rao, V. R.: 1975, Taxonomy of Television Programs Based on Viewing Behavior. *Journal of Marketing Research*, **12**, 355–358.

Richardson, M. and Kuder, G. F.,: 1933, Making a rating scale that measures. *Personnel Journal*, **12**, 36–40.

Sugiyama, M.: 1968, Pattern Analysis of Television Viewing (in Japanese) *NHK Annual Bulletin of Broadcasting Culture Research* No. 13, Tokyo, NHK Broadcasting Culture Research Institute, Tokyo, Japan, 42–65.

Takeuchi, T. et al.: 1989, *Dictionary of Statistics* (in Japanese) Tokyo: Toyo Keizai Shimposha.

Tomomune, Y. et al.: 2000a, TV Station Images in Japan: From A Station Image Survey Conducted in March. (in Japanese) *NHK Monthly Report on Broadcast Research*, July 2000. Tokyo: Nihon Hoso Shuppan Kyokai, 2–25.

Tomomune, Y. et al.: 2000b, Classification of 547 Night Programs by Category: An Attempt at a New Assortment Method (in Japanese) *NHK Monthly Report on Broadcasting Research*, November 2000. Tokyo: Nihon Hoso Shuppan Kyokai, 2–25.

Tomomune, Y. et al.: 2001, Variety Show Programs that Draw Close to Daily Life: Thoughts on the Analysis of Program Content (in Japanese) *NHK Monthly Report on Broadcast Research*, March 2001. Tokyo: Nihon Hoso Shuppan Kyokai, 12–41.

Video Research Inc.: 2000, Examples of Viewer Ratings Analysis Based on Viewer Groupings (in Japanese), *Data Vision 2000+1*, December 4 2000, Tokyo, Video Research Inc.

Webster, J. G. and J. J. Wakshlag: 1983, A Theory of Television Program Choice. *Communication Research*, **10**: 4 (October). Thousand Oaks: Sage Publication, pp. 430–446.

Authors' vitae

Yumiko Hara

Senior Researcher in NHK Broadcasting Culture Research Institute, MORI Tower 16F, 2-5-1, Atago, Minato-ku, Tokyo, Japan, 105-6216.

Ms. Hara received her B. A. in French Literature from the Sophia University in 1977. Joining NHK in 1978, Yumiko Hara has engaged in numerous research projects including 'International Comparative Study of Television Broadcasting,' 'Adult Education and Television Use, ' and 'Audience Behavior and Multimedia.' She is now a senior Researcher in NHK Broadcasting Culture Research Institute,

Yumiko Tomomune

Deputy Secretary General of the Japan Prize, the international educational program contest held by NHK.

Ms. Tomomune received her B. A. in Law from the Keio University. Since joining NHK in 1975, she directed and produced lifestyle and culture programs and worked in satellite broadcasting. She also served in focus group interview research at NHK Broadcasting Culture Institute, studying TV viewers and their preferences. Currently, targeted development of programs interests her.

Maki Shigemori

Ms. Shigemori received her B. A. in French Language from Tokyo University of Foreign Studies. She joined NHK in 1985. Since 1997, she has worked on audience surveys in Programming Bureau in 1999, she moved to the NHK Broadcasting Culture Research Institute in 1999, where she has been engaged in research on relationships between television programs and viewers (mainly qualitative surveys). Now, she works as a Senior Officer in the Corporate Planning Bureau of NHK.

PART 2: BROADCAST NEWS AND PERSONALIZED CONTENT

Chapter 7

Personalcasting: Tailored Broadcast News

MARK MAYBURY, WARREN GREIFF, STANLEY BOYKIN, JAY PONTE[1], CHAD McHENRY and LISA FERRO
Information Technology Division, The MITRE Corporation, 202 Burlington Road, Bedford, MA 01730, USA. e-mail: {maybury, greiff, boykin, red, lferro}@mitre.org. www.mitre.org/resources/centers/it

Abstract. Broadcast news sources and newspapers provide society with the vast majority of real-time information. Unfortunately, cost efficiencies and real-time pressures demand that producers, editors, and writers select and organize content for stereotypical audiences. In this article we illustrate how content understanding, user modeling, and tailored presentation generation promise personal-casts on demand. Specifically, we report on the design and implementation of a personalized version of a broadcast news understanding system, MITRE's Broadcast News Navigator (BNN), that tracks and infers user content interests and media preferences. We report on the incorporation of Local Context Analysis to both expand the user's original query to the most related terms in the corpus, as well as to allow the user to provide interactive feedback to enhance the relevance of selected news stories. We describe an empirical study of the search for stories on ten topics from a video corpus. By personalizing both the selection of stories and the form in which they are delivered, we provide users with tailored broadcast news. This individual news personalization provides more fine-grained content tailoring than current personalized television program level recommenders and does not rely on externally provided program metadata.

Key words. broadcast news, personalization, query expansion, relevance feedback, story selection, user modeling

1. Personalcasting

People are offered vast quantities of news in the form of multiple media (text, audio, video). For the past several years, a community of scientists has been developing news-on-demand algorithms and technologies to provide more convenient access to broadcast news (Maybury, 2000). Applications promising on-demand access to multimedia information such as radio and broadcast news on a broad range of computing platforms (e.g., kiosk, mobile phone, PDA) offer new engineering challenges. Unlike earlier systems which require television content to be manually annotated (e.g., Bove 1983), more recent systems have been developed that automatically index, cluster/organize, and extract information from news. Synergistic processing of speech, language and image/gesture promise both enhanced interaction at the user interface, and enhanced understanding of electronic media such as web, radio, and television sources (Maybury, 2000).

---

[1]Formerly of MITRE, Jay Ponte's current affiliation is Google, Inc., ponte@google.com.

L. Ardissono et al. (eds.), Personalized Digital Television, 177–202, 2004.
© 2004 *Kluwer Academic Publishers. Printed in the Netherlands.*

Unlike traditional broadcasts, which are created in a standard format delivered from a single source (broadcaster) with general content to address a wide range of audience and interests, we define a *personalcast* as a custom created, interactive sequence of stories that are selected based upon specific, individual user interests from a variety of sources and presented in a form tailored to user preferences. Whereas a broadcast is disseminated from one to many, a personalcast is one to one.

In separate research, investigators have developed many different ways to adapt presentations (Brusilovsky, 1996, 2001) including adapting the navigation support (e.g., sorting links, adding/removing/disabling links) or adapting the presentation itself. It has been shown empirically that adaptation can help, in both the speed of navigation/search (Kaplan et al., 1993) as well as in enhancing text understanding (Boyle and Encarnacion, 1994). One would hope the same benefits could accrue with tailored news. Finally, personalization of electronic programming guides (EPGs) (e.g., Ardissono et al., 2001) promises more rapid and custom access to shows of interest to the user.

We claim that a valuable scientific and technological advance would be the integration of methods from user modeling and user-adapted interaction together with news understanding technologies. This combination could enable new services such as the delivery of story alerts to interested users as well as interactive, individual news programs which we call personalcasts. This research is distinct from personalized EPGs in several primary ways:

1. *No metadata.* Metadata about content (programs and stories therein) is unavailable and must be automatically extracted from video sources via speech, text, and image processing.
2. *Linguistic analysis of user query.* User queries are analyzed linguistically, considering the available large broadcast news corpus.
3. *Story-level access.* Tailoring is performed at the story level, and not the program level.
4. *Analytic user tasks.* User tasks are primarily focused on information analysis, and not on entertainment or enjoyment. Users primarily work individually and not in groups.

In addition, this research adds to our knowledge of interactive search and query refinement. Salton and Buckley (1990) showed that automated relevance feedback improves search. Koenemann and Belkin (1996) and Koenemann (1996) showed that relevance feedback that is used for query refinement improves search of text news articles. While we also explore interactive relevance feedback, this research differs in several principal ways.

1. *Short and errorful video stories.* Users are searching short, errorful video broadcast news stories as opposed to longer, edited newspaper articles. The average length of a video story in our corpus is 51 seconds or only 122 words per story. On average, stories contain 5.9 named entities (i.e., proper names such as people, organizations, locations) per story, 4.7 of which are distinct names. Automated speech or manual human transcription introduces significant errors into our corpus which can reduce the performance of automated story segmentation, retrieval algorithms, and human relevance judgments. Stories are also interspersed with (irrelevant) commercials.

2. *Multiple topics.* Whereas prior research tested user performance on 20-minute search tasks on two TREC topics (Topic #162 – Automobile Recalls and Topic #165 – Tobacco Advertising and the Young) from 75,000 Wall Street Journal articles, we explored ten topics selected from a multiyear corpus of nine news broadcasts. As a consequence, while we used fewer subjects (four), each subject was carefully measured in a fully instrumented environment across many topics.

3. *Rich annotation.* Our corpus includes stories that are richly annotated with hierarchically organized topics and named entities.

2. Broadcast News Navigator

To illustrate personalcasting as defined above, we describe the Broadcast News Navigator (BNN). In our research, we have created BNN, a system that exploits video, audio, and closed-caption text information sources to automatically segment, extract, and summarize news programs (Maybury et al., 1997). Figure 7.1(a) shows the results of BNN responding to a user query requesting all reports regarding 'Cuba' between May 17 and June 16, 2001. For each story matching the query, the system presents a key frame, the three most frequent named entities within the story, and the source and date of the story. This display is called a 'Story Skim'.

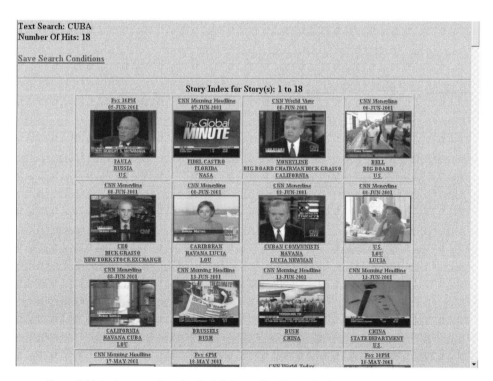

Figure 7.1(a). Automated retrieval of Cuba stories (*Story Skim*).

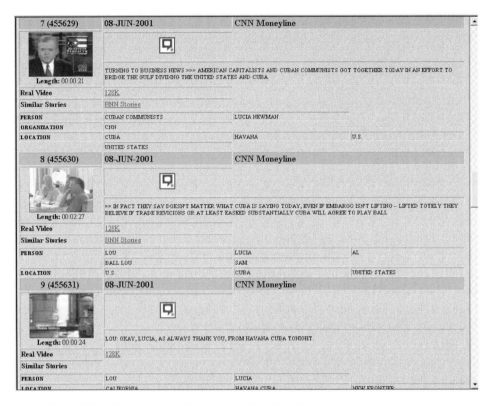

Figure 7.1(b). Details of some Cuba stories (*Story Details*).

This, in essence, provides the user with a 'Cuba' channel of information, personalizing the channel to their information interests. Moreover, the user can create arbitrarily complex queries combining key words, named entities (e.g., people, organizations, locations), sources (e.g., CNN, MS-NBC, ABC), programs (e.g., CNN Prime News vs. CNN Headline New vs. CNN Moneyline, etc.), and time intervals (e.g., specific days, weeks or years). These queries result in selected video stories specific to their interests.

The user can then select any of the key frames to get access to details of the story, such as shown in Figure 7.1(b). In this 'Story Details' presentation, the user has access to all people, organizations and locations mentioned in the story, an automatically extracted one-line summary of the news (the sentence with the most frequently named entities), a key frame extracted from the story segment, and a pointer to the full closed-caption text and video source for review. An empirical evaluation previously reported in Merlino and Maybury (1999) demonstrated that users could enhance their retrieval performance (a weighted combination of precision and recall) by utilizing BNN's Story Skim and Story Details presentations. User satisfaction in that study was 7.8 for retrieval and 8.2 for mixed media display [e.g., story skim, story details, such as those shown in Figure 7.1(a) and 7.1(b)], on a scale from 1 = dislike to 10 = like.

The BNN system provides navigation support, so that the user can select named entities and find stories including them. Further, by employing a clustering algorithm, the system enables the user to select stories similar to the current story.

Television, like other media such as newsprint, radio and the web, is used both for entertainment and informational/educational purposes which range from public health warnings to educational networks such as the Biography or Discovery channels. Focusing on the latter, BNN supports a range of users, topics, and usage models. Users have included experts (e.g., intelligence analysts, political analysts, systems engineers) and casual users (e.g., scientists, managers, secretaries), although our focus has been on expert users. As exemplified by the evaluation topics presented in the Appendix to this article, topics range from ones that interest users of all ages (such as music, sports, weather, and space) to social/adult issues (such as accidental injuries, crime, gambling and investing) and to expert-specific topics (such as bioterrorism and the Mideast conflict).

The BNN prototype has been used in the MITRE Corporation for research, in the military for daily information monitoring, and for open source intelligence analysis. Current users perform both standing queries and ad-hoc searches. A user can subscribe to be alerted (e.g., via email) when a story containing a keyword or named entity is found.

Corporations are beginning to address user needs for content based video access. For example, Virage's VideoLogger[R] and Virage Solution Server[TM] (www.virage.com) incorporate concepts similar to those found in BNN for use by broadcasters, corporate trainers, and analysts. Virage's news on demand system, ViTAP (Video Text and Audio Processing), is used by Government Analysts for retrieval and profile-based alerting of events (Merlino, 2002). It incorporates presentation techniques similar to those found in the BNN, augmented with time synchronized playback tracks for machine translation and keyframes. Related research includes meeting and lecture archiving and retrieval (e.g., Hu, 2003).

The large broadcasters (e.g., CNN, ABC, BBC, C-NBC) continuously repurpose material. Sometimes local programs from the same broadcaster (e.g., CNN) are re-purposed to international (CNN International) or Internet services (CNN Interactive). While current indexing is principally manual, a tool like BNN automates the discovery of specific topics and semi-automates story clip selection.

Video news segmentation performance ranges from 50% to 80% balanced precision and recall. In particular, segmentation algorithms using multimodal cues and trained on a range of broadcast sources such as CNN, MS-NBC or ABC perform with 53% precision and 78% recall (Boykin and Merlino, 1999). Broadcast specific models (e.g., ones using visual anchor booth recognition cues specific to a particular program such as ITN) raise the performance to 96% precision and recall. Story segmentation may occur at the source (e.g., by the broadcaster), at an intermediary (e.g., broadband service provider), or by the end user.

As we discuss in the subsequent sections, the BNN system has been extended to support personalization as well as query expansion using Local Context Analysis (LCA). While many user studies with query expansion have been conducted in the past (Attar and Fraenkel, 1977; Croft and Harper, 1979; Koenemann and Belkin,

1996; Koenemann, 1996, Xu and Croft, 1996, 2000), this research represents the first user study using LCA, the first exploration of LCA in the context of multi-media retrieval on broadcast news (a form of television), and the first user study of personalization and content-based video access.

3. User Modeling and Tailoring

The control flow diagram in Figure 7.2 shows a traditional search session in BNN. The user poses a query and receives a story skim of the kind shown in Figure 7.1(a). The user then selects a story and is provided the details as exemplified in Figure 7.1(b). From this story detail, the user can simply review the summary and all named entities, or explicitly choose a media element to display (such as the full video source or the text transcript). User interest profiles can be created from explicit user input and then used to tailor presentations to the user's interests and preferences.

As shown in Figure 7.3, in Personalized BNN (P-BNN) users can explicitly define user profiles indicating their interests by specifying simple keywords or named entities such as individuals, locations, or organizations. They can also specify preferred broadcast sources to search (e.g., CNN, ABC News). This profile also captures preferences for controlling the display of various media elements by manipulating media properties such as the source, date, time, length, and preference type for media presentation (e.g., key frame only, story details, full video, text summary). The user's interest profiles can be run periodically and the retrieval results sent to the requester as an alert. This alert can be pointers to a story, a story skim or story details like those shown in Figures 7.1(a) and 7.1(b).

Because the original broadcast news source is segmented into its component parts, key elements can be extracted and others summarized. This enables a system not only to select stories based on a user's content interest, but also to assemble them in the manner a user prefers. For example, the user can be presented with only a key frame, with summary sentences, with people or place names, or with the entire source. A natural extension of this work would be the addition of a feedback and collaborative filtering mechanism. An individual user's model could then be modified with each search or within or across sessions, and the user could benefit from searches performed by others in a community.

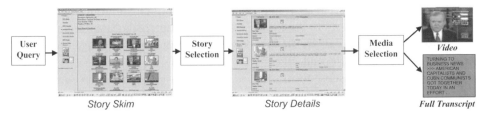

Figure 7.2. Traditional searching using BNN.

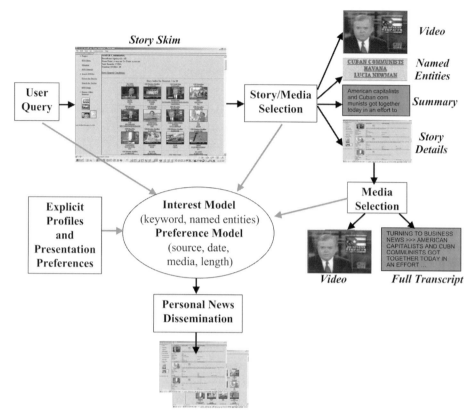

Figure 7.3. User Modeling and Tailored Presentation in Personalized BNN.

4. Query Expansion and Relevance Feedback: Local Context Analysis

We use two methods to find information relevant to users' information needs. First, we expand their original query to the most related terms in the corpus. Second, we allow them to provide relevance feedback, so we can provide stories more similar to those they indicated as being relevant. Neither of these methods takes the user's interest model into account that was described in Section 3. For query expansion, we use a technique called Local Context Analysis (LCA) (Xu and Croft 1996, 2000). Figure 7.4 illustrates the control flow of LCA use. Given a query specified by the user, the system selects those passages containing at least one of the terms and assigns to each of these passages a Retrieval Status Value (RSV) according to the scoring formula employed by the retrieval engine. For all experiments discussed in this article, the Okapi formula (Robertson and Walker, 1994) was used. The Okapi formula is commonly considered one of the most robust and effective formulas developed to date for information retrieval. What is treated as a passage is application dependent. Passages can be paragraphs or paragraph-sized fixed windows of text. Sentences can also be treated as passages. At the other extreme, entire documents

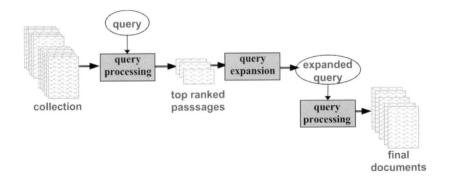

Figure 7.4. Control flow for Local Context Analysis.

can be the passages used for LCA. In this article, a passage is considered as co-extensive with a news story. In the future, however, we plan to run experiments where passages are associated with smaller sections of news stories. This may prove to be more appropriate for collections containing a mix of longer and shorter story segments.

The next step in the process is to mine the top passages for promising concepts that can be used as additional query terms. In the LCA of the BNN version discussed here, concepts are simple words. But concepts can correspond to any lexical, syntactic or semantic marking of documents. An obvious possibility in the context of BNN is to use named entities as concepts. Given an algorithm for the automatic association of named entity tags to snippets of text, named entities can serve as LCA concepts. Alternatively, concepts can be limited to some subset of named entities – persons, for example. An interesting possibility here is the provision of user control over the concept space on a per-query basis. User intuition may deem persons to be critical elements for one information need, where locations are likely to be most helpful for another. Syntactic units, such as noun phrases, can also serve as concepts, assuming the availability of a system component to provide the requisite syntactic analysis.

Once passages have been scored and ranked, LCA selects the top N ranked passages and considers all the concepts appearing at least one time in these top N passages. Each concept is then scored using the following formula:

$$f(c) = \prod_{i-1}^{M} [0.1 + \text{co\_degree}(c, w_i)]^{\text{idf}\,(w_i)}$$

$$\text{co\_degree}(c, w_i) = \text{idf}\,(c) \cdot \frac{\log(\text{co}(c, w_i) + 1)}{\log(N)}$$

$$\text{co}(c, w_i) = \sum_{p \text{ is a passage}} f_{p,w_i} \cdot f_{p,c}$$

$$\text{idf}\,(x) = \min\left(1.0, \frac{\log(N/N_x)}{5.0}\right)$$

The LCA formula for scoring concepts is designed to assign high values to concepts co-occurring with a large number of the query terms in a large number of the top ranked passages. The greater the number of passages, the greater the score. The greater the number of terms it co-occurs with in a given passage, the greater the score is incremented for that passage. The number of times these terms occur, as well as the number of times the concept itself occurs, also affect the degree to which a given passage augments the overall score.

For each of the M query terms, w_i, a value co(c,w_i) is calculated. The co function measures how much the concept c co-occurs with term w_i. Each passage that contains both the concept and the term contributes a value. This value is equal to the product of the number of times c occurs and the number of times w_i occurs in the passage. The log of this measure (1 is added to avoid the possibility of taking the log of 0) is normalized relative to one occurrence of both c and w_i in every passage and then multiplied by idf(c), giving the *co_degree*. The idf statistic is a measure of how rare a word is. The idf fomula used for LCA, a variant of idf weighting used in most modern information retrieval systems, is a function of N_c, the number of passages containing the concept c, out of the total set of passages, which is of size N. The fewer passages containing the word, the greater the idf value. The *co_degree* is a measure of co-occurrence between the concept c and query word w_i. A weighted product of the *co_degrees* (weighted by the idf values for the query words) yields a measure of how valuable the candidate concept c is taken to be relative to the given query.

Once all concepts have been evaluated, a predetermined number of the most highly scoring concepts are chosen. These concepts are then added to the original query terms. If necessary, collection statistics – which may not be pre-computed for concepts as they are for simple query terms – are gathered for the expansion concepts. The enhanced query is then evaluated and the top ranking documents are retrieved. The following are two examples of the top 10 query expansion terms resulting from LCA on the collection of news stories on which this study was based:

initial query 1:   palestinian israeli conflict
query 1 expansion concepts: israel, violence, palestinians, hebron, sources, gaza, gunmen, tanks, city, hamas

initial query 2:   bush budget
query 2 expansion concepts: surplus, medicare, funding, cut, tax, fall, spending, fought, fund, popular

Although LCA was developed for automatic query expansion, and we have explained it in that context, the basic approach can be used in a number of different ways. First, its primary use in BNN is not for automatic query expansion (although this capability is provided), but for suggesting possible query expansion terms to the user, leaving to them the assessment of which combination of the suggested terms, if any, will be most beneficial if used as part of the query (Figure 7.5).

Second, LCA is considered for use as part of relevance feedback, as in Figure 7.6. The explanation of LCA given above can be understood as an application of pseudo-

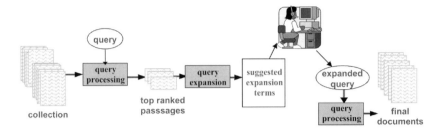

Figure 7.5. LCA produces candidate query terms.

feedback, also known as blind feedback, or as it was called when it was originally proposed (Attar and Fraenkel, 1977), local feedback. With pseudo-feedback, a query is evaluated and then, for the purposes of query expansion and term re-weighting, the top documents retrieved are treated as if they were known to be relevant. That is, they are treated as if these documents were shown to a user and the user feedback indicated that they were all relevant to the information need that motivated the original query. But given a human at the terminal, we need not depend on pseudo-feedback. Actual relevance feedback can be used instead. The user can be shown the most highly ranked news stories and asked to indicate which of them are indeed relevant to their information needs. Then query expansion can proceed as before, but only the stories marked as relevant by the user will be used for selecting expansion concepts in place of the top N stories resulting from the original query.

These alternatives can be combined in various ways. BNN can be made to return both the top relevant documents and a list of suggested expansion terms in response to the initial query. The user can then choose to reformulate the query based on the list of suggested terms (and, possibly a quick review of the top ranked documents to get a sense of how the system responded to the initial query), or simply mark the retrieved documents as to relevance. In either case, the system can respond with both a new set of documents and an updated list of potential expansion terms. This cycle can be repeated any number of times. In addition, during any given interaction, the user can request that the system apply automatic query expansion and return the results of a pseudo-feedback cycle in place of the list of candidate expansion terms and the top ranked documents from the unexpanded query.

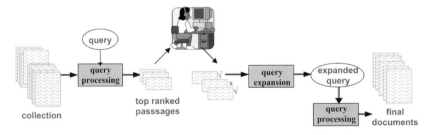

Figure 7.6. Relevance feedback.

One potential limitation of this approach concerns the size of the broadcast news collection. Clearly, discovery of viable candidates for query expansion is dependent upon the existence of reliable co-occurrence statistics. In order that the statistics upon which LCA calculations are based be robust, they must be extracted from a reasonably sized corpus of related stories. This can be problematic but need not be an insuperable barrier. A large number of stories with similar content from the same or similar sources can be presumed to be the ideal resource for uncovering quality expansion-term candidates. If this is not available, however, supplementary resources can be used. If the archive of broadcast news stories is not sufficiently large, but a large collection of, say, contemporaneous newspaper articles is available, the corpus of newspaper articles can be used for the mining of additional query terms, in place of, or in addition to, the broadcast news stories.

5. User Interests and Preferences

There are a number of methods that can be applied to create and exploit a model of user interests and preferences. Regarding user interests and/or information needs, typically these are captured in the form of user profiles explicitly stated by the user. This can occur in a BNN user profile in which a user can specify their information needs either as a list of keywords and/or a list of named entities; that is, people, organizations, or locations, as illustrated in Figure 7.7. Figure 7.7 is the first screen

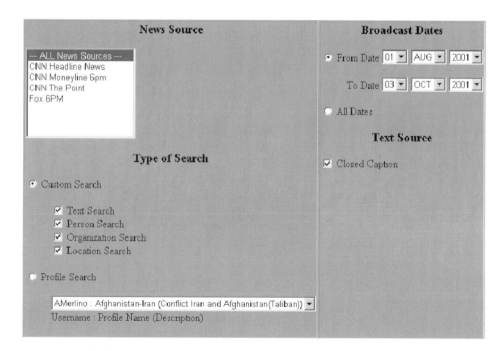

Figure 7.7. Search screen including explicitly stated user profile.

a user sees when they initiate a search in BNN and includes an ability to select program sources, dates, and type of search (e.g., keyword or named entities).

A drop list of stored profiles is displayed in the lower left hand corner of Figure 7.7. Visible is a stored profile for user 'Amerlino' for stories related to conflicts between Afghanistan and Iran. A user can explicitly specify their preferences for particular sources (e.g., CNN, Fox, ABC News) or programs (e.g., CNN Headline News vs. CNN Moneyline), dates (e.g., last three days), time periods, sources (e.g., closed captions, speech transcripts), and type of search (e.g., keyword/text search or named entity search).

Figure 7.8 shows the user manipulating the system's user model (called a profile) of their media presentation preferences. Note that the user can select what types of media (e.g., key frame picture from a clip, text transcript, video), media properties (e.g., clip length), and/or content (e.g., types of named entities, related stories) to display when viewing story details. In Figure 7.8, the user has selected all media elements except for similar stories, clip length, and skimmed results. All of these elements are automatically extracted from source stories by BNN.

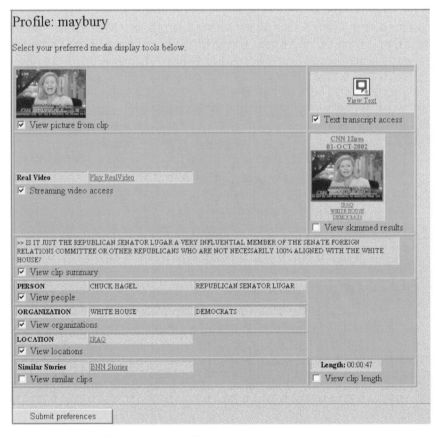

Figure 7.8. User media presentation profile.

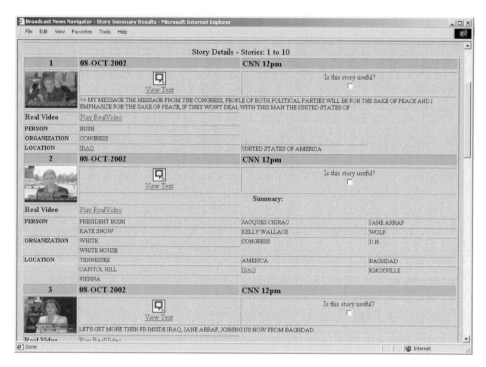

Figure 7.9. Multiple media presentation.

Figure 7.9 illustrates the effect of the media preference profile on the display of stories in the news on October 8, 2002. Based upon preferences selected in Figure 7.8, only two and a half stories can be displayed on the screen. In contrast, if the user had established a profile stating a preference for only one-line summaries, about twice as many stories could be displayed. Note however that the automatically generated one-line summary fails completely in story 2. The user would have no description of this story in a summary-only display.

6. Discovering User Information Needs: Query Refinement in BNN

We can also determine a user's interests not only by what they indicate interest in explicitly (e.g., their search keywords and/or named entities), but also by reasoning about terms and/or entities related to their stated interests. For example, if a user searches for stories about the location 'Iraq', we might look into the story set returned by BNN and notice that the person 'Saddam Hussein' occurs frequently. Or if the person searches for stories in which the name 'Saddam Hussein' and location 'Iraq' appear, she might frequently find the terms 'weapons of mass destruction' or 'UN inspections'.

As in previous versions of BNN, the user initially chooses the set of sources upon which to query, a date range, along with the option to perform either a profile search (saved in a previous session) or a custom search (such as in Figure 7.7). The choices presented to the user in a custom search include options for searching any named entity category (person, organization, location, etc.) as well as a free-form text search.

Having selected sources, time range, and the type of search, the user is presented the detailed search tool [Figure 7.10(a)]. For each category selected in the previous screen, a selectable menu of actual named entities appears with the ability to select one or more elements. Since the text option was selected, a free form text box appears above the selectable menus in Figure 7.10(a). In this example, the user types in the terms 'bush' and 'war'. As show in Figure 7.10(b), the retrieval engine returns a set of stories that are about 'bush' and 'war'.

The user then selects stories that she finds most relevant to her information need, in this case the second story which is about the threat posed by Saddam Hussein in Iraq. The system uses LCA to expand the user's query terms. In particular, the terms 'bush' and 'war' are expanded into a list which is displayed in Figure 7.11(a). It includes person names such as 'donald' and 'rumsfeld', terms such as 'developments' and 'money', adjectival locations such as 'Pakistani', and so on, as described above.

In the example in Figure 7.11(a), the user selects the term 'iraq' from the location menu and then reruns the query, expanded now to include the terms 'bush', 'war', and 'iraq'. Figure 7.11(b) shows the resulting stories retrieved by the expanded query. Notice in Figures 7.10(b) and 7.11(b) that at this stage the user can select via a check box those stories from the returned story list that she deems most relevant to her information needs. The most frequently occurring terms in these selected stories will be added to further refine the user's query. At this point the user can

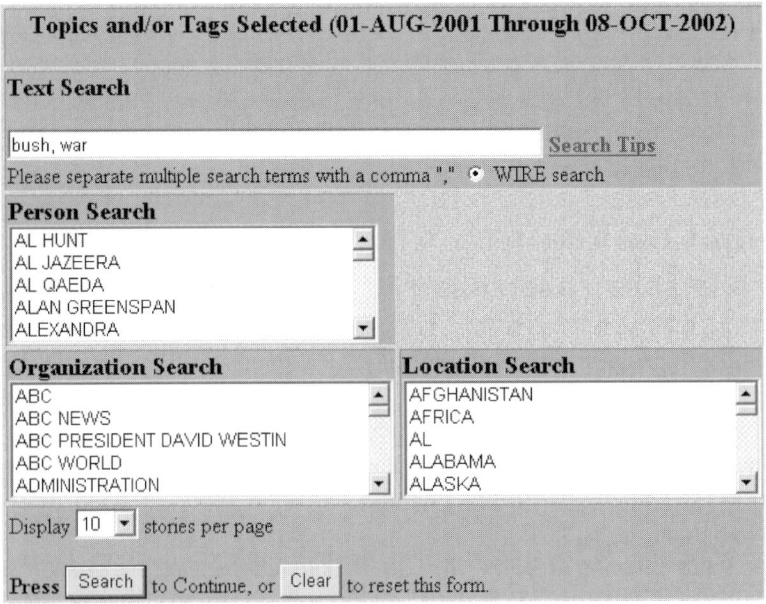

Figure 7.10(a). BNN search.

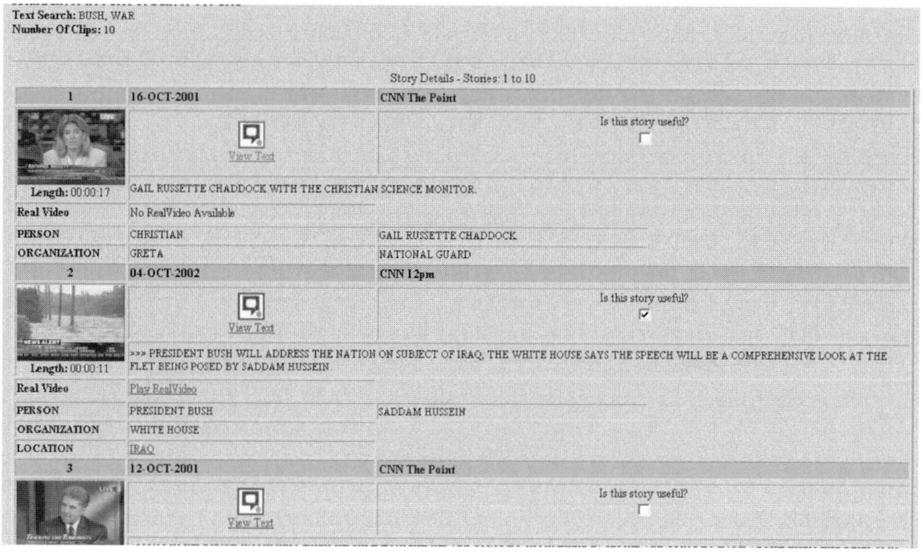

Figure 7.10(b). Relevance selections.

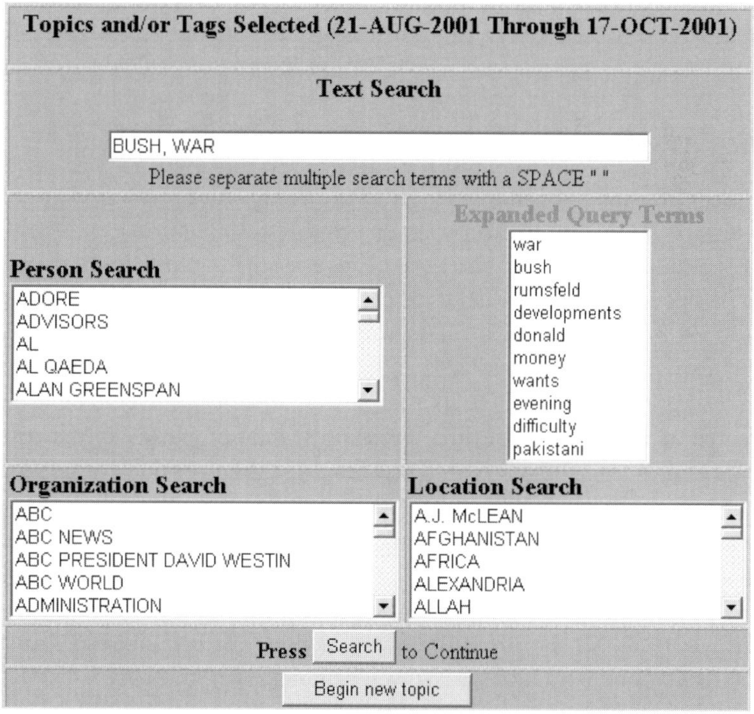

Figure 7.11(a). Results using expanded query.

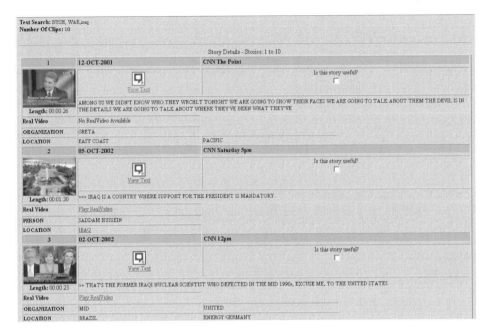

Figure 7.11(b). Selected stories.

further refine her search or simply execute it. The user need not select query expansion terms nor provide relevance feedback, or she can do either or both. A key issue is how relevance feedback affects user performance in searching broadcast news, so we now turn to evaluation.

7. Preliminary Evaluation

Evaluation of user adaptive interfaces is more challenging than typical human-computer interface evaluation, for several reasons. First, the user can influence interface behavior because models of the user change system output and/or behavior. Second, the system's model of the user can influence the behavior of the user (e.g., if it is poor or uncooperative, users can become frustrated; if it is critical or challenging it can inspire new user inferences and behavior). Third, there often is diversity in the task being performed, its complexity, and/or the overall environment. This high degree of variability raises the uncertainty and complexity in the operation of the systems and in their adaptation. This, in turn, makes evaluation challenging.

Because of this complexity, we have evaluated the performance of BNN both in terms of content (type and amount) and the form of delivery. We have found that presenting less information to the users (e.g., story skims or summaries versus full text or video) enables more rapid relevance assessment and story comprehension (Light and Maybury, 2002). For example, using 20 users performing relevance assessments and information extraction tasks, we demonstrated that users exhibit over 90% precision and recall using displays such as those in Figure 7.11(b) in less than half the time required to search digital video sequentially.

Because personalization increases the refinement and focus of a user query, this should translate directly into task performance enhancements. To test this hypothesis, we ran a series of evaluations. We initially tested P-BNN on a collection of 600 news stories (culled out of tens of thousands of stories from several years) primarily in October 2002 from multiple program sources such as CNN Headline News, CNN NewsNight with Aaron Brown, and CNN Moneyline. Based on user queries and user feedback, we returned up to twenty relevant news stories (we interchangeably call documents) which we then had the user assess for relevance. Table I contains illustrative performance evaluations from queries on this collection.

The first column lists the topics investigated in the corpus. The second column reports the precision of documents returned by a single-term user query representing a general information need. The third and fourth columns report the precision of a more specific or focused search which is enhanced by document relevance feedback in the third column and automated query expansion followed by specific term selection in the fourth.

Query precision in Table I is the percentage of documents out of the top twenty returned (or fewer, if less than 20 documents are returned) that the user finds relevant to their information needs. For example, for the first topic where the user is searching for documents about Iraq's foreign minister, whose name they have forgotten, they first search broadly for 'Iraq' and find that all top 20 documents returned are about 'Iraq'. Thus, the precision on the general term 'Iraq' is 20/20 or 100%. However, their information need is unsatisfied as only one story out of 20 (#9) is about 'Tariq Aziz', Iraq's foreign minister. Accordingly, the user continues and selects story

Table I. Preliminary performance evaluation

| | | Performance (Document precision) | |
| | General search | Specific search | |
Topic	Query Precision (query term in parenthesis)	Query plus Document Relevance Feedback (# selected docs)	Query plus Query Expansion Feedback (selected terms in parenthesis)
1. Iraqi foreign minister	20/20 = 100% ('iraq')	1/20 = 5% (1)[a]	100% ('tariq') 100% ('aziz')
2. Weapons of mass destruction	18/20 = 90% ('weapons')	18/20 = 90% (1)	100% ('nuclear') 100% ('inspections')
3. Chief weapons inspector	8/17 = 47% ('inspector')	10/20 = 50% (8)	100% ('blix')
4. Israeli Palestinian conflict	5/19 = 31.5% ('israeli')	8/20 = 40% (8)	95% ('gaza') 95% ('hamas')
5. Washington D.C. sniper	16/20 = 80% ('sniper')	20/20 = 100% (17)	90% ('shooting')
Average	69.7%	57% (7)	97%

[a]This is the performance of relevance feedback on only 1 document (#9), so it is very low.

#9 as relevant and provides this feedback to the search engine. As was detailed in Section 4, LCA extracts a weighted set of the most frequent terms from this document (in this case the terms 'iraq', 'matter', 'telling', 'reiterated', and so on) which P-BNN then uses to invoke another search against the entire story collection, and returns another set of documents that match these weighted terms. Since the user provides only a single document for relevance feedback and the words 'Tariq' and 'Aziz' appear near the end of a twenty term expansion list, the precision performance of this feedback is only 5% (third column of Table I). That is, only 1/20 or 5% of the documents returned after this feedback are about Iraq's foreign minister. Note that depending upon which documents the user selects and the terms contained therein, document relevance feedback can either refine or broaden the search. In all five queries shown document relevance feedback improves precision.

After indicating relevant documents, the user can also ask the system to suggest, based on real-time analysis of these documents, specific terms to expand their query. As shown in the fourth column of Table I, when the user selects either the terms 'Tariq' or 'Aziz' from the term expansion list, the system returns exactly five documents that pertain to the user's original information need, thus achieving a precision of 5/5 or 100%. At this point the LCA models the user's information needs more precisely than a set of weighted terms.

The second query in Table I concerns weapons of mass destruction. The user initially types the simple query 'weapons'. This retrieves $18/20 = 90\%$ or relevant documents about weapons in general. When a document is noted as relevant by the user to their more specific information need of weapons of mass destruction, a real-time analysis of the most frequent keywords in the selected document is performed and is used to retrieve documents, $18/20 = 90\%$ of which are relevant to the user's more specific information needs. In the final step, LCA expansion leads the user to terms such as 'nuclear' or 'inspections' which yield 100% relevant documents.

In the third query example, the user is searching for the lead UN weapons inspector. The user starts with a broad search ('inspector'). However, this yields only 8 out of 17 or 47% relevant documents. Providing user relevance feedback using eight documents raises the performance only slightly, to at least 50%. In fact, relevancy assessment was clear on half of these documents but ambiguous on others. Therefore, we assumed the most conservative interpretation and only counted half as relevant. However, when the user runs LCA query expansion and reviews the list which includes the rank ordered terms 'powell', 'hans', 'secretary', 'weapons', 'the', 'resolution', 'inspectors', and 'blix', the user notes that Hans Blix is the chief weapons inspector and selects the term 'Blix' to find 20 documents which are 100% relevant to their needs.

In the fourth query example, the user is searching for stories about the Israeli-Palestinian conflict. When they type in a general query such as 'israeli', they obtain a low yield (31.5%) of relevant stories. Providing feedback about relevant documents raises the performance somewhat (to 40%) by adding such expansion terms as 'palestinian', 'gaza', 'civilians', 'hamas', 'factions', 'militants', 'sharon', and 'raid'. However, when the user selects specific concrete terms such as 'gaza' or 'hamas', precision rises significantly to 95%.

In the fifth topic area, the user is interested in stories about the sniper attacks in Washington, D.C. Using the term 'sniper', 16 of 20 documents retrieved were about the D.C. sniper (two stories were irrelevant and two others were errors in story segmentation). When the user selects those documents and requests similar ones, the precision rises to 100%. When the user asks for term suggestions based on their relevance assessments, the system indicates that the terms 'sniper, the, police, shooting, maryland, . . .' and so on are the most typical of the document set. If they select the term 'shooting', the precision of the returned document set is 18/20 or 90% (two irrelevant documents are returned about a shooting of a marine and a U.N. protester shooting).

As can be seen from the examples in column two in Table I, the relation of a keyword and the document collection can dramatically influence performance. A specific term like 'iraq' that has many stories in the collection can yield high precision, although users often need to discover these in the search process. Providing document level relevance feedback (shown in column three) using an average of 7 documents improves precision in three out of five cases. However, if only one relevant document is provided (as in query #1), this method performs poorly because of limited evidence to infer the user's information needs. Selection of specific expansion terms by the user (column four) yields a more specific model of their information needs and results in high precision in all five queries which allows the system to retrieve a more relevant set of stories to their interests.

8. Detailed User Evaluation

Motivated by the promise of query refinement for capturing a more accurate specification of user information need, we performed a detailed study to analyze the following variables:

- *Recall.* We were not only interested in the precision of retrieval (i.e., the ability to only retrieve relevant documents), but also the ability to retrieve all of the relevant documents.
- *Scale.* We need to ensure that the promising performance results that we obtained will be sustained in larger collections, in particular in thousands of stories from several months to several years worth of news.
- *Quality.* We need to understand the effects of combining relevance feedback and term selection, to allow users to combine forms of query and document feedback to more accurately specify their needs.
- *Query Characterization and Display.* An effective means for characterizing the effects of various relevance or refinement selections on the weighted term model of the user's information needs is necessary, so the user has a clear characterization of what they are asking for.
- *Speed.* Searches together with refinements take much less than a minute to perform. Nevertheless, we are currently designing user studies to establish the tradeoff between the time necessary to perform query refinement and

document relevance feedback, and increases in precision and recall as a result of finer models of user information needs which reduce time required in post retrieval analysis.

- *User Satisfaction.* We are interested in whether users believe the system to be more enjoyable to use, and whether they perceive it to improve their performance with respect to accuracy, timeliness, and comprehensiveness.
- *Cognitive Load.* While difficult to measure, we are interested in whether query expansion eases or increases the load on the user's attention and reasoning resources. Indirect measurements of these might include time for manual term generation versus term selection from expansion menus, the number of iterations to converge on a query, and so on.

8.1 EVALUATION CORPUS AND TOPIC DEVELOPMENT

We created an evaluation corpus consisting of the closed-captioned text of nine news broadcasts airing between August 21, 2001 and October 17, 2001. The news broadcasts were automatically segmented into stories by BNN, resulting in 502 stories. It is important to note that while (to our knowledge) this is the highest performing story segmentation system, it remains inaccurate (Boykin and Merlino, 1999). A baseline version of the system over a range of broadcast sources (e.g., CNN, MS-NBC, and ABC) performed segmentation on average with 38% precision and 42% recall across all multimodal cues (i.e., textual, audio, and visual cues). In contrast, performance for the best combination of multimodal cues rose to 53% precision and 78% recall. When visual anchor booth recognition cues are specialized to a specific source (e.g., ITN broadcasts that have more regular visual story change indicators), the performance rises to 96% precision and recall. In the current system we were dealing with accuracy in the 50%–80% range.

Each story can contain zero or more topics – zero for those stories that contained no text, or too little text to decipher. To annotate the corpus for topics, an initial pass was made by one annotator who indicated what each story was about, using no predefined topic typology. A senior annotator then reviewed the set of topic labels that emerged, developed a clean typology of 26 topics with subtopics where needed, and made a second pass on the corpus to apply the modified topic labels and to also provide final judgment on the story topics themselves. Figure 7.12 illustrates one of the resulting top-level topics, Terrorism, and some of the sub-topics in this particular corpus.

The second annotator also evaluated each story in isolation and flagged every topic within a story where automatic story segmentation created a section too brief or too removed from context to reasonably understand what the story was about. This resulted in 121 topics being labeled as 'fragments.' In scoring against the stories marked by the subjects in the user study, these fragments were all considered non-relevant.

For the user evaluation we developed 10 topic areas: bioterrorism, U.S. space program, accidental injuries, gambling, investing, Mideast conflict, music, weather, violent crime, and sports. Each experiment topic was manually mapped to the topic

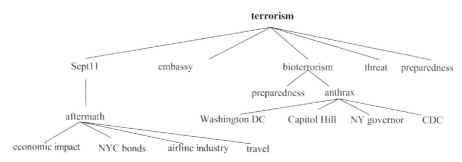

Figure 7.12. Sample topic and subtopic categories in evaluation corpus.

annotations in the evaluation corpus to create a gold standard for measuring user performance. For example, the 'investing' experiment topic mapped to the topic-sub-topic annotations 'economy, stock market' and 'economy, federal reserve rate,' as well as the topic annotation 'investing.' Each topic area was presented in one or more sentences to give the subjects an idea of the stories that were relevant to the topic, for example[1]:

> Bioterrorism: We are interested in any story or story fragment related to bioterrorist events, preparation, threats, or prevention. To be relevant, the biological threat must be initially spread by terrorists, and not by natural processes.

8.2 EXPERIMENT DESIGN

We created a fully instrumented version of BNN to allow detailed comparison of time stamped logs of events in both a baseline system that does not contain query refinement (Configuration A) and one augmented with LCA for query refinement (Configuration B). Since we had previously empirically demonstrated the value of personalizing broadcast news layout (Merlino and Maybury, 1999), our intent was to more extensively and deeply explore the bounds of performance of personalcasting content via query refinement.

At the beginning of the study, four subjects were given an overview of the purpose and design of the experiment, and a demonstration of the experimental task using both system configurations. Subjects were then given personal computers and an opportunity to use the system themselves with several practice topics. The subjects were allowed to ask questions during this training period, but not during the experiment proper. The total training time was approximately one hour. For each of the ten experimental topics, subjects were then asked to find as many relevant stories as possible. For each topic they were given five minutes. They were instructed to work at a normal pace and to try as many different queries as they wished; they were not required to continue searching for the full five minutes if they had no more query ideas. Two randomly chosen subjects used Configuration A for the first five topics, while the other two used Configuration B, and then all switched. While the 10 topics

---

[1] A list of 10 topics can be found in the Appendix.

were randomly ordered, all subjects processed them in the same order. In this way, the conditions under which a given topic was processed were kept as constant as possible. After completing the 10 experiment topics, users were asked to fill out a user satisfaction questionnaire, discussed below.

8.3 RESULTS: COMPARATIVE PERFORMANCE

We based our comparison of the effectiveness of the two system configurations on two metrics: #-correct and recall. The #-correct measure is simply a count of the number of relevant stories found by a given user for a given topic. It does not take into account the number of stories that were considered relevant to that topic. The recall measure, in contrast, is the fraction of relevant stories that the subject was able to find; that is, #-correct divided by the total number of stories in the collection relevant to the topic. We chose not to measure precision, the fraction of stories found by the user that were relevant to the topic. Precision would measure the agreement of the user's assessment of relevance with the judgment as given by the gold standard, which would measure characteristics of the subjects rather than characteristics of the configurations used.

Figure 7.13 shows how each of the subjects performed on each of the topics. The graph on the left shows performance as measured by #-correct, and the graph on the right, performance as measured by recall. The topics are presented in the order of presentation. The scores for a given user are connected, with a different line style for each user. Each point is labeled with an A or B, indicative of the configuration that was used by the associated subject for processing the corresponding topic. For the purpose of visualization, a small amount of random noise has been added to each score in order to make it easier to distinguish overlapping points and lines.

Inspection of the graphs suggests that there may be a difference in ability among subjects. It also suggests that there may be an intrinsic difference in difficulty of some topics as compared with others, although which topics might be considered more

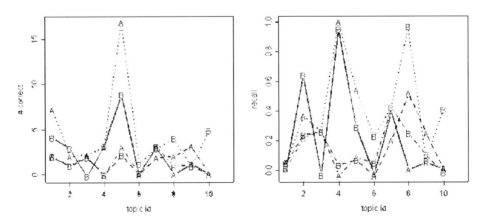

Figure 7.13. Performance across topics and subjects according to: #-correct and recall.

difficult, and which considered relatively easier to resolve, differs according to the metric used. Overall, there is substantial variance in the scores under both metrics, and there does not seem to be any indication that one system configuration dominates the other with respect to either of the two measures studied. Indeed, a statistical analysis of the two configurations showed no significant difference between systems.

However, an analysis of variance showed that, for both metrics, there is a clear effect due to differences in users. Also, for both metrics, the variance attributable to both the user and the topic is far greater than the variance that can be attributed to the different configurations.

8.4 RESULTS: COMPARATIVE SATISFACTION

An anonymous survey was administered to the subjects asking for their assessments on a Likert scale of enjoyment, ease of retrieval, trust in the results, completeness (ability to find all relevant stories), utility, and speed. On average, using System B subjects reported they enjoyed the system 12.5% more, trusted the results 7.7% more, and believed 8.3% more strongly that the results they found were more complete, on average a 9.5% perceived improvement. When asked to explicitly compare System A to System B in terms of ease of use, reliability, and speed, users indicated either no difference or a preference for System B. However, these results are only suggestive as experiments with larger sample sizes are needed to obtain statistically significant findings.

9. Future Research

Many outstanding research problems must be solved to realize automatically created user-tailored news. Important problem areas include:

1. *Automatic logging and inference of user interests.* With users increasingly learning, working and playing in digital environments, monitoring user interactions (e.g., Linton et al., 1999) is feasible and has shown value. In information seeking sessions, detecting selections and rejections of information provides an opportunity to induce individual and group profiles that can assist in content selection and presentation generation. For example, each of the user actions shown in Figure 7.3 (e.g., query, story selection, media selection) affords an opportunity for modeling user interest in the first two actions and/or preference in the last. In addition to explicit user interest collection, an implicit method could build an interest model by watching the user session to track the user's query, selection of particular stories, and choice of media. The system could then automatically construct a content interest and media preference model.

2. *Tailoring.* More sophisticated mechanisms are required to tailor content to specific topics or users. In addition to content selection, material must be ordered and customized to individual user interests. This will require methods of presentation generation that integrate extracted or canned text with generated text.

3. *Information Extraction.* Over the longer term we are working to create techniques to automatically summarize, fuse and tailor selected events and stories. This requires deeper understanding of the source news material beyond extracting named entities, key frames, or key sentences.
4. *Multilingual content.* Because news is global in production and dissemination, it is important to support access to and integration of foreign language content. This poses not only multilingual processing challenges, but also requires dealing with different country/cultural structures and formats.
5. *Cross story fusion.* An important problem is not only the summarization of individual stories, but also summarizing across many stories, possibly from different sources or languages. This is particularly challenging when the sources are possibly inconsistent in content or form. This ultimately requires cross story multimodal presentation generation.
6. *Persistence/transience of interest profiles.* Users' information needs tend to change over time, with profiles rapidly becoming out of date. Monitoring user queries and story selections over time is one method that can address this problem. Generalizing from their specific interests can yield an even richer user model.
7. *Evaluation.* Community defined multimedia evaluations will be essential for progress. Key to this progress will be a shared infrastructure of benchmark tasks with training and test sets to support cross-site performance comparisons.

10. Conclusion

We have designed, implemented, demonstrated and evaluated the Personalized Broadcast News Navigator (P-BNN) that provides tailored content and presentation of broadcast video news. We combine automated video understanding and extraction together with user modeling to provide individualized personalcasts at the story level from weeks of network news. Our system supports explicit user content and media preference profiles, it implicitly reasons about terms co-occurring with user query terms, and it accepts and modifies its model of the user's information need based on user feedback on the relevance of provided content. Accordingly, the system overcomes the fixed organization of news programs produced for stereotypical audiences by segmenting, selecting, and reordering content based on user preferences and feedback. Moreover, it represents an advance beyond program-level electronic program guides that are beginning to find their way into the commercial marketplace by not relying upon any externally provided program metadata and by providing more fine-grained content tailoring at the story rather than program level. Accordingly, we believe this kind of interactive, fine-grained, content-based personalization will be fundamental to television and news understanding systems of the future.

Acknowledgements

We would like to thank Alfred Kobsa and the anonymous reviewers for their detailed and helpful feedback on earlier versions of this article.

Appendix. User Evaluation Topics

1. Bioterrorism: We are interested in any story or story fragment related to bioterrorist events, preparation, threats, or prevention. To be relevant, the biological threat must be initially spread by terrorists, and not by natural processes.
2. U.S. Space Program: We are interested in any story or story fragment related to events and activities associated with U.S. space programs.
3. Accidental Injuries: We are interested in any reports of injuries to people as a result of accidents. Injuries as a result of intentional harmful acts such as crime and terrorism are *not* relevant.
4. Gambling: We are interested in any story or story fragment that reports on gambling, i.e., betting on an uncertain outcome or playing a game for financial gain. Both legal and illegal gambling are relevant.
5. Investing: We are interested in any story or story fragment related to financial investing, such as stock and interest rate reports. Advertisements about financial investing are *not* relevant.
6. Mideast Conflict: We are interested in any story or story fragment that relates to the conflict in the Middle East and efforts to resolve it. To be relevant, the story must center around issues between Middle Eastern countries and/or territories, as opposed to U.S. Mideast relations.
7. Music: We are interested in any story or story fragment about music, including musical compositions, musicians, bands, and concert events.
8. Weather: We are interested in any story or story fragment that reports on or forecasts weather events and phenomena.
9. Violent Crime: We are interested in any story or story fragment about violent criminals and/or criminal actions. Stories about terrorists and terrorism are *not* relevant.
10. Sports: We are interested in any story or story fragment that reports on sporting events or athletes.

References

Ardissono, L., Portis, F. and Torasso, P. 2001. Architecture of a System for the Generation of Personalization Electronic Programming Guides. Eighth International Conference on User Modeling: Workshop on Personalization in Future TV, Sonthofen, Germany. www.di.unito.it/~liliana/UM01/ardissono-etal.pdf.

Attar, R. and Fraenkel, A. 1977. Local Feedback in Full-Text Retrieval Systems. *Journal of the Association of Computation Machinery*, **24**(3): 397–417.

Bove, V. M. 1983. Personalcasting: Interactive Local Augmentation of Television Programming. Master's thesis, MIT, 1983.

Boykin, S. and Merlino, A. 1999. Improving Broadcast News Segmentation Processing. IEEE International Conference on Multimedia and Computing Systems. Florence, Italy. 7–11 June 1999.

Boykin, S. and Merlino, A. 2000. Machine Learning of Event Segmentation for News on Demand. *Communications of the ACM*, **43**(2): 35–41.

Boyle, C. and Encarnacion, A. O. 1994. An Adaptive Hypertext Reading System. *User Modeling and User-Adapted Interaction*, **4**(1): 1–19.

Brusilovsky, P. 1996. Methods and Techniques of Adaptive Hypermedia. *User Modeling and User-Adapted Interaction*, **6**(2–3): 87–129.

Brusilovsky, P. 2001. Adaptive Hypermedia. *User Modeling and User-Adapted Interaction*, **11**: 87–110.

Croft, W. B. and Harper, D. J. 1979. Using Probabilistic Models of Document Retrieval Without Relevance Information. *Journal of Documentation*, **35**(4): 285–295.

Hu, Q. 2003. Audio Hot Spotting. MITRE Sponsored Research Project. http://www.mitre. org/news/events/tech03/briefings/intelligent_information/hu.pdf

Kaplan, C., Fenwick, J. and Chen. J. 1993. Adaptive Hypertext Navigation based on User Goals and Context. *User Modeling and User Adapted Interaction*, **3**(3): 193–220.

Koenemann, J. 1996. Supporting Interactive Information Retrieval Through Relevance Feedback. CHI 96 Doctoral Consortium. http://www.acm.org/sigchi/chi96/proceedings/doctoral/Koenemann/Jk2_txt1.htm.

Koenemann, J. and Belkin, N. 1996. A Case For Interaction: A Study of Interactive Information Retrieval Behavior and Effectiveness. In: *Proceedings of the SIGCHI Conference on Human Factors and Computing Systems*. Vancouver, British Columbia, Canada. ACM Press: NY. pp. 205–212. http://www.acm.org/sigchi/chi96/proceedings/papers/Koenemann/jk1_txt.htm

Light, M. and Maybury, M. 2002. Personalized Multimedia Information Access: Ask Questions, Get Personalized Answers. *Communications of the ACM*, **45**(5): 54–59. (www.acm.org/cacm/0502/0502toc.html). In: Brusilovsky, P. and Maybury, M. (eds). Special Section on The Adaptive Web.

Linton, F., Joy, D., and Schaefer, H-P. 1999. Building User and Expert Models by Long-Term Observation of Application Usage. In: J. Kay (Ed.), UM99: User Modeling: In: *Proceedings of the Seventh International Conference* (pp. 129–138). New York: Springer Verlag. [Selected data are accessible from an archive on http://zeus.gmd.de/ml4um/]

Maybury, M. Feb. 2000. News on Demand: Introduction. *Communications of the ACM*, **43**(2): 32–34.

Maybury, M., Merlino, A., and Morey, D. 1997. Broadcast News Navigation using Story Segments, ACM International Multimedia Conference, Seattle, WA, November 8–14, 381–391.

Merlino, A. and Maybury, M. 1999. An Empirical Study of the Optimal Presentation of Multimedia Summaries of Broadcast News. In: Mani, I. and Maybury, M. (eds.) *Automated Text Summarization*, MIT Press.

Merlino, A. 2002. ViTAP News on Demand. Human Language and Technology Conference, San Diego, CA, March 25, 2002.

Robertson, S. E. and Walker, S. 1994. Some Simple Effective Approximations to the 2-Poisson Model for Probabilistic Weighted Retrieval. In: *Proceedings of the 17th Annual ACM-SIGIR Conference on Research and Development in Information Retrieval*, 232–241. Reprinted in: K. Sparck Jones and P. Willett (eds) 1997, *Readings in Information Retrieval*. Morgan Kaufmann, 345–354.

Salton, G. and Buckley, C. 1990. Improving Retrieval Performance by Relevance Feedback. *Journal of the American Society for Information Science (JASIS)*, **41**(4): 288–297.

Xu, J. and Croft, W. B. 1996. Query Expansion Using Local and Global Document Analysis. In: *Proceedings of the 19th Annual 'ACM-SIGIR Conference on Research and Development in Information Retrieval*, 4–11.

Xu, J. and Croft, W. B. 2000. Improving the Effectiveness of Information Retrieval with Local Context Analysis. *ACM Transactions on Information Systems*, **18**(1): 79–112.

Chapter 8

Media Augmentation and Personalization Through Multimedia Processing and Information Extraction

NEVENKA DIMITROVA[1], JOHN ZIMMERMAN[2], ANGEL JANEVSKI[1],
LALITHA AGNIHOTRI[1], NORMAN HAAS[3], DONGGE LI[4], RUUD BOLLE[3],
SENEM VELIPASALAR[3], THOMAS MCGEE[1] and LIRA NIKOLOVSKA[5]

[1]*Philips Research, 345 Scarborough Rd., Briarcliff Manor, NY 10510, USA.*
e-mail: {*Nevenka.Dimitrova,Angel.Janevski,Lalitha.Agnihotri,Tom.McGee*}@*philips.com*
[2]*Human-Computer Interaction Institute, Carnegie Mellon, Pittsburgh, PA, USA.*
e-mail: *johnz@cs.cmu.edu*
[3]*IBM T.J. Watson, 30 Saw Mill River Road, Hawthorne, NY 10532, USA.*
e-mail: {*nhaas,bolle*}@*us.ibm.com*
[4]*Motorola Labs, 1301 East Algonquin Road, Schaumburg, Illinois 60196.*
e-mail: *dongge.li@motorola.com*
[5]*MIT, Department of Architecture, 265 Massachusetts Avenue N51-340, Cambridge,
MA 02139, USA. e-mail: lira@mit.edu*

Abstract. This chapter details the value and methods for content augmentation and personalization among different media such as TV and Web. We illustrate how metadata extraction can aid in combining different media to produce a novel content consumption and interaction experience. We present two pilot content augmentation applications. The first, called MyInfo, combines automatically segmented and summarized TV news with information extracted from Web sources. Our news summarization and metadata extraction process employs text summarization, anchor detection and visual key element selection. Enhanced metadata allows matching against the user profile for personalization. Our second pilot application, called InfoSip, performs person identification and scene annotation based on actor presence. Person identification relies on visual, audio, text analysis and talking face detection. The InfoSip application links person identity information with filmographies and biographies extracted from the Web, improving the TV viewing experience by allowing users to easily query their TVs for information about actors in the current scene.

Key words. content augmentation, personalization, profile, personal news, video indexing, video segmentation, video summarization, information extraction, TV interface, user interface design, interactive TV

1. Introduction

For many years, people have enjoyed using their televisions as a primary means for obtaining news, information and entertainment, because of the rich viewing experience it provides. TVs offer viewers a chance to instantly connect with people and places around the world. We call this a *lean-back* approach to content consumption. More recently the Web has emerged as a comparably rich source of content. However,

L. Ardissono et al. (eds.), Personalized Digital Television, 203–233, 2004.

unlike TV, which allows users to select only channels, the Web offers users much more interactive access to expanding volumes of data from PCs and laptops. We call this a *lean-forward* approach to content. We explore the process and value of linking content from these two different, yet related, media experiences. We want to generate a *lean-natural* approach that combines the best of these two media and marries it to users' lifestyles.

At a high level we wanted to explore how cross-media information linking and personalization generates additional value for content. We call this research direction *Content Augmentation*. As an example, imagine a user watches a movie that has characters gambling in Las Vegas. A content augmentation application can extract the location from the movie, then, in anticipation of the user's inquiry, it can peruse the Web for supplemental information such as the prices and availability of rooms in the casino featured in the film, instructions for the game the characters play, information on the design and history of the hotel, etc. In addition, this application can employ a user profile, personalizing the linked content by prioritizing the types of links a user most often explores.

To test this model, we developed a pilot system. We began by focus group-testing several concepts, and, based on the group's reaction, designed and implemented a personal news application (MyInfo) and a movie information retrieval application (InfoSip) that enhances the traditional media experience by combining Web and TV content.

This paper details current TV experience (Section 2.1), related work in content understanding and Web/TV information linking (Section 2.2), our user-centered design process (Section 3.1), pilot applications (Sections 3.2 and 3.3), system overview (Section 4), multimedia annotation and integration methods (Section 5), Web information extraction methods (Section 6), and our personalization model (Section 7). We present our conclusions in Section 8.

2. Augmented User Experience

The current TV experience grows out of a 50-year tradition of broadcasters trying to capture a mass audience. They used both demographic data and input from advertisers to determine which programs to play at the various times of day. More recently, the emergence of niche-based TV channels such as CNN (news), MTV (music), ESPN (sports), and HGTV (home and garden) allows viewers more control over when they view the content they desire. In addition, the arrival of electronic program guides (EPGs) have allowed viewers to browse the program offerings by genres, date, time, channel, title, and, in some cases, search using keywords, a big step forward over traditional paper guides that allow access by time and channel only.

2.1. THE CURRENT TV NAVIGATION AND PERSONALIZATION

Current EPGs found in digital satellite settop boxes, cable settop boxes, and personal video recorders from TiVo (www.tivo.com) and ReplayTV (www.digitalnetworksna.

com/replaytv/default.asp) offer users advanced methods for finding something to watch or record. These systems generally hold one to two weeks' worth of TV data, including program titles, synopses, genres, actors, producers, directors, times of broadcast, and channels. Viewers can use EPGs to browse listings by time, channel, genre, or program title. In addition, viewers can search for specific titles, actors, directors, etc. Finally, the TiVo system offers a recommender that lists highly rated programs and automatically records these programs when space is available on its hard disk.

Although TiVo is currently the only commercial product with a recommender, much personalization research has been done in this area. Das and Horst developed the TV Advisor, where users enter their explicit preferences in order to produce a list of recommendations (Das et al., 1998). Cotter and Smyth's PTV uses a mixture of case-based reasoning and collaborative filtering to learn users' preferences in order to generate recommendations (Cotter et al., 2000). Ardissono et al. created the Personalized EPG that employs an agent-based system designed for settop box operation (Ardissono et al., 2001). Three user modeling modules collaborate in preparing the final recommendations: Explicit Preferences Expert, Stereotypical Expert, and Dynamic Expert. And Zimmerman et al. developed a recommender that uses a neural network to combine results from both an explicit and an implicit recommender (Zimmerman et al. This Volume). What all these recommenders have in common is that they only examine program-level metadata. They do not have any detailed understanding of the program, and cannot help users find interesting segments within a TV program.

There has been also research in personalization related to adaptive hypermedia systems (Brusilovsky, 2003). These systems build a model of the goals, preferences and knowledge of each individual user, and use this model throughout the interaction with the user, in order to adapt to the needs of that user.

The Video Scout project we previously developed offers an early view of personalization at a subprogram level (Jasinschi et al., 2001, Zimmerman et al., 2001). Video Scout offers users two methods for personalizing the TV experience. First, Scout can display TV show segments (Figure 8.1). For example, it segments talk shows into host/guest segments, displays musical performances and individual jokes. Second, Scout offers a user interface element called 'TV magnets' (Figure 8.2). If users specify financial news topics and celebrity names, then Scout watches TV and stores matching segments, monitoring the contents of talk shows for celebrity clips and searching the contents of financial news programs for financial news stories. Subprogram level access to TV programs improves the TV experience by allowing users more control over the content they watch.

2.2. RELATED WORK IN CONTENT ANALYSIS AND ENHANCED TV

Recently, there has been increasing interest in hyperlinking video with supplemental information. Examples include Microsoft and CBS's interactive TV (Microsoft

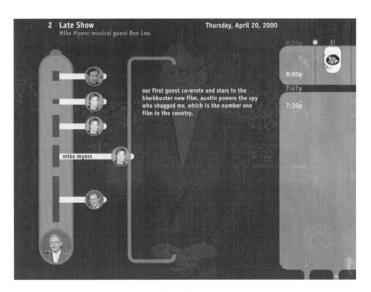

Figure 8.1. Talk show segmented into host and guest segments.

1997), ABC's enhanced TV (ABC 2003), the HyperSoap project at the MIT Media Lab (Dakss), and Jiang and Elmagarmed's work on their Logical Hypervideo Data Model (Jiang et al., 1998).

In 1997 at the National Association of Broadcaster's Expo, we saw Microsoft demonstrate their Enhanced TV concept. This concept allowed users to see Internet data associated with a TV program while watching the program. The Internet content

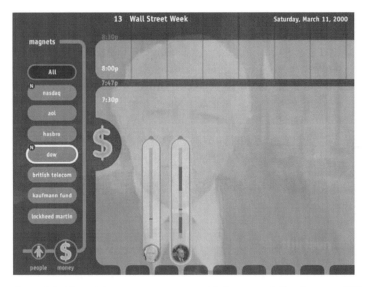

Figure 8.2. Financial news magnet screen with four stored clips from two TV shows.

appeared on the side and bottom of the TV screen while the TV show played. Since then Microsoft has been working with broadcasters such as CBS to deliver interactive TV versions of the Grammy Awards, NCAA Basketball, and even TV dramas like CSI (Microsoft 2000). The current implementation works only for users with WebTV plus service or with a Microsoft UltimateTV settop box.

ABC's enhanced TV broadcasts allow users to view supplemental information such as player statistics for football games, answer questions for game shows, and answer polling questions for talk and news shows (ABC 2003). The interaction takes place on a computer displaying synchronized Webcast data that corresponds to events on the TV show. The current implementation can make it difficult for users, as their attention is needed on two screens simultaneously. In addition, the *lean forward* model of computer use is not completely appropriate for the more *lean back* task of watching TV.

Both the Microsoft/CBS and the ABC products combine Internet content with TV shows. However, neither allows users much freedom to explore. The Internet content is packaged and sent to users by the same people who created the TV program. Also, neither product personalizes either the TV show or the Internet content for individual users.

Another concept called 'HyperSoap' (Dakss et al.) allows TV viewers using a special remote control to point at clothing, props and other furnishings on a soap opera in order to learn how they can be purchased. The research group studied how people interact with hyperlinked video and employed this information in developing different modes of interaction. The design of the system matches current TV viewing in that it allows users to interact with a remote control. However, one clear challenge for this model is how to deal with objects that jump around on the screen as the story jumps from cut to cut.

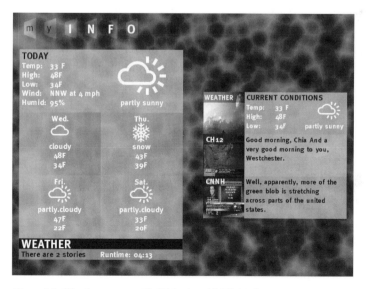

Figure 8.3. Weather screen with Web story highlighted.

Figure 8.4. Headlines screen with TV story highlighted.

Jiang and Elmagarmed have introduced a novel video data model called 'Logical Hypervideo Data Model' (Jiang et al. 1998). The model is capable of representing multilevel video abstractions with video entities that users are interested in (defined as hot objects) and their semantic associations with other logical video abstractions, including hot objects themselves. The semantic associations are modeled as video hyperlinks and video data with such property are called hypervideo. Video hyperlinks provide a flexible and effective way of browsing video data. However, in this system, all the associations are derived manually. Users communicate with the system using a query language. This method of interaction allows them to explore information, but conflicts with the *lean back* model of TV viewing.

Broadcast news analysis and retrieval for various purposes has also been an active area of research for a number of years. We created an initial 'Personal News Retrieval System' in 1996 to test the feasibility of video broadcast filtering in the news domain (Elenbaas et al. 1999). The news broadcasts from different channels were semi-automatically indexed on a server. A client application invoked from a Web browser allows users to search individual stories. Searching is based on anchorperson, broadcaster, category, location, top-stories and keywords.

Merlino et al. developed the 'Broadcast News Editor/Navigator' (BNE/BNN) (Merlino et al., 1997). They rely on the format of the broadcast to be broken down into series of *states*, such as start of broadcast, advertising, new story, and end of broadcast. They use multi-source cues such as text cues ('back to you in New York'), audio silence to find commercials, and visual cues such as black frame and single and double booth anchor recognition.

Hanjalic and his colleagues describe a semi-automatic news analysis method based on pre-selection of categories (Hanjalic et al., 1999). They find anchorperson shots, using a template for matching the shots by matching individual frames. Also, they incorporated a simple word-spotting algorithm to form reports and use this for topic specification. Other systems have been reported in the literature dealing with the news retrieval (Ahanger et al., 1997, Brown et al., 1995, Chen et al., 1997, Maybury 2000). In addition, there is very recent research that performs automated segmentation of news and user modeling to generate personalcasts (Maybury et al., this volume).

Broadcast TV companies have also tried to come up with Internet versions of their content. For example, CNN has a limited number of current stories and an archive of old ones available in Real-video or MPEG-4 (netshow) format. (See http:// www.cnn.com/videoselect/for more details.)

The difference between our applications MyInfo and InfoSip and the cited systems is threefold: (i) our applications integrate both Web and TV content, as opposed limiting users to a single source, (ii) our interface employs a TV-like interaction, and (iii) MyInfo performs extensive prioritization and personalization based on detailed user preferences.

3. Pilot Applications

In order to explore and demonstrate the usefulness of content augmentation, we applied a selective process of filtering initial ideas and concepts. In this section, we present our process and the pilot applications.

MyInfo and InfoSip are both designed to enhance the features of a Personal Video Recorder (PVR) such as a TiVo, ReplayTV, or UltimateTV. These hard disk-based settop boxes currently allow users to easily store large numbers of shows. The segmented news stories, movies and supplemental information from the Web will all be stored on a PVR for access by users using a traditional remote control that has a few additional buttons. These applications are not currently intended to work with live broadcasts.

3.1. THE DESIGN PROCESS

We began by conducting a brainstorming session that included engineers and designers with experience in video processing, Web information retrieval, and Web and interactive TV design. We produced twenty concepts that coalesced into the following themes:

- Connect: Connect users with each other, with their community; with the live world.
- Explore: Support users' ability to move deeper into a specific topic. Allow users to specify the level of detail they require.
- Anticipate: Extract, classify, and summarize information before users request it.
- Summarize: Reduce overwhelming amounts of content (especially redundant content) into appropriate chunks based on user context.

After concept generation, we conducted two focus group sessions. Our focus group consisted of four men and four women living in the suburbs near New York City. They came from different educational, ethnic, and socio-economic backgrounds; however, they all enjoyed watching TV and all had access to and experience with using the Web.

Our first session focused on evaluating and prioritizing the different concepts. In addition, participants shared their current strategies, preferences, and gripes for watching TV and collecting information from the Web. The following two concepts received particularly high ratings from participants:

1. Personal News: the application supplements TV news stories with richer detail obtained from the Web.
2. Actor Info: the application displays Web links for actors in the movie currently being viewed.

Our second focus group employed the same participants, and used a participatory design approach to better define the pilot applications. In exploring the personal news concept, participants revealed that they currently sought out news using a niche surfing technique. When they wanted to know something like the price of a stock, the outcome of a sporting event or the weather, they would tune their TVs to an appropriate channel such as ESPN (sports), MSNBC (finance), or the Weather Channel and then wait for the information to appear. They generally did not use the Web for this sort of high-level news because it required them to abandon household tasks such as making breakfast or folding laundry in order to go upstairs and boot a computer. They desired a system that offered faster access to personal news around the themes of sports, finance, traffic, weather, local events, and headlines. They wanted access to the *freshest* information for these *content zones* from any TV in their home.

In exploring the Actor Info application, participants really liked the idea of viewing supplemental information for a movie, but they did not want to be interrupted. Instead they wanted to be able to easily ask questions such as: Who's that actor? What's that song? Where are they? What kind of shoes are those? etc. They wanted the answers to these questions to appear immediately on the screen in an overlay. This way, they could get the information they wanted without interruption. They did not want links to Web sites. Instead, they wanted much more digested and summarized information. For more detail on the design process, please see (Zimmerman et al., this volume).

3.2. MYINFO

Users access the MyInfo application via a remote control. They can select any of the six content zones identified by the focus group in order to see personal Web extracted data and the latest TV stories that match this zone. In addition, users can press a button labeled 'MyInfo' in order to see a personalized TV news broadcast that displays TV news and Web extracted data from all of the content zones.

The interface displays an expanded story on the left, and a prioritized list of stories on the right. The top story always contains the Web-extracted information, which matches specific request in the user profile. The Web-extracted information includes: for weather, a four-day forecast for the specified zip code; for sports, the latest scores and upcoming games for specified teams; for local events, a prioritized listing by how soon the event will happen, distance from the home, and degree of match to keywords in profile; for traffic, delays for user-specified routes and 'hot-spots'; and for finance, current prices for stocks, change in price, and percent change for indexes, stocks, and funds listed in the profile.

By pressing the NEXT button, users can navigate down in the list of stories. This allows them to effectively skip stories they do not want to hear. In addition, they can press the PLAY-ALL button in order to automatically play all the stories in a single content zone. The interaction supports users' lifestyles, and takes a step towards a *lean-natural* interface. Users can quickly check information such as weather and traffic right before they leave their homes. They can also play back all, or sections of, the personalized news as a TV show, leaving themselves free to carry out tasks in their homes such as eating, cooking, and laundry.

3.3. INFOSIP

The InfoSip pilot application allows users to *sip* information about actors in a scene while watching a movie. Users press the WHO button on the remote control and detailed information appears at the bottom of the screen. Currently, our system provides an image, a biography, a filmography, and current rumors, for all actors in the current scene (Figure 8.5). We manually extract the image from the video, but we hope to automate this process using our actor identification algorithms

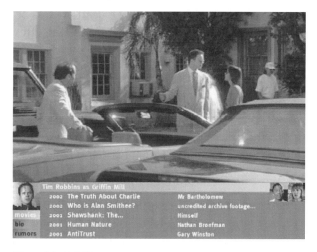

Figure 8.5. InfoSip screen.

(Section 5.5). The descriptive information is automatically extracted from the Web. This application has an advantage over supplemental metadata supplied on DVDs, in that it is always up to date. In the example below, Tim Robbins' filmography details work he did in 2002, even though the source movie, Robert Altman's *The Player*, was released in 1992.

During the collaborative design session, the participants stated that they often saw an actor whom they recognized but could not place. They wanted a simple method of selecting one of the actors, and seeing enough information to help them remember where they had seen that actor before. The decision to display all of the actors in the current scene takes a step towards a *lean-natural* interface by allowing users to both *sip* the metadata and view the movie simultaneously. Listing all actors in the movie would generate too large a list to navigate and would run the risk of drawing the user away from watching the movie. Displaying only the actors currently on screen would often require users to scan back in the movie, because, by the time they realized they wanted the information and grabbed the remote control, the shot with the actor they wanted might have ended. The filmographies have two pieces of additional information that support functionality that was designed but not yet implemented. Their display can be personalized by using a viewing history to highlight movies the user has seen the specific actor in, aiding the recognition task. In addition, when filmographies contain movies that match movies scheduled for broadcast, users can use this interface to select movies for recording.

3.4. DEMONSTRATION

We developed these applications to stimulate conversations between stakeholders in the TV/Web content value chain, from media producers, packagers, distributors to media consumers. The original idea was to develop these applications as demonstrators in order to explore the target applications for consumers. We hoped to use the applications to generate business models and new application concepts with colleagues in the content creation, broadcasting, and distribution domains. However, in the future, we plan to perform a qualitative evaluation of these applications with users.

4. System Overview

The system diagram in Figure 8.6 shows the high-level chain of content processing and augmentation. Unannotated or partially annotated content is delivered to the service provider (e.g. content provider, broadcaster) where generic analysis and augmentation is performed.

Content and (optionally) metadata are delivered to the first step (Feature Extraction and Integration) of the processing chain. At the *server* stage of the augmentation, the system extracts features and summarizes the content, generating descriptive metadata. (A more detailed description of this step is given in Section 5.) The generated

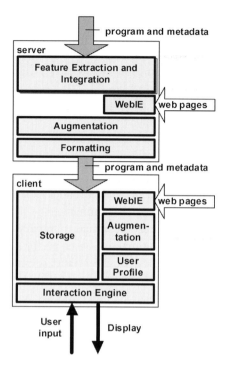

Figure 8.6. Content Augmentation system diagram.

metadata, in conjunction with any existing metadata, is then used to augment the content with additional information from Web sources. This information is provided by using Information Extraction from Web pages (WebIE), as described in Section 6. The augmentation (Augmentation) that occurs at the server side is general, in that it is not based on any personal profile. Following broadcaster augmentation, the content with the complete metadata is formatted and delivered to the consumer device (Formatting).

The remaining augmentation is performed in the *client* stage. Here, a consumer device has the capability of storing content, metadata (in Storage), and user profile (User Profile). The device also has a prioritization module that relies on the user profile. This is used to perform a secondary augmentation (Augmentation) with Web information (WebIE), but this time based solely on user preferences. The information obtained is stored together with the content and is presented to users (Interaction Engine) as if it were a part of the original program. One of the reasons we kept all personalization on the client was to help insure privacy, a major concern of users in our focus group.

There are several delivery pathways for the augmentation data, depending on the implementation of the system and the business model. Encoding metadata with the media is the most straightforward approach to delivering augmentation, but alternative pathways are also possible. Web broadcasts or subscription-based data retrieval can also offer localized or personalized versions of the augmentation data. Finally, the principle division in the server and client stage in Figure 8.6 is mainly to emphasize various aspects of the system. Implementations of the system where various client functions are provided by the server, and, inversely, server functions performed by the client, are possible.

5. Content Processing

Methods for automatic metadata extraction can be divided into coarse- and fine-grain segmentation and abstraction. In this section, we briefly introduce the methods used for our applications. For MyInfo, we coarsely segment the news broadcast into individual stories as described in Section 5.1. Next, each story is summarized by a representative textual summary and a frame that captures the visual summary. Text summarization is described in Section 5.2. Visual summarization is performed by detection shots of the news anchor (as described in Section 5.3) and selection of the most important visual key element (as described in Section 5.4.) For InfoSip, we apply person identification using both face and voice identification, as described in Section 5.5.

5.1. COARSE SEGMENTATION

Our approach exploits well-known, previously reported, cues to segment commercials and news segments from news programs (Merlino et al. 1997 and Boykin et al. 1999). We first find the commercial breaks in a particular news program, and then we perform story segmentation within the news portion. For stories, we use the story break markup ('>>>') in the closed captioning. In addition, we have investigated the detection of story segment boundaries at a macrosegment level (McGee et al. 1999, Dimitrova et al. 2003).

There is a variety of commercial detectors that perform text, audio, and visual analysis to determine if TV programs contain commercial breaks (Blum 1992, Bonner et al., 1982, Boykin et al., 1999, Merlino et al., 1997). Since our domain consists of 'commercial aware' programs, in which the anchors announce that a commercial break is coming up, we were able to use a computationally inexpensive, genre-specific, text-based commercial detector. In part, this relies on the absence of closed captioning for 30 seconds or more, and in part, it relies on the news anchors using cue phrases to segue to/from the commercials, such as, 'coming up after the break' and 'welcome back'. We look for onset cues such as 'right back', 'come back', 'up next' and 'when we return', in conjunction with offset cues, such as 'welcome back' and the 'new speaker' markup ('>>'). We tested commercial detection on US broadcast of four financial news and four talk show programs totaling 360 minutes, with 33 commercials totaling 102 minutes. The financial news programs included four half hour shows of CNN, NBC, and public television programs. The talk shows included four one hour late night shows on the NBC and ABC TV stations. Our algorithm detected

32 commercials totaling 104 minutes. Of these, 25 were exactly right. Only one commercial was completely missed. We detected 4 extra minutes spread out over seven commercials. The resulting recall and precision are 98% and 96% respectively.

5.2. TEXT SUMMARIZATION

Each broadcast news story has to be summarized, in order to use (i) the abstracted data, for matching against the personal profile, and (ii) the summary, for presentation browsing. For MyInfo, a summary consists of a sentence of text and a representative image (key frame), plus a categorization (an assignment of the story to one of our six 'content zones').

The summarization process begins with collection of the closed captioning text – the transcript of the spoken text – sent with each frame of the story. Figure 8.7 presents one such time-stamped transcript.

While this text could be in mixed upper/lower case, just as the sentence you are reading right now is, in practice, it is very commonly mono-case. So recapitalization is performed: the text is put entirely in lower case, and selected words are then capitalized, based on:

- Sentence-terminal punctuation (so the first word of the next sentence will be capitalized)

```
5252  >>> JURORS WILL RESUME
5282  DELIBERATIONS THIS MORNING
5322  IN A TWO-DECADE-OLD MURDER CASE.
5374  NORMAN REED FACES 25 YEARS
5424  FOR THE EXECUTION STYLE MURDER
5473  OF GREENBURG BOOKMAKER,
5513  RUDY WILLIAMS.
5556  HE WAS KILLED BACK IN 1979, BUT
5602  AUTHORITIES FINALLY MADE A BREAK
5658  IN THE CASE LAST YEAR.
5707  POLICE SAY REED AND THREE OTHERS
5744  WENT TO WILLIAMS' HOME
5781  TO STEAL DRUGS AND CASH,
5826  BUT WOUND UP SHOOTING HIM
5866  AND HIS STEPSON INSTEAD.
5961  >> WHEN YOU DON'T KNOW WHO,
6011  YOU KNOW, OR YOU DON'T KNOW WHY,
6100  THEN YOU WONDER IF THIS IS
6192  NOT GONNA COME TO YOU,
6235  OR IS IT GONNA DAMAGE YOU
6274  AND DAMAGE YOUR FAMILY?
6324  SO WE'RE LIVIN' IN FEAR.
6383  >> THE DEFENSE MAINTAINS REED
6419  WAS AT THE SCENE FOR A DRUG DEAL
6459  AND TOOK OFF WHEN THE OTHERS
6505  INVOLVED STARTED SHOOTING.
```

Figure 8.7. Time-stamped transcript of a news story, as collected from the closed captioning. ('≫' indicates 'change of speaker').

- Lists of:
  First names of people
  People name 'particles' (e.g., von, del, ben)
  Titles and honorifics ('Judge', 'Senator', 'Esquire')
  Names of places:

- Geographic regions (rivers, mountains, etc)
- Political entities (cities, counties, states, provinces, countries, etc)
- Terms used to denote streets, squares, bridges, parks, etc

  Acronyms
- Simple heuristics governing capitalization of words preceding or following words in these lists. These produce, e.g., 'Brooklyn Bridge', rather than 'Brooklyn bridge', and 'George Washington' rather than 'George washington'.

Figure 8.8 shows the result after the recapitalization step.

Our own algorithm was used, which was adequate for our needs, but not perfect. The reader should note the mistaken capitalization of 'and' and 'was', because the surname 'Reed', being also a common first name, is in the first names list, and a heuristic that texts always contain persons' full names fired. Better algorithms have been developed (Brown et al., 2002) which first capitalizes the whole text, and then de-capitalizes those words in a list of common English words.

The IBM INTELLIGENT MINER FOR TEXT ('TextMiner') document summarizer (Boguraev et al., 2000) is then applied, to select the N sentences in the story which summarize it best. (We use N = 1.) 'Best' in this context is a weighted metric, involving the 'salience' (position) of the sentence in the document, its length, and other factors. Usually, the first sentence of a news story ends up being the one selected; given how news stories are written, this sentence is normally both a comprehensive summary and a good introduction to the story. However, sometimes a non-useful sentence occurs first ('Hello, I'm Dan Rather'.); TextMiner often catches these cases and makes a better selection.

Jurors will resume deliberations this morning in a two-decade-old murder case. Norman Reed faces 25 years for the execution style murder of Greenburg bookmaker, Rudy Williams. He was killed back in 1979, but authorities finally made a break in the case last year. Police say Reed And three others went to Williams' home to steal drugs and cash, but wound up shooting him and his stepson instead. >> When you don't know who, you know, or you don't know why, then you wonder if this is not gonna come to you, or is it gonna damage you and damage your family? So we're livin' in fear. >> The defense maintains Reed Was at the scene for a drug deal and took off when the others involved started shooting.

Figure 8.8. The recapitalized text.

For the story in Figure 8.8, the text summarization found is:
'Jurors will resume deliberations this morning in a two-decade-old murder case.'
We also use the TextMiner document classifier. It works on the basis of frequency of occurrence of words within the story, and similarity of such frequency distributions to canonical examples. The classifier engine is domain-independent; to use it, we trained it off-line with a corpus of exemplar stories for our six 'information zones'. In the case of the story in Figure 8.8, the computed categorization is:

15.2041 headlines
12.8685 future announcements ('teasers')
11.6219 commercials
11.4269 local news

where the numbers on the left are confidence scores, which have no metric interpretation; simply, larger values are to be preferred to smaller values.

A third TextMiner engine, the 'feature finder', is used to extract proper names from the story. These names could be matched against entries in the user profile, to determine the story's relevance for the user.

Name, person: Norman Reed 4708 25
Name, unknown: Greenburg 4820 13
Name, person: Rudy Williams 4847 42
Name, person: Reed Was 5743 15

Here, the numbers to the right of the names of persons, places, and unknown things are the locations and durations of their occurrences in the story (in units of characters). The number of occurrences of a given name, and its salience in the story, could further contribute to calculation of a story's relevance for the user.

The TextMiner classifier was evaluated as part of the NIST Tipster SUMMAC text summarization evaluation of 1998 (Mani et al., 1998). It was found to have a precision of 0.68 and a recall of 0.47.

5.3. ANCHOR DETECTION

We have an anchorperson detection module, which is an important contributor to multi-modal segmentation, because stories often begin and/or end with in-studio (anchorperson-present) shots, rather than during *reportage* segments (shots of reporters and/or interviewees, commonly taken 'on location', or at the reporter's 'desk'). This module is also important for story summarization, since it helps in choosing representative keyframes for the stories that do not include anchor images. This module is composed of three main blocks:

1. Shot detection
2. Face clip finding
3. Anchorperson shot detection

5.3.1. *Shot Detection*

We compute the cumulative probability distribution of each of the red, green, and blue channels from their histograms for each frame (Hampapur et al., 1994). The distance between two cumulative probability distributions is found by using the Kolmogorov-Smirnov (KS) test. First- to fourth-order differences, and two types of tests, are used to make shot boundary detection robust with respect to various video effects (wipes/fades/dissolves) and flashes.

We compute KS distances between consecutive frames and between those separated by 1, 2, and 3 frames. The first test is based on ratio combinations of each of these distances. Each of the ratios (and/or the distances) must be larger than predetermined thresholds. In order to prevent false shot break detections due to flashes, we also check the KS distance of the following frame to the previous frames before declaring the current frame as the starting point of a new shot. Second- and third-order differences, and different thresholds on the distances and their ratios, are used for this. Again, the ratios (and/or the distances) must be larger than thresholds. For example let $D(n, n-2)$ denote the KS distance between frames n and n-2. If

$$D(n, n-2)/D(n-2, n-3) >= \text{thr1} \text{ and}$$
$$D(n, n-3)/D(n-3, n-4) >= \text{thr2} \text{ and}$$
$$D(n, n-3) > \text{thr3} \text{ and } D(n, n-2) > \text{thr4},$$

one of the two acceptable conditions is satisfied and the same test is applied for the following frame (by replacing n with $n + 1$) before declaring the current frame (frame n) as the beginning of a shot. The same threshold values are used for all videos.

5.3.2. *Face Clip Finding*

We process the video sequence to find video clips containing faces. For each clip, the following information is saved: the frame numbers of the first and last frames of the clip, and the coordinates of the bounding rectangle of the largest face in view, in each frame in the clip. These clips are, in general, subsets of the shots found in step 5.3.1. In cases where the clip spans two shots; it is broken into two clips, at the shot boundary. Where multiple video clips containing faces occur within a single shot, they are merged. We use a face detection algorithm which is based on flesh tone-finding followed by high chroma detection and horizontal texture detection (Connell, 2002).

5.3.3. *Anchorperson Shot Detection*

The next step is matching the face in one clip with those in others. For each face clip, the largest face (as determined by its rectangular bounding box) is used. To make the matching more robust with respect to head motions, especially roll (rotation in the image plane), we expand the original bounding box so that it is twice as large in both width and height, in order to include the hair region of the head and some of the shoulder region, also. Thus, more color information is incorporated, in addition to just flesh tone. The enlarged rectangle is then divided into 6 regions: one for each side of the head, one for the original face box and the hair on the top, and three for the shoulder and neck region. See Figure 8.9.

For each frame, the cumulative distributions of the red, green, and blue channels are calculated for each of the six regions; these are then averaged over all the frames of the clip. This gives us a representative distribution for that clip. Although this is quite a slow process, non-real time performance can be tolerated in the MyInfo application.

To find the canonical anchorperson clip, we look for one clip whose representative distribution is very similar to those of a large percentage of the other clips. We compute the pairwise KS distance between the representative distributions of each pair of clips, and, if the distance is less than a threshold, we consider them to be different image sequences of the same person and background. As this calculation is of order n^2 in the number of clips, we employ an early-termination scheme to ignore some of the clips. First we start with the representative distribution of a clip and find the KS distance of this distribution to those of the other clips. If we find that $m\%$ of the clips have distances that are less than a threshold t, we group them together, and sort the list in ascending order according to their distances to the distribution we have started with. We call this group the *initial list*, and then we start pruning this group. We take the first clip we started with and the one which is at the top of the *initial list*, and put them in a new group called the *anchor shots list* which will be the pruned version of the *initial list*. To start pruning, we take the first

Figure 8.9. Face, with original (inside box) an expanded and partitioned (outside box) bounding box.

Table 8.1. Results from anchor detection

	Number of detected shots	Number of detected face clips	Number of true anchor shots	Number of false positives	Number of false negatives	Accuracy of the shot beginning points
CNN1			7	0	1	100%
CNN2	102	68	7	0	2	100%
Ch12_1	201	63	5	1	1	100%
Ch12_2	132	99	7	0	1	85.7%

distribution in the *initial list* and find the KS distances of the others in the list to it. We keep the ones whose distances are less than *t* in the *initial list* and remove the others and again sort the list. We then put the first element of this list in the *anchor shots list* and repeat the process. This way we make sure that every clip in the *anchor shots list* will be within distance *t* of each other.

In our experiments, the percentage threshold *m* was 25–35%. In its current state, the algorithm can only deal with clips in which there is one anchorperson, but it can be extended to work on other more general cases also.

We performed some experiments on four news segments to test the performance of the algorithm (see Table 8.1). The algorithm was tested on 56,500 frames of news videos from CNN and local news channel in Westchester, NY. In this data set, there were 26 true anchor shots. (Note that in the test data, there are some shots in which more than one anchorperson appears. As the current version only works for single anchorperson in a shot, the shots with multiple anchorpersons have not been counted in the true anchor shots.) The algorithm found one false positive and five false negatives. The percentage of anchor shots whose starting frame was detected correctly by the shot detection algorithm was 96.15%. If some special effect is used for transition from one shot to another, detection of beginning of the new shot is delayed. In all these experiments, the same KS distance threshold was used.

5.4. SUMMARY IMAGE SELECTION

In order to find a representative visual key element, we find a representative keyframe for each news story. This image has to be the most representative frame from the story. Figure 8.10 shows an example of the summarization process for a news story. At the top, a film strip consisting of 8 families of video frames is presented, showing the length of each family along with its cumulatively averaged histogram. For finding important segments, we use the uniformly colored segments generated by family histogram clustering; the frames are weighted by the duration of the family they belong to. We use Family Histograms (Dimitrova et al., 1999) to find uniformly colored video clips. These correspond to shots, or parts of shots.

For each feature, we find a value between zero and one that gives the 'desirability' of that feature. The figure shows the various visual features that are extracted for

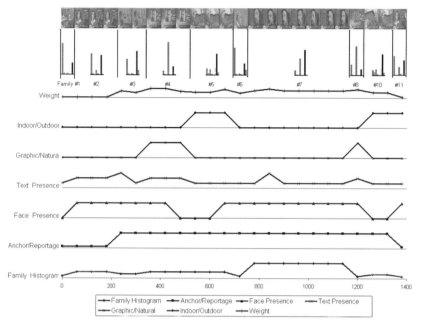

Figure 8.10. Representative image selection.

summary image selection. For the family histograms, the importance of a frame is derived by the duration of the family it belongs to and divided by the longest family in the news story. The bottom curve shows the importance based on family histograms. The second curve shows the anchor vs. reportage class. The news story initially starts with the anchor, goes on to reportage and ends with the anchor. Each story is usually composed of an anchor shot followed by reportage shot(s). The anchor shots are similar for all stories, so they do not provide any value in representing the story. In order to select an image from only the reportage, an anchorperson detector is used (see Section 5.3.3). In this curve, the value of anchor is 0.1 and that of reportage segment is 1. The third curve from bottom shows presence or absence of faces. The value of this feature is 0 if no faces are present, and 1 if one or more faces are detected. The next curve gives the text importance in the video. This is derived by the number of lines of text in the frame divided by the maximum number of lines in the news program. Presence of both faces and text is desirable in the selected image. The next curve in the graph shows presence of graphic vs. natural scene video. Graphic information relates to shots that contain graphs, slides, and other computer-generated screens. We include a graphic image if available. The second curve from top gives the indoor vs. outdoor information. For news programs, we feel that outdoor shots are more important for news stories than indoor shots. We use the indoor/outdoor detector developed by Naphade et al. (2002). In the above curves, the value is 1 for graphic and outdoors and 0 for natural and indoor frames. We select a frame that is deemed to be the most 'interesting' by the algorithm that considers all the above attributes. An importance score is computed for each frame as following:

$$FrameScore = AR^* \left(\sum_{i=1}^{6} W_i F_i \right)$$

where AR is 1 for reportage segment and 0.1 for anchor segment. The W_i is the weight given to each of the features F_i: F_1 is Face, F_2 is videotext, F_3 is anchor or reportage, F_4 is graphics or no graphics, F_5 is outdoors or indoor, and F_6 is weight of family histogram. The top curve in Figure 7.10 gives an importance score based on all the input features for each frame. For our system, presently we use equal weights for all the features. A frame from family #3 is selected as the most representative for the story.

We performed an empirical benchmarking of our method in the following way. We found two representative images, one using our image selection algorithm, and another image using the 'middle image pick method' as taking the image occurring at the middle of the story. We watched the news story and determined which image summarized the news best. Based on this viewing, we decided the 'desirability' of the image selected on a scale of 1 to 5. On this scale, if the image selected was the one that we felt summarized the news story the best, we gave it a 5; in the other extreme where the image was not desirable at all, we gave it a rating of 1.

Based on this system, we analyzed a total of one hour of news stories consisting of half-hour each of CNN Headline News and Channel 12 news (local news channel). A total of 33 news stories were selected to be presented to the user for evaluation. The Table 8.2 shows the number of votes for the ratings of the middle image pick and summary image selection algorithms. Overall, the algorithm does better than the mid method. The average rating of the image selected by the algorithm is 4.27, vs. 3.87 using the mid method. Also, the standard deviation of the algorithm is only 0.87, compared to 1.17 of the mid method, which means that the algorithm consistently gives better images.

Table 8.2. Results of the middle image vs image selection method

Rating	Mid method votes	Algorithm result
5	14	16
4	5	12
3	12	3
2	0	2
1	2	0
Average	3.87	4.27
Std Dev	1.17	0.87

5.5. PERSON IDENTIFICATION

A rich 'frequently asked question' – answering application relies on manual annotation or automatic detectors. For example, to answer the 'who is this person?' question in a movie, documentary or home video, we need to know which people are present in each scene. The major challenge is to robustly identify persons from different views, distances, lighting conditions, in the presence of various background noise conditions. We used automatic face and voice identification methods for this task (Li et al., 2001).

A person identification approach is constructed, based on the joint use of visual and audio information. First, in the *analysis* phase, we perform visual analysis for detection, tracking and recognition of faces in video. Face trajectories are first extracted and the Eigenface method is used to label each face trajectory as one of the known persons in the database. Due to the limitation of existing face recognition techniques and the complex environmental factors in our experimental data, the visual recognition accuracy is not high. Next we employ audio segmentation and classification to find the speech segments. Film often has music background or environmental noise in the soundtrack, and this factor makes the audio identification a challenging process. Speaker identification using Gaussian Mixture Models is applied to the speech segments. Both audio and visual analysis have their advantages under different circumstances, and we studied how to exploit the interaction between them for improved performance.

In the fusion phase, two strategies have been employed (Li et al., 2001). In the first strategy, the *audio-verify-visual(AVV) fusion* strategy, speaker identification is used to verify the face recognition result. The second strategy, the *visual-aid-audio fusion* (*VAA*) strategy, consists of using face recognition and tracking to supplement speaker identification results. In our testing we used a database, which consisted of 100 video clips (dialog, non-dialog, and silent clips) from the sitcom 'Seinfeld.' In the experiment, speaker identification gave recall of 54.6%, and precision of 76.9%, while the face recognition gave recall of 15%, and precision of 35%. The AVV strategy yielded 12% recall, and 92.9% precision, while the VAA strategy yielded 62.9% recall and 82.4% precision. We see that AVV has a slightly lower recall than the face recognition and best precision which is good for surveillance type of applications. VAA generates the best overall identification performance and is suitable to TV content analysis applications such as InfoSip.

In addition, we use textual information extracted from closed caption or video caption. We have a name spotting process that extracts role names that appear in each video scene, and assigns a score for each detected role name according, to the frequency of its own appearance as well as that of those that closely relate to it. These scores, together with our audiovisual detection results, are used in a final voting process to decide which role(s) appear in the scene. The integration is based upon the belief values of different candidates, using a single layer Bayesian network. The ones with highest integration belief will then be justified as top characters appearing in the scene.

For narrative content where there is more than one talking face on the screen each time, and sometimes non-related voice over, we need to use a talking head detection process, which automatically detects the face(s) on the screen that has corresponding speech in the synchronized soundtrack. Such information can then be used in the fusion process to integrate the speaker identification results with the corresponding face trajectory. A cross-modal association method called Cross-modal Factor Analysis (CFA) is proposed and used for our talking head detection (Li et al., 2003). CFA achieves 91.1% detection precision in our experiments, while our two other implementations based on Latent Semantic Indexing (LSI) and Canonical Correlation Analysis (CCA) achieve 66.1% and 73.9% detection precision respectively using the same set of testing data.

6. Web Information Extraction

Unlike in-depth Natural Language Processing, Information Extraction (IE) 'skims' the input text, finds relevant sections and then focuses only on those sections in the subsequent processing in order to find targeted information (Cardie 1997). In other words, IE systems (1) take as input a document that contains unrestricted text, (2) find useful information about the domain from the analyzed text, and (3) encode the information in a structured form (e.g. suitable for populating databases). We will refer to IE in the context where the input is a Web document as Web Information Extraction (WebIE). An introduction to IE, WebIE, and additional references are given in (Janevski, 2000).

Our system implements a framework in which instantiations of modules called *IE rules* can be plugged in and executed for each acquired document. We developed two collections of rules: tag-based and content-based. Tag-based rules utilize the encoding of the documents (tags), while content-based rules apply natural language processing techniques over the text and operate at various levels starting from keyword matching to in-depth syntax analysis. We will refer to IE rule instantiations as *IE tasks*.

6.1. LASER WEBIE

We distinguish two types of WebIE – Diffusion and Laser. In Diffusion WebIE, tasks require broad search over a large number of sites and time is not critical. A Laser WebIE system extracts and formats information from a well-defined set of Web sources. Our content augmentation system executes instantiations of Laser WebIE rules that retrieve information on news headlines, weather, traffic, sports games and scores, stock quotes, and movie cast information. Furthermore, most IE tasks are customized for every instantiation. Specifically, the weather information is tied to the user's zip code; traffic information is dependent on the user's route to work; sports and stock depend on user's personal preferences; movie cast information depends on the cast member currently present in the scene. We will use the segment of the user personal profile in Table 8.3 to illustrate the WebIE tasks in this section.

Table 8.3. Part of user profile – a sample

Zip code	10510
Traffic hotspots	Taconic Pkwy; Bear Mountain Bridge; Route 100; Tappan Zee Bridge
Stock symbols	PHG; IBM
Favorite Actors	Bening, Annette; Spacey, Kevin; Redford, Robert

6.2. DOCUMENT ACQUISITION AND IE RULES

Once WebIE task(s) are instantiated, the results must be delivered quickly while the video context is still active. Even with high-speed access to the Web, it could take considerable time to retrieve, process, and present information to the user. For this purpose, the source URLs are given in advance and WebIE tasks directly acquire the Web pages, thus avoiding a search through numerous pages. To bootstrap the augmentation, a list of predefined URLs for each of the queries is embedded in the system. Since content augmentation is likely to be delivered as a service, content creators and/or distributors can encode these pointers with the content, or have them delivered to the system ahead of the broadcast delivery of the content (or during delivery). Moreover, in a scenario where all content processing is performed locally, 'generic' URLs (pointers) would provide enhancements for various WebIE tasks. The URL for the information source is given partially, and is then customized based on the WebIE task arguments and the information from the personal profile. An example local weather URL is given in Table 8.4a) where at least part of the URL (in bold) is dynamically generated. Another example is extraction of actor information in Table 8.4b) using the generic URL and customizing it with the actor name Robert Redford (in bold).

For the design of Laser WebIE tasks, we assumed a relatively static content presentation style since Web site structures remain stable for a period of time. The IE tasks take advantage of this and use identifiable references specific to the information source. However, the number and the uniqueness of each source of information argues against the desire to build as few WebIE rules that can instantiate as many tasks as possible. All IE rules are built on the same principle, and use a similar set of parameters to identify an IE rule. First, the boundaries of a segment are specified. Second, the boundaries of the extracted information are given. And, third, the format of the output data is defined. The segments and the extracted information can be defined through HTML tags or specific contents such as keywords, numbers, dates, and other data types. In addition, IE rules can take advantage of the segment

Table 8.4. WebIE: weather and actor information extraction – a sample

(a)	http://weather.com/weather/local/<**zipcode**>
	http://www.weather.com/weather/local/**10510**
(b)	http://www.imdb.com/Name?<**last**>,+<**first**>
	http://www.imdb.com/Name?**Redford,+Robert**

structure (e.g. tabular information representation), and use it to identify a segment and/or the information that needs to be extracted.

In Table 8.5, we show two IE task examples with the corresponding URLs, the segments and the extracted information. The Stocks task will acquire a document from a URL that contains the stock quote for Philips (PHG) – the customized part is given in bold. Then, the segment is isolated, based on specific HTML tags also given in bold. Finally, the task extracts texts from two such regions shown in gray background. The extracted texts contain the current stock price, the absolute and the relative change in value. The execution of Headlines, also shown in Table 8.5, will access a URL customized with the fragment in bold – the number 11 stands for Westchester County. The segment is isolated based on two keyword phrases provided in the task definition. The result is extracted between the two characteristic HTML tags. 'White House press briefings', one of the extracted headlines, is shown on a gray background. For each extracted headline the task will also return the URL of the document that contains the complete story – all segment tasks look for links within the extracted region, and if one is found, the URL is returned with the result.

While all WebIE task examples show Web pages written in English, in general, the WebIE rules and tasks are easily portable to other languages. For rules and tasks that are based on keywords and property of the page content, porting to another language is straightforward. In the cases where in-depth syntax analysis is performed to extract information, a larger effort would be required to integrate corresponding language processing tools, such as syntax parsers, with the system. The applicability of the system described depends heavily on the robustness and performance of the information extraction components. Once defined, Laser WebIE tasks are very accurate, as long as the structure of the source Web page(s) remains unchanged. In our tests, we ran a combination of about fifteen WebIE tasks daily for thirty days and obtained 100% accurate extracted information. Laser WebIE tasks have such high accuracy and robustness because they were defined for specific type of target Web pages. The properties of the WebIE tasks depend highly on the content delivery business model. Narrowly defined Laser WebIE tasks are suitable for a setup where a dedicated service maintains the annotation and augmentation.

Table 8.5. Information extraction from stocks and headlines – a sample

Stocks	URL	http://qs.money.cnn.com/apps/stockquote?symbols=**phg**
	Segment	\<td ...class=ıstockheaderı\>31.13\</td\>\<td ...\>
	Extracted text	{\<td ...\>31.13\</td\>, \<td ...\>\<img ...\>0.90 / +2.98%\</td\>}
Headlines	URL	http://www.news12.com/CDA/0,2033,**11**,00.html
	Segment	What You Need To Know ... White House press briefings ...
		National & International News
	Extracted text	\<a href=ı/CDA/...00.htmlı\>White House press briefings\</a\>
	Extracted URL	/CDA/Articles/View/0,2049,11-11-22511-258,00.html

7. Personalization

Personalization provides one of the greatest benefits and one of the greatest risks to content augmentation applications. During our focus group sessions, participants constantly stressed their desire for personalized and easy to use information, along with a need to feel in control. However, they were very wary of any system that made them feel watched. They were all quite uncomfortable with the idea of broadcasters and advertisers gaining access to their detailed information about their media consumption habits, patterns and preferences. Our approach to the personalization challenge was to use our focus group to help identify areas of greatest benefit, and then to balance this with technological capabilities and privacy protection. Based on these requirements we designed the MyInfo application to personalize news in two ways. For the Web data, the system parses and extracts information from Web sites according to requests in the user profile. For TV news stories, the application prioritizes individual stories based on time of broadcast (freshness of this news), topics of interest listed in the user profile, and cues broadcasters use to indicate a story's importance.

7.1. PERSONALIZING WEB DATA

In discussions with our focus group, participants stressed that they did not want to spend a lot of time configuring their system in order to get personalized information. They claimed that difficulty in setup (or perceived difficulties) as well as the requirement to share personal information kept them from using current Web news personalization systems like myYahoo (www.myyahoo.com). Therefore our system places all of the personalization in the client device (settop box in the home) and focuses on providing maximum, targeted information with minimal input. We present screen shots of expanded Web stories for financial news, traffic, local events, and sports in Figure 8.11.

The weather information and sports allow minimal interaction by using the zip code data users enter into their settop boxes while configuring their channel lineups. MyInfo automatically extracts the weather information for this zip and extracts the latest sports scores and upcoming games for local teams. If users desire, they can edit their profile and request weather for a different zip and select other sports teams to track.

Financial news and traffic require more input from the user, but the resulting feedback makes the effort worthwhile. For traffic, the profile contains a set destinations and a set of 'hot spots'. Destinations include towns or prominent structures such as malls, stadiums, airports, etc. Hot spots include points of constriction like bridges and tunnels, which notoriously have traffic delays. Once selected, the system extracts Web traffic information on the specific hot spots and on the major roads between the users home and the selected destinations. For financial news, the profile must contain a list of the stocks, mutual funds, and financial indexes the user wishes to

Figure 8.11. Expanded Web stories for financial news, traffic, local events, and sports. These panels display on the left-hand side of the MyInfo application. For a view of a whole screen, see Figure 8.3.

track. The system then displays a listing of the item, its current price, change in price, and percent change.

For local events the profile contains a set of keywords describing events users like most such as 'music, jazz, fairs, plays, theatre . . .'. The system displays a prioritized listing of these events based on how soon they will take place, their distance from the user's home, and the match to the keywords.

The personalized Web information improves the traditional TV news experience in two ways. First, it reduces the amount of time required to retrieve this information from either a traditional TV or Web site. For example, if users just want to know the current temperature or a stock price, the information is a single button push away. They don't even have to wait for the news anchor to tell them and they don't have to type in a URL and then enter their zip code. Second, the Web-extracted data adds personalization to the TV experience. For the first time, the TV can immediately provide users with specified information on demand. For example, the local TV news can only afford to devote so many minutes of broadcast time each day for traffic information. This prevents them from relaying information on all routes during a traffic segment; forcing them to often skip routes that are important to an individual user. The personalized Web data creates a more personal and meaningful experience, while still allowing users to also view the traditional TV traffic news, which provides a nice overview of the whole traffic situation and information on the worst spots in their area. The personalization of this information helps generate the new lean-natural experience.

7.2. TV NEWS PERSONALIZATION

MyInfo personalizes TV news stories through segmentation, classification, and prioritization. Segmentation cuts the TV news into individual stories and classification places each story into one of the six content zones. These processes allow users to manually personalize the TV news by allowing them to quickly select and skip individual stories, a big improvement over the traditional TV news viewing experience. Prioritization takes this a step further by organizing individual stories within a content zone.

In prioritizing stories, the system balances topics specified in the profile, time sensitivity, and cues the broadcaster uses to indicate a story's importance. Different formulas are used for the different content zones (See Table 8.6).

Use of the broadcaster information is very important, particularly for the headlines zone. Users have no way of predicting every kind of news story that might be important to them. They may know they are interested in China, and therefore add this topic to their profile. However, it is hard for them to predict major events that affect

Table 8.6. Metadata sample

Zone	Profile match	Broadcaster importance	Time sensitivity	Time sensitivity rule
Traffic, Sports, Financial News, Weather	40%	50%	10%	Time since or until event
Local Events	60%	20%	20%	Time until event
Headlines	40	50	10%	Length of time since/until event

many people, such as earthquakes, gas leaks, trial outcomes, etc. By allowing the broadcasters' editorial content decisions to play a role, users get a much better mix of information.

MyInfo determines broadcaster importance of a story from three different characteristics: (i) duration, (ii) location in the newscast, and (iii) teaser announcing a story will play later in the broadcast. Since broadcast time is limited, a longer story will be more important. Location in the broadcast and use of a teaser are subtler. The most important TV news stories generally appear at the beginning; however, broadcasters place other stories they think many viewers want to see at the end. Then they use teasers to keep the viewers from switching channels. At this time, we have designed the broadcaster importance method but it has yet to be implemented and evaluated. Currently our prototype only considers the profile in prioritizing the TV news stories.

7.3. INFOSIP: PERSONALIZED/AUGMENTED NARRATIVE

InfoSip is an example of a 'frequently asked questions' answering application. It unobtrusively serves actor information related to the scene. During focus group testing, participants indicated that they wanted supplementary information for movies and TV shows, but they did not want it to interrupt viewing. With our system, users interact by selecting a specific query on the remote control. InfoSip uses predefined categories of questions/buttons such as 'who', 'where', 'what', 'when', 'why', and 'how much'. For example, users press the 'who' button to ask 'who's that actor?' The system displays a list of all of the actors in the current scene using annotated data from person identification (see Section 3.3) and supplemental data about each one obtained through Web IE (Figure 8.5). Web IE allows InfoSip to improve upon supplemental information currently found on DVDs in three ways: (i) it always extracts the latest information, (ii) it can personalize information based on a user profile, and (iii) it can consult information sources other than the original content creator.

Filmography information can be personalized based on the user's viewing history. Highlighting movies in which users have seen an actor increases the chances that they will remember why this person looks familiar. The design of the menus on the overlays can also be reconfigured based on a personal profile. For example, 'bio', 'filmography', and 'rumors' are the three menus available for person interested in gossip, but 'bio', 'filmography', and 'references' are menus available for people more interested in references this movie is making to other movies.

8. Conclusions

In this chapter we presented personalization aspects for content augmentation applications that combine content from multiple media sources. Our pilot applications MyInfo and InfoSip show promise that the technology has come of age. Web

Information Extraction and the segmentation, indexing, and retrieval of video at a subprogram level both offer new tools for TV personalization developers. These technologies can improve the viewing experience by both better understanding the TV content and by retrieving related material that is more focused at individual users. In the future we plan to evaluate our pilot applications with real users, continue developing video and Web retrieval and extraction algorithms and generate more content augmentation concepts.

Acknowledgements

We thank Lesh Parameswaran, Jeanne de Bont, Henk Lamers, and Giang Vu of Philips Design for help with the user interface design of the content augmentation project.

References

Ahanger, G. and Little, T. D. C.: 1997, A System for Customized News Delivery from Video Archives, In: *Proceedings of ICMCS'97*, (June 3–6) IEEE Press.

Ardissono, L., Portis, F. and Torasso, P.: 2001, Architecture of a System for the Generation of Personalized Electronic Program Guides, Eighth International Conference on User Modeling: *Workshop on Personalization in Future TV*. Sonthofen, Germany.

Blum, D. W.: 1992, Method and Apparatus for Identifying and Eliminating Specific Material from Video Signals, US patent 5,151,788, September.

Boguraev, B. and Neff, M.: 2000, Lexical Cohesion, Discourse Segmentation, and Document Summarization, *Proc. RIAO International Conference*. April, Paris.

Bonner, E. L. and Faerber, N. A.: 1982, Editing System for Video Apparatus, US patent 4,314,285, February.

Boykin, S. and Merlino, A.: 1999, Improving Broadcast News Segmentation Processing, *IEEE International Conference on Multimedia and Computing Systems*. Florence, Italy, 7–11 June.

Boykin, S. and Merlino, A.: 2000, Machine Learning of Event Segmentation for News on Demand, *Communications of the ACM* **43**(2), 35–41.

Brown, M. G., Foote, J. T., Jones, G. J. F., Jones, S. K. and Young, S. J.: 1995, Automatic Content-Based Retrieval of Broadcast News, In: *Proceedings of ACM Multimedia 95*. San Francisco, CA: ACM Press, pp. 35–43.

Brown, E. W. and Coden, A. R.: 2002, Capitalization Recovery for Text, In: A. R. Coden, E. W. Brown, and S. Srinivasan, (eds.): *Information Retrieval Techniques for Speech Applications*. Springer, pp. 11–22.

Brusilovsky, P.: 2003, Adaptive Navigation Support in Educational Hypermedia: The Role of Student Knowledge Level and the Case for Meta-Adaptation. *British Journal of Educational Technology* **34**(4), 487–497.

Chen, L. and Faudemay, P.: 1997, Multi-Criteria Video Segmentation for TV News, In: *Proceedings of IEEE First Workshop on Multimedia Signal Processing*. Princeton, NJ.

Connell, J.: 2002, Face Finding, http://www.research.ibm.com/ecvg/jhc.proj/faces.html.

Cotter, P. and Smyth, B.: 2000, PTV: Intelligent Personalized TV Guides, *Seventeenth National Conference on Artificial Intelligence*. Austin, TX, USA, pp. 957–964.

Cardie, C.: 1997, Empirical Methods in Information Extraction, *AI Magazine* **18**(4), 65–79.

Dakss, J., Agamanolis, S., Chalom, E., Bove, V. M., Brooks, K., Nemirovsky, P. and Westner, A.: HyperSoap: http://www.media.mit.edu/hypersoap.

Das, D. and ter Horst H.: 1998, *Recommender Systems for TV. Technical Report WS-98-08 Recommender Systems*, Papers from the 1998 Workshop, Madison, WI. Menlo Park, CA: AAAI Press, pp. 35–36.

Dimitrova, N., Martino, J., Agnihotri, L. and Elenbaas, H.: 1999, Superhistograms for Video Representation, *IEEE ICIP*. Kobe, Japan.

Dimitrova, N., Agnihotri, L. and Jasinschi, R.: 2003, Temporal video boundaries, In: *Video* A. Rosenfeld, D. Doermann, and D. Dementhon (eds.): *Mining Book*. Kluwer, pp. 61–90.

Elenbaas, H., Dimitrova, N. and McGee, T.: 1999, PNRS–Personalized News Retrieval System, *SPIE Multimedia Storage and Archiving Systems*.

Haas, N., Bolle, R., Dimitrova, N., Janevski, A. and Zimmerman, J.: 2002, Personalized News Through Content Augmentation and Profiling, In: *Proceedings of International Conference on Image Processing 2002*. Rochester, NY: IEEE Press, September 22–25.

Hampapur, A., Jain, R. and Weymouth, T.: 1994, Digital Video Segmentation, In: *Proceedings of the ACM International Conference on Multimedia*. San Francisco, pp. 357–364.

Hanjalic, A., Lagendijk, R. L. and Biemond, J.: 1999, Semiautomatic News Analysis, Indexing and Classification System Based on Topic Preselection, *SPIE Storage and Retrieval for Image and Video Databases VII* **3656**, January pp. 86–97.

IBM Intelligent Miner for Text℗

Janevski, A. and Dimitrova, N.: Web Information Extraction for Content Augmentation, In: *Proceedings of ICME'02*. Lausanne, Switzerland: IEEE Press, August 26–29.

Janevski, A.: UniveristyIE: Extracting Information from University Web Pages, MS Thesis, University of Kentucky, Lexington.

Jasinschi, R., Dimitrova, N., McGee, T., Agnihotri, L. and Zimmerman, J.: 2001, Video Scouting: An Architecture and System for the Integration of Multimedia Information in Personal TV Applications, *IEEE Conference on Acoustics, Speech, and Signal Processing (ICASSP)*. Salt Lake City, UT, USA, May 7–11, pp. 1405–1408.

Jiang, H. and Elmagarmid, A. K.: 1998, Spatial and Temporal Content-Based Access to Hypervideo Databases, *VLDB Journal*, **7**(4), 226–238.

Li, D., Wei, G., Sethi, I. K. and Dimitrova, N.: 2001, Person Identification in TV Shows, Journal on Electronic Imaging, Special Issue on Storage, Processing and Retrieval of Digital Media, October.

Li, D., Dimitrova, N., Li, M. and Sethi, I. K.: 2003, Multimedia Content Processing Through Cross-modality Association, *ACM Multimedia*. November 2–5, Berkeley.

Kubey, R. and Csikszentmihaly, M.: 1990, Television and the Quality of Life: How Viewing Shapes Everyday Experiences, *Lawrence Erlbaum Associates*. Hillsdale NJ, USA.

Maybury, M. (ed.): February 2000, News On Demand, *CACM* **43**(2): 33–34, 35–79.

Mani, I., House, D. et al.: 1998, Tipster SUMMAC Text Summarization Evaluation, Final Report, October 1998. Mitre Technical Report MTR W980000138 and Technical report, DARPA.

McGee, T. and Dimitrova, N.: 1999, Parsing TV Program Structures for Identification and Removal of Non-story Segments, SPIE Conference on Storage and Retrieval for Image and Video Databases VII (ei24).

Merlino, A., Morey, D. and Maybury, M.: 1997, Broadcast Navigation Using Story segmentation, In: *Proceedings of ACM MM '97*. Seattle, WA: ACM Press, November, pp. 381–388.

ABC Enhanced TV: http://heavy.etv.go.com/etvHome/.

Microsoft NAB demo of enhanced TV: http://www.microsoft.com/presspass/exec/craig/nab97.asp

Microsoft/CBS interactive TV: http://www.microsoft.com/presspass/press/2000/Sept00/CBSpr.asp

Naphade, M. R., Kozintsev, I. and Huang, T. S.: 2002, A Factor Graph Framework for Semantic Video Indexing, *IEEE Transactions on Circuits and Systems for Video Technology* **12**(1), 40–52.

Zimmerman, J., Marmaropoulos, G. and van Heerden, C.: 2001, Interface Design of Video Scout: A Selection, Recording, and Segmentation System for TVs, In: *Proceedings of Human Computer Interaction International (HCII)* **1**, New Orleans, LA, USA, August 5–10, pp. 277–281.

Chapter 9

ContentMorphing: A Novel System for Broadcast Delivery of Personalizable Content

AVNI RAMBHIA, GENE WEN and SPENCER CHENG
e-mail: {avni, gene, spencer}@morphbius.com

Abstract. Truly personalized, interactive multimedia broadcast remains an unfulfilled promise. Technologies such as TVGuide Interactive and Personalized Video Recording (PVR) have attempted to push the frontier, but remain limited in their scope and applicability. Specifically, any recording fixes the 'storyline', i.e. the sequence of events in the presentation. In this paper, we describe a novel method for personalized content broadcast that enables personalization at different levels, from conventional program-by-program to minute-by-minute granularities. Instead of one linear presentation, we enable the parallel broadcast and/or storage of multiple variations of the same presentation, any one of which can be chosen for viewing at a given time. This is done by a synthesis of several techniques, including modeling and representing the presentation as a trellis graph. Recorded content captures one or more of these versions depending on user interests. Suitable (pre-existing) metadata schemes are harnessed to describe the content segments and user profiles, and to match the same. During any viewing session, a user first chooses (as usual) to view one presentation from the available broadcast and recorded options. Using our technology and the metadata engine, the user can then further choose between different versions of this chosen presentation.

Key words. adapative content, content morphing, interactive personalization, multi-theme broadcast, trellis

1. Introduction

In this paper, we first examine the current state of technologies dealing with interactive and personalized multimedia broadcast. We then introduce a vision of the capabilities enabled by our system, which we call ContentMorphing. We describe a novel method of modeling interactively personalizable content as an acyclic directed graph. We also describe where to embed metadata to characterize the content and facilitate automatic and manual interactivity. We call the resulting content AdapativeContent.[1] Methods to author AdapativeContent in real world scenarios are discussed. We describe the authoring, protection, playback and storage of AdapativeContent, as well as the manner in which any metadata engine is harnessed to describe and filter AdaptiveContent. Finally, we summarize our discussion and discuss avenues of future work.

---

[1] The ContentMorphing system, AdaptiveContent and related technologies are protected by patents and pending patents issued to Morphbius, Inc. and/or its subsidiaries and/or affiliates.

L. Ardissono et al. (*eds.*), *Personalized Digital Television*, 235–255, 2004.
© 2004 *Kluwer Academic Publishers. Printed in the Netherlands.*

2. Existing Personalization Technology

The aim of this section is twofold – to acknowledge existing attempts to enable personalized content, and to emphasize the static nature of the experience currently enabled.

Content creation and delivery technology has remained fundamentally unchanged since the invention of television and, later, the VCR. Whether broadcasted (analog or digital), viewed via a DVD or streamed, programs in today's 800-channel digital universe remain essentially static and unchanged in nature from programs 50 years ago. Not even the invention of the personal computer with all of its potential has significantly altered the presentation of multimedia material. Various attempts of making the television viewing experience a more proactively 'pull' experience along the lines of Internet browsing have not been overwhelmingly successful. However, it has clearly been recognized, as indicated by the success of dedicated, 24×7 news and sports channels, that personalization of content should be addressed.

Technologies such as TV Guide Interactive™, VCR-Plus™, MbTV™, TiVo's Wishlist™, interactive DVD and PVRs have been developed to capitalize on this opportunity, and do provide a form of such personalized and dynamic content. However, issues such as coarse granularity (program level) or high levels of human intervention hold back their widespread adoption.

Existing personalization technologies operate very much in an all-you-get-is-what-you-see (AYGIWYS) mode. A program recorded on a videocassette recorder (VCR) or personal video recorder (PVR) is very much what was broadcast. DVDs offer some additional material, but a fixed storyline. The user is thus constrained to view a presentation judged suitable for the average target audience. There is little opportunity to target specialized audiences via existing distribution channels due to prohibitive transmission, management and maintenance overheads for each thematic variant. Some recent new services do provide the user with some interactivity in choosing specific content and its delivery. However, such interaction is 'non-versatile', i.e. once the content is delivered and recorded, the capability of interaction with the content is lost and the personalization becomes 'permanent'. This AYGIWYS mode limits the evolutionary horizon.

3. Existing Complementary Technologies

The ContentMorphing scheme assumes the existence of a metadata engine, and a distribution infrastructure.

Any implementation of the ContentMorphing system is specific to the underlying distribution mechanism being used – the method for multiplexing various program streams, for associating segment header information with specific segment(s)' audio and visual components and the timing mechanism are all derived from such a mechanism and are designed to allow seamless compliance of AdaptiveContent with such a system. Thus, only the authoring and playback modules need to be aware of ContentMorphing – the broadcast and/or streaming components and file formats need not be altered in any way. That this is possible has been demonstrated by the MPEG-4 mapping of ContentMorphing described in [Rambhia 2003]. Other transmission mechanisms of interest to us are MPEG-2 based broadcast systems such as DVB.

For the purposes of tagging each segment with description information, creating and updating user profiles and matching a profile (or collection of profiles) with a segment description, we assume the existence of a metadata engine. The choice of metadata engine is usually determined by the transmission infrastructure being used – as an example, for MPEG-4 [Avaro 2000], the metadata engine would probably be based on MPEG-7 [José 2001] or a subset thereof.

While a specification of the exact details of the metadata engine and its specific means of integration with a ContentMorphing system implementation are out of scope of this paper, we introduce below some promising technologies that could provide suitable starting points for a metadata engine.

[Boll 1999] describes an adaptive metadata scheme specifically designed to support a scenario fairly close to our own. Significant differences exist between their metadata system and ContentMorphing – their system is geared toward online retrieval of documents, does not support a conventional broadcast and channel surfing scenario, and does not provide for building a variety of storyline options into a specific presentation – i.e. it also provides only one-shot interactivity. Nevertheless, theirs is a unique metadata and search system that is specifically designed for fine-grained content representation and user profiling and thus provides for a useful metadata engine. [Hjelsvold 2001] describe a fairly mature and complete system for classifying and describing video clips on-line, and for matching content profiles against user profiles. While applicable only to single-storyline presentations stored for online retrieval, we believe it could be easily adapted to describe segments and support real-time broadcast-level interactivity. [Karadkar 2002] describes a dynamic metadata scheme that supports content description and smart responses to content queries. For purpose of clarity, note that their trellis hypertext model is unrelated to our technique of modeling interactive content as a trellis graph.

4. Contribution of Paper

In this paper, we introduce and substantiate a fundamentally new paradigm of content creation, distribution and playback. As discussed in the previous section, there are several excellent technologies in existence relating to TV personalization. However, unlike ContentMorphing, they are mostly one-shot techniques – i.e. personalization is achieved once, during serving/transmission or recording, and never again. ContentMorphing, on the other hand, provides continuous interactivity from broadcast to recording to playback, although possibly with diminishing amounts of choices at each stage. ContentMorphing is not simply a document container or just a description mechanism supporting search and retrieve. It is a paradigm and technique which allows different programs, or a single program with multiple variations, can be multiplexed into a single-channel program. Using Content

Morphing, this single-channel program can be browsed, stored and viewed as multiple (though usually related) programs, based on intelligent user interaction. Significantly, the internal complexity of the resultant AdaptiveContent bitstream is invisible to the transportation mechanism – the composite stream appears as a single channel program to the broadcast infrastructure. Only the head-end needs additional complexity to unravel and intelligently present the various options within each program. ContentMorphing does not require bi-directional communication between the client and broadcast center.

ContentMorphing does require a metadata scheme for describing content and user profiles, and a related set of rules for matching the two. However, this metadata scheme, while complementary to ContentMorphing, does not form an integral part of its philosophy. Our implementations use existing schema most applicable to the underlying system – e.g. MPEG-7 descriptions for MPEG-4 content and systems.

The following discussion attempts to provide the reader with a glimpse of the ContentMorphing experience, and its fundamental difference from current interactivity technology. Again using the coverage of the Olympic games as an example, the broadcasters are already receiving the full video feed from all concurrent events but have only one channel to broadcast this data over. Currently, they choose one video feed at a time and transmit it over this channel. A much better coverage than this could be achieved by using ContentMorphing and organizing several, or even all, of these feeds into AdaptiveContent and broadcasting that so that each viewer can then choose to view the event of his choice from this collection. Depending on how comfortable a specific viewer is with respect to interacting with content, the personalization and the filtering of content can be fully automatic or with varying degrees of human intervention. Furthermore, the user can switch to viewing a different event *within* the same presentation. Where the player offers recording capabilities, the user can even move back and forth in time and in between several events in the presentation.

While mainly developed for and described from a streaming media broadcast, recording and playback point of view, ContentMorphing can be adapted for use with static media such as multimedia web pages and documentaries. However, there are other excellent technologies that are built specifically for this purpose. Content-Morphing, in this case, serves the additional purpose only of providing a unifying framework for both static documents and broadcast (dynamic) multimedia.

5. Sample Applications

In this section, we describe some sample scenarios to illustrate the types of applications that ContentMorphing enables, and its exquisitely simple feasibility.

5.1. OLYMPICS FOR EVERYONE

In the case of large events such as the Olympics, there are always concurrent events. Specific subsets of audiences may have a specific interest in one particular event or another. A network that has to choose to telecast only one event at a time risks alienating the fans of the other event. Using the ContentMorphing framework, telecasts of each event can be captured separately, and then multiplexed and simultaneously broadcast over a single channel. Metadata is inserted as required, and the ContentMorphing system assimilates it into the overall presentation package. Within each household, preferences can be set to select and view the specific event or events of interest. With slightly advanced provisions, a network provider can even provide a listing or set of thumbnail displays of all available events. The user can then interact with this menu to select an event to view at any point of time. Alternatively, the user can specify a set of events of interest, record all applicable alternatives, and then play them back one at a time at the user's leisure. The format for recording and the mechanism for playback (including key management, revised tagging and buffer optimization) is provided by ContentMorphing.

Note that for this application, separate telecast material for each event already exists. Typically, there is also infrastructure in place to tag the output of each camera with the appropriate metadata. This description metadata typically remains static for the duration of the telecast. Where the underlying infrastructure supports remote location of streams (such as MPEG-4), the segment headers and associated metadata can be updated over time, allowing for more complex interactivity a day or a few days after the events, once the content owner has had time to fully analyze and tag the video streams.

5.2. WHAT'S YOUR ANGLE?

Rapid-action sports such as basketball or soccer are characterized by highlights such as a goal or an impressive tackle. Replays of such events are of extremely high interest, especially from different camera angles. Using conventional broadcast, such replays necessarily preclude the telecast of the normal course of the game for the duration of the replay. Thus, the replay can occur for limited amounts of time only. Also, only one camera angle can be displayed at a time.

Using CM, feed from multiple cameras can be tagged, multiplexed and transmitted. Each viewer can choose, say, one camera angle of primary interest. However, around high-interest events, all angles can be locally stored. Then the user may view the highlights from as many angles as available. The user may choose to interrupt her view of the event to review the highlights, or may choose to wait until the event is over or in recess before viewing the replays. In fact, the network could choose to have several more camera angle feeds available for significant moments, but only a few during the normal course of the game. Of course, interactivity is not required for the user to experience the content – a default (conventional) presentation is automatically available if no user input is provided, or if interactivity is explicitly turned off at the player end.

Similar to the previous section, for this application as well, content for the different paths is readily available from each camera. The description metadata is static insofar as the description of the camera angle. However, on-the-fly tagging is required to identify highlights and newly available or unavailable camera angles.

5.3 RATED A FOR ANYTHING

It is common practice nowadays to make multiple versions of a movie, with a few localized edits to accommodate theatre viewing vs. TV viewing needs, for example. However small the variations between the versions, each version must be maintained separately. Having purchased or rented one version, a user cannot view a different version. While the bulk of the movie runs along a single storyline, there are local scene variations that are different. Using a single AdapativeContent presentation, these variations can be tagged and then transmitted/stored in parallel, but common parts of the storyline are only tagged and stored once. Thus, the overall size of the presentation can be made comparable to that of a single movie. The exact same disk can be used to view the movie at a chosen rating, with the Player automatically choosing and skipping appropriate scenes. Along similar lines, it is possible to create educational material targetted for different talent levels within similarly grouped students. For example, in a video discussing chemistry, the 'general' storyline may include a longer introduction with a shorter presentation of advanced applications, while the 'advanced' storyline may skip the introduction in favor of including additional segments on advanced applications. The benefits of such content are similar to those just discussed for multiple-rating movie or other entertainment content.

In these cases, content must be specifically created and edited with such personalization in mind. However, our paradigm opens up a vast new realm of possibilities, including interactive movies along the lines of interactive novels. For example, instead of automatically or semi-automatically switching to a certain segment when multiple alternatives are available, the presentation could explicitly pause for user input to determine how the storyline should progress.

6. Description of Framework

Consider any presentation as an interactive novel. At specific points in the story, a set of alternative future storylines is available, and the reader can choose any one. Depending on the alternative chosen, a new set of alternatives may be subsequently available, and so on. If each story segment is treated as a node, then we can construct an acyclic directed graph from these nodes. From one node to a valid succeeding node, we draw an edge in the graph. Thus, each path in this graph represents a valid storyline of the overall presentation. Eventually, certain (or all) paths may merge to share a common conclusion or set of further alternative storylines.[2]

---

[2]The absolute duration of the presentation along a certain path from start to end is not of direct concern to us, as designers and implementers of the system. Content length is an authoring issue. Where preservation of absolute length is important, the content should be authored so as to enforce such a requirement.

We use this approach to model customizable audio-visual presentations. The basic idea is that the directed acyclic graph consists of all possible audio-visual content accessible to a user. Each node represents a self-sufficient media segment of definite length and is characterized by a well-structured description of the content segment. This description is created from a well-defined semantic grammar. Each edge represents a connection to a valid successor node. One node may connect to several others (to each via an edge) at a juncture where more than one storylines are available. Any of these nodes are valid successors to the current node.

For intelligent content consumption, we describe a means to create a user preference profile using the same grammar as that used to describe the nodes. The profile criteria are applied to the node descriptions of incoming data. Using suitable matching techniques, nodes of potential interest are extracted from the graph. These are then assembled to create a seamless personalized presentation.

In the following two sections, we formally describe the modeling of the presentation as a graph and the conveyance of the graph structure information along with the media.

7. The Trellis Paradigm

Consider any media presentation to be a sequence of limited-time segments. With traditional presentations, only one segment is a valid representation of the content at a given time, and only one segment is a valid successor to a given segment. Thus, if we were to represent this content as a graph, it would be a trivial linear series of single nodes, with each node connecting only to the next node in the sequence.

However, with AdapativeContent, more than one segment may be valid at a given point of time, and one of several segments can be a valid successor to a given segment. All valid segments at a given time are alternative to each other, and a concatenation of any sequence of successive segments is a *storyline*. We model AdapativeContent as a directed acyclic graph (in the graph theoretical sense). Each individual content segment is represented by a unique node in the graph. Each node lies in a specific column on the grid that holds the graph. Each column designates a specific time offset from the previous column. Thus, the column a node is in designates the relative time instance the corresponding content segment could be used. Permissible transitions from one segment to the next are represented by the edges of the graph, with the direction of the edge being from the previous node to the succeeding node. Any set of connected edges along a given direction forms a storyline. Figure 9.1 shows an arbitrary media presentation embedded into such a directed graph. A-B-C-D-E, A-B-F-G-C-D-E and J-G-H-I-E are all valid storylines for the depicted content.

Note that in order for some legitimate transitions which go 'backward' in relative time, i.e. to previous columns of the graph [dotted arrows in above diagram], to occur,

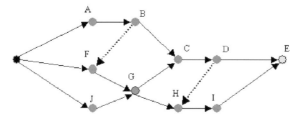

Figure 9.1. Embedding of presentation in directed acyclic graph.

the presentation device must be able to store the necessary content segments until they are no longer required.

To remove the above restriction of requiring local storage in order to present the content, we prefer to use a subset of the directed graph, known as a trellis graph. The main difference between a trellis and a general directed graph is that a path through a trellis is always moving forward in relative time. In practical terms, use of the trellis model removes the requirement for local storage on the presentation device when processing AdapativeContent. Figure 9.2 depicts the same presentation as Figure 9.1, but embedded into a trellis. Note again that content segments are represented by the nodes in the graph, the column a node is in designates the relative time instance the segment could be used and the permissible transitions from one segment to another are represented by the edges of the graph.

As should be apparent from Figure 9.2, the major disadvantage of the trellis model is that segments that are flexible enough to appear at different time instances must be duplicated, whereas in the directed graph approach, such segments only need to be transmitted once as long as they can be refreshed from the local playback cache. The duplication overhead becomes more and more severe as the number of segments that can be connected to 'backwards' increase. In either the directed graph or the trellis case, the caching and the presentation timings of the segments need to be carefully managed so as to guarantee that all necessary segments are available at the required time, along with any other information required for decoding the media. Since AdapativeContent does not guarantee that a specific segment will be viewed

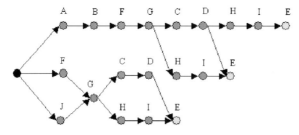

Figure 9.2. Embedding of presentation in trellis graph.

at a specific time, special considerations are required to guarantee the availability of content under all viewing conditions.[3]

The structure of the trellis, and information specifying the location of a segment (which forms a node in) the trellis, is conveyed using segment headers. In addition to location and timing information, segment headers also contain metadata[4] describing the segment, using the overall application's metadata scheme of choice. The reconstruction of the trellis is done using segment headers. The selection of any one of the permissible paths through a directed graph or a trellis is done based on the metadata within each segment header. Segment headers are structured as a series of 'tags'. Specific tags associated with a given segment indicate the position of the corresponding node in relation to the presentation trellis. Other tags provide adequate information for the presentation device to automatically determine the most appropriate path to select for presentation. Information that a metadata tag could describe includes well-defined concepts like movie rating (G, PG13, R, X), as well as any arbitrary information deemed appropriate by the content provider and supported by the chosen metadata scheme.

In the overall system, the role of the content provider is to (a) tag the content segments with appropriate metadata and (b) optionally select a set of designated paths through the graph from all possible paths to match specific personalization criteria. The role of the presentation device is to locate or to construct the most appropriate path for a particular user, and then to recover correctly synchronized multimedia information for decoding, composition, interaction and display.

7.1. FOR EXAMPLE

Suppose we have a CNBC viewer whose main interest is the chip business. She (unfortunately) has most of her portfolio invested in NASDAQ stocks and is also watching mortgage rates since she is thinking about re-financing. Thus, the user interest can be described in terms of the tags 'Chips', 'NASDAQ' and 'Interest'.

Suppose that at some point of time, the following clips are available on her channel:

A news clip 1 (Light Grey Block) – 'MSFT ups Xbox shipment forecast', that is tagged as 'MSFT', 'NSDAQ', 'Xbox', and 'Graphics Chips'.

A news clip 2 (Dark Grey Block) – 'Goldman Sachs downgrades Intel', tagged as 'INTC', 'NASDAQ', 'Semi-conductor'.

A news clip 3 (Medium Grey Block) – 'MLB labor disputes', tagged as 'Sports', 'MLB'.

These are broadcast concurrently, according to the time line shown below:

---

[3]As an example, suppose a given segment is encrypted and requires a decryption key to be viewed. In traditional Conditional Access systems, all keys are synchronized using time stamps and rotating flags. In the case of AdapativeContent, this scheme is no longer reliable. Hence, a different scheme using the metadata tags or a parallel tagging mechanism is required to associate keys with their specific content segments.

[4]As indicated in the review of existing technology, our discussion of such metadata in this paper is at a purely functional level.

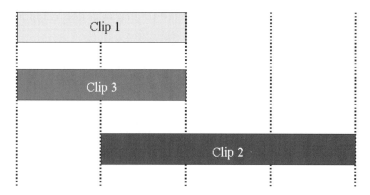

Figure 9.3. Media clips superimposed on trellis columns.

Moving from left to right: Clip 1 (the MSFT story) and Clip 3 (Medium Grey Block) are available alternatives. Since Clip 3 does not match the user's interest, it is filtered out by the system. Hence the user sees the MSFT story. At the end of Clip 1, Clip 2 (the Intel Story) is available and matches the user interest.

However, playback of this starts mid-way, as shown below.

The experience is as if the user watched the MSFT story on CNBC and then switched to Bloomberg, which is carrying the Intel story half way through. The user experience can be improved if the broadcaster produces clips of standard length, buffers stories with similar tags and/or 'carousels' important clips. In case the Player had sufficient memory, persistent or otherwise, it is possible that the Intel story (Clip 2) was buffered from its starting point since a close match of interest was detected. In this case, the user sees the following:

In fact, depending on the relative priority of the clips (e.g. by examining weights of different tags), Clip 2 can be played back by interrupting and time shifting the remainder of Clip 1.

Briefly, here is what the player does:

1. For each time instance, designated by the column width of the trellis, makes a local selection of the available clips (valid paths) that can be concatenated so that the concatenated time equals duration between adjacent columns.
2. The available clips include buffered clips, local static image and graphics data that don't have explicit timing, and upcoming clips in the same stream.
3. Then from the available clips, selects the 'best' one based on some pre-defined criteria.

8. Segment Header Structure and Embedding

As described above, each segment header consists of a number of tags. Tags contain the following categories of information:

1. Timing information
2. Description of the node contents
3. Trellis position for the node that this content segment represents, including
    a. Reference number for the current node
    b. Reference numbers of valid predecessor nodes

The reference number of the current node and the numbers of the nodes it connects from effectively define the structure of the trellis relative to the node being defined. The exact mechanism is discussed later in this section. Node references are unique in scope down one column of the trellis. Where a single stream crosses several trellis columns, its nodes in each column will typically carry the same reference number.

Information for each tag is encapsulated inside a tag container. The segment header for a given node may contain one or more such tag containers. The figure above

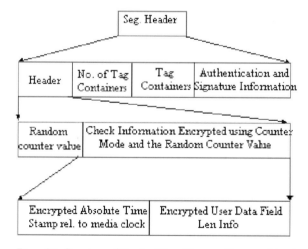

Figure 9.4. Structure of ContentMorphing-specific segmet header.

depicts the structure of one segment header, not including metadata tags. As shown, the header's header and authentication information envelope the actual tags. Authentication and signature information is included as shown to ensure that the segment header is received correctly at the user end. The segment header can also be encrypted to prevent unauthorized use. The header's header contains a random counter value that is used to seed and signal the encryption mechanism. It also contains the time stamp at which it becomes active, and header length information.

Figure 9.5 depicts the process of inferring the structure of the presentation trellis from tag information.

The first (root) node is special, in that it does not contain connectivity information, but simply initializes the graph. It does so by indicating the IDs of each node that will start off a path in the first column of the trellis. Thus, it also effectively tells the player the number of nodes it will have to deal with at the start of the presentation. After the root node, the principle is simply that of connect-the-dots. Each node is identified by a number unique to its column. Each node in a column carries a list of (predecessor) nodes in the previous column that it is a valid successor to. Connecting the dots backwards in terms of predecessors, rather than forward in terms of successors, is essential for broadcast-like scenarios where the future of the transmission is unknown but the past is determinate. One edge in the trellis exists for each such predecessor, and is drawn from the predecessor node to the current node.[5] Where a single edge needs to extend beyond one column, a 'dummy' node is created for each spanned column. The dummy node connects to only the spanning node, the next dummy node to this dummy node, and so on until the node branches out to 'real' nodes in the future trellis columns. Note that the Node numbered 1 in the third column of the trellis above is a dummy node.

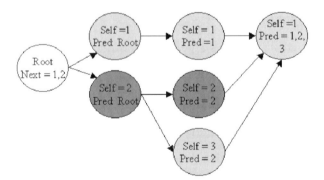

Figure 9.5. Derivation of trellis from segment header information.

---

[5]While simple, this technique offers one powerful advantage: there is no inter-column dependence beyond adjacent columns. This makes the technique inherently suitable to broadcast transmission.

9. Realization of the System

Thus far we have discussed the tools and techniques we use to model AdapativeContent, and the CM system. This section describes general issues related to a practical realization of the system, keeping in mind that the specific details will depend on the underlying transmission mechanism, content format and metadata engine chosen for the implementation.

9.1. AUTHORING ADAPATIVECONTENT

Apart from determining the content segments themselves (each of which forms a node in the trellis), the following tasks must be fulfilled to generate AdapativeContent:

1. Insert root trellis information,
2. Insert node-related media information,
3. Insert node metadata information and
4. Associate the metadata information with the media information.

Root trellis information indicates resource requirements for the trellis. It also establishes a time base, sets up any information required for key mechanisms and identifies ownership and payment information. Most importantly, it provides information to initialize the trellis graph. Root trellis information is included in the segment header for the root node of the trellis presentation. Depending on the presentation, the root node may or may not refer to actual multimedia information. A generic description of the content to establish the generic subject(s) of the presentation, authored via the metadata engine, is inserted here.

All subsequent nodes in the trellis contain some media data, constituting the segment. Several types of media will typically constitute a segment – the simplest example being audio media and visual media for a conventional audio-visual segment. Additionally, text, graphics or value-added media material may constitute or augment a segment.

As discussed earlier, a segment header encapsulates each segment. Timing information for the segment, key information (and possibly key rotation information), trellis position information and any authentication information are calculated/defined and inserted into each segment header. Additionally, descriptive metadata is generated by the metadata engine and inserted into the header by the ContentMorphing implementation. The exact format of the time, the mechanism for the key rotations, and the syntax for the metadata header and content segment itself depend on the underlying transmission framework. Where such framework allows for remote content inclusion, part or all of the segments and/or segment headers may be stored and updated remotely, and pushed to or pulled by the client upon request (and possibly payment). For example, for a live telecast of a game, only very basic events may be sent along with the live feed. However, after the game is over, post-analysis can add tags for all key highlights of the game. If the trellis information is remotely posted, then this richer granularity and corresponding metadata can be leveraged by a player to provide richer interactivity with the content when it is replayed by the viewer. Applications can use further use the remote location feature, if available, to provide (at possibly higher cost) more heavily tagged presentations or more varied presentations to a viewer.

9.2. DELIVERING ADAPATIVECONTENT

Typically, delivery of AdaptiveContent proceeds in identical manner to conventional content designed for the underlying transmission mechanism. Whether broadcast, multicast, unicast, streamed, downloaded or written to static media – no special considerations are needed to deliver the correspondingly authored AdaptiveContent. Of course, where a delivery framework is specifically designed and implemented for AdaptiveContent in a ContentMorphing-aware manner, further optimizations and dramatic performance and capacity improvements are obviously possible.

9.3. CONSUMING ADAPATIVECONTENT

The need for processing of ContentMorphing places additional complexity requirements on the playback device, over and above the requirements of the underlying transmission mechanism. However, if the device is software or firmware enabled, and provides local storage, the additional complexity and related cost is not unreasonable.

A ContentMorphing player extracts relevant media from a 'universal' AdapativeContent broadcast stream in two stages. At stage 1, a coarse filtering is done to extract all segments of potential interest from the universal stream. The result is stored locally for immediate or subsequent use. At stage 2, this coarsely filtered presentation is finely filtered based on the current user specifications. The fine filtering effectively causes an experience of the content along one trellis path, i.e. storyline. Both filtering processes are essentially implemented by the metadata engine – typically in terms of a true-false interface. The ContentMorphing system feeds data to the engine, and acts upon the results to modify the content or influence the player behavior, as applicable.

9.3.1. *Coarse Filtering*

An incoming presentation in our framework contains media information pertaining to all possible nodes in the presentation trellis. At the coarse filtering stage, media corresponding to all nodes that are of no possible interest to the household are discarded. Such rejection can either be done at the presentation level (i.e. the entire presentation is not of interest) or at a branch in the storyline (e.g. for a household with no children, R rated segments may be discarded in favor of more restrictive ratings). The filtering utility is fed with incoming descriptions and user profile(s), and returns results of matches. Accordingly, the ContentMorphing component of the player edits out all superfluous nodes and corresponding media data. In case of interactive streaming, the rejected media streams are never requested. In the broadcast case, all incoming data pertaining to the rejected streams is ignored. When the mismatched objects/ streams are removed, their segment headers are removed as well. Thus, no metadata tags are received for their nodes, and, as a consequence, the filtered trellis automatically does not contain the rejected nodes and paths. Thus, coarse filtering prunes the broadcast or global trellis, retaining only those nodes whose descriptions match the collective household profile.

All streams that are accepted by the Player after coarse filtering are evidently of some potential interest to one or more users within the current household. In case of delayed playback or recording, these streams are reassembled by the Content-Morphing component of the player into a suitable storage format and stored locally on disk or a similar storage medium. In case of live playback, the streams are immediately sent on for further processing.

The local storage format will usually significantly differ from the incoming format. For example, in the broadcast case, trellis and metadata information is usually cycled to enable mid-program channel switching. For local storage, global trellis and meta-data information need be stored only once per file. Also, specific content protection methods may be applied to locally stored content. The coarse filtering process includes all these transformations.

9.3.2. *Fine Filtering and Switching*

Fine filtering occurs during actual playback of the content. Effectively, fine filtering determines which storyline from the trellis is chosen to experience the content. The storyline chosen depends on the specific interests and interactive inputs of the current viewer. Depending on the application and method of content authoring, fine filtering may reject all material unrelated to the current path, or retain thumbnails of material from other paths to aid interactive methods of jumping across storylines in the future.

Fine Filtering is done just before feeding a simple device-interpretable program stream to the native playback logic. The latest segment header information for each current node is extracted by the ContentMorphing component of the player and used to infer the current state of the trellis as well as to determine a match between the user interest and the current Object. If no match is detected, that branch of the trellis is ignored for purposed of the current playback. At each branch in the trellis, proprietary tools can be used together with or independently of automatic selection to decide which branch to take. In addition, mechanisms are provided to process any user interactivity and feed the same to the metadata engine to translate into a change of user preferences where required. All of these inputs ultimately provide for targeted selection of the next media segment experienced by the viewer. This process constitutes fine filtering.

Independently of fine filtering, browsing utilities can also be provided for smart browsing of all available content, to begin a presentation or arbitrarily switch into a specific storyline. For example, it is possible for a player to be programmed to display other alternatives in a side menu. In this case, a viewer could interact with that interface to switch to an arbitrary random-access point in the presentation. The switch would take effect at the time instance corresponding to the next trellis column. Similarly, the viewer could then resume viewing the presentation where she left off. Note that these switches are taking place without switching channels. Issues related to graphical user interface issues for these components are obviously not trivial. However, a detailed discussion of such interfaces and their operation relative to the playback device architecture is outside the scope of this paper. Our aim here is only to demonstrate that such operations are feasible within a ContentMorphing system, and to point out the capabilities and associated complexities of such an implementation.

While switching nodes in and out [whether due to fine filtering or interactive requests], the player also keeps track of local presentation time, arranges for decryption as required and maintains media buffering. It also maintains synchronization between the various streams by correctly offsetting the internal time stamps by its knowledge of timeline based on the current presentation context. A full description of the working of this component is both tedious and unoriginal. The issues involved are fairly obvious, as are the solutions.[6] The critical parts of the system relate to the authoring, selective storage and player-side unraveling of AdaptiveContent as described above.

10. Complexity and Open Issues

10.1. AUTHORING

10.1.1. *Compression*

The system described in this paper reflects a significant paradigm shift from the traditional AYGIWYS broadcast model. The multiplicity of storylines necessitates the simultaneous transmission and storage of multiple concurrent and alternative streams, as well as associated metadata, per A/V presentation. This represents significant overhead as opposed to conventional programs that have one audio and one video stream per presentation. As such, the following are now required:

1. A new means of compressing A/V content,
2. Low price, high volume, random access storage medium
3. More efficient means of utilizing existing bandwidth

The last is very critical for applications such as broadcast TV, where resources such as spectra have already been allocated.

---

[6]The structure and working of the underlying platform on which the ContentMorphing system is implemented strongly affects such an implementation, and may in fact directly provide several modules needed for the same.

Fortunately, with recent developments and breakthroughs in all related areas, the capability of transmitting and/or storing AdapativeContent economically is, to a very large extent, already available. For example, the latest video compression standards such as MPEG-4 and H.264 have reported dramatically improved efficiency over the 'legacy' MPEG-2 standard, which is used for both digital television (standard and high definition) and Digital Versatile Disks (DVDs). New modulation schemes and improvements in VLSI technology have made wide adoption of more sophisticated modulation schemes feasible. Low cost, high volume, random access storage devices and media such as Blue ray DVD, memory cards and re-writeable DVDs have also become more and more easily available.

There are challenges to content authoring as a result of very flexible content delivery (interactive vs. non-interactive coarse filtering) and consumption (switch between alternative edges, random access and channel surfing) modes that CM enables. One of the major challenges is managing buffer fullness in such an environment under all circumstances. Even though buffer management in video coding is relatively well studied in theory and practical guidelines are well established, existing theories and guidelines deal almost exclusively with handling a single stream from a single video input, with the exception of splicing in digital TV (DTV). In DTV, various combinations of compressed A/V content are frequently 'spliced' into other materials. The challenge in buffer management when bit stream splicing happens is due to the fact that compressed A/V content is, by its nature, variable rate, which in turn results in a time varying nature of buffer fullness. The buffer fullness corresponds to a delay, i.e. the amount of time a byte spends in the buffer. Consider the instant when splicing happens and the system switches from one bit stream to another. If the bit stream from which the switch is initiated was encoded with an assumption of nearly full buffer, but the bit stream to be switched to was encoded with an assumption of a nearly empty buffer, buffer overflow may occur. This is because the encoder for the second bit stream may attempt to take advantage of the presumed buffer emptiness and produce more bits than the decoder could consume and the buffer could store. In the exact opposite scenario, buffer underflow could also occur.

Many mechanisms have been proposed to overcome this issue, including:

1. Emptying the buffer when splice occurs. This solves the overflowing problem, but is less effective for under-flowing. It also causes uneven delay and disruption of the presentation.
2. Restricting the location of splicing points so that they only occur when the buffer fullness is roughly 50%. This makes potential splicing points few and far between.
3. Inserting splice flags [Cugnini 1997] to designate points in the bit stream where splicing can occur without causing artifacts or discontinuity in the presentation. This necessitates identification of such points in the encoding process, and knowledge of the time varying buffer fullness of streams. For many network-to-affiliate feed operations, the required splice points are well known.

4. Creating transition clips with transition clip generators (TCGs), around the point where splice occurs, by decoding and re-encoding some (usually a few frames) of the materials involved to enable a seamless splice.

However, these solutions are not directly suitable for applications to ContentMorphing as the system inherently necessitates frequent and flexible switches between streams. For example, consider the solution of flagging splice points. In CM, switching between legacy and live materials is a valid possibility. In this case, the knowledge of the corresponding buffer fullness for bit streams generated by different parties at different times is lost, and the splice points may no longer be valid. Even the TCG solution may become problematic in terms of complexity and overhead when splicing and switching occur frequently. One possible improvement to TCG that might be applicable to ContentMorphing is to fully utilize the capabilities provided by new audio-visual compression standards for bit stream streaming (mostly for applications in network streaming where the bandwidth is not stable), such as SP frames in H.264, and divide the information into baseline and enhancement information so as to reduce the processing and bandwidth overhead. Such an approach may necessitate some changes to the underlying standard(s) and at this point forms an open problem for research, in our opinion. Another technique is to force constant bit-rate (CBR) encoding as frequently as possible. Where spikes in bit rate are necessitated by virtue of the nature of the content, switching into and out of the stream is disabled until the bit rate can be re-stabilized. This essentially is the inverse of the splice flags technique in that the flags indicate the beginning and end of non-switchable rather than switchable intervals on the stream.

SMPTE 321M defines constraints on the encoding and packetization of MPEG-2 transport streams so that they can be spliced without modifying the PES payload. We foresee similar guidelines recommended by SMPTE or similar organizations.

10.1.2. *Real-time Analysis and Tagging*

As we have touched upon before, tagging and analysis of content in real time is currently limited to pre-created, or very slowly varying, tags and descriptions. However, for non-real time transmission, more detailed tagging can be done after automatic or manual off-line analysis. Several pattern matching and recognition tools, notably those developed in the context of MPEG-7, can be harnessed for this purpose. This enhanced metadata, along with suitably edited audio-visual streams can be re-telecast some hours after the live event ends. Alternatively, latest versions can continually be posted at some designated remote location so the user always has the latest tag stream for the same audio-visual streams that were originally telecast. Staggered fee structures may also be applied depending on the level of segment information detail offered. For example, for a soccer game, different camera angles could be tagged in real time automatically. After the game has been broadcast, for subscribers, a more detailed set of tags could be broadcast (through data channels in analog or DTV) so that the users, when watching the game again (or when watching a delayed, taped game), could select to see only the highlights and/or significant goals, or follow a certain set of players.

An important distinction to note between ContentMorphing requirements and most current content profiling technology is the following. In the CM system, we ask, 'Given the following content descriptions, which one is most likely to be preferred by the viewer?', as opposed to the more widely researched problem of, 'Given this specific user profile, which pieces of content are available in some content pool that may be interesting to the user?' Thus, real-time modules should be able to profile generic content based upon the metadata engine's vocabulary to enable meaningful real-time tagging of AdaptiveContent.

As advanced metadata engines emerge and are adapted for use within the ContentMorphing environment, and AdaptiveContent-aware authoring tools become an integral part of the live-content generation workflow, detailed real-time tagging of content will become possible.

10.2. USER END

The additional processing in a ContentMorphing-enabled terminal as compared with a 'traditional' single-stream terminal includes parsing the segments and their tag information, identifying and linking the correct bit streams to their node(s), possible authentication, authorization and decryption for protected metadata streams and media streams, decoding of media streams, and composition. However, at any given time, only one storyline is actually rendered. Thus the amount of the most computationally expensive operations in the terminal, namely the decryption and decoding of the media streams, remains largely unchanged on average. The only major additional overheads that ContentMorphing imposes are the use of the metadata engine, and the implementation of the selection interface.

ContentMorphing does create significant potential for manufacturers to provide value-adds over and beyond what is offered by currently popular standards such as MPEG. In fact, ContentMorphing allows manufacturers to go beyond ContentMorphing itself! As an example, consider the 'quarterback cam' used in recent Super Bowl coverage, in which images from different cameras are organized and warped so as to form a seamless rotation at the control of the user. This effective gives the viewer a 360-degree view of the field. With ContentMorphing, a similar application is possible using an incoming AdapativeContent presentation if the network transmits an adequate number of camera angles. Recall that in AdapativeContent, images from these different cameras are appropriately compressed, tagged and transmitted over to the user. Conventional ContentMorphing allows the user to view his/her favorite angle and even a mosaic of images from different angles. However, a terminal can also choose to geometrically transform the images and stitch them, giving the user the capability of using his/her remote control and navigate in a complete 360-degree view in real time. In this case, the image the viewer sees is not directly one of the images transmitted, but rather a transformed view enabled by the enhanced capability of the terminal.

11. Conclusion and Future Work

In this paper, we have described a system capable of creating, serving and providing an experience of interactive personalized multimedia at a granularity in time and space that is not currently available, with minimal additional infrastructural requirements. It allows content providers to present unified content suitable for a more varied audience than traditional broadcast, with users truly having control over how they experience a presentation. We address one of the great barriers to user personalization by removing the overriding needs for massive up-stream server farms and a pervasive network to permit household-specific and user-specific personalization.

A mapping of the entire system to MPEG-4 has been presented in [Rambhia 2003]. The newly specified DASE application framework [ATSC 2003] is a client-side standard that enables rich presentations and interactivity via XML-like templates as well as Jave-based applications, and is another interesting system that our system may be mapped to. Future work includes adaptation of existing metadata frameworks to produce metadata engines that can be used in the real world to tag and describe AdapativeContent. Future work also includes development of efficient mechanisms of carouseling trellis information to maximize switching performance while minimizing overhead. As discussed in the previous section, buffer management is also an open issue. Finally, we also plan to examine the role of IPMP and DRM in the system, and methods and means by which it can be incorporated to protect not only the audiovisual content but also the metadata and trellis structure.

References

Avaro, O., Eleftheriadis, A., Herpel, C. et al.: 2000, Multimedia Systems – Overview. In: A. Puri, (ed.): *Multimedia Systems, Standards and Networks*. Dekker: New York.

ATSC Standard A/100: *DTV Application Software Environment – Level 1 (DASE-1)*, March 2003.

Blaszak, L. et al.: September 2002, Performance of H.26L/JVT Coding Tools. ICCVG. 2002, Zakopane, Poland, pp. 25–29.

Boll, S. and Klas, W.: 1999, ZYX, A Semantic Model for Multimedia Documents and Presentations. In: *Proceedings of the 8th IFIP Conference on Data Semantics (DS-8): Semantic Issues in Multimedia Systems*. Kluwer Academic, Rotorua.

Breznican, A.: 2001, *DVD Creates Devoted Cinephiles*, September 11, Los Angeles Times.

Cugnini, A.: 1997, MPEG-2 Bitstream Splicing. In: *Proceedings of Digital Television '97 Conference*, Overland Park, Intertex: Publishing Kansas.

DCMI Usage Board (eds.): Dublin Core Metadata Initiative, Multiple Recommendations. Published online at http://dublincore.org/documents/.

Healey, J.: 2001, *Next-Generation DVD Players Ready to Flex Their Brain Power*. September 20, Los Angeles Times.

Hjelsvold, R., Vidyagiri, S. and Leaute, Y.: 2001, Web-based Personalization and Management of Interactive Video. In: *Proceedings of the Tenth International World Wide Web Conference*, Hong Kong, May 1–5 pp. 129–139.

José, M.: MPEG-7 Overview. Official MPEG-7 document online at http://www.mpeg-industry.com/mp7a/w4980_mp7_Overview1.pdf

Karadkar, U., Na, J.-C. and Furuta, R.: 2002, Employing Smart Browsers to Support Flexible Information Presentation in Petri Net-Based Digital Libraries. In: *Research and Advanced Technology for Digital Libraries: 6th European Conference, ECDL 2002, Proceedings, Lecture Notes in Computer Science (LNCS) 2458*, Springer, pp. 324–337.

Kennedy, S.: 2001, *Southland's Become a Driving Force in Manufacturing DVDs*, August 6, Los Angeles Times.

Maybury, M., Greiff, W., Boykin, S., Ponte, J., McHenry, C. and Ferro, L.: 2004, Personal-Casting: Tailored Broadcast News. In: L. Ardissono, A. Kobsa, and M. Marybury, (eds.): *Personalization and User-Adaptive Interaction in Digital TV*. Kluwer Academic.

MBTV, Inc.: White Paper on MBTV Technology. http://www.mbtv.com/whatismbtv/whatismbtv.htm.

Nardon, M., Pianesi, F. and Zancanaro, M.: 2002, Interactive Documentaries: First Usability Studies. In: *Proceedings of TV'02: the 2nd Workshop on Personalization in Future TV in conjunction with the 2nd International Conference on Adaptive Hypermedia and Adaptive Web Based Systems*, Malaga, pp. 73–84.

Rambhia, A., Wen, J. and Cheng, S.: September 2003, MPEG-4-Based Automatic Fine Granularity Personalization of Broadcast Multimedia Content, VLBV 03, Madrid, pp. 139–147.

Taylor, J.: 1998, *DVD Demystified*. McGraw-Hill.

TiVo, Inc.: White Paper on TiVo Technology. http://www.tivo.com/flash.asp?page=discover_index.

van Setten, M., Veenstra, M. and Nijholt, A.: 2002, Prediction Strategies: Combining Prediction Techniques to Optimize Personalization. In: *Proceedings of TV'02: the 2nd Workshop on Personalization in Future TV in conjunction with the 2nd International Conference on Adaptive Hypermedia and Adaptive Web Based Systems*, Malaga, pp. 23–32.

Whitaker, J.: 2001, *DTV Handbook*. 3rd Edn. McGraw-Hill.

Whitaker, J.: 2001, *Interactive Television Demystified*. McGraw-Hill.

PART 3: ITV USER INTERFACES

Chapter 10

Designing Usable Interfaces for TV Recommender Systems

JEROEN VAN BARNEVELD and MARK VAN SETTEN
Telematica Instituut, P.O. Box 589, 7500 AN, Enschede, The Netherlands.
e-mail: {Jeroen.vanBarneveld, Mark.vanSetten}@telin.nl

Abstract. To ensure that TV recommender systems become successful, much attention should be paid to the user interface. This chapter describes an iterative design process in which users were involved from the onset. It was performed to design a user interface for a TV recommender system and to develop guidelines for the design of such user interfaces. The focus of the design process lies on those aspects that are specific to recommendations: presenting predicted interests, presenting explanations of the predictions, and ways in which users can provide feedback. The design process with its various analysis, design and evaluation methods as well as the resulting guidelines are discussed in detail.

Key words. design, personalization, recommender systems, TV, usability, user interfaces

1. Introduction

Due to developments such as digital television, more and more TV channels and programs are becoming available. TV recommender systems (Smyth & Cotter, 2000; Baudisch & Brueckner, 2002) are potentially important tools in aiding viewers to choose what they will watch on TV. TV recommender systems support users in determining how much they will probably like certain programs, and help them to quickly identify those programs that they will probably find worth watching.

To ensure that TV recommender systems live up to these expectations, significant attention must be devoted to the user interface. Buczak et al. (2002) performed usability tests for a personalized Electronic Programming Guide (EPG), which showed that an intuitive, easy-to-use interface for browsing and searching TV show listings and recommendations is essential for this kind of application. Consumers will only utilize interactive, personalized digital TV when they perceive additional benefits in comparison with their current TV. An intuitive, easy-to-use interface is also one of the unique selling points (van Vliet, 2002), and will be a key to the success of TV in the near-term future as an interactive device (Aaronovitch et al., 2002).

In order to create an intuitive, easy-to-use interface for a TV recommender and develop guidelines for designing such an interface, we initiated an iterative design process in which users were involved from the onset. In this design process, focus

L. Ardissono et al. (eds.), *Personalized Digital Television*, 259–285, 2004.

was placed on those aspects that are specific to recommendations. Generic EPG and TV user interface issues were only addressed where necessary. A good source for such generic guidelines can be found at http://www.gsm.de/musist/mstyle.htm

In this chapter, both the iterative design process itself and the resulting guidelines are discussed. First, however, some user interface aspects that are specific to (TV) recommender systems will be discussed, followed by a description of the iterative design approach applied. After this, the experiences and results from our user interface design process will be described.

1.1. USER INTERFACE ASPECTS OF A TV RECOMMENDER

The main task of a TV recommender system is to help viewers find programs that they will find interesting or fun to watch. In order to achieve this, recommender systems predict how interesting each TV program will be for the current viewer using one or more prediction techniques. Examples of prediction techniques are social filtering (Shardanand & Maes, 1995; Herlocker, 2000), techniques from case-based reasoning (Jackson, 1990), techniques from information filtering (Houseman & Kaskela, 1970), item-item filtering (Rashid et al., 2002), and genre Least Mean Square (van Setten, 2002).

Figure 10.1 shows a generic model of a prediction technique. For a given user, each prediction technique calculates a predicted interest value (the prediction) of a piece of information, in this case a TV program. This prediction is based on knowledge stored in the user profile, on data and metadata of the information, and on profiles of other users (van Setten et al., 2003). Prediction techniques learn the interests of users from feedback they receive from them; some techniques provide users with explanations about their reasoning. Validity indicators are used by the recommender when combining multiple prediction techniques in order to improve predictions. These indicators are employed within the recommender and are therefore not visible to the user (van Setten et al., 2003).

This section mainly focuses on three aspects of this model that are directly part of the user interface, namely: predictions, feedback and explanations. Several chapters in this volume discuss various approaches to the prediction part of TV recommender systems in greater detail (Ardissono et al., 2004; Masthoff, 2004; O'Sullivan et al., 2004; Smyth & Cotter, 2004; Zimmerman et al., 2004).

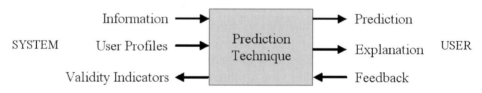

Figure 10.1. Generic model of a prediction technique.

1.1.1. *Predictions*

A prediction is the result of a prediction technique that indicates how interested the user will be in a specific TV program. In general, the predicted value is a number on some scale, e.g. the interval [1,5] or the normalized bipolar interval [−1, 1]. How TV viewers prefer to have predictions presented to them is investigated in detail in this chapter.

1.1.2. *Feedback*

Prediction techniques are capable of learning from users in order to optimize future predictions. In the case of TV recommenders, they learn users' interests in TV programs by gathering feedback from the users. There are two ways to acquire feedback from users: by analyzing the usage behavior, which is called implicit feedback (Lieberman, 1995), and by using explicit relevance feedback (Roccio, 1965; O'Riordan & Sorensen, 1995). With implicit feedback, the TV recommender gathers information about people's actions while using a TV. These can range from global actions, such as the amount of time spent watching certain TV programs, to detailed actions such as each button click on the remote control. Such actions are used to infer how interested the user is in the program. With explicit feedback, in contrast, a user explicitly evaluates the relevance of the TV program, which is generally done by rating it.

Because providing feedback distracts users from watching TV, it should be as unobtrusive and easy as possible. The manner in which users prefer to give feedback is therefore the second aspect investigated in this chapter.

1.1.3. *Explanations*

If we have any doubt about a recommendation provided by someone else, we usually ask for a justification of the recommendation. By doing so, the reasoning behind the suggestion can be analyzed, and we can determine for ourselves whether the evidence is strong enough. Most existing recommender systems behave like black boxes: there is no way to determine what the reasons are behind a recommendation.

Explanations provide transparency by exposing the reasoning and data behind a prediction, and can increase the acceptance of prediction systems (Herlocker et al., 2000). Users will be more likely to trust a recommendation when they know the reasons behind that recommendation (Herlocker et al., 2000; Sinha & Swearingen, 2002). Simple early experiments by Sinha and Swearingen (2002) indicated that users generally like and place more confidence in recommendations that they perceive as transparent. There is another positive effect of explanations in recommender systems: Zimmerman and Kurapati (2002) assume that providing explanations promotes understanding the recommender system and creates a sense of forgiveness if users do not like recommended new items. To get a high sense of forgiveness, however, the user must have reason to believe that the recommender is not likely to make the same mistake again in the future.

If explanations are to be understandable, they must be presented in a way that best suits the user. For this reason, the way explanations should be presented according to TV viewers is also investigated in this chapter.

1.2. ITERATIVE DESIGN

In the past, software design and user interfaces were driven by the new technologies of the time. This is called system- or technology-driven design. Users were not taken into account much in the design. They were given software functions with whatever interface developers were able to come up with.

Research has shown, however, that it is very important to actually consult users or to involve them in the design process rather than designing for a fictitious user. As Spolsky (2001) puts it: 'At a superficial level we may think we're designing for users, but no matter how hard we try, we're designing for who we think the user is, and that means, sadly, that we're designing for ourselves...' In the early 1980 s, focus therefore shifted towards user-centered design (Norman & Draper, 1986), in which the usability for end-users is a prime design goal. Designing usable products usually involves four main phases (Faulkner, 2000; Lif, 1998; Nielsen, 1993):

- Analysis of tasks and users.
- Usability specification in which a number of (measurable) goals are identified.
- The actual design of the product.
- Evaluation of the usability of the design.

To obtain the highest possible level of usability, design and evaluation usually take place iteratively. The purpose of reiteration is to overcome the inherent problems of incomplete requirements specification by cycling through several designs, incrementally improving upon the current product with each pass (Dix et al., 1998). Tognazzini (2000) states that iterative design, with its repeating cycle of design and testing, is the only validated method in existence that will consistently produce successful results, i.e. usable interfaces. Iterative testing is necessary because one cannot always be certain that modifications will actually improve the usability of a product. Changes can sometimes introduce new problems, which can only be detected by retesting (Lindgaard, 1994; Nielsen, 1993).

While user-centered design puts the users into the middle of design considerations, their role was still quite passive, namely that of a target for user task analysis and requirements gathering. Following the 'Scandinavian' approach to software systems design (Floyd et al., 1989; Ehn, 1992), part of the human-computer interaction community recently moved to a new framework called participatory design (Muller & Kuhn, 1993). In this, users are considered to be active participants and partners in the design process (Mandel, 1997).

In order to acquire proper understanding of their wishes and demands as well as a feeling of what their ideas are for a TV recommender's user interface, we especially involved users in the first phases of the design process, resulting in rough designs by the users and detailed opinions on interface elements. In the later phases, we involved users in the validation of the detailed designs, but not in the design process itself as full participatory design can be very costly and time consuming; it asks a lot from the users involved.

1.3. THE USER INTERFACE DESIGN PROCESS FOR A TV RECOMMENDER

Several design and evaluation techniques can be used during the cycles of an iterative user interface design process. Depending on the iteration phase, some techniques are more suitable than others. Techniques such as brainstorming and interactive design sessions are well suited for gaining global insight into the wishes, demands and ideas of the target users in early stages of the design phase. At intermediate stages, techniques focused on specific details and design questions (such as surveys) are more suitable. Techniques that evaluate the whole integrated design come into play during the last stages of the design process. The iterative nature of the entire process makes it possible to return to techniques previously used in order to re-investigate design decisions.

Our user interface design process consisted of the following activities:

- Analysis of the tasks, users and interfaces of existing systems (see Section 2).
- A brainstorming session was organized with different types of TV viewers to explore their expectations for a user interface of a TV recommender, and an interactive design session was held resulting in a number of crude mockups created by the TV viewers themselves (see Section 3).
- An interactive on-line survey was conducted among a larger group of users to investigate various widgets for visualizing the three user interface aspects (see Section 4). Based on the brainstorming results, the interactive design session and the survey, an initial prototype was developed for the TV recommender interface.
- Using heuristic evaluation methods, the first prototype was evaluated together with usability experts (see Section 5). The prototype was improved based on the results of this evaluation.
- Various sets of usability tests were conducted with several users (see Section 6).
- Based on the results of the various design and evaluation steps, a final prototype was developed (see Section 7).

2. Analysis

A user interface design process starts with a thorough analysis to define the tasks that need to be facilitated, the users, and what users want and need. Two approaches were employed: a formal task and user analysis (Dix et al., 1998; Lindgaard, 1994; Nielsen, 1993) and an analysis of existing EPGs, TV systems and other recommender systems.

Results of the task analysis will not be further discussed here because they are reflected in the three aspects of recommender systems (discussed in Section 1.1) that were selected based on the results of the task analysis.

2.1. USER ANALYSIS

A typical user of a TV recommender system is familiar with the concept of color television and knows how to operate a television with a remote control. Our target group consists of users between roughly 15 and 60 years of age. We believe that interfaces for children need to take their different needs and behaviors into account, while older people may have difficulties dealing with the new technologies that TV recommender systems are based on. Separate research is therefore necessary to determine good user interfaces for TV recommender systems for children and the elderly. Because TV is used by a wide variety of people with various backgrounds, it must be possible for a wide variety of users with varying levels of education and experience to use the interface.

2.2. EXISTING SYSTEMS

Because several EPGs, interactive TV systems and other recommender systems already exist, we did not need to start from scratch but could learn from them. The systems we examined include: omroep.nl (www.omroep.nl), tvgids.nl (www.tvgids.nl), DirectTV (www.directtv.com), YourTV (www.yourtv.com.au), PTVplus (www.ptvplus.com), Tivo (www.tivo.com), TVScout (Baudisch & Brueckner, 2002), a prototype EPG by Philips (Gutta et al., 2000; Zimmerman & Kurapati, 2002), Sony EPG (www.sony.co.uk/digitaltelevision/products), Movielens (movielens.umn.edu), Netflix (www.netflix.com), TiV (van Setten, 2003), Amazon (www.amazon.com), Libra (www.cs.utexas.edu/users/libra), Yahoo Launch (launch.yahoo.com), Jester (shadow.ieor.berkeley.edu/humor), Epinions (www.epinions.com), and imdb (www.imbd.com).

Based on the analysis of these systems, we identified a set of factors that appear to influence the design of the three interface aspects of a recommender system. For the presentation of a prediction, these factors are:

- Presentation form: this is the visual concept used to present a prediction. Examples include the use of a bar, a number of symbols or a numerical score.
- The scale of the prediction: Continuous versus discrete, range (e.g. 1 to 5 or 0 to 10), precision (e.g. $\{1, 2, 3, 4, 5\}$ or $\{1, 1.5, 2, 2.5, 3, 3.5, 4, 4.5, 5\}$), and symmetric versus asymmetric (-2 to 2 versus 1 to 5).
- Visual symmetry or asymmetry: even though the scale may be symmetric, a prediction can still be presented asymmetrically (e.g. a scale of -2 to 2 can be presented by five thumbs, with the third thumb representing the neutral value zero).
- Use of color to represent the prediction: some systems use different colors to distinguish between lower and higher predictions.

The factors for user feedback are the same as for predictions, with two additions:

- Scale used for prediction and feedback: Is the scale used for feedback the same as that for presenting the predictions?
- Integration of prediction and feedback: To what extent is the presentation of the feedback integrated with the presentation of the prediction?

Identified factors for explanations are:

- Level of detail: how detailed is the explanation, e.g. is it only coarse or does it include a lot of examples and detailed descriptions of the reasoning?
- System transparency: does the explanation reflect the internal working of the prediction techniques?
- Modality: what modalities are used to present the explanations? (e.g. text, graphs, tables, images, spoken language).
- Integration with the prediction: is the explanation presented directly with the prediction or must the user specifically ask for an explanation?

We investigated the preferences of TV viewers regarding these three main aspects of a TV recommender system's user interface and their different impact factors. We started at a general level with a brainstorming session followed by an interactive design session.

3. Brainstorming and Interactive Design Sessions

The purpose of the brainstorming session was to explore users' basic expectations for user interfaces of TV recommender systems.

3.1. APPROACH

We invited potential users with no specific knowledge of recommender systems to participate. A total of 19 people participated in two sessions. The group consisted of 9 males and 10 females with various backgrounds, between the ages of 20 and 56. All people participated on a voluntary basis. To ensure that older people with relatively little knowledge of new computing applications would not be intimidated by younger people with more technical experience, we divided the session into two separate groups: one for younger participants and one for participants older than 45. The same approach for identifying user expectations was used in both groups.

In order to ensure that the participants would not be influenced, they did not receive any special instructions about recommender systems, except for an introductory general explanation about such systems. None of the results of the analysis as described in Section 2 were provided to any of the participants beforehand. The session started with a brainstorming phase on the user interface. Ideas on the three main topics were generated, written down, and posted visibly for every participant. These ideas were then clustered to get a better overview. After a short discussion on the various ideas during which new ideas could still be added, groups of three to four participants were formed for the design session. Each group was asked to design and present a mockup TV recommender interface, based on the ideas from the brainstorming session that they liked most. At the very least, the interface had to be able to present a set of recommendations, give users a way to provide feedback on recommendations, and allow them to obtain an explanation of why a certain recommendation was made.

3.2. RESULTS OF THE BRAINSTORMING SESSION

The initial brainstorming resulted in a broad collection of ideas and recommendations for TV recommender interfaces. We grouped the results based on the three main user interface aspects of recommender systems, and added a group for ideas that went beyond these three aspects. As expected, the ideas and comments resulting from this session were rather broad and not very detailed:

- Predictions: The user should always be in full control. If desired, the user should be able to turn off recommendations. The user should have influence on a range of settings, including the level of personalization, the number of recommendations, and their level of detail.
- Feedback: Providing feedback on recommended items should be as unobtrusive as possible. It should be easy and quick, and should require only a small amount of effort by the user. Implicitly generated feedback would be preferable, for instance by measuring the viewing time of certain programs or analyzing uttered comments on programs.
- Explanations: Explanations based on peer users' interests and on similarities with the user's favorite programs were both considered to be interesting. Not everyone wants to see explanations all the time. For this reason, explanations should only be given when requested, and they should be easy to interpret. Textual explanations should be short; most users even preferred visual explanations such as charts.

In addition to ideas and comments on the three main aspects of a TV recommender, some more general ideas also arose:

- The TV recommender system should be available on a variety of devices, such as personal computers, PDAs/handhelds, mobile phones and TVs. This would enable the user to consult the recommender system irrespective of his/her location.
- Watching TV is seen as a social activity. The possibility of multiple people watching TV and controlling the recommender system should be taken into account.
- Integration with a TV guide that offers information on all TV programs, and not only on recommended programs, is desirable.

3.3. RESULTS OF INTERACTIVE DESIGN SESSION

The design process for TV recommender interface mockups resulted in a wide variety of drawings and descriptions (two mockups are shown in Figures 10.2 and 10.3). Several important similarities between the different mockups could be observed:

- Although participants stated that a TV recommender system should be available on a range of different devices, almost all mockups were based on a TV with a remote control as the operating device. One group proposed the use of a separate device (a hybrid of a PDA and a tablet PC) that facilitated the TV recommender interface and that could simultaneously be used to operate the TV.
- Every mockup sorted recommendations by genre, while some provided alternative sorting options by time, channel, etc.
- As some participants remarked during the initial brainstorming session, a TV recommender interface should ideally facilitate the use by groups, because watching television is often a social event. A mockup reflecting this idea is shown in Figure 10.3.
- In virtually all mockups, the initiative for displaying recommendations lies on the side of the user. One group proposed unsolicited recommendations (pop-ups in the bottom of the TV screen or via instant messaging mechanisms on a PDA or mobile phone) to alert the user of a recommended TV program that is about to be aired.
- Most of the mockups provided an easy way for users to supply feedback on the recommended items. Most common was a 5-point scale ranging from 1 to 5 (visually asymmetric; the symmetry of the scale was not mentioned in the mockups), operated by the remote control. Other options included a sliding continuous scale and voice recognition.

Among the various mockups, two main interaction types could be distinguished. The first is based on the assumption that a user wishes to plan a couple of hours of TV watching. Recommended programs can be selected and placed in a 'personal TV guide' or 'watch list'. More detailed information on recommended TV programs can be obtained, and these programs can be rated when watched. The mockup in

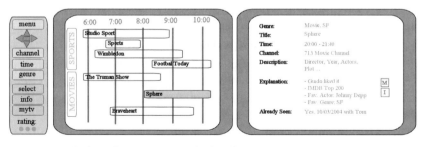

Figure 10.2. Mockup of a TV recommender interface.

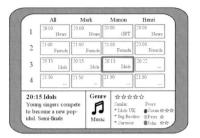

Figure 10.3. Mockup of a TV recommender interface for groups.

Figure 10.2 is an example of an interface of this type. The second type of interaction is based on the idea that a user wants to watch a TV program that best fits his interests right now. These mockups provide a simpler type of interaction because fewer actions have to be performed: only the programs currently being aired are listed. In our design, we attempted to offer both tasks within a single interface.

After the brainstorming and design sessions provided us with global guidelines for designing the user interface of a TV recommender system, our next step was to investigate the preferences of users for the three aspects in more detail. This was done by means of an on-line survey.

4. On-line Survey about Interface Widgets

Our analysis of existing (TV) recommender systems and the ideas generated in the brainstorming session provided some interesting directions and guidelines for the user interface of a TV recommender system. Based on the analysis, a variety of possible interface widgets with different parameters were identified for visualizing each of the three interface aspects of recommender systems. We investigated their usefulness in detail based on an interactive on-line survey.

4.1. EVALUATION BY ON-LINE SURVEY

We wanted participants to make a well-founded choice between different interface options for the interface widgets we investigated. For this reason, rather than using a survey on paper, we created an interactive on-line survey. In this survey, participants could easily try the different widgets and were thus better able to determine the ones they preferred the most. The survey also supported branching: after certain choices participants received extra questions, or questions about parameters were tailored to the answers already given. The survey was completed by 106 people (43 female, 63 male) ranging from 15 to 70 years of age (average age 33) and with different types of education and occupation. Of those people, only 5.6% had ever used an EPG while 29.9% had used a TV guide on the Internet. Most people used paper TV guides (58% regular TV guides and 48% program listings in newspapers). Note that participants could select multiple sources for their TV program information. The survey questions can be accessed on-line at http://tiv.telin.nl/duine/tv/survey

4.2. RESULTS

4.2.1. *Predictions*

The survey results indicate that most people prefer either to have the predictions integrated into a normal EPG (59%) or to have two separate views (39%): one with the normal EPG and one with their recommendations. Only 2% believed that a list of recommendations alone would be enough.

We also asked people to choose between four different interface elements to present predictions (see Figure 10.4): a group of symbols where more symbols express a higher predicted user satisfaction, a thermometer-like bar, a numerical score, and a smiling/sad face symbol. Most people opted for the group of symbols (69%), with the bar in second place (19%). The main reason people gave for this choice was that both the group of symbols and the bar provide a clear and orderly presentation of a prediction while allowing for easy comparison between multiple predictions.

Of those who preferred a group of symbols, most people liked to have stars presenting the prediction (85%), while only a few (7%) opted for thumbs. The others had no opinion or provided their own suggestions. When asked about the number of symbols that should be used in presenting a prediction, the majority chose a scale of 5 symbols (89%), by which 63% indicated that the center symbol (e.g. three stars) should be seen as a neutral value. A neutral center value indicates that most people prefer a symmetrical scale for a prediction (using both positive and negative values and with equal lengths for the positive and negative sides), but an asymmetrical visual representation.

The use of color in presenting the predictions was valued as an improvement by 91% of the participants. They noted that color improves transparency, is more orderly and distinct, and provides a quicker overview of the predictions. However, attention should be devoted to color-blindness; the presentation of the prediction must be clear, even for people who cannot distinguish colors. We also asked participants which color they believed should be used to express that a program fits their interests poorly, neutrally or well. Most people associated red with a predicted low interest (57%) and associated orange (31%), yellow (26%) and blue (19%) with a predicted neutral interest. The prediction that the user would find the program interesting was predominantly associated with green (62%), although some people also indicated that red (15%) or yellow (14%) might be used. When prompted to select color triplets for expressing predicted low-neutral-high user interests, the most popular combinations were red-yellow-green (15%), red-orange-green (15%) and red-blue-green (13%).

Figure 10.4.   Interface elements presenting predictions: group of symbols, bar, numerical score and smiling/sad face symbol.

It can be concluded from these results that people prefer conventional and well-established patterns for presenting predictions: one to five stars to present the prediction (with three stars being neutral), and color combinations that resemble those of traffic lights. Please note that this preference may be influenced by culture. When different established patterns exist in other cultures, it might be best to use those patterns instead.

4.2.2. Feedback

Although implicit feedback was preferred by the participants of the brainstorming session, the survey focused on explicit feedback because explicit feedback is reflected in the user interface and implicit feedback is not.

When presented with six different widgets for providing explicit feedback (see Figure 10.5), participants' stated preferences were less in agreement than for the elements representing predictions. The three most popular widgets were the ratings slider (26%), the group of stars (24%) and the numeric score with plus and minus buttons (21%). The results were also inconclusive regarding their preference for a symmetric rating scale (that has both positive and negative numbers) or an asymmetric scale (with only positive numbers): 48% preferred a symmetric scale, 43% the asymmetric scale, and the rest did not have a preference.

When asked whether the feedback widget should be separated from or combined with the presentation of the prediction, 55% chose to have the two combined, while only 33% preferred to separate the two completely (the others were indifferent). Although most people preferred integration, about 53% opted for loose integration only (widget B in Figure 10.6) in such a way that the combined widgets for feedback and predictions could still be identified separately. This way, the user can still see the original prediction when providing feedback. The other respondents selected one of the three other integration options; the more integrated they were, the less people preferred them.

We believe that the same scale should be used for the presentation of predictions and user feedback, because there was no clear preference for a symmetric or an asymmetric scale, because participants preferred to have the presentation of the prediction and the feedback loosely integrated into a single widget, and because consistency

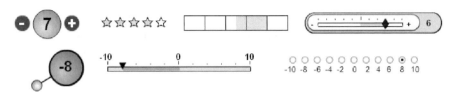

Figure 10.5. Various widgets for giving feedback. From left to right and top to bottom: numeric score with plus and minus buttons, group of stars, rating bar, rating slider with numeric score, volume knob, simple rating slider, and radio buttons.

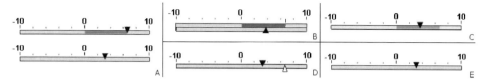

Figure 10.6. Five levels of combining feedback and prediction widgets, ranging from completely separated (A) to full integrated (E).

is an important generic usability requirement. When looking at the granularity of the rating scale, it appears that people like a low to medium number of values. On both the symmetric and asymmetric scales, a range of 10 had a large preference (65% on the asymmetric scale and 21% on the symmetric scale), although on the symmetric scale, a range of 20 had the largest preference (33%). This might again be culturally influenced, in this case by Dutch school grades that are on a 10-point scale. The range of 20 on the symmetric scale had a maximum of +10 and a minimum of −10. When providing feedback, participants also preferred the use of color in the feedback widget (82%).

From these results and the general consistency principle, it can be concluded that it is best to use the same type of presentation and scale for predictions and feedback, namely a symmetrical scale mapped onto 5 stars. Because feedback requires a granularity of at least 10, half stars should also be supported. The neutral value should be the median of the range, i.e. 2.5 stars. For consistency reasons, the range for predictions should then be the same as that for feedback (otherwise when a user gives a feedback of 3.5 stars for a program, the same program could be recommended to him with 3 or 4 stars). Furthermore, the feedback widget should be loosely integrated with the presentation of the prediction and should use color to present the given feedback value.

4.2.3. *Explanations*

Participants indicated that a recommender ought to be able to explain its predictions (45% indicated that it was important and 28% that is was very important). Most people (56%) prefer clear explanations, without wanting to know much about the inner working of the prediction engine. However, there are some people who prefer more detailed explanations (22%), while others prefer minimal explanations (22%).

To determine what types of explanations people trust the most, we provided four different types. The first explanation was based on the similarity between this TV program and another TV program the user liked: 'you will like 'Angel' because you also like 'Buffy The Vampire Slayer''. This explanation was preferred by 25%. The second explanation was based on what the user's friends thought about the program: 'Your friends Menno, Cristina and Ingrid liked this program'. Only 6% of the participants had trust in this explanation, which was explained by one of the participants as 'although they are my friends, it does not mean that we have the same taste'. Most people (34%) preferred the third type of explanation, which was based on the idea of social filtering: 'people who have tastes similar to yours liked this program'. Also explanations based on program aspects, such as actors, genres or the director, were preferred by many people (32%), e.g. 'This movie is directed by Steven Spielberg and Tom Cruise plays one of the main characters'.

When looking at the modality for presenting explanations, we offered participants three different modalities: a graph, a table and a textual explanation, and asked them to choose the preferred modality. Most people opted for the graph (46%) or table (44%), while very few preferred the textual explanation (2%); the rest had no preference. This result confirms Herlocker's (2000) findings regarding the modality of explanations.

90% of the participants preferred receiving an explanation only when they explicitly requested one and not automatically with every prediction. Merely 6% wanted to see explanations with all predictions, while 4% did not want to see explanations at all.

It can be concluded from this survey that people find it important for a recommender system to be able to explain its predictions, although only when requested. The explanations themselves must be clear without too much detail about the inner working of the prediction engine. There is no clear preference for the type of explanations, although explanations based on people's friends are trusted the least. This also implies that it is possible for different prediction techniques to provide their own type of explanation, as long as the explanation is easy to understand. The modality of the explanations should at least contain a graph or table and not only textual information, because graphs and tables allow people to quickly understand explanations.

4.2.4. *First Prototype*

Based on the results of the brainstorming session and the interactive on-line survey, a first prototype of the user interface of the TV recommender was developed (see Figure 10.7). In this design, predictions are presented by a group of stars. The scale of the prediction consists of five stars with a granularity of 0.5 stars, where 2.5 stars, being the median of the five stars, represents the neutral value, making it numerically symmetric, but visually asymmetric. The traffic-light pattern of red-yellow-green is also used within the presentation of the predictions as fill color for the stars (e.g. in Figure 10.7 the program 'De Bovenman' has 4.5 green stars, while the program 'Kruispunt' has only a half red star). Feedback is given using the same scale as that for the predictions: the feedback widget is a combination of five stars with precision 0.5 and a rating bar below the original prediction, thus providing redundancy of interaction. Explanations are presented on the feedback pop-up screen by a short textual description and a graph that depends on the used prediction technique(s). We developed the recommender system's interface to be used on a tablet PC because we believe that such devices, with integrated remote control functionality for the

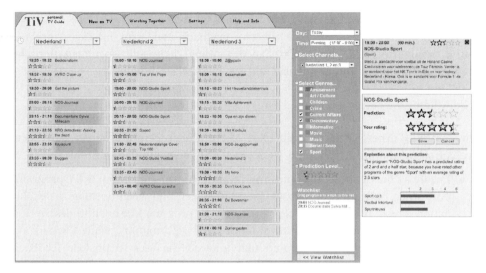

Figure 10.7. First prototype: main screen, pop-up of detailed TV program description and pop-up for feedback and explanations.

TV, will become common in about ten years; however, it can also be used on a regular PC without any changes.

Because the focus of this research was placed on predictions, feedback and explanations, we only used a table view EPG layout in this prototype and did not investigate alternatives, such as a grid layout or 3-D layouts, e.g. time pillars (Pittarello, 2004). These could present better program-guide layouts when many more channels are available to the user. We also did not study other aspects, such as various sorting options for the EPG, group recommendations (Masthoff, 2004) and interfaces for multiple devices.

5. Heuristic Evaluation of the First Prototype

A formal heuristic evaluation involves having a small set of evaluators (often usability experts) examine and judge the user interface with recognized usability principles (or heuristics). With heuristic evaluation it is possible to identify many usability problems early in the design phase (Nielsen, 1993; Lif, 1998).

Although the focus of our research was placed on the three main aspects of recommendations, the heuristic evaluation also gave us insight into usability issues that affect the entire user interface of the TV recommender.

5.1. HEURISTICS

The heuristics that were used in evaluating the prototype are (Harst & Maijers, 1999; Shneiderman, 1998; Nielsen, 1993): provide task suitability, employ consistency throughout the interface, evoke a strong sense of controllability, reduce the user's short-term memory load, provide effective feedback and error messages, provide useful, straightforward and well-designed (on-line) help and documentation, be considerate in layout and aesthetics, and use color with thought.

5.2. RESULTS

Two usability experts who were not part of the design team performed a heuristic evaluation on the prototype. They discovered the following design problems:

- Ensure a consistent way of accessing detailed information about a TV program, both when opening the feedback (pop-up) screen and when opening the explanation screen. In our prototype, clicking on the program title or short description would open a pop-up window with detailed information, while clicking on the prediction opened a pop-up that allowed the user to provide feedback and see the explanation. This might confuse users. In the revised design, clicking anywhere on the TV program creates a pop-up window in which the detailed information, the feedback and the explanation can be accessed separately using tabs. The tab that is displayed still depends on the location of the click. This form of presentation allows users to easily switch between the three aspects.
- Provide clear visible clues of what actions a user can perform. In our interface, users could drag programs to their own 'watch list'. Although the location where the user had to place the stylus in order to drag the program was clearly marked (Figure 10.8), it could be made clearer by changing the cursor symbol when it is above or near such a handle, thus making its affordance more easily visible.
- Make the functionality of buttons very clear. Our TV guide has two display modes: one in which the times of programs on the different channels are not synchronized (as shown in Figure 10.7), and one in which the times are synchronized in blocks of one hour. To switch between these two modes, users had to activate or de-activate a clock-like symbol that was unclear and wrongly positioned. In the new design, a checkbox was used instead that is located just below the time selection field.
- Clearly show what information is currently displayed. In our first prototype, the date of the TV shows currently being displayed was only visible in the drop-down fields in the selection column. It should also be visible at the top of the listed programs.

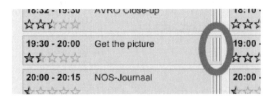

Figure 10.8. Visual indication that a program can be dragged.

- Bring explanations to the point; elaborate explanations are more difficult for users to understand.
- Make the explanations consistent with the presentation of predictions. Predictions in our prototype have a granularity of 0.5. However, explanations described the average interests with a different granularity, e.g. 1.6 stars. The granularity of the two should match.
- In our first prototype, after providing feedback the user had to press a save button to actually store the rating. According to one of the usability experts, this was unnecessary because using the feedback widget should be enough: users should not have to press an additional button. We therefore removed the save button and made the application save the rating automatically.
- Allow users to scroll to different channels instead of requiring them to select channels in a pull-down menu. Because this would create a completely different grid-like display of TV programs, we decided to wait for the results of the usability tests before making such a drastic change.
- The experts were in disagreement about the use of colors for the predictions and feedback: one expert found the colors (traffic-light model) non-intuitive and unclear while another expert found them to be intuitive and very useful, because they made high predictions more easily detectable. Because the survey also indicated a preference for the traffic-light model, we decided to leave it untouched until the usability tests gave a more definite answer.

The experts also provided us with insight into the positive aspects of our design. They believed that most goals of TV viewers are easy to achieve using the interface. Sometimes several different actions lead to the same result (redundancy), meaning that no extra shortcuts were needed. Both experts also indicated that they felt they were in control of the system. They believed that users would have little difficulty using the interface and would also have a feeling of control. The layout was perceived as generally clear and logical. However, some minor changes were recommended, e.g. in the placement of labels and the alignment of certain interface elements. These changes were taken into account in the subsequent prototype. Experts commended the sparse and hence effective use of colors. General items are displayed in neutral (grayish) colors, while more important or highlighted items are shown in more striking colors.

6. Usability Testing

Figure 10.9 shows our new prototype, in which we addressed the problems that were uncovered in the heuristic evaluation while preserving the strong points of the interface. With this new version we performed two series of usability tests with five users each. Usability testing with real users is the most important evaluation method. In a certain sense, it is irreplaceable because it provides direct information about how people use computers and what their exact problems are with the concrete interface being tested (Nielsen, 1993).

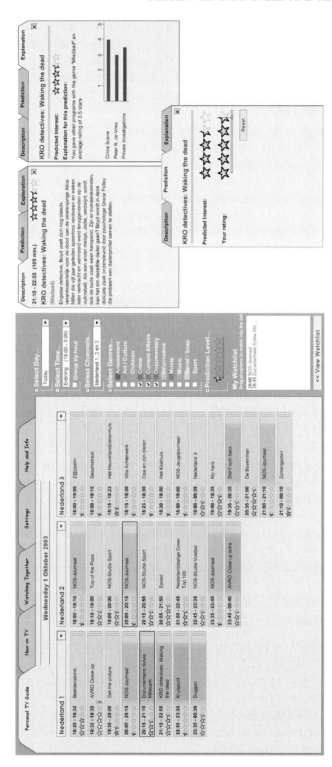

Figure 10.9. Improved prototype before usability tests: main screen, pop-up of detailed TV program description with three tabs.

Dumas and Redish (1993) state that usability tests share the following characteristics:

- The primary goal is to improve the usability of the product; each successive test will have more specific goals.
- The participants represent real users and do real tasks.
- Everything participants do and say should be observed and recorded.

The resulting data is analyzed, the real problems are diagnosed and changes to fix those problems are recommended.

6.1. SETUP OF THE USABILITY TEST

Our first usability test was conducted with three male and two female participants in individual sessions. One participant was in the age group of 15–20, two were 21–30, one was 31–45 and one was older than 45. All participants were familiar with the usage of TVs and had used a PC before: some had limited PC experience, the others average. They were provided with a tablet PC containing the TV recommender. Before starting the session, they were allowed to practice the use of the tablet PC with a stylus as an input device by playing a few games.

All actions performed by the participants were recorded on a VCR by capturing the image of the tablet PC. The participants were asked to go through several assignments on their own, without any help from or communication with the observer, and to think aloud. To ensure that the participants had real goals when using the personalized EPG, the assignments included questions they had to answer, e.g. 'How well do you think the program 'Newsradio' suits your interests, according to the system? (in your own words)'. Participants were clearly instructed that we were evaluating the user interface and not them, so that if they were unable to carry out an assignment it was not their fault, but a fault of the interface. In order to assess the *perceived* quality of the user interface, participants were asked to fill out a small questionnaire (16 questions on a 5-point Likert scale). After finishing all assignments, they had a brief discussion with the observer.

Before our usability test, we defined the following quantitative usability goals:

- All participants must be able to perform all assignments on their own, without intervention by the observer.
- Each assignment must be completed within a specified time, which was determined by measuring our own use of the system (adding a safety margin because we were well acquainted with the interface) and based on a few small tests with different people. The participants were not aware of this predefined maximum time; they could continue until the assignment was completed, or abort the current assignment if they felt the system was not responding properly.

The qualitative usability goals were:

- The user interface must be easy to use.
- The interface should be intuitive.

- How the system presents a prediction and the meaning of the prediction should be clear.
- It should be easy for users to provide feedback on predictions.
- It should be simple for them to find explanations of predictions, and these explanations should be easy to understand.

6.2. RESULTS OF THE FIRST USABILITY TEST

All participants performed all assignments without help from the observer. However, not all participants accomplished all assignments within our predefined maximum time (all reported times are true 'interaction times' and do not include time spent reading the question). In particular, we identified the following problems:

- In the used prototype, the stars of a listed program turned white to indicate that this was not a prediction but feedback provided previously by the user for that same program. This appeared to be unclear: it took three participants more than one minute each to figure out how the interface displayed this information.
- Users could drag programs to their watch lists by clicking on a handle pane next to each listing (see Figure 10.8) and then dragging the listing(s) to their watch lists. Based on the heuristic evaluation, we had already changed the mouse cursor symbol to indicate that the user could initiate a drag operation when hovering over this area. Participants nevertheless assumed that a program could be dragged by clicking at any point in its display area. It took two participants more than 1.5 minutes each to complete the assignment.
- Finally, knowing how to find out which programs are in a certain genre was not intuitive (once again it took two participants more than 1.5 minutes each to complete this assignment the first time). However, when asked a second time, all participants completed this assignment well within the maximum time allotted.

The measured times also indicate that participants quickly learned how to use the interface. For instance, it took our five participants an average of 49 seconds to highlight genres the first time they had to do this. On a second occasion, it took them only 19 seconds. All participants were able to work out how to deal with this particular aspect of the interface, and easily remembered and applied this knowledge later.

Decreasing execution times for similar tasks were also seen in assignments in which participants had to drag programs to their watch lists. The first time it took them an average of 120 seconds, and the second time only 12 seconds. Because the average time for completing this assignment the first time greatly exceeded the maximum allowable time limit, we changed the way programs could be dragged to the watch list: dragging could now be initiated by clicking anywhere in the display area of a program, rather than a dedicated handle only.

6.2.1. *Presentation of Recommendations*

All participants instantly understood the meaning of the stars that indicated their predicted interest in a particular program. Also, when looking for more information on a certain program, they intuitively clicked on the program in question. Participants agreed that the interface clearly indicated whether or not a program would meet their interests (score 4.2 out of 5). The use of colors (green, yellow and red stars) was seen as explanatory and clarifying (score 4.6 out of 5). This calmed the concern that arose in the heuristic evaluation; users do appreciate the use of colors for presenting predictions.

In our design, the difference between a recommendation and a program for which the user had already provided feedback was expressed by replacing the prediction with the feedback of the user, and visually changing the color of the stars to white. This only appeared to be clear to two of the participants. One of the other three noticed it later in the test. We made this clearer in the next version of our prototype, by adding a small icon of a person beside the stars if the rating was based on feedback given by the user (the color still changed to white) and by making it clearer when providing feedback (see next section).

6.2.2. *Providing Feedback on Recommendations*

All participants were able to quickly access the part of the interface with which they could give feedback on a program recommendation. The way to do this with the feedback widget was purposely kept redundant: users could use the slider or directly click on the stars. Three participants used the slider only, one participant clicked on the stars only, and one participant used both options.

After rating a program in a pop-up window, four out of five participants were insecure about how to close the window. One participant pressed the 'Reset' button, while others eventually used the 'X' button in the top-right corner of the pop-up. One of the participants reopened the pop-up window in order to make sure that his feedback was saved properly. During the discussion, four participants indicated that they expected some explicit feature to save their feedback, such as a save button. The lack of specific feedback from the system on their actions resulted in insecurity. This finding is in contradiction with the opinion of one of the usability experts in the heuristic evaluation. It appears that although it takes an extra action, users prefer to be certain that their feedback is saved. We changed this in the user interface by reintroducing the save button. The save button is only enabled when the user has given or changed a rating. Pressing the button changes two visual states: the stars of the feedback widget changes by turning the color of the stars to white (the same color that is used for the stars in the program listing for a program the user had already given feedback on) and the save button becomes disabled.

According to the final questionnaire, four participants agreed that giving feedback on a recommendation takes little effort (score 4.75 out of 5) while 1 participant was indecisive about this matter.

6.2.3. *Explanations of Recommendations*

All participants were able to quickly access the part of the interface with which they could find explanations about a prediction. This was also confirmed by the final questionnaire, in which all participants agreed that the explanations were easy to find (score 4.8 out of 5). Participants also indicated that explanations were visualized in a good way (score 5 out of 5) and that the explanations serve their purpose well, because they clarify the recommendation (score 4.6 out of 5). Participants also indicated that they found the explanations to be relatively credible (score 3.8 out of 5). However, some participants indicated that they would like more detailed explanations. The survey also indicated that some people prefer minimal explanations, while others prefer more details. Therefore, in our next prototype we allowed users to ask for more details when desired.

6.2.4. *Interaction with Various Interface Components*

In general, participants found that the interface was easy to use (score 4.2 out of 5) and that they were in control of it (score 4.6 out of 5). This conclusion is also supported by the measured times it took participants to complete the assignments.

Separating the interface into different main functions on tabbed 'file cards' (see Figure 10.9) also appeared to be a good design decision. All participants managed to find information on these file cards quickly, and knew intuitively how to use the tabs. Finally, the pop-up window with extended program information, feedback and explanations appeared in a fixed position relative to the program on which the user clicked. Some participants mentioned that this obstructed the programs listed below the selected program, and suggested making the window draggable. This was changed in the follow-up prototype.

6.3. ITERATION

Because some of the changes to the original prototype were not trivial (e.g. how user ratings are saved and how they are visually presented), iterative design theory requires another evaluation test, which could focus on the revised parts of the interface. Another usability test was therefore performed that was similar to the one described in the previous section. Five different participants were asked to participate (one in the age group of 15–20, two in the group 21–30, one in the group 31–40 and one well above 41). The usability goals of this test corresponded with the usability goals of the previous test but focused on the changed aspects of the interface.

This second evaluation attested significant improvements in the usability of the prototype. All participants were able to perform all assignments within the estimated time limit without help from the observer. Measured times for completing the assignments show that the changes made to the prototype greatly simplify the tasks that proved to be too difficult in the first usability test. Dragging four programs of their own choice to the watch list took participants an average of 79 seconds (compared to 137 seconds in the first usability test). Participants felt that dragging programs could be done very intuitively because a drag action could be initiated from any point on a TV program display. Another important result was that participants instantly recognized the programs they had given feedback on; they all understood that the presence of a white person-like icon, which was added to this last prototype, indicated that they had given feedback on that particular program. This was a considerable improvement, considering that users had troubles figuring out what programs they had rated previously during the first usability test; this took them an average of 117 seconds. During the second usability test, the same task was completed in an average of 8 seconds.

Results of the second evaluation indicate that the usability problems identified during the first test were resolved. No new usability problems were identified, which is why no further adjustments to the prototype were necessary.

6.4. FUTURE EVALUATIONS AND RESEARCH

The usability tests described in this section were the last tests we performed on the prototype interface. However, before a TV recommender system and its user interface as described in this chapter can be marketed commercially, more extensive usability tests should be performed involving usage in real-life household settings with a substantial larger number of users and over a longer period of time. The usage on multiple devices, individual user characteristics (such as color blindness), and integration with devices such as digital video recorders should also be taken into account. Additional usability problems could then be uncovered that remain unnoticed in a more laboratory-like environment.

7. Conclusions

This chapter has addressed the issue of the design of a usable interface for a TV recommender system, with a focus on three aspects of a recommender system that are reflected in the user interface, namely the presentation of predictions, the presentation of explanations, and the provision of feedback to the recommender. In order to develop an intuitive, easy-to-use interface and to develop guidelines for TV recommender system interfaces, we conducted an iterative design process. The chapter focused on both the design process itself and the results of the various design steps and evaluations, resulting in a number of guidelines for designing user interfaces of TV recommender systems.

7.1. USER INTERFACE DESIGN PROCESS

Regarding the user interface design process itself, we can conclude that an iterative design process is indeed necessary for creating high-quality user interfaces. Different analysis, design and evaluation techniques all contribute to improving the design of the interface. Some methods (such as brainstorming and interactive design sessions) are very suitable early in the design process because they help to gain good general insight into users' expectations and wishes.

Following well-established guidelines for interface design very strictly from the beginning of the process will result in fewer usability problems at a later stage. Much attention should be devoted to this point: even though we paid close attention to these established guidelines, some usability problems were still discovered later that could be traced back to a lack of compliance of the design with these guidelines.

Surveys are an excellent means for asking users their opinions on user interface widgets, especially when using an interactive on-line survey in which users can realistically test different options. Heuristic evaluations should be performed on the first prototypes, because these can quickly identify several usability issues without having to bother users with them. When these issues have been resolved, it is time to involve users in the evaluation process again by performing usability tests. In these tests, the most important problems that real users have when using the interface are uncovered. In order to resolve any remaining or newly introduced usability problems (due to changes made to correct problems identified previously), any improved version of the user interface should be re-tested.

In this design process, we also discovered the necessity of using different evaluation techniques. Sometimes conflicts between the results of different tests arose, indicating a latent usability problem that needed to be investigated in more detail. The different design and evaluation techniques also allow customization options to be identified that manifest themselves as differences in opinions between different groups of users. When customization options are based on such differences, the options offered to users are based on user's customization wishes, and not on what could be referred to as postponed design decisions (these are problems in the design about which designers are indecisive and which are often turned into options so the user can make the decision).

7.2. THE USER INTERFACE

During the entire process, we identified several guidelines for the design of a TV recommender user interface, the details of which have been discussed in this chapter. In summary, the main guidelines concerning the three investigated aspects of a TV recommender system are as follows:

- When designing a user interface for a TV recommender system, one should use well-established patterns in presenting predictions and providing feedback – in this case present predictions using five stars, with the center star representing the neutral value – and if the user wants to use color for the predictions, use the traffic light pattern. A clear distinction should also be made between the presentation of a prediction and the presentation of feedback already given on a program.

- Concerning feedback, it is best to use the same type of presentation and scale as that for presenting predictions (consistency), although some interaction redundancy in providing feedback can improve the feedback process. Consistency means that not only the scale of prediction and feedback should be the same, but also their granularity. Furthermore, the feedback widget should be loosely integrated with the presentation of the prediction and the use of color should be similar for both predictions and feedback. Also clearly indicate when the user's feedback has been stored in his profile. Allowing the user to explicitly save the feedback, thus preventing uncertainty, might do this.

- Recommender systems should be able to explain their predictions, although only when requested. Most people want explanations to be concise, without too much detail on the inner working of the prediction engine. However, some people want more detail than others, making it wise to allow users to obtain additional explanatory data upon request. Again, make sure that consistency exists between the prediction, feedback and explanations. The modality of the explanations should at least contain a graph or table.

In order for TV recommenders to have a clear additional benefit for customers as compared to their current TV systems, a usable interface is crucial. We hope that our guidelines will help others in their design process. We also hope that designers will nevertheless employ an iterative design process and involve users wherever possible, because every user interface will be different, with a different visual look and perhaps additional functionality (e.g. integrated digital video recorders). In this chapter, we primarily focused on the user interface aspects of the recommendation part of a TV recommender system. Other parts of a fully interactive personalized digital TV system also need to be designed for usability.

The final prototype can be found on-line at http://tiv.telin.nl/duine/tv/ui.

Acknowledgements

This research is part of the PhD project Duine (http://duine.telin.nl) at the Telematica Instituut (http://www.telin.nl) and the Freeband project Xhome (http://www.freeband.nl). The authors would like to thank Harry van Vliet, Betsy van Dijk, Ynze van Houten, Johan de Heer, Anton Nijholt, Mascha van der Voort and Andrew Tokmakoff for their comments, support and help in this research project. We would also like to thank all participants of the brainstorming and design sessions, the on-line survey and the usability tests.

References

Aaronovitch, D., Bazalgette, P., Benn, T., Cramer, C., Enriquez, L., Erwington, T., Foster, R., Graham, A., Hughes, J., Hundt, R., Kelly, J., Lovegrove, N., Marshall, C., Oliver, M., Plain, M., Smith, C. and Thompson, M.: 2002, Television and Beyond: the next ten year. ITC 67/02, Independent Television Commission, London, UK, On-line: http://www.itc.org.uk/latest_news/press_releases/release.asp?release_id=626.

Ardissono, L., Gena, C., Torasso, P., Bellifemine, F., Chiarotto, A., Difino, A. and Negro, B.: 2004, User Modeling and Recommendation Techniques for Personalized Electronic Program Guides. In this volume.

Baudisch, P. and Brueckner, L.: 2002, TV Scout: Lowering the Entry Barrier to Personalized TV Program Recommendations. In: P. De Bra, P. Brusilovsky and R. Conejo (eds.): *Adaptive Hypermedia and Adaptive Web-Based Systems: Proceedings of the Second International Conference.* May 29–31, Malaga, Spain, Springer, Heidelberg, pp. 58–68.

Buczak, A. L., Zimmerman, J. and Kurapati, K.: 2002, Personalization: Improving Ease-of-use, Trust and Accuracy of a TV Show Recommender. In: L. Ardissono and A. L. Buczak (eds.) *Proceedings of the Second Workshop on Personalization in Future TV.* Malaga, Spain, May 28, pp. 3–12.

Cayzer, S. and Aickelin, U.: 2002, A Recommender System Based on the Immune Network. In: *Proceedings of the 2002 Congres on Evolutionary Computation,* Honolulu, USA, May 12–17, pp. 807–813. On-line: www.hpl.hp.com/techreports/2002/HPL-2002-1.pdf

Dix, A. J., Finlay, J. E., Abowd, G. D. and Baele, R.: 1998, *Human-Computer Interaction.* 2nd ed. London: Prentice Hall, Europe.

Dumas, J. S. and Redish, J. C.: 1993, *A Practical Guide to Usability Testing.* New Jersey, USA: Ablex Publishing Corporation.

Ehn, P.: 1992. Scandinavian Design: On Participation and Skill. In: P. S. Adler and T. A. Winograd (eds.): *Usability: Turning technologies into tools.* New York: Oxford University Press, pp. 96–132.

Faulkner, X.: 2000, *Usability Engineering.* Hamsphire, UK: Palgrave.

Floyd, C., Mehl, W. M., Reisin, F. M., Schmidt, G. and Wolf, G.: 1989, Out of Scandinavia: Alternative Approaches to Software Design and System Development. *Human-Computer Interaction* **4**(4), 253–350.

Gutta, S., Kurapati, K., Lee, K. P., Martino, J., Milanski, J., Schaffer, D. and Zimmerman, J.: 2000, TV Content Recommender System. In: *Proceedings of 17th National Conference on AI,* Austin, July 2000, pp. 1121–1122.

Harst, G. and Maijers, R.: 1999, *Effectief GUI-ontwerp.* Schoonhoven, The Netherlands: Academic Service.

Herlocker, J.: 2000, *Understanding and Improving Automated Collaborative Filtering Systems.* PhD thesis, University of Minnesota.

Herlocker, J., Konstan, J. A. and Riedl, J.: 2000, Explaining Collaborative Filtering Recommendations. In: W. Kellogg and S. Whittaker (eds.): *Proceedings of the 2000 ACM Conference on Computer Supported Cooperative Work,* Philadelphia, Pennsylvania: ACM Press, New York, pp. 241–250.

Houseman, E. M. and Kaskela, D. E.: 1970, State of the art of selective dissemination of information. *IEEE Trans Eng Writing Speech III* 78–83.

Jackson, P.: 1990, *Introduction to Expert Systems.* Reading: Addison-Wesley.

Lieberman, H.: 1995, Letizia: An Agent that Assists Web Browsing. In: *Proceedings of the fourteenth International Conference on AI.* Montreal, Canada, August, pp. 924–929.

Lif, M.: 1998, Adding Usability—Methods for modelling, User Interface Design and Evaluation. Technical Report 359, *Comprehensive Summary of Dissertation,* Faculty of Science and Technology, University of Uppsala, Uppsala, Sweden.

Lindgaard, G.: 1994, *Usability Testing and System Evaluation.* London: Chapman & Hall.

Mandel, T. W.: 1997, *Elements of User Interface Design.* New York: John Wiley & Sons, Inc.

Masthoff, J.: 2004, Group modeling: Selecting a Sequence of Television Items to Suit a Group of Viewers. In this volume.

Muller, M. and Kuhn, S. (eds.): 1993, Special issue on participatory design. *Communications of the ACM* **36**(4).

Nielsen J.: 1993, *Usability Engineering*. San Francisco: Morgan Kaufmann Publishers.

Norman, D. A. and Draper, S. W.: 1986, *User Centered System Design: New Perspectives on Human-Computer Interaction*. New Jersey: Lawrence Erlbaum.

O'Riordan, A. and Sorensen, H.: 1995, An Intelligent Agent for High-Precision Text Filtering. In: *Proceedings of the Fourth International Conference on Information and Knowledge Management '95*. Baltimore, USA, November 29–December 2, pp. 205–211.

O'Sullivan, D., Smyth, B., Wilson, D., McDonald, K. and Smeaton, A. F.: 2004, Interactive Television Personalisation–From Guides to Programmes. In this volume.

Pittarello, F.: 2004, The Time-Pillars World. A 3D Paradigm for the New Enlarged TV Information Domain. In this volume.

Rashid, A. M., Albert, I., Cosley, D., Lam, S. K., McNee, S. M., Konstan, J. A. and Riedl, J.: 2002, Getting to Know You: Learning New User Preferences in Recommender Systems. In: *Proceedings of ACM Intelligent User Interfaces 2002*. January 13–16, San Francisco: ACM Press, New York, pp. 127–134.

Roccio, J. J.: 1965, Relevance Feedback in Information Retrieval. In: G. Salton (ed.): *Scientific Report ISR-9, Information Storage and Retrieval*, National Science Foundation, pp. XXIII-1–XXIII-11.

Shardanand, U. and Maes, P.: 1995, Social Information Filtering: Algorithms for Automated Word of Mouth. In: I. R. Katz, R. Mack, L. Marks, M. B. Rosson & J. Nielsen (eds.): *Proceedings of Human Factors in Computing Systems (CHI'1995)*. May 7–11, Denver, New York: ACM Press, pp. 210–217.

Shneiderman, B.: 1998, *Designing the User Interface, Strategies for Effective Human-Computer Interaction*, 3rd ed. Longman, USA: Addison Wesley.

Sinha, R. and Swearingen, K.: 2002, The Role of Transparency in Recommender Systems. In: *Extended Abstracts Proceedings of Conference on Human Factors in Computer Systems (CHI'2002)*. April 20–25, Minneapolis, Minnesota: ACM Press, New York, pp. 830–831.

Smyth, B. and Cotter, P.: 2000, A Personalised TV Listings Service for the Digital TV Age. *Knowledge-Based Systems* **13**, 53–59.

Smyth, B. and Cotter, P.: 2004, The Evolution of the Personalized Electronic Programme Guide. In this volume.

Spolsky, J.: 2001, *User Interface Design for Programmers*. Berkeley, USA: Apress.

Tognazzini, B.: 2000, If They Don't Test, Don't Hire Them. On-line: http://www.asktog.com/columns/037TestOrElse.html

van Setten, M.: 2002, Experiments with a Recommendation Technique that Learns Category Interests. In: P. Isaías (ed.): *Proceedings of the IADIS International Conference www/Internet 2002*. Lisbon, Portugal, November 13–15, pp. 722–725.

van Setten, M., Veenstra, M., Nijholt, A. and van Dijk, B.: 2003, Prediction strategies in a TV recommender system—Methods and Experiments. In: P. Isaías and N. Karmakar (eds.): *Proceedings of the Second IADIS International Conference www/Internet 2003*. Faro, Portugal, November 5–8, pp. 203–210.

van Vliet, H.: 2002, Where Television and Internet Meet: New Experiences for Rich Media. *E-View* **2**(1). On-line: http://comcom.kub.nl/e-view/02-1/vliet.htm.

Zimmerman, J. and Kurapati, K.: 2002, Exposing Profiles to Build Trust in a Recommender. In: *Extended Abstracts Proceedings of Conference on Human Factors in Computer Systems (CHI'2002)*. Minneapolis, Minnesota: ACM Press, New York, April 20–25, pp. 608–609.

Zimmerman, J., Kurapati, K., Buczak, A. L., Schaffer, D., Martino, J. and Gutta, S.: 2004, TV Personalization System—Design of a TV Show Recommender Engine and Interface. In this volume.

Chapter 11

The Time-Pillar World
A 3D Paradigm for the New Enlarged TV Information Domain

FABIO PITTARELLO
*Dipartimento di Informatica, Università Cá Foscari di Venezia, Via Torino 155,
30172 Mestre (Venezia), Italia*

Abstract. This study discusses a paradigm for exploring the digital TV information domain, characterized by a large number of channels. The proposal is based on the introduction of ambiguous schemes for organizing information related to the TV domain; these schemes, already popular and successful for seeking information on the web, are here introduced for helping people who appreciate iterative and interactive search, involving mechanisms of associative learning. Serendipity is here used as an approach complementary to exact organization schemes and useful especially for *zappers* who browse the TV domain without knowing, in advance, what they are looking for. The TV domain is here presented as a fully navigable 3D world populated by visual counterparts of TV channels, called *time-pillars*. These artifacts are composite objects that offer simplified access to TV information and a number of related functions. The paradigm introduced in this study supports users who prefer the explorative approach for navigating TV streams, and in particular the part of the TV domain that is not supported by any Electronic Program Guide (EPG) or other complementary information services. The 3D metaphor can be used also as an interface for EPGs, in order to obtain a less fragmented view of the whole TV domain. The impact on users has been validated with an iterative procedure, i.e., a pilot study and a subsequent more detailed experiment, which have confirmed the usefulness of the approach and given useful hints for future development.

Key words. 3D, convergence, cooperation, digital TV, information visualization, serendipity, virtual worlds.

1. Introduction

The new digital TV domain is characterized by the availability of hundreds of channels, both general and thematic. While this abundance offers new information opportunities to the average TV viewer, content-seeking tools currently available on consumer TV sets have not evolved much and often do not enable TV viewers to cope with information overload problems.

In recent years, a number of researchers have proposed different solutions for filtering channel information; an interesting overview of such techniques is proposed in this volume (Smyth et al.). These methodologies cope with the problem of information overload by recommending a selection of TV streams or a list of opportunities ordered by rank on the basis of static user profiles and dynamic usage information.

L. Ardissono et al. (eds.), Personalized Digital Television, 287–320, 2004.
© *2004 Kluwer Academic Publishers. Printed in the Netherlands.*

Unfortunately, these approaches cannot be easily extended to the whole TV domain, because today there is no comprehensive source of information associated with TV streams that can be used as an input to those recommendation engines. Besides, a significant part of the broadcasters do not provide complementary information sources associated with their video streams.

Finally, filtering techniques are less useful for TV viewers who prefer to browse the TV domain with an explorative approach. The user categorization proposed by Hara (Hara et al., in this volume) shows that this category includes a significant part of TV viewers. They are referred to as *diversion-seeker zappers*. This study addresses the needs of this significant category of users, who appreciate browsing through the entire TV domain, including in particular that part which is not supported by any Electronic Program Guide (EPG) or alternative information services.

According to Rosenfeld and Morville (Rosenfeld et al., 2002), known-item search (seeking information knowing exactly the target) is not the only modality for seeking information. Users who know the exact label of what they are searching for and want to find it as quickly as possible use this paradigm. However, in other cases, users have a vague idea of what they are looking for, and if they are enabled to explore the domain, they may learn about information they had not considered before starting browsing.

Rosenfeld and Morville suggest that these modes of finding information are not mutually exclusive, but they are both successful search modalities for web information. Users browsing through the web switch between known-item search and serendipitous[1] navigation.

While known-item search characterizes most consumer TV interfaces, and filtering techniques are applied by many recommender systems to reduce the number of perceivable streams, this work introduces serendipitous browsing as a complementary means of exploring the new enlarged TV domain. A new 3D paradigm that allows sophisticated exploration behaviors with a simple user interface is presented and discussed in the following sections.

Concerning TV content, this study helps TV viewers to be informed about those channels that are not supported by complementary information sources, and are therefore invisible to the filtering engines. This is not an infrequent situation: digital technology has lowered broadcasting costs and many small TV stations broadcast their content, often without any information associated with their streams. The advent of new efficient compression schemes, such as MPEG4 (Pereira et al., 2002), will probably enhance this trend.

The paradigm and the underlying architecture proposed here allow the user to monitor the content of these channels. Monitoring channels simply allow the user to record and see what has been broadcast in the past few hours or days, and does not give the opportunity of being informed about upcoming streams. Anyway, it

---

[1]Serendipity is the faculty of making fortunate discovery by accident. The term was coined by the English author Horace Walpole after the title of a fairy tale, called *The Three Princes of Serendip*; according to Walpole, *as their highnesses traveled, they were always making discoveries, by accidents and sagacity, of things which they were not in quest of.* (Lewis, 1960).

is the only opportunity of enlightening a consistent part of the TV domain when other information sources are lacking.

An extended architecture using media convergence and the same interaction paradigms is presented to considerably augment the quantity of monitored channels. While the main part of this study is related to *hidden* channels, this extension also allows TV viewers to use the system as an EPG, open to the contribution of broadcasters who want to collaborate actively to spread information about their future shows.

In conclusion, this paradigm will allow users to have a less fragmented vision of the TV domain.

This chapter is organized as follows: Section 2 illustrates the main features of the 3D informative environment for the exploration of the TV domain. Section 3 discusses the *time-pillar*, the main component of the 3D environment. The user interface of the prototype implementation and the underlying system architecture are described in Section 4. Section 5 illustrates how the proposal can be greatly enhanced by a cooperative approach using media convergence. Section 6 discusses the proposal, comparing the design choices with related literature. Section 7 evaluates the 3D interface. Section 8 draws the conclusion and suggests future developments.

2. A 3D Approach for Exploring the TV Domain

The introduction of serendipitous browsing for the TV domain is here associated with a 3D metaphor. Precisely, a topical and metaphor-driven ambiguous scheme (Rosenfeld et al., 2002) is used to organize information and allow users to browse it.

While the topical scheme is a well-known method for grouping items of a specific domain, the association of topics with a visual representation guarantees additional advantages, such as an intuitive approach and a progressive and easier development of mental maps for the visited domain. Section 6 gives better insights about the rationale for such a choice.

The paradigm for the exploration of the TV domain is based on the 3D environment shown in Figure 11.1. This environment does not aim to compete with the known-item search approach in the trivial task of selecting a specific channel. Rather, it suggests a different way of navigating channel information, more similar to Internet browsing than to the traditional interaction with a TV set. The underlying idea is to provide an interface that allows users to move through an information-rich environment and to encounter serendipitously channel streams and related data. Two classes of object characterize the 3D scenario:

- Higher scale objects (mainly architectural or symbolic entities such as a theatre, a stadium, etc.), visible from a distance, that mark the different zones of the environment. These landmarks are associated with specific topics for thematic channels, e.g., sports, music, news and culture, or languages for the general channels, e.g., Italian, English and French.
- Visual counterparts of TV channels, called *time-pillars*.

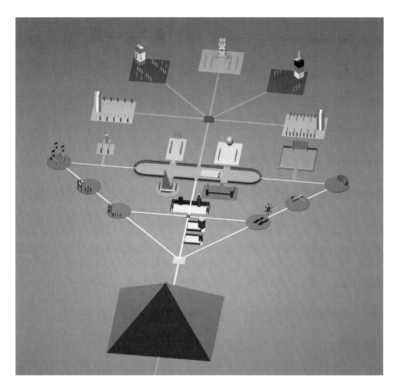

Figure 11.1. A 3D world for the TV domain.

The time-pillars are sophisticated artifacts placed in the different zones character-ized by the landmarks, according to thematic or language criteria. For example the time-pillars representing channels related to the theme *theatre* are displayed next to a simplified representation of a theatre. The resulting landscape is a 3D environment articulated in venues with a specific morphology and connected by a grid of visible paths.

3. The Time-pillars

The time-pillars (Figure 11.2) that populate the 3D environment are articulated objects that offer simplified access to information and a set of related functions. Each time-pillar is associated with a TV channel: the broadcaster's name is visualized on the base of the pillar. A quick overview of the content that is broadcasted is seen in real time by clicking over the cube on the summit of the pillar. The central part of the pillar addresses content exploration and summarization. Indeed, the time-pillar allows the recording and retrieval of audio and video streams; this feature gives the user the chance to monitor a specific channel for a period.

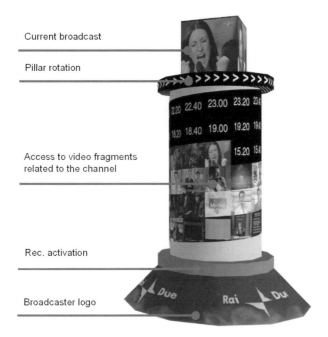

Current broadcast

Pillar rotation

Access to video fragments
related to the channel

Rec. activation

Broadcaster logo

Figure 11.2. The time-pillar.

The time-pillar is conceived for a 3D environment that can be freely navigated by users, therefore it can be seen from different directions. Users can manage the partial visual occlusion of the content by clicking on the upper part of the time-pillar to rotate the central part of the spiral.

The spiral scheme is taken from the tradition of Roman art, in particular that relating to the narration of historical events, such as *Trajan's Column* (Bianchi Bandinelli, 1970). This column, conceived in the 2nd century A.D., contained more than 2,000 figures illustrating episodes of the Dacian war. The novelty of this monument was the idea of representing the war scenes using an helicoidal band of figures spiralling up.

Each pillar is the visual counterpart of a specific channel and each recorded video sequence has a counterpart in its spiral. Users can click on the snapshots on the spiral to visualize the related video fragment. The insertion order on the surface of the pillars reflects the temporal order of the recorded video events.

Figure 11.3 illustrates a monitoring session. The user activates the recording activity by clicking on the base of the pillar. At regular time intervals (about 20 minutes), short video fragments of the selected channel are recorded by the underlying hardware. A snapshot of the recording is generated for each fragment and visualized on the time-pillar surface; finally the snapshot is linked to the stored video stream. In 24 hours the entire surface of the pillar is textured with *active* snapshots that can be examined by the user.

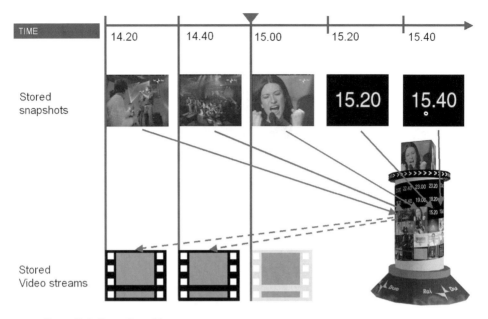

Figure 11.3. Recording video streams.

4. User Interface of the Prototype

Figure 11.4 illustrates the visual interface of the prototype. The 3D environment occupies the right part of the screen. The upper part of the screen is reserved for a text label indicating the zone of the 3D world the user is navigating. The lower part of the screen is reserved for the navigation controls (automated tour, guided

Figure 11.4. The interface of the prototype.

tour, free walk and map). The zone for broadcast playback occupies the left part of the screen; each time the user selects a snapshot of the spiral or the cube on top of the pillar, the related video stream is played in this area. Finally, the lower left part of the screen is reserved for text information related to the selected channel.

Four paradigms are available for navigation:

- Automatic tour: this allows the automatic exploration of the whole 3D environment using a predefined path and viewpoints. The user can click the *Zones* button in order to activate a panoramic navigation through the thematic and general zones. This modality allows the user to navigate quickly through the available zones without examining the time-pillars in detail. The user can also click the *TV Channels* button to get an exhaustive and more detailed navigation through all the available pillars. The users may switch seamlessly between the two modalities in order to examine in detail only the zones they are more interested in, speeding up the whole navigation process. In both cases, the transition between different zones and pillars is scheduled by the system.
- Guided tour: this paradigm enables the user to explore the whole TV domain systematically, using the same predefined path and viewpoints of the previous paradigm. In this case, the user is required to control each step in the path, moving from zone to zone (i.e., *Zone+* and *Zone-*buttons), or from channel to channel (i.e., *TV Channel+* and *TV Channel-*buttons).
- Free walk: this is conceived for wandering freely through the TV domain, using four directional buttons. In this case the user may choose the preferred viewpoint.
- Map: when the user clicks on the *Map* button, a miniature of the 3D world is visualized on the lower right part of the screen. The user may directly reach a specific venue by clicking on this map.

The interface proposed is adaptable (see Section 6.4): users may take advantage of all the four paradigms by switching between the different navigation modalities according to their needs.

Figure 11.5 shows a typical interaction sequence in the time-pillar world. First (Figure 11.5A), the user explores the TV world by using one of the four available navigation paradigms. Next, the user reaches the *Economics* zone (Figure 11.5B), which hosts all the channels related to this theme. The identity of the zone is marked by the presence of a big textured monolith; when the user reaches this zone only the time-pillar on the right is partially filled with content. In Figure 11.5C the user approaches the *CanaleLavoro* (a job opportunities related channel) time-pillar and clicks on its base to activate recording. After a few hours the user again reaches this time-pillar (Figure 11.5D), which is partially mapped with snapshots showing the result of the monitoring activity. At this point, the user may click on these snapshots in order to view the recorded fragments.

Figure 11.6 illustrates the components of the software architecture required to implement the time-pillar world. The *3D visualization component* presents the 3D

Figure 11.5. A – Navigating the time-pillar word. B – Overview of the *Economics* zone. C – The *CanaleLavoro* time-pillar. D – The *CanaleLavoro* time-pillar after the monitoring activity.

metaphor and receives the input from the *interaction component*. When the user decides to monitor a specific channel, the interaction component sends the *update component* a request to activate the recording.

The update component activates the *scheduler*, which starts the recording according to a specific algorithm (fixed scheduling) and stores the recorded streams in the *media repository*. At the same time, the update component modifies the

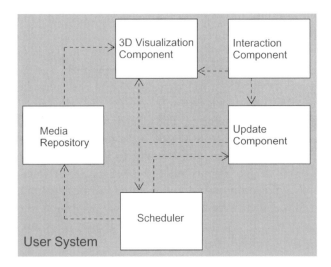

Figure 11.6. Stand-alone software architecture.

3D world by revising the pointers to the video snapshots and streams progressively available in the media repository.

We have developed a prototype for the evaluation of the time-pillar proposal running on a personal computer with a 3D accelerated graphics card and a DVB-S card for satellite TV. Concerning the standards and the languages suitable for building the 3D metaphor, MPEG4 (Pereira et al., 2002) was considered as one of the most interesting candidates for its ability to integrate different media, including 3D content. Unfortunately, the research performed so far has not led to implementations useful for a prototype. Therefore the application was implemented using VRML (Carey, 1997).

5. Information Sharing

Our prototype allows a single user to navigate the TV domain by monitoring the broadcasts of specific channels. Unfortunately, it is possible to explore only a small quantity of channels because the decoder included in the system can monitor only one channel. Therefore, the usefulness of our solution for an extensive navigation inside the TV domain is limited.

In this section, an extension to the software architecture, using the same paradigm described in the previous sections, is discussed.

The convergence with Internet, combined with a cooperative approach, offers the chance to monitor a large number of channels by avoiding the hardware constraints of stand-alone configurations. The proposal can be realistically applied, given the capabilities of the recent video compression schemes and the progressive diffusion of DSL and fiber technologies for the network.

In order to fill the time-pillar world with information, two additional typologies of content contributors are considered: remote users, sharing on the network the result of their channel monitoring activity, and official broadcasters, filling the time-pillars with previews of forthcoming programs (excluding live shows). In the latter case, the time-pillars are used as EPGs. As discussed in Section 7, our evaluation study has confirmed the users' interest in the introduction of this function.

The networked version of the system allows the users to view a variety of information sources with the same interface. In this scenario during their exploration the users find a large number of pillars already filled with content, ready to be explored.

Figure 11.7 shows an example of the resulting 3D environment. The boxes represent the different zones that characterize the 3D scene. The colors of the pillars identify the origin of the content:

- red pillars for content recorded on the local user system;
- grey pillars for content monitored by other users, recorded on their remote systems and shared over the network;
- yellow pillars for content delivered by official broadcasters, related to forthcoming programs.

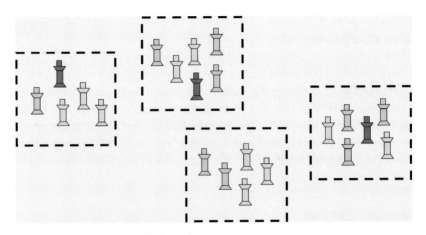

Figure 11.7. Time-pillars and information sources.

5.1. EXTENDED ARCHITECTURE AND COMMUNICATION PROTOCOL

Opening the system to external contributions requires the definition of additional software components distributed over the network. The dynamism that characterizes the TV domain suggests the introduction of an independent *coordination server* (Figure 11.8), which plays the role of a unified and updated source, capable of managing all the remote contributions.

The coordination server is not only the passive repository of information sent by remote data sources; it is also responsible for maintaining a list of all the TV channels. The official broadcasters and the remote users can fill in only the time-pillars related to channels in this list. Finally, the team of the coordination server is responsible for determining the morphology of the 3D world, including the layout of the time-pillars. Individual personalization of the 3D geometry might be considered for a future version of the system, even if this is problematic in a shared environment (see Section 6.1).

The architecture of the stand-alone system described in Section 4 is updated by adding a *communication component* for network communication.

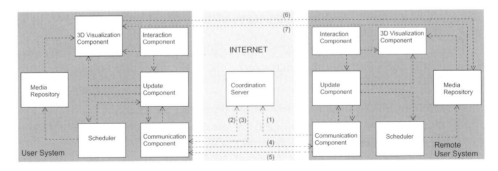

Figure 11.8. Retrieving a video stream from a remote user.

Figure 11.8 shows two personal systems using the same architecture and communication protocol that share information over the network.

Figure 11.9 illustrates the communication protocol for retrieving content from a remote user. Each remote user, after registration with the coordination server, periodically sends information about the channels it has monitored, i.e., the URLs of the video streams available in its media repository (step 1). The coordination server verifies in its private repository the availability of alternative sources for these channels. If no official broadcaster source or more recent recorded streams from other remote users are available, the server updates the public repository of information pointers with the new contribution. Otherwise no update occurs and the new data is stored only in the private repository of the server for future use.

When the local user system (Figures 11.8 and 11.9, on the left) starts, or at periodic time intervals, its communication component retrieves from the coordination server information about the morphology of the 3D world and all the remote users registered on the coordination server (steps 2 and 3 in Figure 11.9). If any modification of the 3D world structure has occurred, the update component of the user system updates its own local version.

Then, the remote users are queried in order to verify if they are up and running (step 4). After the acknowledgement (step 5), the snapshots and the video URLs associated with the time-pillars are updated in the local user system; finally the local user system requests the multimedia data from the remote users (steps 6 and 7).

The broadcaster's contribution allows the system to extend its own functionality by providing the opportunity to use the time-pillar interface also as an EPG for forthcoming programs.

Figure 11.10 shows a personal system retrieving information from a broadcaster. The software architecture of a broadcaster sharing content on the network is composed of: a *media repository* storing multimedia streams; a *content management component* that builds the EPG and updates the content on the media repository; a *communication component* that receives the EPG from the content management component and sends it to the coordination server over the network.

The communication protocol described in Figure 11.9 is still valid for retrieving streams from a broadcaster. Official broadcasters have priority over the monitoring activity performed by remote users on the same channel. Therefore, the coordination server will always update its public repository of pointers with more recent information coming from the broadcasters.

The implementation effort of the distributed architecture has been devoted so far to analyzing and experimenting the best combination of supporting technologies. A prototype under development uses coordination technology to exchange information between the components distributed on the network. By using VRML and coordination languages (Gelertner, 1985), we have implemented, for evaluation purposes, a prototype of a virtual world shared by some remote users. The prototype demonstrated the technical feasibility of putting together all the technologies needed for the extended architecture and will be used as a basis for future development.

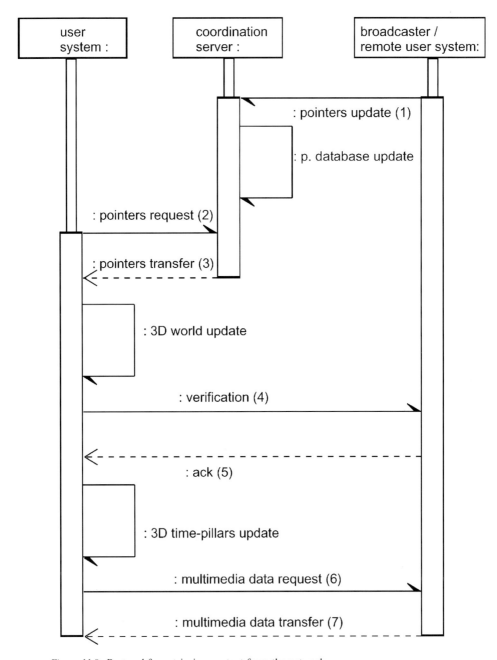

Figure 11.9. Protocol for retrieving content from the network.

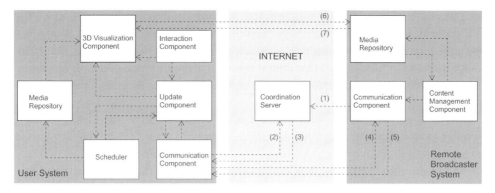

Figure 11.10. Retrieving a video stream from a broadcaster.

6. Discussion and Related Work

The development of the proposal has been guided by the principles of user-centered design (ISO 13407, 1999; Kreitzberg, 1996; Norman et al., 1986). This approach is characterized by at least three activities (analysis, design and evaluation) that must be performed iteratively in order to achieve good usability results.

The analysis phase was characterized by the identification of a major user need, i.e., coping with the complexity of the new enlarged TV domain, characterized by severe information problems. While the recognition of this issue constitutes the initial motivation of a significant number of proposals in this volume (O'Sullivan et al.; Smyth et al.; Zimmerman et al.), our analysis focused also on the additional needs of a particular class of users: the so-called *zappers*, who prefer an explorative approach to channel filtering for browsing the TV domain. Searching the TV domain is often difficult, because only a few of the broadcasters provide metadata associated with TV streams that may be used as input by search engines for retrieving content.

Recalling what was discussed in Section 1, our analysis led to the definition of a paradigm supporting users who prefer the explorative approach, addressing that part of the TV domain not supported by the EPGs.

The proposal introduces ambiguous schemes and serendipitous browsing as an approach complementary to exact organization schemes. This approach is here associated with a 3D visual metaphor. Most of this section discusses the motivation for the specific design choices that led to the development of the prototype described in the sections above, comparing it with related work.

6.1. THE 3D METAPHOR

By choosing a 3D explorative paradigm for browsing the TV domain we deliberately went back to the origin of the serendipitous approach, characterized by the subjective involvement for seeking information and by the reduction of the cognitive distance between users and the objects of their search.

The explorative approach was selected to cope with the wide extension of the TV domain, which could hardly have been presented to users with a static viewpoint without recurring to intermediate abstract schemes (see Nikolovska et al., 1998, described later in this section) that inhibit associative presentation of details belonging to different channels and therefore one of the most interesting aspects of serendipitous search.

Interaction in 3D environments characterizes the lives of all humans beings. Therefore using the same paradigm for accessing information may be suitable for a wide range of people, including casual users.

Moreover, the visual metaphor allows users to conjugate exploration with the progressive accumulation of knowledge. The ability of human beings to remember objects when they are placed in a structured visual context has been extensively exploited since the origin of Western civilization, leading to different effective memorization methodologies, such as the *method of loci*. Orators extensively used this method and its derivations during the Classical period. Further development occurred during the Renaissance, when memory specialists developed sophisticated schemes to help memorization (Yates, 1966). In recent times the memory empowerment provided by visual stimuli has been confirmed by the modern neurosciences (Baddeley, 1998).

The purpose of the time-pillar world metaphor is to give users a stimulating environment, where they are free to wander around and *encounter* information. At the same time, they progressively build a mental map of the scenery, the objects within it and their mutual spatial relationships. The cognitive effort guides them in subsequent navigations and allows them to retrieve themes and channels, without preventing them from encountering unexpected new information.

Recent studies empirically investigate spatial memory performance across 2D and 3D visual interfaces. While some of these studies (Cockburn et al., 2002) do not confirm the superiority of 3D interfaces for rapid retrieval of data items from static-perspective abstract spatial organizations, others (Ark et al., 1998), considering the task of object retrieval on flat 2D backgrounds or in 3D *ecological* representations, show improved performances for the latter situation. Interestingly, even studies that do not recognize the supposed superiority of 3D interfaces (Cockburn et al., 2001) find higher subjective user ratings for 3D.

Another significant study (Ware et al., 1996) shows that 3D interfaces with the ability to change the viewpoint outperform 2D display in tasks related to the comprehension of complex abstract structures.

Considering commercial products, we can notice that 3D based interfaces for managing office tasks are shifting from solutions based on static-perspective (Alspach et al., 1995) to paradigms characterized by an explorative approach with dynamic change of the viewpoint, corresponding to the subjective vision of the user wandering into the scene (Win3D).

Concerning 3D interfaces for TV content, a remarkable attempt comes from the *NewsNow* prototype (Marrin et al., 2001). The project explores the scenario of a new content paradigm for interactive TV, breaking with the traditional video presentation and proposing personalized news combining video fragments in a 3D world. Unfortunately, rather than being the proposal of a new metaphor for channel exploration, it is focused on personalizing the content of a specific broadcaster.

A group of researchers (Nikolovska et al., 1998) has proposed an approach for exploring TV channel data in a 3D information environment. Each program is represented on a 2D plane as a box marked with a color associated with a specific genre (e.g., film, sport, etc.). Users can browse the 2D plane or they may use a search tool that allows them to query the system by category and time. The third dimension is used to evidence the programs resulting from the query and to allow users to shift among the different days of the current week; other planes are used for displaying the query tool and for giving a preview of a specific program chosen by the users.

Users access TV data changing dynamically their viewpoint on the 3D scene, but the authors fail to explain the navigation mechanisms of their interface. Navigation is a fundamental activity for interfaces based on the explorative approach that has been considered as a primary issue in the time-pillar world.

While the authors claim that their approach may be used for a large number of channels, the metaphor adopted does not seem to be useful for examining such a large number of data on a 2D plane. The snapshots shown by the authors illustrate a scenario with a limited number of channels (about 20). The interface does not seem able to give, in a single view, a complete panorama of the 500 TV channels proposed by the authors without losing all the significant details for identifying them. This is an indirect confirmation of the difficulty in representing the complex TV information domain using a single viewpoint on the scene.

The snapshots show that, to cope with this problem, users are required to zoom on specific areas for viewing details; but, acting this way starting from a large information 2D plane they would lose the context, feel disoriented and without any reference, such as labels or images associated with TV programs, helping them to know where they are.

Finally, viewing a preview of the programs content requires the users to shift from the location of the specific program on the 2D plane to a specialized area where all the previews are visualized. Users who want to access several previews are subject to several changes of context. The time-pillar world is characterized by a smoother approach supporting associative vision of streams belonging to different channels. This approach does not give such an unusable overview of the TV domain and favours the immediate vision of content without requiring any change of context. Users can immediately access the information associated with a given channel and can easily access the content of the neighbouring channels.

Another important issue in the making of the time-pillar world was to establish the responsibility for designing the scene and disposing the time-pillars. The solution proposed currently takes advantage of an organized pool of collaborating authors who, along the same lines as in the *Yahoo* team, establish the taxonomy of the TV domain and consequently the relations between the 3D objects on the scene. A modest level of personalization for the time-pillars might be implemented in a future version (this was one of the features suggested by some of the volunteers participating in the evaluation test, see Section 7), but it should be considered very carefully in order to avoid unnecessary cognitive overload. Furthermore, geometry personalization would be problematic in a multi-user 3D world that might be a possible extension for the time-pillar metaphor.

6.2. NAVIGATION PARADIGMS

Due to the navigational nature of the interface, the establishment of simple and consistent navigation metaphors becomes a primary goal for the time-pillar world; the issue of navigation inside virtual environments has been explored only in recent times (Modjeska, 2000), and still represents a challenge for human interaction research (Brutzman, 2002).

Recent studies show that navigation in 3D worlds can benefit from the definition of tools that guide the user in the scene (Haik et al., 2002). Research for automatic path computation to assist 3D navigation of complex synthetic environments has produced interesting results (Salomon et al., 2003), avoiding problems related to the movements of an unconstrained camera in the scene.

The time-pillar world, however, has gone beyond this navigation scheme by implementing four different navigation paradigms that could give users with heterogeneous skills the possibility of using the same 3D interface. According to Pejtersen and Rasmussen (Pejtersen et al., 1997), interface learning is an important part of the interaction process. During the interaction process users learn the interface, gradually shifting from knowledge-based behaviors, characterized by analytical reasoning, to skill-based behaviors, characterized by automated subconscious execution of tasks. A successful interface should provide different interaction modalities and should allow the users to shift between different behaviors and cognitive styles, according to their profiles and to the dynamic evolution of their skills.

The introduction of higher scale objects or landmarks, functioning as reference points (Vinson, 1999), was an additional help in making navigation easier.

6.3. THE TIME-PILLAR

The time-pillar is the most important and complex artifact of the 3D environment. This Section will explain the rationale for the choice of the time-pillar scheme, comparing it with other schemes taken from information visualization research.

The starting requirement for its design was suitability for representing temporally-ordered visual information in a compact way, without hiding the surrounding context. A number of studies demonstrate the importance of having visible landmarks to avoid disorientation in 3D environments. This requirement seems particularly important for women, as has been shown in an interesting study (Czerwinski et al., 2002), which suggests the use of larger displays that allow users to see a larger number of landmarks and context-related information, thus diminishing the cognitive effort.

While the linear and grid schemes currently used in graphical interfaces for managing video streams (Tse et al., 1999) hide a significant percentage of the interface area, the spiral scheme proposed in this work has smoother requirements, see Figure 11.11.

It should be noticed that, although the basic scheme for the time-pillar artifact comes from ancient times, the approach is comparable with modern information visualization techniques (Card et al., 1991). Similar to the cone trees (Hemmje, 1995; Robertson et al., 1991) the perspective wall (Mackinlay et al., 1991) and the fish-eye (Sarkar, 1994) schemes, the spiral scheme shows a portion of the information in detail; adjacent information is displayed at a coarser, but still understandable level of detail. Using this technique, it is possible to see a significant amount of information while reducing the reserved display space.

Due to the explorative nature of the environment, an additional requirement for the artifact was its suitability to properly display information from different viewpoints without requiring additional user motion for examining all the content. The linear and grid schemes, usually conceived for WIMP interfaces, are problematic. Their insertion in a 3D environment would require the definition of additional interactive behaviours to automatically head such artifacts towards the users. Moreover, given the usual screen ratio, the linear scheme would require additional animation for moving the artifact laterally, in order to let the user to see all the video frames without moving from the initial location.

The shortcoming of these solutions is that they modify significantly the spatial relations between the objects of the 3D world, causing disorientation and therefore navigation problems.

The adoption of the time-pillar solution makes it possible to present video-temporal information without modifying the overall morphology of the artifact. The technique adopted is similar to that used in the cone trees approach (Robertson et al., 1993) and makes it possible to animate only the central part of the artifact, while preserving the integrity of the time-pillar object.

In terms of the organization of the spatio-temporal content of the time-pillar, the design choice was to maintain the integrity of the relations between a given TV channel and the video fragments accessible from the pillar interface.

While providing a personalized EPG was not considered a primary goal for the development of the time-pillar world metaphor, different content aggregations might

 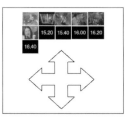 

Figure 11.11. Linear, grid and spiral schemes.

be interesting (e.g., a time-pillar collecting thematic suggestions for a given day) and these might be considered in a future extension of the interface.

6.4. ADAPTABLE AND ADAPTIVE TECHNIQUES FOR SIMPLIFYING ACCESS TO
     INFORMATION

In recent years a number of techniques have been developed for simplifying access to computer-mediated information.

Adaptivity, i.e., automatically adapting the system on the basis of the user profile and/or usage data, and adaptability, i.e., allowing the user to change explicitly some system parameters, approaches have been developed in the area of hypermedia (Browne et al., 1990; Brusilovsky et al., 1998; Brusilovsky, 2001; Fink et al., 1998; Perkowitz et al., 2000; Schneider-Hufschmidt et al., 1993; Stephanidis, 2001).

The extension of these techniques to 3D paradigms is a less explored issue. Recent works propose adaptive architectures for generating dynamically personalized 3D worlds. All the proposals (Chittaro et al., 2002; Guinan et al, 2000; Walczak et al., 2002) offer examples of 3D virtual stores, created exploiting user profiles based on preliminary questionnaires or monitoring user activity.

All these systems personalize the set of 3D objects and their placement in the scene. Adaptivity is problematic when these 3D worlds are shared by different users; the authors seem to be aware of this contradiction, but reserve the solution of this problem to future research.

The advantages and the drawbacks of the different approaches were considered for the time-pillar world design. According to Fink et al. (1998), it is possible to distinguish techniques that adapt the available information, as well as approaches that adapt the user interface.

Concerning the first issue, a number of researchers have proposed different adaptive approaches to the TV domain, helping the user to cope with the information overload problem (Baudisch et al., 2002; Buczak et al., 2002; Cotter et al., 2000; Lee et al., 2002; Meuleman et al., 1998; Smyth et al., in this volume). Personalized EPGs that filter the available information using static user profiles and dynamic usage data allow TV viewers to have useful suggestions without being overwhelmed by the volume of data.

Unfortunately, this approach requires the knowledge of metadata associated with TV streams and is limited therefore to that part of the TV domain supported by complementary information. Moreover, some users, such as the zappers, seem to be attracted by a different explorative approach involving associative search mechanisms. This was the reason why we developed an approach based on serendipitous browsing.

Concerning the user interface, the time-pillar world approach avoided adaptive geometry personalization, which is interesting but deserves further analysis in order to understand its drawbacks in the creation of a mental map of the environment. This study emphasizes the role of navigation as the most relevant interaction activity and suggests an adaptable approach for it.

We avoided explicit associations between a single paradigm and a certain level of expertise (e.g., automatic navigation for novices and free walk for experts). All the users shift seamlessly among the available navigation modalities. The evaluation study discussed in Section 7 has confirmed this choice, showing that there is no trivial relation between a specific navigation paradigm and the user's expertise; instead, there are different groups that use different subsets of the navigation features.

6.5. RECORDING SCHEMES

The recording scheme used for monitoring the channels broadcast (fixed scheduling) is very simple and in certain cases is not able to monitor all the events. The shortest transmissions, such as weather forecasts, are the most problematic. However, even this simple mechanism can be a valuable tool, because it allows the user to build a visual map of the content. The user can see programme times at a glance and can roughly identify the typology of information (news, entertainment, films, etc.). By clicking on the snapshots to activate the video fragments, the user can then refine this first level of information. A more accurate approach could be given by more sophisticated techniques of video stream segmentation and summarization (Gunsel et al., 1998; Kobla et al., 1997; Lienhart et al., 1997; Tsekeridou et al., 2001).

Some interesting applications of techniques for automatically segmenting broadcast news are shown in this volume (Dimitroval et al.; Maybury et al.; O'Sullivan et al.) and could be integrated in the time-pillar system as an alternative to fixedscheduling.

As for the audio-video streaming standards, there are substantial studies which aim to give a structure to the video stream and to allow information retrieval within it (Nack et al., 1999a; Nack et al., 1999b). Future versions of the time-pillar world may take advantage of this.

6.6. COORDINATION LANGUAGES

The implementation of the extended architecture is based on coordination languages, which offer an easy paradigm for coordinating activities and sharing information (Gelertner, 1985). In recent times a number of infrastructures have extended the coordination approach to the web, using a set of Java classes (Ciancarini et al., 1997; Freeman et al., 1998; IBM TSpaces). These infrastructures are particularly interesting for sharing information among different subjects distributed over the Internet. These implementations also offer integrated services for discovering the presence of new components on the network. This is an interesting feature for the time-pillar world architecture, which is based on the dynamic contribution of different subjects on the net.

Some of these implementations present additional security features for accessing data on a specific server. These features are a fundamental component of a system that may be further extended (e.g., broadcasters could give basic information to everyone connecting to their servers and more extensive services to the subscribers of TV channels) and might be used in future versions of the time-pillar world.

7. Evaluation Study

We iteratively evaluated the time-pillar interface by means of a preliminary pilot study and a subsequent evaluation experiment characterized by a modified, more accurate version of the 3D environment, the same procedure, a higher number of volunteers and revised questionnaires aimed at obtaining higher accuracy. This section mainly focuses on the discussion of the second evaluation experiment that confirmed the good results obtained by the preliminary study.

The goal of the evaluation study was to determine the impact on users of the proposed interface. While a complete usability evaluation based on the ISO 9241-11 (ISO 9241-11, 1998) definition should consider effectiveness, efficiency and user satisfaction, our works focuses primarily on the last topic. The reason is that the main interest was to evaluate the user appreciation of an approach that introduces in the TV domain ambiguous classification schemes as a complementary approach to the techniques that support exact classification schemes. While effectiveness and efficiency are fundamental in known-item search, their role is less important in a complementary approach that gives the users the opportunity of *making discoveries, by accidents and sagacity, of things they were not in quest of* (Lewis, 1960). Future work will include an evaluation of these items and a comparison with known-item search, as a prerequisite analysis for integrating the different paradigms. This integration already characterizes the web and may be proficiently extended to the TV domain, in order to increase the number of potential users of the time-pillar world.

Physical constraints led to implementing a software simulator of the system, in order to let the users perform the test in a laboratory room equipped with normal personal computers without satellite card or other special hardware. Some system features were inhibited (e.g., the recording feature), and a number of pre-recorded streams were used to give the user the chance to interact with the time-pillar interface. In spite of the approximations due to the partial inhibition of the system features, the results obtained were very useful in evaluating the impact of the work done and to receive feedback for future extensions.

The 3D world was organized, as in the original prototype, in 22 thematic zones and populated with about 100 empty pillars. Some of the pillars were filled with content from satellite channels.

7.1. DESIGN

Sixteen subjects participated in the pilot study and 49 different subjects participated in the second experiment. In both cases the subjects were recruited among the participants in multimedia and industrial design courses held in Italy. The mean age for the second test was 22.14 years. The participants had sufficient basic computer skills to complete the assigned task autonomously. The experimental conditions were the same for each subject.

7.2. PROCEDURE

The participants interacted individually with our system. Before starting the main part of the evaluation experiment, they were asked to fill in a preliminary questionnaire related to TV viewing. Then the test coordinator introduced the prototype, which was presented as an alternative way of accessing TV content. The participants were guided to understand the nature of the time-pillar artifacts and the interaction modalities, and the different cognitive paradigms for moving through the world were explained.

After the briefing, the test takers started their own interactive session. Each participant had a personal computer with the 3D simulator installed and was given 30 minutes to interact with the system.

The users were asked to perform two main tasks: browse the time-pillar world by exploiting the four navigation paradigms offered by the interface and access information stored in the time-pillars, trying out the different functionalities of these active artifacts.

A test coordinator was available in the room to answer the test takers' questions and resolve technical problems. After the interaction phase the test takers were required to fill in the post-test questionnaire (see Appendix).

7.3. THE QUESTIONNAIRES

The preliminary questionnaire was organized in two sections: a section for terrestrial TV viewers (all the test takers) and a section reserved to satellite TV viewers. Both sections were aimed at analyzing the behavior of TV viewers, considering time spent watching TV, preferred programs and satisfaction with the current interaction paradigms.

The preliminary questionnaire included 2 items for personal data, 10 items based on a Likert Scale, 22 yes/no questions and 4 open-answers for integrating previous questions with additional comments.

The post-test questionnaire (Table 11.1) was organized in six parts related to the structure and navigation modalities of the 3D world, adaptation and personalization issues, current and future functionalities of the time-pillars.

The questionnaire included 23 items based on a Likert Scale, 6 yes/no items and 4 open-answers to collect additional comments about the interface.

Table 11.1. Structure of the final questionnaire

Part	Description
1	3D world metaphor
2	Navigation paradigm
3	Personalization functionalities for the 3D world interface
4	Automatic personalization
5	Current time-pillars functionalities
6	Future time-pillars functionalities

The 4-point Likert scale, used for the preliminary study, was replaced in the second experiment by a 5-point Likert scale, including a mid-point neutral rating.

7.4. ANALYSIS OF THE RESULTS

7.4.1. *Preliminary Questionnaire*

All the participants completed the first part of the preliminary questionnaire, while only 16 test takers filled in the second part about satellite TV.

57% of the test takers said that they watched TV up to an hour per day, while 40% watched TV 1–3 hours per day. Only one test subject watched TV more than 3 hours per day. Users expressed their preference for 8 different types of programming using an 11-point Likert scale (from 0 = strongly uninterested to 10 = strongly interested).

Film was the most appreciated type of programming (mean > 8.8); positive grades were assigned to *Music* (mean = 7.2), *News* (mean = 7.1), *Documentary* (mean = 7.1) 7.1) and *Sports* (mean = 6.0); lower grades were assigned to the other categories of programming: *Soap* (mean = 4.9), *TV Series* (mean = 4.7) and *Variety Shows* (mean = 3.4).

The most interesting results are related to the interaction paradigm. The answers (see Table 11.2) show that while most terrestrial TV viewers select channels by pressing the appropriate number on the remote control or using *channel surfing*, satellite TV viewers give more importance to different techniques, such as favorites or all-inclusive channel lists.

An open-answer devoted to user suggestions about interaction showed that systems characterized by a larger number of channels push the users to try paradigms that allow a preliminary description of the channels before selection.

Another item suggested that user satisfaction about existing channel selection paradigms diminishes for satellite TV viewers who navigate among twenty or more channels. Unfortunately, only a few test takers said they used satellite TV to navigate a higher number of channels; therefore the answers to this item, although interesting, deserve a more accurate analysis on a larger group of volunteers.

7.4.2. *Post-test Questionnaire*

Part 1. Table 11.3 shows how test takers evaluated the 3D metaphor as a whole, expressing their opinion in terms of seven qualitative attributes. The central columns

Table 11.2. Selecting channels

	Select channel number on remote control	Channel surfing	Favorites channel list	All-inclusive channel list	Other methods
Terrestrial TV	71.4%	79.6%	14.3%	4.1%	0.0%
Sat TV	62.5%	50.0%	50.0%	25.0%	6.2%

Table 11.3. Attributes describing the 3D metaphor

	Strongly disagree	Somewhat disagree	Neutral	Somewhat agree	Strongly agree	Mean	Sd
Useful	0	4	8	21	16	4.00	0.91
Interesting	0	0	0	20	29	4.59	0.50
Pleasant	0	2	7	29	11	4.00	0.74
Beautiful	2	10	13	22	2	3.24	0.97
Easy	0	8	12	21	8	3.59	0.96
Appropriate	0	5	16	19	9	3.65	0.90
Relaxing	6	13	18	8	4	2.82	1.11

show the number of test takers agreeing with the evaluation evidenced by the column label; the last two columns on the right show the mean and standard deviation (Sd) obtained from the answers given by each users (from 1 = strongly disagree to 5 = strongly agree). Similar structures are used in Tables 11.4, 11.7, 11.9 and 11.10.

In general, test takers had a positive feeling about the interface; all the participants judged it *interesting* (mean = 4.59 Sd = 0.50) and most of them evaluated it as *useful* and *pleasant* (mean = 4.00). Lower, but still positive, evaluations (mean > 3, Sd < 1) were given to the *beautiful, easy* and *appropriate* attributes. Only the *relaxing* attribute gained a modest evaluation (mean = 2.82).

We may infer from the results that the interface had a good impact on the test takers; lower satisfaction values for the *beautiful, easy* and *appropriate* attributes and the negative result for the *relaxing* parameter may be related to the limits and roughness of the prototype. In particular, several volunteers expressing low eva-luations for the *relaxing* attribute specified in a following answer (question 10, see Appendix) that the most frustrating problem was that the time-pillars made a complete rotation after the initial click, without any possibility of stopping them for a deeper examination of the snapshots.

Part 2. In Section 6.2 we highlighted the importance of allowing the users to choose from different cognitive styles for moving inside the 3D environment. This point of view, which led to the design of four different navigation paradigms, has found significant confirmations from the answers of the test takers. Table 11.4 shows that the most appreciated paradigms were the *guided tour* and the *map* (mean > 4). *Automatic tour* and *free walk* gained lower evaluations (mean ~ 3), showing also higher data dispersion (Sd > 1).

Table 11.4. Navigation paradigms

	Total aversion	Partial aversion	Neutral	Partial appreciation	Total appreciation	Mean	Sd
Automatic t.	3	19	8	12	7	3.02	1.22
Guided t.	0	3	8	23	15	4.02	0.85
Free	4	20	5	11	9	3.02	1.31
Map	2	2	3	17	25	4.24	1.03

The results show a general appreciation for paradigms that combine guidance with freedom, i.e., controlled motion along a path or control from a graphical map. Both these paradigms allow users to move at their own pace, without the passivity of the automatic tour or the complete freedom of a free walk. The result is a confirmation of studies showing that navigation in 3D worlds can benefit from the definition of tools that guide the user in the scene. However, it would be wrong to conclude that these paradigms are the only ones worth considering for the final implementation of the interface.

An additional item underlined the diversity of behaviors that characterize different users. The test takers were asked to indicate one or more motion paradigms to discard, but had also the chance to indicate no paradigm, if they felt it was important to maintain all of them. A significant percentage of users indicated to discard *automatic tour* and *free walk* (see Table 11.5), but none of the test takers indicated to discard both of them. In general, no one indicated more that one paradigm to discard; 12.2% of participants were satisfied with all the paradigms and therefore indicated no navigation modality to discard.

These results led to consider the hypothesis of distinguishing three different groups of test takers, characterized by (1) aversion for free walk, (2) aversion for automatic navigation and (3) appreciation for both paradigms.

Cluster analysis, based on k-means and the initial hypothesis of three clusters, was applied to the evaluations given by the test takers about the four interaction paradigms. Table 11.6 shows the results: the values characterizing the centre of each cluster are expressed using the same scale used by the test takers for evaluating the navigation paradigms (i.e., 5-point Likert scale from $1 =$ total aversion to $5 =$ total appreciation). The results confirm the existence of three user groups with features consistent with the initial hypothesis:

- the *organized tour lovers (21 members)*: a group characterized by a preference for paradigms that automate navigation. Although they prefer guided navigation (4.00), they do not consider total automation a negative feature (3.48); on the contrary, they have a negative opinion about free navigation (1.95);
- the *control supporters (19 members)*: a group characterized by a preference for free (3.63) and partially free (guided) navigation (4.00). The members of this group consider automatic navigation as a paradigm that brings an unbearable loss of control and therefore give it a negative evaluation (1.89);

the *Swiss-knife enthusiasts (9 members)*: a smaller group of individuals that appreciate having many different navigation paradigms at their disposal (automatic tour $= 4.33$, guided tour $= 4.11$, free walk $= 4.22$).

Table 11.5. Navigation paradigms to discard

Automatic tour	Guided tour	Free walk	Map	None
18 (36.7%)	2 (4.1%)	21 (42.9%)	2 (4.1%)	6 (12.2%)

Table 11.6. Final cluster centers

	Cluster 1 ($n = 21$) Organized tour lovers	Cluster 2 ($n = 19$) Control supporters	Cluster 1 ($n = 9$) Swiss-knife enthusiasts
Automatic tour	3.48	1.89	4.33
Guided tour	4.00	4.00	4.11
Free	1.95	3.63	4.22
Map	3.67	4.63	4.78

The map value shows that all three groups, consistently with what emerged from Table 11.4, appreciate this support.

Part 3. Users were asked to express their opinion about some possible extensions of the interface. All the proposed extensions aim at personalizing interaction inside the 3D world, at different levels. The first two proposals would allow the users to save a list of positions corresponding to interesting locations for direct return, and the option of building customized guided tours on the basis of thematic selections.

The second set of extensions would allow the user to customize the morphology of the 3D world, by moving the time-pillars to make personalized groups, or building additional areas inside the 3D world.

As illustrated by Table 11.7, the test takers showed a very positive attitude towards the extensions that allow personalization of their experience in the 3D world (mean > 4, Sd < 1). A very low percentage judged these extensions not interesting.

These proposals stimulated the users to suggest additional functionalities in a following open-answer item (question 5); for example some users suggested populating the environment with additional visual artifacts representing the digital radio channels.

Part 4. This part of the questionnaire covered an important complementary issue: the role of techniques for automatic personalization of content. These techniques collect information about the users using either questionnaires in order to generate

Table 11.7. Proposal of additional functionalities for the 3D world

	Strongly disagree	Somewhat disagree	Neutral	Somewhat agree	Strongly agree	Mean	Sd
Save position for direct return	0	1	1	28	19	4.33	0.63
Guided tour on the basis of thematic selection	0	1	7	20	21	4.24	0.78
Move pillars for building personalized groups	1	2	4	19	23	4.24	0.92
Build parts of the 3D world	0	1	7	11	30	4.43	0.82

static user profiles or monitor users during the interaction phase to generate dynamic user profiles. The test takers were asked to express their opinion about these methods (see Table 11.8).

A significant percentage of the test takers said they were against automatic personalization of the 3D world, whether obtained on the basis of preliminary questionnaires (77.6%) or by monitoring the user's activity (57.1%). This result is only apparently in contradiction with the personalization request that emerges from the answers in Part 3.

The reason for this result can be found in an additional open-answer question (question 8), where the users had to explain the reasons for their feelings about automatic personalization. Most users were not confident that the system would be able to identify their preferences. They were also concerned that automatic choices driven by the system would lead them to miss some important novelty in the TV domain. Finally, they claimed the right to have different opinions on different days.

In conclusion, the answers given in Parts 3 and 4 suggest that personalization is a relevant issue for the group of test takers, but a significant number of them want to have full control over the personalization process. Some of them prefer to browse the whole TV domain and to encounter information to select, rather than receiving the final result of a black box personalization engine. That is the approach that characterizes the time-pillar world and it is similar to Zimmerman's proposal (Zimmerman et al., in this volume); in fact, their system, rather than proposing a limited number of recommendations, creates a prioritized list of *all* TV shows that allows users to browse both highly and lowly rated programs.

The lesson to bear in mind for the future is that any personalization engine conceived for the system should help users without overwhelming them. The users should have the chance, at any time, to switch off the personalization system for navigating freely.

Part 5. This part collected opinions about the current functionalities of the time-pillars. The implemented functions had a substantially positive evaluation (Table 11.9, with a mean 3.63÷4.39 for the different items).

Some of the test takers, in an open-answer question for describing positive features and drawbacks in using the time-pillars (question 10), suggested expanding the rotation function, for example allowing rotation in both directions or stopping in order to observe more closely the snapshots mapped on the surface.

Part 6. This part evaluated opinions about the future functionalities of the pillars (see Table 11.10). The first two items are related to the enhancement of traditional

Table 11.8. User profiling

	Profile from preliminary questionnaire	Profile from behavior monitoring
Agree	22.4%	42.9%
Disagree	77.6%	57.1%

Table 11.9. Current time-pillars functionalities

	Total aversion	Partial aversion	Neutral	Partial appreciation	Total appreciation	Mean	Sd
Visualize live broadcast	0	2	3	18	26	4.39	0.79
Visualize snapshots	0	4	11	22	12	3.86	0.89
Visualize video fragments	2	8	8	19	12	3.63	1.15
Pillar rotation	0	5	6	17	21	4.10	0.98

TV viewing. The test takers expressed appreciation for the idea of using the time-pillar surface for mapping the EPG of the forthcoming programs or accessing the full registration of selected programs (PVR function); Table 11.10 shows a mean = 3.82 3.82 for EPG and a mean = 4.10 for PVR.

The second group of functionalities belongs to the area of convergence between different media, TV and Internet. The underlying hypothesis behind these items is to consider the 3D world connected to the network. Although using time-pillars as pointers to Internet sites related to specific channels received a positive evaluation (mean = 3.63) from the test takers, the option of using these artifacts as a social interface for exchanging opinions with other users was not considered to be so important by some of them (mean = 2.88).

In conclusion, the test takers appeared to be more interested in functionalities that enhance the traditional TV viewing, while access to Internet sites and chat rooms received lower grades. This may be related to the general attitude of considering TV viewing as an activity that does not require active participation.

The pilot study provided an opportunity to measure the impact on users of the time-pillar paradigm. The results were encouraging and confirmed most of the design choices made for the interface.

As far as navigation is concerned, some of the test takers considered very important some paradigms that other users would have discarded. The variety of opinions confirmed the need to maintain different navigation paradigms from which to choose. In this way, access to the 3D interface and, most of all, satisfaction during interaction, may be guaranteed to a wider category of users. Moreover, the study led to the identification of three different user groups which hold different behaviors but share a common feature: they appreciate interaction with more than one navigation paradigm.

Table 11.10. Proposal of additional time-pillars functionalities

	Strongly disagree	Somewhat disagree	Neutral	Somewhat agree	Strongly agree	Mean	Sd
EPG	0	3	12	25	9	3.82	0.81
PVR	2	2	5	20	20	4.10	1.03
Internet links	2	6	9	23	9	3.63	1.05
Chat	4	18	11	12	4	2.88	1.13

Finally, the evaluation study suggested that adaptive features might be implemented in the system, but they should not overwhelm the users, giving them the chance to switch off the personalization system for navigating without additional limitations.

8. Conclusion

In this work we have proposed a paradigm for exploring the digital TV information domain, characterized by a wide number of channels. Ambiguous schemes for organizing TV-channel content have been introduced as a complementary approach to exact organization schemes supporting known-item search.

The 3D paradigm introduced is targeted at users who prefer an explorative, serendipitous approach for navigating TV streams, in particular those that are not supported by any EPG or other complementary information services. However the 3D metaphor can be used also as an interface for an EPG, in order to obtain a less fragmented view of the whole TV domain.

An iterative evaluation with two groups of volunteers confirmed most of the design choices. The users appreciated the introduction of the time-pillar metaphor to access the TV domain, and they suggested improvements to the proposed interface.

Additional evaluations will be performed in order to measure the effectiveness and the efficiency of the time-pillar approach, as a preliminary step in merging this paradigm with known-item search facilities such as favourite lists. The possibility of seamlessly switching between the different search paradigms may be an interesting opportunity for widening the number of potential users, as demonstrated by the experience of the web search engines.

Concerning the interface, the volunteers' comments will be exploited to achieve a smoother and more relaxing interaction in an improved version of the time-pillar world.

The user evaluation performed so far was based on volunteers with a basic knowledge of personal computer interfaces. A more extensive evaluation will involve casual users lacking these skills, in order to test the suitability of the interface for additional classes of TV viewers, and to receive feedback about possible interface modifications.

The proposal of extending the time-pillar functionalities in order to use them as pointers to Internet sites related to specific channels received a positive grade from the test takers; that opportunity might be interesting not only for providing complementary information sources but also for giving to *active* TV viewers additional services related to the broadcasting; e.g., TV viewers browsing the *CanaleLavoro* channel (see Section 4) could be enabled, using the time-pillar interface, to get in touch directly with the firms offering job opportunities. Extending the time-pillar interface to host active services will be a part of future development.

Finally, watching TV is often a group activity (Masthoff, in this volume) where people meet, share opinions and hints about TV shows (Chuah, 2002). The 3D approach used in this work offers an intuitive metaphor for social activities that is successfully used in multi-user web 3D worlds (Adobe Atmosphere; Blaxxun). A possible extension of the time-pillar metaphor may include social interaction as an optional opportunity for those TV viewers that appreciate it.

Appendix – The Post-Test Questionnaire

The time-pillar interface has given you a chance to access the content of a number of TV channels navigating through a 3D scene. Read the following statements and express your personal opinion about them.

Part 1

1 – Express your personal opinion about the interface using the following seven attributes (*5 point scale*)

	Strongly disagree	Somewhat disagree	Neutral	Somewhat agree	Strongly agree
Useful					
Interesting					
Pleasant					
Beautiful					
Easy					
Appropriate					
Relaxing					

Part 2

2 – The time-pillar world has given you the chance to use 4 different navigation modalities. Did you appreciate them? (*5 point scale*)

	Total aversion	Partial aversion	Neutral	Partial appreciation	Total appreciation
Autom. tour					
Guided tour					
Free walk					
Map					

3– Indicate one or more navigation paradigms to discard (if any) (*yes/No*)

Automatic tour
Guided tour
Free walk
Map

Part 3

4 – Express your opinion about possible future extensions for the interface (*5 point scale*):

	Strongly disagree	Somewhat disagree	Neutral	Somewhat agree	Strongly agree
A – Feature for saving viewpoints on the scene (e.g., a channel or a thematic zone) and allowing subsequent direct return to them					
B – Automatic or guided tour through a selection of themes (e.g., if you are interested in news or sports, the tour will guide you only through these themes)					
C – Possibility of moving time-pillars, in order to build personalized groups of them					
D – Possibility of customizing other 3D features of the time-pillar world (e.g., possibility to build a new zone for time-pillars)					

5 – Suggest additional functionalities for the time-pillar world (*open question*)

Part 4

6 – Would you like the system to automatically choose a path for you in the time-pillar world on the basis of a preliminary questionnaire? (*yes/no*)

7 – Would you like the system to automatically deduce your preferences from your movements in the time-pillar world, for example by noting how long you spend on a certain time-pillar or zone? (*yes/no*)

8 – Give the reasons for your answers to questions 6 and 7 (*open question*)

Part 5

9 – The time-pillars make it possible to manage different functionalities related to a single TV channel. Express your personal opinion about the following functionalities (*5 point scale*):

	Total aversion	Partial aversion	Neutral	Partial appreciation	Total appreciation
A – Visualization of the current broadcast					
B – Visualization of the snapshots related to the monitoring activity					
C – Visualization of the video fragments					
D – Rotation of the time-pillars for visualizing the recordings without changing viewpoint					

10 – Describe positive features and drawbacks in using the time-pillars (*open question*)

Part 6

11 – Express your level of interest about the following possible functionalities for the time-pillar interface (*5 point scale*):

	Strongly disagree	Somewhat disagree	Neutral	Somewhat agree	Strongly agree
A – Links to Internet sites related to that TV channel					
B – Electronic Program Guide (EPG)					
C – Full registration of selected programs (PVR)					
D – Chat with other users to exchange opinions about that channel					

12 – Describe other information services and/or functionalities that you would like to find on the time-pillar interface (*open question*)

References

Adobe Atmosphere, http://www.adobe.com/products/atmosphere/main.html

Alspach, T. and Alspach J.: 1995, Microsoft Bob. Indianapolis: Alpha Books.

Ark, W., Dryer, D. C., Selker, T. and Zhai, S.: 1998, Representation Matters: The Effect of 3D Objects and a Spatial Metaphor in a Graphical User Interface. In: *HCI'98 Conference on People and Computers XIII*. Sheffield, UK, pp. 209–219.

Baddeley, A.: 1998, *Human Memory: Theory and Practice*. New York: Allyn & Bacon.

Baudisch, P. and Brueckner, L.: 2002, TV Scout: Guiding Users from Printed TV Program Guides to Personalized TV Recommendation. In: *2nd Workshop on Personalization in Future TV*. Malaga, Spain, pp. 151–160.

Bianchi Bandinelli, R.: 1970, *Rome: The Center of Power. (The Arts of Mankind)*. New York: Braziller.

Blaxxun, http://www.blaxxun.de

Browne, D., Totterdell, P. and Norman, M. (eds.): 1990, *Adaptive User Interfaces*. London: Academic Press.

Brusilovsky, P.: 2001, Adaptive hypermedia. *User Modeling and User Adapted Interaction* **11**(1–2), 87–110.

Brusilovsky, P., Kobsa, A. and Vassileva, J. (eds.): 1998, *Adaptive Hypertext and Hypermedia Systems*. Dordrecht: Kluwer Academic Publishers.

Brutzman, D.: 2002, Teaching 3D Modeling and Simulation: Virtual Kelp Forest Case Study. In: *7th International Conference on 3D Web Technology*. Tempe, Arizona, USA, pp. 93–101.

Buczak, A., Zimmerman, J. and Kurapati, K.: 2002, Personalization: Improving Ease-of-Use, Trust and Accuracy of a TV show Recommender. In: *2nd Workshop on Personalization in Future TV*. Malaga, Spain, pp. 1–10.

Card, S. K., Robertson, G. G. and Mackinlay, J. D.: 1991, The Information Visualizer, an Information Workspace. In: *ACM CHI'91 Conference on Human Factors in Computing Systems*. New York, USA, pp. 181–188.

Carey, R. and Bell, G.: 1997, *The Annotated Vrml 2.0 Reference Manual*. Reading: Addison-Wesley.

Chittaro, L. and Ranon, R.: 2002, Dynamic Generation of Personalized VRML Content: A General Approach and its Application to 3D E-commerce. In: *7th International Conference on 3D Web Technology*. Tempe, Arizona, USA, pp. 145–154.

Chuah, M.: 2002, Reality Instant Messenger: The Promise of iTV Delivered Today. In: *2nd Workshop on Personalization in Future TV*. Malaga, Spain, pp. 59–68.

Ciancarini, P. and Rossi, D.: 1997, Jada – Coordination and Communication for Java Agents. *Lecture Notes in Computer Science* **1222**, 213–226.

Cockburn, A. and McKenzie, B.: 2001, 3D or Not 3D? Evaluating the Effect of the Third Dimension in a Document Management System. In: *ACM CHI 2001 Conference on Human Factors in Computing Systems*. Seattle, USA, pp. 434–441.

Cockburn, A. and McKenzie, B.: 2002, Spatial Cognition: Evaluating the Effectiveness of Spatial Memory in 2D and 3D Physical and Virtual Environments. In: *ACM CHI 2002 Conference on Human Factors in Computing Systems*. Minneapolis, USA, pp. 203–210.

Cotter, P. and Smyth, B.: 2000, PTV: Intelligent Personalised TV Guides. In: *12th Innovative Applications of Artificial Intelligence Conference*. Austin, TX, USA, pp. 957–964.

Czerwinski, M., Tan, D. S. and Robertson, G. G.: 2002, Spatial Cognition: Women take a Wider View. In: *ACM CHI 2002 Conference on Human Factors in Computing Systems*. Minneapolis, USA, pp. 195–202.

Fink, J., Kobsa, A. and Nill, A.: 1998, Adaptable and Adaptive Information Provision for All Users, Including Disabled and Elderly People. *The New Review of Hypermedia e Multimedia* **4**, 163–188.

Freeman, E., Hupfer, S. and Arnold, K.: 1999, *JavaSpaces Principles, Patterns, and Practice*. Reading: Addison-Wesley.

Gelertner, D.: 1985, Generative Communication in Linda. *ACM Transactions on Programming Languages and Systems* **7**(1), 80–112.

Guinan, T., O'Hare, G. M. P. and Doikov, N.: 2000, ENTER: The Personalisation and Contextualisation of 3-Dimensional Worlds. In: *8th Euromicro Workshop on Parallel and Distributed Processing (EURO-PDP 2000)*. Rhodes, Greece, pp. 142–149.

Gunsel, B. and Tekalp, A. M.: 1998, Content-based Video Abstraction. In: *IEEE International Conference on Image Processing*. Chicago, IL, pp. 128–132.

Haik, E., Barker, T., Sapsford, J. and Trainis, S.: 2002, Investigation into Effective Navigation in Desktop Virtual Interfaces. In: *7th International Conference on 3D Web Technology*. Tempe, Arizona, USA, pp. 59–66.

Hemmje, M.: 1995, LyberWorld: A 3D Graphical User Interface for Fulltext Retrieval. In: *ACMCHI'95 Conference on Human Factors in Computing Systems*. Denver, Colorado, USA, pp. 417–418.

IBM Tspaces, http://www.almaden.ibm.com/cs/TSpaces/

ISO 9241–11: 1998, Ergonomic Requirements for Office Work with Visual Display Terminals (VDTs) – Part 11: Guidance on Usability.

ISO 13407: 1999, Human-Centred Design Processes for Interactive Systems.

Kobla, V., Doermann, D. and Faloutsos, C.: 1997, Video Trails: Representing and Visualizing Structure in Video Sequences. In: *5th ACM International Conference on Multimedia* Seattle, WA, USA, pp. 335–346.

Kreitzberg, C.: 1996, Managing for Usability. In: A. F. Alber (ed.): *Multimedia: A Management Perspective*. Belmont, CA: Wadsworth, pp. 65–88.

Lee, H., Lee, H., Nam, J., Bae, B., Kim, M., Kang, K. and Kim, J.: 2002, Personalized Contents Guide and Browsing Based on User Preference. In: *2nd Workshop on Personalization in Future TV*. Malaga, Spain, pp.131–150.

Lewis, W. S (ed.): 1960, *Horace Walpole's Correspondence: Sir Mann, November 1748–September 1756*. New Haven: Yale University Press.

Lienhart, R., Pfeiffer, S. and Effelsberg, W.: 1997: Video Abstracting. *Communications of the ACM* **40**(12), 54–62.

MacKinlay, J. D., Robertson, G. G. and Card, S. K.: 1991, The Perspective Wall: Detail and Context Smoothly Integrated. In: *ACMCHI'91 Conference on Human Factors in Computing Systems*. New York, USA, pp. 173–179.

Marrin, C., Myers, R., Kent, J. and Broadwell, P.: 2001, Steerable Media: Interactive Television via Video Synthesis. In: *6th International Conference on 3D Web Technology*. Paderborn, Germany, pp. 7–14.

Meuleman, P., Heister, A., Kohar, H. and Tedd, D.: 1998, Double Agents – Presentation and Filtering Agents for a Digital Television Recording System. In: *ACM CHI'98 Conference on Human Factors in Computing Systems*. Los Angeles, CA, USA, pp. 3–4.

Modjeska, D. K.: 2000, Hierarchical Data Visualization in Desktop Virtual Reality. PhD dissertation, University of Toronto, Toronto, Canada.

Nack, F. and Lindsay, A. T.: 1999, Everything You Wanted to Know About MPEG-7 – Part 1. *IEEE Multimedia* **6**(3), 65–77.

Nack, F. and Lindsay, A. T.: 1999, Everything You Wanted to Know About MPEG-7 – Part 2. *IEEE Multimedia* **6**(4), 64–73.

Nikolovska, L. and Martino, J.: 1998, Spatial Browsing to Retrieve Multimedia Information. *IEEE Multimedia* **5**(2), 78–83.

Norman, D. A. and Draper, S. W.: 1986, *User Centered System Design: New Perspectives on Human-Computer Interaction*. New Jersey: Lawrence Erlbaum.

Pejtersen, A. M. and Rasmussen, J.: 1997, Ecological Information Systems and Support of Learning: Coupling Work Domain Information to User Characteristics. In: M. G. Helander, T. K. Landauer and P. V. Prabhu (eds.): *Handbook of Human Computer Interaction*. Amsterdam: Elsevier, pp. 315–346.

Pereira, F. and Ebrahimi, T.: 2002, *The MPEG-4 Book*. New Jersey: Prentice-Hall.

Perkowitz, M. and Etzioni, O.: 2000, Adaptive Web Sites. *Communications of the ACM* **43**(8), 152–158.

Robertson, G. G., Mackinlay, J. D. and Card, S. K.: 1991, Cone Trees: Animated 3D Visualizations of Hierarchical Information. In: *ACMCHI'91 Conference on Human Factors in Computing Systems*. New York, USA, pp. 189–194.

Robertson, G. G., Card, S. K. and Mackinlay, J. D.: 1993, Information Visualization Using 3D Interactive Animation. *Communications of the ACM* **36**(4), 56–71.

Rosenfeld, L. and Morville, P.: 2002, *Information Architecture for the World Wide Web (2nd edition)*. Sebastopol, CA: O'Reilly & Associates.

Salomon, B., Garber, M., Lin, M. C. and Manocha, D.: 2003, Interactive Navigation in Complex Environments Using Path Planning. In: *2003 Symposium on Interactive 3D Graphics*. Monterey, USA, pp. 41–50.

Sarkar, M. and Brown, M. H.: 1994, Graphical Fisheye Views. *Communications of the ACM* **37**(12), 73–83.

Schneider-Hufschmidt, M., Kühme, T. and Malinowski, U. (eds.): 1993, *Adaptive User Interfaces: Principles and Practice*. Amsterdam: Elsevier Science.

Stephanidis, C.: 2001, Adaptive techniques for Universal Access. *User Modeling and User Adapted Interaction* **11**(1–2), 159–179.

Tse, T., Vegh, S., Marchionini, G. and Shneiderman, B.: 1999, An Exploratory Study of Video Browsing User Interface Designs and Research Methodologies: Effectiveness in Information Seeking Tasks. In: *62nd Annual Meeting of the American Society for Information Science*. Medford, NJ, USA, pp. 681–692.

Tsekeridou, S. and Pitas, I.: 2001, Content-Based Video Parsing and Indexing Based on Audio-Visual Interaction. *IEEE Transactions on Circuits and Systems for Video Technology* **11**(4), 522–535.

Vinson, N. G.: 1999, Design Guidelines for Landmarks to Support Navigation in Virtual Environments. In: *ACMCHI'99 Conference on Human Factors in Computing Systems*. Pittsburgh, Pennsylvania, USA, pp. 278–285.

Walczak, K. and Cellary, W.: 2002, Building Database Applications of Virtual Reality with X-VRML. In: *7th International Conference on 3D Web Technology*. Tempe, Arizona, USA, pp. 111–120.

Ware, C. and Franck, G.: 1996, Evaluating Stereo and Motion Cues for Visualizing fInformation Nets in Three Dimensions. *ACM Transactions on Graphics* **15**(2), 121–140.

Win3D, http://www.clockwise3d.com

Yates, F. A.: 1966, *The Art of Memory*. Chicago: University of Chicago Press.

HUMAN-COMPUTER INTERACTION SERIES

1. E.H. Chi: *A Framework for Visualizing Information.* 2002   ISBN 1-4020-0589-X
2. J. Schreck: *Security and Privacy in User Modeling.* 2003   ISBN 1-4020-1130-X
3. M.A. Blythe, K. Overbeeke, A.F. Monk and P.C. Wright (eds.): *Funology.* From Usability to Enjoyment. 2003   ISBN 1-4020-1252-7
4. M.Y. Ivory: *Automated Web Site Evaluation.* Researchers' and Practitioners' Perspectives. 2003   ISBN 1-4020-1672-7
5. C.-M. Karat, J.O. Blom and J. Karat (eds.): *Designing Personalized User Experiences in eCommerce*   ISBN 1-4020-2147-X
6. L. Ardissono, A. Kobsa and M. Maybury (eds.): *Personalized Digital Television.* Targeting Programs to Individual Viewers. 2004   ISBN 1-4020-2163-1

KLUWER ACADEMIC PUBLISHERS – DORDRECHT / BOSTON / LONDON